COMPARATIVE AND INTERNATIONAL EDUCATION

Globalisation, Framework and Difference

COMPARATIVE AND INTERNATIONAL EDUCATION
Globalisation, Framework and Difference

Divya Sharma

MD PUBLICATIONS PVT LTD
NEW DELHI
www.mdppl.com

Published by :

MD Publications Pvt Ltd
"MD House", 11, Darya Ganj,
New Delhi - 110002
Phone : +91-11-45355555
E-mail : contact@mdppl.com
Website: www.mdppl.com

ISBN: 978-81-7533-362-8

Published and Printed by Mr. Pranav Gupta on behalf of **MD Publications Pvt Ltd** at Mohit Enterprises, Delhi.

PREFACE

Comparative Education is the comparative study of educational theories and practices in various countries. Comparative education attempts to use cross-national data to test propositions about the relationship between education and society and between teaching practices and learning outcomes. Comparative education considers the implications of comparative studies for the formation and implementation of policies in education, social, national and international development. Comparative education invites contributions from associated disciplines in the fields of government, management, sociology and technology and communications which affect educational research and policy decisions.

Much of the justification for undertaking comparative education studies prior to 1960 was in terms of their potential either for countering parochialism or ethnocentrism, or for assisting in the improvement of education at home.

In this change of emphasis comparative education is clearly following a course already charted in economics, sociology and political science. Economics has ventured furthest, perhaps. It has now left far behind its earlier preoccupation with the identification and description of economic institutions and has become a complex endeavour to explain and predict behaviour connected with making choices among alternatives. Sociology, similarly, has moved beyond the description and classification of social units to analysis and prediction of their interaction. And, just at the present time, some of the most fruitful work of relevance for comparative education is currently appearing from political scientists pursuing a cross-national approach. Clearly, these parallel developments have not occurred simply by chance: they express a common reaction to a common set of methodological potentialities and problems. The challenge to move from the particular to the general, from identification description classification to hypothesis-testing, theory building and prediction is pervasive.

One test of the progress of a science is its acquisition of a terminology. In developing "technical terms", words are often borrowed from everyday use, and then more precisely defined for technical purposes. One thinks immediately of the use in physics of the term "velocity"; or, in economics our attempt to define "demand" as "ability and willingness to pay", and not simply to retain its common meaning of "need" or "desire". Indeed, on occasion the most far-reaching result of scientific study of a phenomenon appears to be the recognition of a new, more powerful, albeit more limited, definition of a term.

Comparative education has mistakenly come to be identified either with the study of education in another country, or with studies using data drawn from more than one country.

This view of what constitutes comparative education enjoys the sanction of both common usage and common sense. One finds out what is going on abroad and compares it with what is happening at home, often with a practical programme of amelioration in view. Certainly, many essays in comparative education are of this type. Alternatively, one uses a collection of multi-national data to identify, describe, and compare relationships within education, or between education and other social phenomena. Again, I must emphasise that to call such studies "comparative" agrees with common sense and usage. But the weakness of that position is that it establishes as the criterion for classification as a comparative study the mere presence or absence of foreign or multi-national characteristics of data, and by implication ignores, or even denies, the existence of a characteristically comparative method.

Comparative education is often incorrectly assumed to exclusively encompass studies that compare two or more different countries. In fact, since its early days researchers in this field have often eschewed such approaches, preferring rather to focus on comparisons within a single country over time.

I am very thankful to Mr. Pranav Gupta, Director of MD Publications Pvt Ltd, New Delhi, for his kind cooperation and support for this book.

Divya Sharma

Contents

1

Comparative Education: Theory and Processes

INTRODUCTION

At the outset of what has been called the 'Global Century' there is much evidence of a revitalisation of the field of comparative and international education that few would have envisaged even a decade ago. The impact and implications of intensified globalisation and rapidly changing geopolitical relations underpin much of this revitalisation, as do dramatic advances in information and communications technology, paradigmatic challenges and developments across the social sciences, and the relative ease of international travel that has come to characterise our times.

A RESEARCH ORIENTATION

A research orientation is evident in this revitalisation and in the emergence of related research centres and research training initiatives. These trends are well documented by directories such as those produced by Dyer and King and Altbach and Tan; and by related reviews of organisational developments, institutional capacity and the growth of national comparative education societies. To this we can add evidence of the buoyant expansion of the World Council of Comparative Education Societies (WCCES), the emergence of new specialist journals, the research impact of international development agency involvement in the South, and the growing influence of large scale, collaborative research initiatives. Indicative of such developments are the various African Education Research Networks, the vibrant Northern Policy Research and Advisory Network on Education and Training (NPRANET), the European Union funded PRESTIGE initiative and the globally influential International Association for the Evaluation of Educational Achievement (IEEA).

International interest in the latter, large-scale, comparative studies of educational achievement, and in the methodologies employed in their design, is often motivated by concern for system differentials in performance notably, as revealed in school subject league tables. Intensified global economic and educational competition has thus helped to heighten the prominence of comparative and international research and involved a wider range of stakeholders in both the research process and in the interpretation of findings. So too has the international application of related studies concerning school improvement and school effectiveness; inspired by the apparent 'lessons to be learned' from the economic transformations and educational achievements of Pacific Rim states, such as Taiwan and Singapore. Indeed, the high profile and controversial nature of such studies have been instrumental, in themselves, in involving a wider range of formerly mainstream educationalists in comparative and international research. Alexander, for example, has challenged the school effectiveness studies by extending his contextually grounded work on primary education in the United Kingdom to new multi-level studies of culture and pedagogy in England, France, India, Russia and the United States. From a more macro-oriented stance, well known analysts such as Ball have also begun to apply their own distinctive, and theoretically inspired, policy perspectives within a comparative framework, and sociologists, including Green and Dale are increasingly exploring comparative implications as they engage directly with the processes and mechanisms through which globalisation affects national systems of education. Planners, funders and consumers of education are, moreover, increasingly expressing keen interest in international and comparative studies as they seek ways of dealing with the implications of competitive league tables, market forces, multiple innovations, and demands for ever more cost effective ways of increasing access and improving the quality of educational provision. This resurgence is visible, at all levels, within and beyond the framework of formal national systems of education and it encompasses, for example, non-formal provision, adult and continuing education, distance and life-long learning, community projects and a diversity of private sector initiatives.

More broadly speaking, it is pertinent in the post-September 2001 era to emphasise renewed worldwide preoccupation with the need to improve cross-cultural dialogue and understanding. Such goals, as we shall argue later, have long underpinned the rationale for much work in the field of comparative and international education. They were especially prominent in studies carried out following the two world wars, but the centrality of the humanitarian dimension of the field has remained visible in its consistent engagement with concerns that include, for example, development studies, health related initiatives and the implications of HIV/AIDS, work with refugees and migrants, liberation theory and peace education. Adding renewed stimulus, world leaders today can be observed, with some urgency, to be calling for international development issues to be more clearly seen as priorities for all in society to engage with – as we try better to understand the causes of international conflict and work towards a 'safer world'. This was, for example, a core theme in a speech delivered by the Secretary of State for International Development in the United Kingdom, in March 2002. In this global context, implications for the rethinking of development strategies, and for comparative and international research in the fields of education, development and beyond, cannot be underestimated. Other pertinent issues could be mentioned, but these examples are clearly indicative of the contemporary widening of interest in the potential and processes of comparative and international research in education worldwide.

The present volume is designed both to contribute to, and further stimulate, this resurgence of interest and activity, at what is clearly a strategically important time for research and scholarship that transcends national and cultural boundaries. In doing this, however, it is argued that comparative and international research in education must also be fundamentally reconceptualised in ways that better articulate and demonstrate its continuing relevance for the future. The field's diverse history and traditions, for example, deserve both celebration and challenge while its multidisciplinary origins and nature position it well for further advancement in a world in which the socio-cultural analysis of global trends and developments requires concerted attention.

The case for such reconceptualisation is developed within a conceptual framework that recognises that the processes of globalisation are advancing simultaneously with a variety of poststructuralist challenges to the Enlightenment project, positivistic science, modernisation theory and rationalism itself. Tensions between the ideas and developments that underpin globalisation on the one hand, and theoretical perspectives that prioritise difference on the other, it is argued, generate what may be the most fundamental of all intellectual challenges of the present day. The implications of this for comparative and international education are profound because concern with global trends, the dilemmas of international transfer, and the concepts of cultural and contextual difference lie at the very heart of both the traditions and the aspirations of the field. Indeed, capturing the contemporary discourse well, Arnove and Torres portray the re-emergent intellectual agenda for comparative education as one that, most pertinently, focuses upon the 'dialectic of the global and the local'.

Our own perspectives on these core issues have developed from extensive professional and academic experience in different capacities and contexts across the globe. This cumulative experience consists of periods of long-term work and residence in Australia, Papua New Guinea, Kenya, Bangladesh, Poland, Iran, Thailand and the United Kingdom. It includes intensive periods as researchers, consultants and teachers in countries such as Belize, St Lucia, Botswana, Tanzania, Canada, the USA, India and China; and senior professional and administrative responsibilities within, or for, a wide range of universities, international agencies, professional associations and non-governmental organisations. We also bring together a range of different intellectual traditions, substantive interests and areas of professional expertise. These include specialist interests in research and evaluation capacity for development, globalisation and education, education in small states, language policies in ethnically and linguistically plural societies, educational policy, planning and administration and most pertinently here – theoretical and methodological developments in the field of comparative and international education.

The present volume thus draws upon a combination of theoretical analysis, critical reflection upon practical and professional experience, and extensive engagement in empirical research in a wide variety of professional and cultural contexts worldwide. This combination of theory, methodology, policy and practice also underpins much of the reconceptualistion thesis advanced throughout the present work. We therefore argue that, to a great extent, a more effective bridging of the worlds of theory and practice lies at the heart of contemporary efforts to improve both the quality of educational development and the quality and impact of educational research itself. These arguments are developed more fully in subsequent chapters in ways that build cumulatively upon the previous work of both writers.

CONCEPTUAL FRAMEWORK

In the light of the above, and given the extent of contemporary challenges to the nature and impact of both social and educational research, this book is designed to develop a meta-level analysis directly related to the socio-economic transformations, intellectual shifts and educational priorities that characterise the outset of the twenty-first century. This is intended as a stimulus and benchmark for others to build upon in shaping what is emerging as a new period of development for the field of comparative and international education as a whole. In saying this, we acknowledge the teleological dangers and limitations of attempts to demarcate phases of development in any arena. The reconceptualisation proposed here therefore argues for a more cumulative building upon the valuable traditions of the field, while articulating a challenging and future-oriented critique that is informed by contemporary social and intellectual developments.

First, we present an historically informed review of the nature and evolution of the combined field of comparative and international education, from its nineteenth-century foundations to the present day. In doing so we explore the differing origins and foundations of diverse comparative and international traditions; identify the changing motivations and purposes that have generated various periods of growth; chart major paradigmatic shifts of emphasis; and examine the nature of the challenges that currently command critical attention.

Second, a critical analysis is undertaken of the implications of the literature relating to globalisation, post-modernism and post-colonialism for the future development of comparative and international research in education.

Third, throughout the book an assessment is made of the significance of the current, and internationally prominent critique of educational and social research, with particular regard to its relevance for (i) the improvement of educational policy and practice and (ii) the theoretical and methodological advancement of future comparative and international research and development initiatives.

In developing the overall framework, we examine the changing nature of problems encountered within the field. Ideas derived from the various theoretical and methodological analyses are also applied to an identification and examination of the substantive issues and priorities that have dominated the research agenda during the past decade and to those that we believe will continue to command attention well into the twenty-first century. This incorporates a critical review of recent developments and problems encountered within the field and further consideration of the professional and intellectual implications of the globalisation and other theoretically-inspired debates. Particular attention is given to the impact of globalisation and changing geopolitical relations upon the nature and role of influential bilateral and multilateral development assistance agencies. We examine how such bodies have influenced the research process, their part in the shaping of educational policy worldwide, and how they have impacted upon varied educational contexts and systems in practice.

In doing this, we address specific geopolitical changes that have taken place in major regions of the globe such as East Asia, Southern Africa and Eastern Europe. The book thus examines the impact of rapid socio-political change upon dramatic educational transformations worldwide, and demonstrates how new research priorities, challenges and opportunities have opened up as a result. This is linked to a discussion of pertinent and contemporary research studies and to a more focused examination of the implications of changing priorities and agendas in the arena of international development co-operation. As indicated above, this is informed by the analytical framework generated by the globalisation, post-modern and post-colonial debates – and by our evolving critique of the uncritical international transfer of education policy and practice. Indeed, at the heart of the rationale for the book lies our concern with the dilemmas generated by the increasingly rapid, and uncritical, transfer of educational theory, policy and practice from one context to another. Moreover, we argue that the complexities of this issue have become increasingly problematic as multilateral and bilateral development agencies have sought to collaborate in the formulation of internationally agreed educational policy agendas. While many benefits can, indeed, be derived from such co-ordinated efforts, these have often been achieved at the expense of important contextual considerations. Dadey and Harber have, for example, shown how many of the findings of Western school effectiveness research do not apply well in African contexts. The same can also be seen to apply to much of the Western literature on curriculum change, decentralisation, teacher professionalism and school autonomy. In the course of later chapters we examine a number of these substantive topics in greater depth. Here, however, we first draw attention to the more fundamental need for all those engaged in comparative and international initiatives to accord such issues and contemporary challenges the disciplined and critical attention they deserve worldwide.

Perhaps it should not come as a surprise that, when faced with the turbulence of successive waves of economic and social change, policy-makers, practitioners and consumers of education, alike, look to the successful experiences of others for guidance and advice. We have already noted, for example, how policy-makers in the United Kingdom have purposefully examined the experience of Pacific Rim nations, in the light of their reported 'superior performance' in international surveys of educational achievement. Much can certainly be learned from comparisons with the work of others and from the international experience, but many distinguished comparativists have long pointed out that major problems lie in any simplistic transfer of educational policy and practice from one socio-cultural context to another. To cite Sir Michael Sadler's seminal lecture, appositely delivered at the turn of the last century:

> We cannot wander at pleasure among the educational systems of the world, like a child strolling through a garden, and picking off a flower from one bush and some leaves from another, and then expect that if we stick what we have gathered into the soil at home, we shall have a living plant.

Many are familiar with Sadler's socio-cultural and interpretative perspective, but it justly deserves re-consideration here as we increasingly recognise the importance of cultural influences on learning, and assess the future potential of the field as a whole. Indeed, it is especially pertinent in a global era where economic imperatives, neoliberalism, and positivistic assumptions currently dominate much social policy and where the diverse challenges of, for example, post-modern and post-colonial perspectives help to highlight the extent of contested terrain, and the (multi)cultural forces and factors that underpin human progress. As argued elsewhere, context matters and comparative and international research in education is especially well placed to demonstrate this. On the other hand, while the field of comparative and international education has many professional and intellectual traditions that deserve both recognition and celebration, it must also face concerted internal and external challenges if it is to prove to be of continuing worth and influence for the future. Chief of the field's traditional strengths are its multidisciplinary character and 'time honoured commitment to policy-oriented research relevant to the world around it'.

A RATIONALE FOR RECONCEPTUALISATION

New developments and challenges to the established traditions of comparative and international research in education are becoming visible on many fronts but, to date, their cumulative impact and potential has not been coherently articulated in a way that directly examines the implications and complexities of globalisation. The time, however, is ripe for a comprehensive re-assessment of the field as a whole. This is demonstrated well by the many strategically significant arguments for change that can be marshalled to build on those already outlined above.

First, the timing is most propitious, following both the 100th anniversary of Sadler's lecture, and the start of a new century. For many analysts of trends the end of a century, and especially of a millennium, provides a useful opportunity to take stock, although we emphasise here that the year 2000, in itself, is a Eurocentric perception. Societies such as China or India, whose civilisations go back several millennia, or the Islamic world, which also has its own calendar, do not accord the year 2000 the same significance as do Western nations. This was not their millennium. Such a fundamental difference points to the limitations of any field, but it is especially significant and revealing in studies concerned with cross-cultural issues, and those that have been dominated by Western theoretical perspectives, methodologies, literatures and personnel. As Bray points out, recent years have seen the greatest growth of professional interest in comparative education occur beyond the English speaking world – in countries with increasingly large and vibrant comparative education societies, such as China and Japan. He goes on to note how development agency involvement in research has also stimulated calls for renewed growth throughout the South.

This includes the UNESCO Principal Regional Office for Education in Asia and the Pacific, which during the 1980s and early 1990s had declined in visibility but which is making renewed efforts to play an active role. It also includes the Asian Development Bank, which has emerged as a major figure in the education sector. Thus considerable work is being conducted outside universities as well as within them.

Second, the influence of intensified globalisation and changing geopolitical relations has profound implications for the nature of our discourse and for the ongoing relevance of many previously taken for granted terms and conceptual distinctions. The continuing appropriateness and utility, for example, of distinctions between the 'first' and 'third' worlds, and between 'developed' and 'developing' countries, are clearly increasingly problematic in the post-colonial era and following the dramatic decline of the Soviet Union. Indeed, many post-colonial writers challenge the implicit values, analytic assumptions and over-generalisations that underpin such 'dualistic' classifications in principle. The same can be said for commonly used generic terms such as 'Western', 'Northern' and 'the South'. While recognising the intellectual limitations and dangers of such terminology, we argue here that our aim to engage with a wide spectrum of contemporary debates (and varied stake-holders) as our reconceptualisation thesis demands is still often facilitated by their use. We therefore prefer to adopt a critical stance, in sympathy with the post-colonial critique, wherever possible; however, throughout the text, we retain use of more commonly applied terminology and distinctions where it is pragmatically necessary to communicate with as wide a range of readers as possible. In the light of these developments it is, nevertheless, clear that any contemporary reconceptualisation must find more effective ways of incorporating difference, and divergent cultural perspectives into the basic canon of comparative and international research and scholarship.

Third, the contemporary Western critique of mainstream educational research points to problematic divisions between the professional cultures of research, policy and action. Critiques are being generated within professional circles as well as by governmental agencies, policy-makers, funders, practitioners and a wide spectrum of other stakeholders. In this politically charged debate, calls are being made for educational research to be more cumulative and authoritative to be more directly relevant, useful and accessible to both policy-makers and practitioners and to be more cost effective as budgets tighten and accountability is ever more emphasised. Comparative and international research faces similar challenges and must find ways of bridging the professional cultures that have often separated academic theorists from the work of those more directly engaged in matters of policy and practice. Ways in which this might be achieved are explored later, but here it is perhaps more pertinent to note that, in the United Kingdom, 1997 saw indications of positive organisational developments in the formal inauguration of the British Association for International and Comparative Education (BAICE).

This significant and symbolic advance came about from the merger between two formerly distinct professional associations, the British Comparative and International Education Society (BCIES) and the British Association of Teachers and Researchers on Overseas Education (BATROE). This new start reflects many of the widespread professional concerns that we have identified here. In particular the merger represents the further bringing together of two distinctive communities – those that have tended to specialise in detached, comparative study (often of Western industrial nations), and those whose primary interests lie in 'international' educational policy and practice and active involvement in the direct experiences of developing countries. While both sides of the combined field have frequently been concerned with educational reform, it is often the case that those who have traditionally perceived themselves as 'comparativists' saw their work as less directly practical in nature, than that of the 'internationalists', and as more of an academic, research-based activity. Since such rapprochement holds multiple potential for the future of research, policy and practice worldwide we will return to this issue and to the history of the field and its implications in more detail later. In doing so, however, it should be noted that a more global history of comparative education also emerges in our analysis, highlighting the ongoing significance of complexity and diversity.

The above arguments are all the more pertinent given that many large-scale educational reforms of recent decades - in many different contexts - have been markedly less successful than intended. There is therefore an urgent and current need to take stock of what has happened, where, and with what results, if we are to contribute to the generation of improved understanding and greater success at the level of implementation. As Watson points out there are now:

> Too many pressures from governments and aid agencies for research to be focused on the present and for the immediate future rather than taking a longer time perspective. Our time frames are too short. Comparative historical experience of what has been tried elsewhere and with what success or failure, such as in the fields of community education or the vocationalised curriculum, is rarely called upon in policy recommendations, often with depressing consequences.

While there is therefore a need for comparative and international research to bridge the theory-practice divide, there is also a strong case for a reconsideration of the potential to be gained from the renewed application of historical research perspectives. As Hobsbawm observes:

> The destruction of the past, or rather of the social mechanisms that link one's contemporary experience to that of earlier generations, is one of the most characteristic

and eerie phenomena of the late twentieth century. Most young men and women at the century's end grow up in a sort of permanent present, lacking any organic relation to the public past of the times they live in.

To some extent this critique points to the need for comparative and international education to re-value connections with its own intellectual past - 'to re-establish its unique role in providing comparative historical insights for future policy action' (Watson 1999b:235). More recently, for example, Kazamias has made an impassioned plea for 'reinventing the historical in comparative education' as a means of tackling what he sees as its 'humanistic impoverishment'.

In a related way there are equally significant dangers that too much contemporary comparative and international research remains blind to important theoretical and methodological issues and debates that have characterised the field in the past. This is a particularly sensitive and pertinent issue for researchers new to cross-cultural work, and given the recent exponential growth of international consultancy work that is increasingly carried out by personnel with little formal training in the pitfalls of undertaking comparative and international studies. As Cowen points out, while comparative education is currently attracting renewed attention, it is also 'going through a dangerous moment' with the re-emergence of 'cargo-cult' assumptions about the transferability of policy and practice, and the 'advocacy discourse of politics'.

Finally, it is pertinent to return to the growing influence of globalisation and modern information and communication technologies on the nature and concept of education itself. Is, for example, formal education as we currently know it the best means for educating the millions of people – young and old currently denied access? Given the rapid development of new technologies, the growth of private sector initiatives and the changing role of the media, much potential for new forms of teaching and learning is emerging in what is now increasingly seen as the learning society. Thus Broadfoot and Jarvis both argue for a further broadening of scope in our frames of reference, to include all forms of learning, in any redefinition of the field of comparative and international education. This we also endorse and pursue in our subsequent review of the field, and in our proposals for the future.

CONCLUSION

In conclusion it is argued that the outset of the twenty-first century is a particularly apposite time for a critical, reflective and forward-looking review of comparative and international research in education. There is already much evidence of a revitalisation of the field, stimulated by intensified globalisation, rapid geopolitical change and a broadening of interest from the mainstream educational and social science research communities. In this book we argue that if the potential of these developments is to be fully realised, a fundamental reconceptualisation of comparative and international research in education is essential and that this process has theoretical, methodological, substantive and organisational implications. In the following chapters we further develop and articulate this reconceptualisation thesis in the light of an analytical framework derived from the relevant literature relating to globalisation, and to post-modern and post-colonial perspectives on the significance of context, culture and difference. To paraphrase Miller's words, quoted at the outset; so many streams of thought have now begun to come together that their collective 'encounter' makes such 'transformational' change an urgent priority for all engaged in comparative and international research in education worldwide.

❏❏❏

2

Comparative and International Education

INTRODUCTION

The early foundations of comparative education have been described as 'travellers' tales' because they consisted of little more than observations about how young people were educated or trained in different societies. For example, the ancient Greeks and Romans admired the discipline of Spartan education. The Romans marvelled at the debates in ancient Persia concerning what future government employees should learn and how they should be assessed. Indeed, there is a remarkable contemporaneity about many of these specific topics! The Italians of the early medieval period were intrigued by the tales brought back by Marco Polo of how the Chinese taught their children and administered their vast country. The *Codex Mendoza* reveals how Mexican children had a differentiated curriculum for boys and girls in what would now be classified as the primary years. Ibn Batuta, a well documented traveller from Morocco, wrote fascinating accounts of society in much of fourteenth-century Islamic North Africa and the Middle East. However, these various works provided general social vignettes and did not comprise serious or systematic studies of education in other societies.

Brickman has described these early developments and insights as the 'prehistory' of comparative education, yet they reveal that man's ongoing curiosity about what happens in different parts of the world has very deep roots. To some extent this explains why, in an age of increased global pressures for uniformity, the differences and diversity of communities continue to attract serious attention. Going beyond Western constructions of the field's history that have, to date, dominated the English language literature, more truly global foundations and traditions are thus increasingly visible today. Wilson and Bray, for example, draw attention to these multiple origins of the field, and highlight significant Chinese and Japanese historical foundations and antecedents.

The roots of comparative education as an academic field, however, are generally acknowledged to go back only to the beginning of the nineteenth century, as, also, do the origins of international education. Because these two parallel and somewhat complementary sub-fields have traditionally had different foundations and purposes, their approaches to research have often been predicated on different sets of assumptions. These differences can generate both confusion and misunderstanding. Moreover, since the two fields have become so closely entwined that they are now often seen as one, it is even more pertinent for their different foundations to be well understood by those engaging in such work today.

In the Western literature it is widely claimed that systematic comparative education had its origins with Marc-Antoine Jullien's proposal in 1817 that governments should provide statistical information concerning different facets of their education systems. This would include data on educational finance, student enrolments at different levels of the system, numbers of teachers and so on, in order 'to deduce true principles and determined routes so that education would be transformed into an almost positive science'. Jullien is certainly acknowledged for first using the term 'comparative education' and for many Western writers, he is seen as the founding 'father' of this dimension of the field. Over a century later Jullien's vision came closer to reality with the creation of the International Bureau of Education (IBE) in Geneva in 1925. This was followed in the post-World War II period with the annual production of collections of international statistics on education by bodies such as the United Nations Educational, Scientific and Cultural Organisation (UNESCO), the United Nations Development Programme (UNDP), the Organisation for Economic Cooperation and Development (OECD) and the World Bank. Such annual reports and statistics have now become essential tools for analysts, policy makers and practitioners in comparative and international education. The growth of international data collection also led academics such as Anderson, Holmes and Robinsohn and Noah and Eckstein to try to establish comparative education more firmly as a positivistic (social) science. This was to have major implications for the nature and form of much analysis in the field, especially as many national policies at that time were based on the belief that educational reforms introduced in one country could be transferred to another with little regard to the different national contexts. However, as Halls argued in challenging the dominance of such thinking:

The truth is that if we borrow macro-concepts from other systems their application in our own system is almost bound to fail. The most telling example of this is where implantation was forcibly imposed, as in the colonial territories.

The origins of international education, on the other hand, can be traced back to Cesar Auguste Basset, another Frenchman, who in 1808 called for scholars who were free from national preconceptions and who could observe education outside France with the intention of making recommendations for the reform of the French education system. This was just then beginning to evolve as a result of the Napoleonic Code and the creation of the Universite de France. For many researchers international education gradually came to mean looking at education systems within the socio-economic, political and cultural context of a particular country, a far cry from the positivistic trends pursued by Anderson and Noah and Eckstein. However, differences also emerged in the way international education came to be seen, and in the USA, especially following World War II, international education became closely associated with study tours to different countries, and with the express purpose of improving international understanding and awareness of other cultures and societies. More recently some writers have begun to use the term to describe the work (and study of) 'international schools' across the globe, schools which might be located in any country but whose student intake may come from a wide range of nationalities. In many cases these students will take the International Baccalaureate or the European Baccalaureate, will be prepared for employment anywhere in the world, and will be expected to develop an understanding of different cultures, as well as good relations with people of different nationalities and languages. Indeed, in 2002 a new journal with this more specific focus was launched, titled the *Journal of Research in International Education,* by Sage publications in collaboration with the International Baccalaureate Organisation (IBO).

Further differences emerge because of the characterisation of comparative education with academic analyses of education in the industrialised world, both East and West, and international education with more applied studies carried out in developing countries. As we have already seen, both traditions have, to some extent, been brought together under the overarching umbrella of the composite term 'comparative and international education'. This was illustrated, for example, by the pre-BAICE redesignation, in 1979, of the British Comparative Education Society as the British Comparative and International Education Society (BCIES), modelled on the earlier 1969 reformulation of the Comparative and International Education Society (CIES) in the USA. However, it needs to be recognised that, while this merger of the twin fields has major intellectual implications for all involved in such work, in conceptual and organisational terms it is not a universal phenomenon. Many European countries have thus not seen a need to change the title of their 'comparative' societies. The same is true, for example, of the comparative education societies of China, Hong Kong, Japan and Taiwan and, indeed, of the World Council of Comparative Education Societies (WCCES). In Southern Africa there is also a strong historical connection in the character and focus of the Southern Africa Comparative and History of Education Society (SACHES).

To return to the core argument being developed here, however, Epstein suggests that because many scholars have lost sight of the differing roots of the main arenas within this multidisciplinary field of study, confusion has prevailed in much of the recent literature. This is apparent in the following comments from leading writers in the field of comparative education. Arnove, for example, in seeking to justify a 'world systems' approach, argues that 'world systems analysis restores the international dimension to the field of comparative and international education by providing a framework that is essential to an understanding of educational developments and reforms that are simultaneously sweeping many countries of the world'. R.M. Thomas, writing from a different perspective, argues that the work of bilateral and multilateral agencies and many non-governmental organisations (NGOs) is applied 'international comparative education'. Paulston generates further possible confusion when he suggests that 'international' education is 'a new branch of comparative education' which addresses the problems of educational planning, development and theory construction in macro-studies of education and social change, especially in the 'Newly Industralised Countries (NICs)'.

The significance of this debate extends well beyond logistics and semantics because, for the best part of a couple of centuries, it has underpinned two very different approaches to the study of education in different societies. These, as we have noted, can be seen as the more detached academic approach often characteristic of the 'comparativists', and the more directly applied work conducted under the 'international' banner. It is true to say, however, that some pioneers in the field, most notably Sadler, were able to operate equally well in both the theoretical and applied arenas. Indeed, in his work as Director of the Office of Special Inquiries and Reports within the then United Kingdom Department of Education, Sadler always strove to ensure that any comparative study with which he was involved was both sensitive to cultural context and had an emphasis on the practical application of his findings. Reflecting on the purpose of his Office, he had this to say in 1903. The chief purpose of comparative research is:

> *(1) ... to collect, summarise, and publish various kinds of educational experience, with a view to getting what is sound and true from a number of discrepant opinions; (2) informing the nation how it stands in regard to educational efficiency as compared with other nations; (3) promoting, as far as possible, general consent and agreement as to the wisest and most fruitful line of development in national education.*

It is little wonder that Sadler is often remembered as a farsighted and clear thinking figure and that, in the words of **Magnussen**, '*He made his office a powerful research bureau and virtually founded the study of comparative education in the process*'. Sadler was keenly aware of the need to consider the context for each education system. This made each system unique, and helped Sadler to recognise how questionable it is to transfer educational models and policies from one system to another. As we shall see below, his views were shared by many other pioneers of comparative education.

Returning therefore to the basic distinctions between the comparative and international traditions, Epstein's analysis helps to clarify the picture further. He thus maintains that, comparative education 'is primarily a field of study that applies historical and social science theories and methods to international problems in education' and, as a result, 'is primarily an academic and interdisciplinary pursuit'. On the other hand, he argues that 'international education fosters an international orientation in knowledge and attitudes' by bringing together teachers and scholars in academic exchange or interchange. He goes on to say that whereas 'comparativists are primarily scholars interested in explaining why educational systems and processes vary and how education relates to wider social factors and force ... ', international educators, on the other hand, 'use the findings derived from comparative education to understand better the educational processes they examine and thus to enhance their ability to make policy relating to programmes such as those associated with international exchange and understanding'. We now look at the nature of some of the most pertinent early work in more detail, before further exploring the purposes given for comparative and international education, as traditionally articulated in the field's own core literature.

DEFINITIONS AND PURPOSES

The elements of confusion surrounding the terms comparative and international outlined in the previous section pervade the differing definitions that have appeared over the years. They also reflect the particular concerns of the individual authors, demonstrating how identified priorities are related to the standpoint of the commentator – be they, for example, researchers, teachers, policy-makers or practitioners. Starting with Sadler's much quoted address delivered in Guildford in the United Kingdom in 1900, he justified comparative education in the following terms:

> *The practical value of studying in a right spirit and with scholarly accuracy, the working of foreign systems of education is that it will result in our being better fitted to study and to understand our own.*

This theme of 'being better fitted to understand our own' has been a hallmark of comparative education for much of the past century. So also has the aim of trying to explain differences. This can be seen from the comments of another of the early pioneers, Isaac Kandel, who stressed explanation and analysis as key features. **Kandel** wrote:

> *The chief value of a comparative approach to educational problems lies in an analysis of the causes which have produced them, in comparison of the differences between the various systems and the reasons underlying them, and finally in a study of the solutions attempted.*

Hans, on the other hand, was at pains to stress the reformative element of comparative studies:

> *Comparative education is not only to compare existing systems but to envisage reform best suited to new social and economic conditions Comparative education quite resolutely looks into the future with the firm intent of reform.*

This was very much the thrust of King's work, though as the popularity of his best-selling book *Other Schools and Ours,* which went into five editions, testifies, he never lost sight of the need to see education within its particular social, cultural and historical context. This view was shared by Bereday who took the focus of social and cultural contexts as his main thrust when he said that 'comparative education seeks to make sense out of the similarities and differences among education systems'. Mallinson wrote in a similar vein when he argued that 'the highest goal of comparative education must be to describe, explain and compare educational systems in terms of their cultural totality'. He elaborated this in the following terms:

> *By the expression 'comparative study of education' we mean a systematic examination of other cultures and other systems of education derived from those cultures in order to discover semblances and differences, and why variant solutions have been attempted (and with what result) to problems that are often common to all.*

More recently, **R.M. Thomas**, has stated that:

> *In its most inclusive sense, comparative education refers to inspecting two or more educational entities or events in order to discover how and why they are alike and different. An educational entity in this context means any person, group or organisation associated with learning and teaching. An event is an activity concerned with promoting learning.*

Thomas thus takes the debate away from being simply concerned with the comparison of education systems to the comparison of any educational activity, and Bray and Thomas extend and represent such thinking most effectively in multi-level diagrammatic form.

Their framework for comparative education analysis thus demarcates seven geographic/ locational levels, ranging from the individual to world regional, six non-locational demographic groups and seven aspects of education and society. In calling for multi-level analyses they argue that 'many studies neglect discussion of the ways in which patterns at lower levels in education systems are shaped by patterns at higher levels, and vice versa'.

The above arguments relate well to the views of several other writers in the field. For example **Farrell**, argues that:

> *... there can be no generalising scientific study of education which is not the comparative study of education [since the latter ...] attempts to study a class of phenomena usually called education which seeks to explain the complex web of inter-relationships which can be observed within education systems and other kinds of systems.*

Raivola develops a similar case, suggesting that no general theory or hypothesis can be developed from the study of one situation alone. Thus 'all research that seeks to offer general explanations must be comparative'. This is a theme that other more contemporary commentators are increasingly advancing, including **Phillips** who maintains that:

> *It is, after all, in the very nature of intellectual activity to make comparisons. Comparing is a fundamental part of the thought processes which enable us to make sense of the world and our experience of it. Indeed, it can be argued that only by making comparisons can we properly defend our position on most questions of importance which require the making of judgement.*

Finally, **Postlethwaite's** definition and his distinction between the comparative and international dimensions of the combined field, add a valuable degree of clarity to the debate. This is both useful, and largely consistent with the position that we adopt in the present volume. He writes:

> *Strictly speaking to 'compare' means to examine two or more entities by putting them side by side and looking for similarities and differences between or among them. In the field of education, this can apply both to comparisons between and within systems of education. In addition, however, there are many studies that are not comparative in the strict sense of the word which have traditionally been classified under the heading of comparative education. Such studies do not compare, but rather describe, analyse or make proposals for a particular aspect of education in* one country *other than the author's own country. The Comparative and International Education Society introduced the word 'international' in their title in order to cover these sorts of studies.*

Despite the various definitions noted above, major dilemmas remain because the combined field can be seen to be so all-embracing that it is almost impossible to pin it, and its parameters of study, into any neat description. Writing from the early 1980s researchers such as Arnove thus argued that the field of comparative and international education was characterised by much methodological debate and diversity of opinion relating both to its subject matter and orientation. They went on to say that comparative and international education is thus 'a loosely bounded field held together largely by a belief that education can serve and bring about improvements in society and that lessons can be learnt from developments in other societies'. **Kelly** went even further in her analysis of the state of the field by maintaining that:

> *Comparative education remains an ill-defined field whose parameters are fuzzy. No simple theory or method guides scholars and the importance of culture and historical specificity continues to be debated. The field has no*

centre, rather it is an amalgam of multidisciplinary studies, informed by a number of different theoretical frameworks.

This, therefore, is a complex, multifaceted field that is both difficult to define and challenging to engage with. Greater clarity, however, surrounds the purposes and reasons for comparative and international education that have typically been identified in the literature. These are certainly easier to identify and have traditionally been seen as to:

1. gain a better understanding of one's own education system;
2. satisfy intellectual and theoretical curiosity about other cultures and their education systems; and better understand the relationship between education and the wider society;
3. identify similarities and differences in educational systems, processes and outcomes as a way of documenting and understanding problems in education, and contributing to the improvement of educational policy and practice;
4. promote improved international understanding and co-operation through increased sensitivity to differing world views and cultures.

We reconsider this long-standing rationale in the light of more contemporary developments, the expectations of different stakeholders, and our own critical analysis. Here, however, it is pertinent to conclude, by noting that much of what has come to be seen as the traditional canon of writing within the field sources such as those cited above currently stems from largely Western sources and personnel. This is, however, only a partial picture and one that, as we look to the future, warrants further challenge in its own right. Moreover, for many, this construction is closely associated with somewhat dated mid-twentieth-century traditions of comparative education conceptualised largely as area studies and encyclopaedic teaching about the nature of education in other countries often within programmes for teacher education and training. While this perspective reflects the persistence of a fixed, and often inaccurate and unhelpful, historical snapshot, it does draw attention to the importance of current and future work more clearly articulating the nature and potential of contemporary changes and developments. These are all issues that we return to later, as we go beyond the historical foundations reviewed here.

A MULTIDISCIPLINARY FIELD

In the light of the above it is argued that comparative and international education is certainly a diverse, multidisciplinary and ever-changing field to which contributions from many disciplinary perspectives have long been welcome. Literature on the field's evolution clearly demonstrates the early dominance of historical and philosophical approaches to research, although more positivistic epistemologies have clearly also long underpinned important developments. Similarities, for example, exist between the positivistic assumptions made in the early work of Jullien, and more recent 'scientific' advances in the post-World War II era. In identifying periods that represent the development of the field, authors such as Trethewey and Brickman point to historical phases that can be broadly classified as those of (i) travellers' tales, (ii) cultural borrowing, (iii) cultural context and (iv) empirical social science. We will return to the implications of this for more recent periods of time later, but from this historical perspective, phase (or strand) one is characterised by the unsystematic travellers' tales that we have already noted. Phase two is perhaps best represented by the nineteenth and early twentieth-century preoccupation with the 'borrowing' (or imposition) of metropolitan models of education in the colonial territories of the South – the direct transfer of policy and practice from one cultural context to another. Phase three, often seen (in Europe and North America) to begin at the start of the twentieth century, is closely associated with Sadler's critique of uncritical international transfer, and his advocacy of the systematic study of education within its socio-cultural context. It is here that the historical and philosophical approaches and related epistemological frameworks rose to prominence. These, in turn, were later challenged by the more positivistic emphasis that underpinned the post-World War II dominance of the empirical social sciences and disciplines such as political science and economics.

More recent developments within the field both add to, and challenge, this type of phases representation. For the time being, however, this remains helpful in sketching out basic changes in emphasis during the broad span of the field's history. From the outset, nevertheless, we recognise that the demarcation of phases oversimplifies many issues that will later assume greater significance in our own analysis, and raises many questions about the details of both the process and substance of comparative and international research in education. For example, the phases are not necessarily linear or consistent across time, cultures or individuals. Moreover, throughout the history of the field many have asked if there is such a thing as 'the' correct comparative method, and whether researchers should be concerned with one or many countries and systems. The pursuit of the ideal comparative method thus characterises the influence and the writings of B. Holmes. On the other hand, and writing in the same era, E.J. King was notable for challenging the influence of positivistic science and for rejecting the direction of comparativists to any one 'correct method'. To cite **Kay and Watson's** pertinent interpretation of King's standpoint:

> *... we must get inside the skin of other people as nearly as we can. We must learn the 'language of life' as far as possible. We must 'make sense' of their conditioning and concerns in their idiom ... a holistic contemplation of a national education system could be compared with the aesthetic appreciation of a work of art: the complete experience is of more value than the discussion of the parts which compose it.*

While King had a major influence during the post-World War II period, he clearly did not seek to make comparative and international research 'scientific'. Nor did he pursue law-like generalisations, arguing that improved cultural integrity is of paramount importance for the field. In many ways this demonstrates a clear and ongoing link with the interpretive and hermeneutic foundations that inspired earlier writers such as Sadler and Kandel. Indeed, Kandel, himself, described comparative education as the continuation of the history of education into the present.

A variety of research approaches may thus be seen to operate within periods most characteristically represented by one dominant paradigm or group of disciplines. Our own use of any notion of phases is therefore pursued with considerable caution, but in a way that, hopefully, highlights dominant trends in an accessible way.

Other complications in reviewing the history and nature of the field result from questions relating to matters of substantive focus. Should, for example, researchers be concerned with formal systems and their interaction with society, politics, the labour market and other aspects of socio-economic development, or should more emphasis be placed on non-formal education, or sub-sectors such as primary schools, secondary education, teacher training, technical and vocational training or higher education? Should comparativists be concerned with the processes of education in different societies: what happens within the schools or the classrooms; the teacher-learner interaction; the way in which the curriculum is constructed or conducted; or the ways in which a school is organised? Or should they be more concerned with the measurable outcomes of the system: examination results; numbers of graduates; or the numbers going into different branches of the economy? Should the unit of analysis be the nation-state, as has traditionally been the case, or should this be smaller to focus on practice or wider in scope to include whole regions like the European Union (EU), the Southern African Development Community (SADC) group of countries, the Association of South-East Asian Nations (ASEAN), or East Asia? If it is to be the latter, is the concern to identify similar trends or problems, or to examine key issues across a whole region of countries? Alternatively, should comparative study be only related to the present or to a particular historical period, or can different historical periods be examined simultaneously, as demonstrated by Phillips?

The point being advanced here is that all of the above have, at different times, been seen as legitimate areas for comparative and international research in education over the years, and each position has been vigorously defended. Much thus depends upon the standpoint of the commentator and the purposes of the various investigations. This diversity, nevertheless, has generated a wide range of critics. There are those, like Farrell and Psacharopoulos, who have argued that there has been too much concern for theoretical considerations and not enough emphasis on the practical lessons to be learnt. Others, like Halls, Rust and Torres, maintain that too many studies have been overly descriptive and have lacked a substantial theoretical foundation. Rust also argues that there is currently too little knowledge about the early pioneers in the field, and that insufficient attention is given by new researchers to the ongoing implications of important methodological debates that were pursued by past generations. This would accord with Hobsbawm's observation that too many commentators are now growing up 'in a sort of permanent present' with little or no historical perception. This is a view shared by other writers, such as Cowen and underpins the rationale for the historical dimension of this volume itself.

EVOLUTION OF THE FIELD

In this section we return to the evolution of the field by examining in more detail the changes of emphasis reflected across the main periods of historical development. In doing this we relate, albeit cautiously, to the four phases identified above, but also go more deeply into an examination of specific initiatives and changes in distinctive strands of enquiry. We begin briefly with work characteristic of the phases of cultural borrowing and cultural context, but pay most detailed attention to the later institutional growth of the field and to developments in the initial post-World War II period that was, in many contexts, dominated by the influence of the empirical social sciences.

Promoting cultural borrowing

For most of the nineteenth century and the early part of the twentieth, many writers in the field of comparative education, regardless of whether they saw their roots in the comparative or the international traditions, were primarily concerned with what came to be known as cultural borrowing. Thus Horace Mann, Secretary of the Board of Education in Massachusetts in the USA from 1848, studied education in Prussia, France and England with the express intent of borrowing those ideas that he felt could most easily be transplanted to the USA. He is often called the father of American public education as a result. Ushinsky, whose study of Prussian education led to faltering reforms in Tsarist Russia, and Matthew Arnold, whose examination of education in France, Germany (especially Prussia) and Holland pointed up the deficiencies of education in England, and had a direct influence on the 1870 Education Act in England and Wales, were also in the mould of cultural borrowing. Although since Sadler many others have argued that it is not possible to borrow educational policy and practice from one context and transfer to another with any real hope of the transplant being successful, many governments and international agencies still do not appear to recognise this today. Cultural borrowing has thus continued in practice as decision-makers adopt such perspectives and seek directly to transplant models of, for example, school choice, school improvement, higher education governance and finance, non-formal provision or vocational qualifications from one system to another.

Understanding cultural context

Under the influence of Sadler, for much of the early part of the twentieth century many researchers in the field of comparative and international education became more critical of such assumptions, and were increasingly concerned to show that an education system could only be understood in the light of a particular culture and society. As Sadler was at pains to point out, 'what happens outside the school is more important than what happens inside because it shapes and influences what takes place inside'. Writers in this genre were Kandel, Hans, Bereday, Mallinson and E.J. King. Not only did they stress that it was essential to understand the language of a particular society in order to appreciate the underpinning philosophy of the school system, but there was also a concerted attempt to understand the 'forces' (Kandel), 'factors' (Hans), 'national character' (Mallinson) and 'cultural philosophy' (King), that had helped to shape an education system. Until the 1960s, including the pre- and post-World War II periods, there was, perhaps understandably, a preoccupation with conflict and ideological competition. Much of Kandel's work, for example, aimed to highlight the superiority of democratic systems over totalitarian ones, and his book titled *Studies in Comparative Education* is still regarded as a classic in this regard. All of the above mentioned authors, however, were largely descriptive and historical in their approach. They saw their role as encouraging international understanding and helping to bring about educational reform by showing what was happening in different countries. Their *modus operandi* was comparison, their framework for study was the nation-state, and their cultural perspective was decidedly Western.

It was during this early period that the establishment of a number of seminal university courses specifically designed to teach comparative education studies was achieved. Amongst the leading organisations were Teachers' College at Columbia University, New York, and Syracuse and Michigan State Universities in the USA; the University of London Institute of Education in the United Kingdom and other centres throughout Europe. Wilson notes that the first Western textbook, titled *Comparative Education,* was published by Peter Sandiford in London in 1918. There were other important developments associated with the creation of specialised yearbooks and journals. Most notable of these were the *Education Yearbook*; the *World Yearbook of Education*; the *International Review of Education,* founded in 1931; and the *International Yearbook of Education,* founded in 1933. By the late 1930s, therefore, the field of comparative education was firmly established on both sides of the Atlantic but its scope was still rather limited and it consisted essentially of historical attempts to understand and explain how and why a particular system of education had developed along the lines it had. Further afield, as Hayhoe and Bray and Gui emphasise, the parallel development of a specifically Chinese comparative literature had also emerged, with origins around the start of the twentieth century. There are also other pertinent histories of the field that have yet to receive appropriate attention, as we will argue later in this volume.

Organisational developments and the dominance of the empirical social sciences

World War II was to prove a watershed in more ways than one, though it was not until the late 1950s and 1960s that its impact on the field of comparative and international education was to become so noticeable. The creation of many international bodies concerned with rebuilding a world shattered by war; the desire on the part of individual governments to redesign their education systems to take into account the changed social climate; and the beginnings of the end of the European colonial empires were all to lead to a ferment of ideas about education's role in social and economic development. Along with this came renewed interest in educational experiments and reforms in different countries.

In 1956, the Comparative Education Society was formed in the USA, to be redesignated the Comparative and International Education Society (CIES) in 1969. In Europe the Comparative Education Society in Europe (CESE) was created in 1961, with individual countries forming their own national sections. Japan followed suit in 1964 with the creation of its own national society, while in Vancouver, in 1968, an International Committee of Comparative Education Societies was convened with the express purpose of furthering interest in the field. This led to the establishment of the World Council of Comparative Education Societies (WCCES) in 1970, with a remit to bring together representatives from around the world for a World Congress to be held every few years.

Significantly, of the five societies that initially established the WCCES, two were from Asia-the Japanese Comparative Education Society and the Korean Comparative Education Society.

Several of what were to become the leading comparative and international education journals also appeared during this period: *Comparative Education Review*; *Comparative Education*; and *Compare*. More recently, in 1979, the *International Journal of Educational Development* was launched with the main purpose of bringing comparative and international education research perspectives to bear specifically on the educational problems facing less developed countries. Subsequently the serial *Oxford Studies in Comparative Education* was founded in 1990 indicating the growth of the field itself within that university. These, however, are all initiatives originating in the Western world. Reflecting wider organisational growth, more recent times have seen the emergence of other journals world-wide, often emphasising comparative and international research or dealing with educational development in specific countries and regions. Illustrative examples include the *Comparative Education Review* (Beijing), the *Papua New Guinea Journal of Education*, the *Journal of Comparative Education and International Relations in Africa*, the *Revista Española de Educación Comparada* (Spanish Comparative Education Review), and the *Journal of Education and Development in the Caribbean*. According to Altbach and Tan's global inventory of programmes and centres in comparative and international education, by the mid-1990s there were at least 28 national societies and other regional bodies, and specialist comparative programmes were taught in 71 institutions situated in every continent of the world. This, moreover, was only a partial world survey, despite the authors' intention to be more global in scope. Bray more recently records the further growth of the WCCES to comprise 30 societies by 2002, along with its ongoing expansion and the regular publication of selected World Congress proceedings.

While the post-war ferment of ideas and creativity led to much organisational development and the establishment of numerous journals and societies, there emerged an equally creative debate relating to methodology and focus. This led to the development of new strands in the way in which comparative and international research was conducted. Because much of the work carried out during the cultural borrowing and cultural context phases was largely historical, descriptive and explanatory, it faced much criticism from the new generation of post-war educational planners. Farrell, for example, argued that much of this work was 'of little use to or little used by policy makers'. In the light of such criticisms new approaches were formulated that more directly reflected the influence of the empirical social sciences. The early critics Anderson, Bereday, Noah and Eckstein emerged from the positivist school of social sciences developing in the USA. Such writers argued that the previously dominant historical and cultural approach lacked scientific rigour because it failed to draw causative links between schools and society, and especially with the labour market. They therefore focused upon the connections between education and society, to see if it was possible to identify 'laws' governing this relationship. Bereday's approach was undoubtedly the most complex, and it is questionable if it has ever been successfully applied, but all were forerunners of the later applied aspirations and intentions of bodies such as the World Bank and UNESCO. Their work also coincided with the growing concern for studying the outcomes of education, rather than the internal workings of schools or universities as institutions.

In the United Kingdom, B. Holmes sought to refine the scientific model by creating what he called the 'problem' approach to comparative education. Greatly influenced by Karl Popper's concept of 'critical dualism', Holmes believed it was possible to establish 'laws' governing school-society relationships, if it could be shown that where certain conditions existed then certain outcomes could be predicted. On this basis he argued that it was possible to transfer educational policies and educational practices from one society to another where the problems were very similar. Difficulties in identifying 'problems' (whose problems?) and in translating this method into context-sensitive practice underpin subsequent critiques raised by writers such as E.J. King and Kay.

A rather different approach to the above debate was taken by Anderson. He wanted to see if it was possible to develop theories of school-society relationships that could be tested in different contexts and that might generate general 'rules' that could be of use to policy makers and planners. He also believed that it was important to undertake in-depth studies in more than one country. Perhaps his most enduring contribution to the evolution of the field is that he did not see either the nation-state or national school systems as the main focus of research. He therefore argued that it was just as legitimate to explore social stratification or educational achievement in the light of political philosophies or against economic growth, as it was to look at any other aspect of education. Researchers would thus isolate certain variables for observation and analysis. According to Kelly, Anderson's work had a profound influence on the development of comparative and international research in this period, and led to further significant advances in the field.

Adopting a political science perspective, other writers at this time argued more strongly than before that one could only understand a nation's education system, and the ways it was administered, if there was a clear understanding of the underlying political philosophy. Thus any appreciation of education in the USSR or Eastern Europe was not possible without knowledge of Marx's thinking and the development of Lenin's application of this philosophy. Likewise it was argued that one could only understand education in the USA with reference to the early founding fathers, such as Jefferson and Franklin, or education in China with reference to Mencius and Confucius as well as to Mao and Marx. Influenced by such thinking, a series of books on education, culture and politics in Eastern Europe, France, West Germany, and the USA began to appear in what many now see as a high point of visibility for the Anglo-American constituency of the field.

Further advances were, however, to be made during this phase of development by social scientists who were both keen to generate empirical data and committed to the application of new development perspectives – initially that of modernisation theory. By the 1950s and 1960s the dominant paradigm influencing the field, and much social science thinking about education, was that of structural-functionalism, out of which came various shades of modernisation theory. These assumed that because education systems were part of the social, economic and political structures of a nation then investment in education would bring about enhanced economic growth. Education was also increasingly recognised as a means of socialising the younger generation into the norms and values of the country of their birth, of preparing them for the labour force and for their position in society. Evidence for the role of schooling in modernisation came from the way certain countries Turkey, the Soviet Union, Japan, China were seen to have deliberately used their education systems to foster this process. Many other writers, economists of education in particular, were also arguing in favour of investment in education for economic as well as modernisation purposes. As the process of de-colonisation began to accelerate, others began to argue in favour of educational investment as the quickest and most reliable means of national development, by which was meant not only economic growth but also changed attitudes to work, industrialisation and social development. This brought in many researchers, human capital theorists and international agency personnel who would not explicitly have seen themselves as in the vanguard of advances in comparative and international education.

Within a few years this perspective was also being rigorously challenged for a number of reasons. First, because many Western societies were becoming transformed by immigration into ethnically, religiously and linguistically plural societies, the traditional functional patterns of education were seen to hold true no longer. Second, the launching of the first space satellite, *Sputnik,* by the USSR in 1957, and the defeat of the USA in Vietnam in 1975 were symbolically important. Such events shattered, at least for a time, the illusions fostered by the Western powers that Western democratic systems of government, and hence education systems which fed into these, were necessarily the best, or indeed, the only way forward to economic and social development. Third, and perhaps the most compelling reason, was the fact that, despite much educational investment in developing countries, much of it financed by foreign aid, the gap between high-income countries and low-income countries, measured by a whole range of indicators, was seen to be growing rather than diminishing. Economic growth was, at best, very uneven. In many countries equality of opportunities was a mirage. As for democracy taking root and new attitudes being inculcated, the evidence for this was very mixed. If anything, political and social unrest were growing and modern schooling was viewed increasingly as an instrument for maintaining the inequalities within and between societies. By concentrating on the social, political or economic impact of education, rather than on its pedagogic, academic and cognitive outcomes, others also argued that much educational research had failed in its primary task of writing about, and encouraging governments to engage in, educational reforms. New approaches were seen to be needed for the comparative analysis of education systems.

By far the most damning, and consequently influential, criticisms of the modernisation school came from critical theorists who argued that the effect of promoting the Western functionalist view of schooling was to lead, not to greater economic freedom and growth, but to economic and educational dependency. Moreover, it was argued that many comparativists had been too concerned with the industrialised world: Europe, North America, Japan and the USSR. When Anglophone writers had taken an interest in the less developed countries of the South, their insights and observations were seen to have been largely based on the English speaking countries of Africa and Asia, thus ignoring, and remaining ignorant of, others that were not English speaking. French, Spanish, and other European writers did take into account Francophone and Lusophone contexts, and, importantly, some of their contributions significantly helped dependency theory emerge as a major alternative strand of comparative enquiry. Paulston describes such neo-Marxist critics as 'radical functionalists' because they argued that modern education was repressive, highly selective to ensure the dominance of the existing political and social elites, and wasteful insofar as those who did not succeed in the system were condemned to menial tasks. Writers in this vein included Fanon, Freire, Carnoy, Bowles and Gintis and Althusser.

Marxist and neo-Marxist critiques of the 1960s and 1970s thus generated a range of new theoretical perspectives to help explain education's role in society, and these had a major influence upon comparative and international research in education at this time. For example, correspondence theory argued that education and employment opportunities were not only closely inter-related but that school structures and curriculum options help to maintain society's social and economic structures.

Acknowledging the above criticisms, from the 1970s increased attention began to be paid to the study of the educational problems of less developed countries from a greater variety of theoretical perspectives. These studies were partly historical, exploring the impact of colonialism on society, administrative structures, schooling, language and literacy, and partly contemporary, seeking to explain why, in spite of massive investment, and the huge expansion of education, many new nation-states were falling further behind the high-income countries. Indeed, the de-colonisation process created so many new states that this factor, in itself, generated new interest in comparative and international research and new national units for analysis. British East Africa, for example, became Kenya, Uganda and Tanzania and throughout the rapidly expanding Commonwealth 12 new small states (with less than 1.5 million people each) were founded between 1965 and 1977 alone. Critical analyses and their conclusions highlighted the naïve neo-colonial transplantation of education systems in the colonies, a form of cultural borrowing but one that was imposed and therefore unwillingly accepted. The dominance of colonial languages, colonial curricula, foreign textbooks and examinations, and links with metropolitan universities all led, it was argued, to an educational dependency as insidious as colonialism itself.

Inspired by changing times, and much of the same critical theory, related challenges to the dominance of the empirical social sciences rapidly emerged in diverse forms that ranged from gender studies to critical ethnography, cultural studies, legitimation theory and the post-modern critique. These are, however, major themes that are more appropriately addressed in the following chapters, as we move beyond our historical analysis and deal with more contemporary issues and developments.

SUMMARY

It is argued that while empirical social sciences can be seen to have played a dominant role in reshaping the nature of much of the immediately post-war comparative and international research in education notably in the Anglo-American literature the more recent history of the field has been characterised by concerted challenge and considerable epistemological and theoretical diversity. Some of these more contemporary trends were initially stimulated by the impact of increased interest in the relationship between education and national development and by the work of writers living and working in the South. Others reflected the widening of the research constituency, and the influence of specialists from different disciplines. This more contemporary history and its impact on the field is the focus of subsequent chapters. It is apposite here, however, to note that any conception of phases for the development of the field must certainly highlight the profusion of late twentieth-century challenges to the dominance of the empirical social sciences. Writing in 1997, Mitter thus saw five paradigmatic phases through which he believed the field had passed. He identified the 1980s as the 'post-modern revolt' and the 1990s as a period characterised by 'universalism versus cultural pluralism'. While this usefully acknowledges recent trends in some contexts, our own historical review draws attention to the dangers and limitations of the demarcation of all broad forms of categorisation. In particular, such thinking can mask the ongoing diversity of perspectives that has long invigorated the variety of the many different comparative and international educations that have jostled for dominance throughout each stage of the field's history.

In concluding this chapter it is, therefore, argued that, although the assumptions of the empirical social sciences have had a marked and lasting impact upon the historical evolution of the field, reactions to the dominance of such approaches to research, and to the positivistic epistemologies that underpin related theoretical frameworks, have, in turn, inspired much of the contemporary intellectual landscape that we must now engage with. Without encroaching too far upon ground to be covered in detail later, it is pertinent to foreshadow how, in challenging the post-war dominance of empiricism, leading comparative and international researchers came to pioneer critical advances in, for example, development studies, multicultural and multilingual research, gender studies, post-colonialism, and world systems analysis. Thus, for example, by the 1970s the study of education and international development had become well established as a legitimate specialisation within the broader multi-disciplinary field. With regard to gender, although there had been a rapid increase in studies of the impact of education on gender stereotyping and job opportunities in the Western world, there had been remarkably little systematic work done on a comparative basis until writers such as Kelly and Nihlan and Kelly pointed this out. Their complaint was that hitherto much comparative work ignored the role of education in reproducing gender inequalities and in encouraging male domination in society and the economy. Subsequently there have been numerous cross-cultural studies, as well as in-depth country analyses, undertaken so that gender issues are now also very much a specialist sub-section of the field. While this is not universal in its application and impact, it points to the diversity of international perspectives, is a revealing and culturally sensitive issue in its own right, and is an arena that now increasingly acknowledges the dangers of both male and female marginalisation. Given the international community's expressed concern to equalise the opportunities available to all throughout the world, especially in those parts of the globe that have been adversely affected by poverty, it is clear that challenging, and critically informed, comparative research on education and gender is continuing to advance rapidly.

The emergence of the debate relating to world systems analysis is perhaps most appropriate in an illustrative capacity here, given the centrality of the more recent intensification of globalisation to our contemporary analysis of the field. The main thrust of the world systems thesis is that global social, economic and political linkages need to be better understood since these have an increasingly powerful bearing on any individual country and its education system. Early comparative work of this nature was carried out by Arnove and Ramirez and Boli-Bennett, anticipating the growing convergence of educational systems, the perceived commonality of many problems and the similarity of trends in related policy and practice. Given increased recognition of the powerful role played by international agencies in shaping influential educational debates, global frameworks of analysis have thus assumed enhanced explanatory power and legitimacy. These are therefore all issues that we will look at in considerably more detail in later chapters.

From the above discussion it can be seen that while the twin fields of comparative and international education have different roots, origins and purposes, they also have a great deal in common. Moreover, together, there is much to suggest that each tradition has much to offer the other. As a combined and multidisciplinary field of enquiry, comparative and international education has a rich collective history, a diversity of purposes and foundations, a global institutional network and a distinguished and well-established literature. The evolution of this multidisciplinary field well demonstrates its responsiveness to both changing geopolitical relations and to advances in disciplinary and paradigmatic thinking. Chief of the distinctive concerns that are visible across the various strands and phases of the field's development are sensitivity to cultural context (at macro, societal and micro institutional levels) and critical concern with the international transfer of educational policy and practice.

Because comparative and international research in education is influenced by many different intellectual, disciplinary and professional foundations it cannot lay claim to any one single theoretical or methodological perspective that sets it apart from other areas of educational or social science research. Perhaps not surprisingly, therefore, the history of the field demonstrates as many vigorous debates about theories and methods as it does about changes in substantive areas for sustained enquiry. The complexity that such multidisciplinarity generates remains a perpetual challenge for those engaged in research, as we shall argue in the next chapter. It is, however, also the source of much of the creativity and enthusiasm that has so well sustained growth and renewal throughout the field's substantial and distinguished history.

Comparative education is a fully established academic field of study that examines education in one country (or group of countries) by using data and insights drawn from the practises and situation in another country, or countries. Programs and courses in comparative education are offered in many universities throughout the world, and relevant studies are regularly published in scholarly journals such as *Comparative Education,*

International Review of Education, Mediterranean Journal of Educational Studies, International Journal of Educational Development, Comparative Education Review, and Current Issues in Comparative Education. The field of comparative education is supported by many projects associated with UNESCO and the national education ministries of various nations.

According to Harold J Noah and Dr. Farooq Joubish, comparative education has four purposes:

1. To describe educational systems, processes, or outcomes.
2. To assist in the development of educational institutions and practices.
3. To highlight the relationships between education and society.
4. To establish generalized statements about education that are valid in more than one country.

Comparative education is often incorrectly assumed to exclusively encompass studies that compare two or more different countries. In fact, since its early days researchers in this field have often eschewed such approaches, preferring rather to focus on comparisons within a single country over time. Still, some large scale projects, such as the PISA and TIMSS studies, have made important findings through explicitly comparative macro analysis of massive data sets.

□□□

3

Changing Research Agendas in Comparative Education

INTRODUCTION

We have also begun to examine the implications of this analysis for the ways in which such research is carried out. In this chapter we build upon these theoretical and methodological perspectives to focus more directly upon their implications for the substantive educational issues and priorities that warrant concerted attention in current and future work. In doing this, we acknowledge that it is both unrealistic, and inappropriate, to attempt to present any form of definitive or comprehensive research agenda for all. Indeed, more in tune with the spirit of the book as a whole, we argue that – especially in times of rapid socio-cultural change – newly emerging issues and priorities deserve clearer articulation and consideration from a wider variety of intellectual and cultural perspectives. We, therefore, contribute our own assessment of emergent issues and priorities to this broader discourse, to help stimulate further critical thinking, and to encourage others actively to engage in advancing the debate. This is done in a way that is consistent with the evolving critique of the field and with our associated reconceptualisation thesis. We, therefore, do not attempt to cover every substantive issue that merits contemporary attention, but we do hope our own construction of priorities will both help to illustrate the potential of the broader critique that we develop here, and prove stimulating for others in its own right.

In the interests of clarity and coherence, we group related substantive issues together. This helps to focus our suggestions around a number of potential research themes that best demonstrate the significance of our related theoretical and methodological arguments. In this respect the chapter underpins our argument for a closer 'bridging' between the diverse worlds of educational research, theory and practice. This, in turn, points to what we argue is the increasingly important role of philosophical, epistemological and cultural factors in shaping both research agendas and educational development priorities for the future. It extends some aspects of the analysis begun here, where the issues and priorities raised relate more directly to changing global agendas and to their implications for international development co-operation.

While a combination of rapidly changing geopolitical relations and paradigmatic challenges may have stimulated the need for change, in earlier chapters we have noted how the field of comparative and international education now has an expanded audience and a wider constituency of actors to satisfy. This, in itself, has implications for the shaping of the research agenda and generates related tensions concerning the maintenance of theoretical priorities and the advancement of critical scholarship. To cite Apple's recent contribution to the rethinking of priorities for comparative education:

> *As Pierre Bourdieu reminds us, one of the most important activities scholars can engage in during this time of economic rationalism and imperial neo-conservatism is to analyse critically the production and circulation of these discourses and their effects on the lives of so many people in so many nations.*

Elsewhere in the same article Apple goes on to argue that:

> *All too often, analyses of globalisation and the intricate combination of neo-liberalism and neo-conservatism remain on a meta-theoretical level, disconnected from the actual lived realities of real schools, teachers, students and communities. While such meta-theoretical work is crucial, its over-use has left a vacancy.*

It is in this spirit that our contribution to the construction of new agendas and priorities for the attention of comparative and international research is made. Firstly, however, we re-connect with our historical review, and reflect upon what we see as the dominant issues that have attracted most recent research attention – in the light of the broader historical, contemporary and contextual factors to which they are related.

CHANGING ISSUES AND PRIORITIES

The last two decades of the twentieth century were, in many ways, dominated by economic concerns that had a major influence upon social and educational trends and priorities worldwide. The focus of much social science research thus reflected the nature and tone of the dominant economic discourse, and the competitive, assessment and accountability culture that it generated. Indeed, as the challenges raised by the 2002 British Broadcasting Corporation (BBC) Reith Lectures on the theme of trust so well demonstrate, we are today grappling with the human impact and social implications of what has been called the 'assessment society'. Work by Broadfoot and Little illustrates the contemporary and global significance of the latter issues well, and the enduring pertinence of Dore's 'diploma disease' thesis demonstrates the seminal influence of comparative studies in this arena.

Comparative and international education research priorities that dominated this period across a variety of contexts connected closely, and often critically, with sustained efforts to link education to improved economic competitiveness. In this climate the education policy agenda has been progressively oriented towards training needs, skills development strategies and the promotion of an efficient and adaptable workforce. The term 'human resource development' captures this emphasis well, and illustrates how fundamental changes in professional cultures and values influence both the substance and the language the discourse that is adopted. In England and Wales the recent governmental re-branding of its own education department as the Department for Education and Skills (DFES) is, itself, revealingly symbolic. Much attention has, as indicated earlier, also been paid by policy makers, both in the North and the South, to the implementation of educational reforms. This has, in turn, provided a focus for much comparative and international research that examined the imperative for reform, the impact of culture and context on learning, and the similarities and differences in the change strategies applied within and between education systems.

The international influence of the performativity culture has been advanced by the rapid globalisation of neo-liberalism and marketisation, to the extent that the possibility of alternative development models has, for many, been almost eclipsed. The demise of the former Soviet Union, and the subsequent transfer of 'turbo' capitalism into Eastern Europe, for example, helped inspire Fukuyama's 'end of history' thesis and underpinned the rapid, but problematic, adoption of neo-liberal educational policies, in transitional societies such as Estonia, Poland and the former East Germany.

Supporting the broadly neo-liberal market philosophy came increased attention to effectiveness and accountability via new modes of evaluation, performance indicators, the prioritisation of leadership and management training, the previously noted emphasis on examinations and assessment, and the use of comparative league tables. Reflecting such trends are studies by, for example, Dalin on school improvement strategies; research by Reynolds *et al.* on school effectiveness; Levin and Lockheed's application of school effectiveness research in developing countries, and Harber and Davies' more critical standpoint taken to the transfer of Western management and effectiveness models to the South. Since comparative league tables have come to feature particularly prominently at the local, national and international levels in recent years, they deserve special mention here.

Indeed, it could be argued that national enthusiasms for school, university and other public sector league tables was stimulated by the assumed potential of international league tables generated by the early IEA studies of school performance. The first of these were conducted and attracted attention long before investment in national and local league table systems became accepted as a useful strategy for quality assurance. Since the IEA studies are perhaps the most well known and highly resourced comparative studies in the arena of education, the influence of comparative research carried out from the 1970s can thus with dubious honour be seen to have had a marked impact worldwide.

Also connected to changing economic circumstances, European studies of post-compulsory education carried out by writers such as King reflected growing awareness of the increased speed of change, and of the need to prepare new generations for uncertain futures. E.J. King's concern with 'uncertainty', indeed, anticipated later developments that are now reflected in contemporary conceptions of the 'risk society'. Work carried out within the last two decades of the twentieth century is also notable for its attention to feminist theory and gender and for recognition of the increased plurality of societies worldwide. This included attention to the educational implications of multiculturalism and the needs of minorities, indigenous peoples and diverse language groups. Despite this, however, economic priorities, perhaps inevitably, continued to dominate many core policy and research agendas alike.

The last two decades have also seen much global convergence in terms of educational policies and priorities resulting from the combined influence of international development agencies such as UNESCO, UNDP and the World Bank. Edited collections published by Buchert and King and Buchert help to chart such trends, but these developments deserve closer attention in the light of the globalisation dilemmas being considered here. We also examine the rise to prominence of the commitment of global agencies to basic education throughout the South, to poverty reduction strategies, to gender equality and inclusivity, and to the quality and relevance of educational provision. These are all issues of such contemporary importance that they will inevitably continue to dominate educational policy and research agendas worldwide for the foreseeable future.

More recently, however, widespread policy deliberations have also begun to focus upon newer issues, such as the impact and application of new information technologies, the concepts of lifelong learning and the learning society and most pertinently here – the implications of intensified globalisation for the reform of education and training. In the context of these and related developments, we now explore what, in the light of our own analysis, we see as new and emergent priorities that could make a creative, stimulating and helpful contribution to the advancement of the field of comparative and international research as a whole.

EMERGENT AND FUTURE PRIORITIES

Reflecting on concern with the relationship between globalisation, context and difference that runs throughout this volume, we first, and most fundamentally, argue that future comparative and international research agendas have much to gain from more concerted efforts to promote increased cultural and contextual sensitivity. At the broadest level this points to the need for more in-depth and critical analyses of the diverse implications of globalisation for education in different cultural contexts. Green, for example, has shown how Western conceptions and assessments of globalisation currently dominate the existing literature and the related policy discourse. His work also demonstrates how, in many Western nations, skills formation is rapidly assuming increased prominence in educational policy, to the detriment of the more human, aesthetic and liberal aspects of education – whereas values and social and cultural objectives remain more clearly visible in Asia. As indicated earlier, however, little in-depth, empirical work has been done on differing local and national conceptions of globalisation, and of related perceptions of the implications for education and training. The result is that Western perspectives and Western research in this relatively new arena are currently in danger of overly dominating policy considerations elsewhere – to the possible detriment of both improved success in policy implementation and further theoretical advancement. A growing awareness of such issues is visible in work by writers across a wide range of disciplines including political science, economics, sociology and cultural studies but, as we argue throughout this volume, the field of comparative and international education is particularly well placed to make a more substantial contribution to such research. We have already noted, for example, how, to date, few in-depth and critical studies relating to the implications of globalisation have been carried out within Sub-Saharan Africa. This is despite the fact that development co-operation agencies are already advancing new 'skills for development' initiatives, founded largely upon existing Western interpretations of the potential benefits of globalisation for the South as a whole. Here is a crucial arena for future multidisciplinary, comparative and international research that holds significant applied and theoretical potential, to explore how beneficial such 'skills for development' really are. It may be, for example, that local craft skills, communities and cultures are being threatened by the economic forces of globalisation. A social 'mapping' of community views, as advocated by Paulston, may thus be helpful in documenting differing perspectives perhaps conducted through collaborative and participatory strategies of field research. Preliminary collaborative research carried out in Tanzania and Rwanda by one of the present writers, and colleagues certainly demonstrates the multi-level implications of such analyses revealing how the perceived impact of globalisation differs between social groups at the local level. Tanzanian stakeholders from the educated urban elite thus perceive greater opportunities stemming from increased globalisation in Tanzania than do research informants from poorer, more isolated rural community contexts. The potential for further in-depth ethnographic and comparative studies, as advocated by Crossley and Vulliamy, thus emerges forcefully from this work. So too does the significance of studies undertaken by, or in collaboration with, local researchers familiar with the cultures and contexts in question.

At the international level the engagement with globalisation highlights the enduring significance of the comparativist's critique of the processes of international transfer. Building upon Dale's work on the mechanisms of globalisation, empirically grounded studies of the new architecture of international development co-operation, and of the implications of bodies such as the World Trade Organisation (WTO) and the General Agreement on Trade in Services (GATS), therefore have much to contribute. As Robertson argue, GATS interprets education as a private and commercial enterprise, and failure to critique the application of market principles in this arena ignores the political foundations and neo-colonial implications of such global enterprises.

Moreover, such analyses point to the differences identified between internationalism and globalisation, and to attendant concerns about democratic prospects worldwide. As Jones pertinently observes:

> *The logic of globalisation contrasts markedly with that of internationalism. The latter, with its intrinsically democratic foundation, looks to a world ordered by structures supportive of that functionalism which is embedded in accountability. Globalisation, by contrast, implies few logical imperatives in favour of accountability, but rather looks to the pursuit of interest on the global level through the operation of unfettered capitalism.*

Connecting with our consideration of priorities for future attention, Jones goes on to maintain that:

> *Those interested in promoting or studying education in international perspective will find a more complex world order than ever before, with the logic of internationalism under threat from an increasingly differentiated and anarchic framework for the conduct of international relations ... Of particular importance is the need to think afresh about the nature and importance of democracy, democratic institutions and accountability.*

It concern with democracy also points to future priorities for comparative and international research on a variety of other theoretical, methodological and substantive levels. A recent special issue of *Compare,* the journal of the British Association for International and Comparative Education (BAICE), for example, suggests ways forward by looking at *Changing Contexts For Democracy And Citizenship,* and highlighting 'evidence of the challenges to education for democracy and citizenship that are posed by changes in the world order'. Contributors to this special issue identify threats to democracy generated by the reproduction of a 'dominant culture, which is increasingly becoming influenced by the global economic market'. While Jarvis is specifically concerned to maintain the democratic and radical foundations of adult education traditions, other contributors explore implications for feminist perspectives on citizenship and governance; the democratisation and decentralisation of education in South Africa and in Taiwan and analyses of educational reform, culture and citizenship in Germany and Brazil. Pertinently, the potential benefits of multi-level analyses are also usefully demonstrated by this collection of studies emphasising the relationship between global, national and local trends and issues.

Linking to notions of diversity and difference that underpin much of our analysis, cultural issues, it is argued, deserve greatly increased attention in future comparative and international research. To some extent this reflects earlier emphasis pursued within the field, and relates to the importance of the context sensitivity arguments articulated above. It is also connected, for example, to growing awareness of the role of cultural identity in facilitating learning, acknowledgement of the place of values in education and in an ever more mobile world the increased demand for educators able to deal with the learning needs of multicultural groups of students. Perhaps even more pertinently for our own analysis, the emergence of a diversity of new comparative and international literatures often stemming from different cultural perspectives – points to major new intellectual arenas for the future. Illustrating the potential of such developments is Hayhoe and Pan's work on Knowledge Across Cultures and Bray and Gui's seminal study of comparative education traditions across Greater China the Mainland, Taiwan, Hong Kong and Macau. The latter is a study that draws upon many rich and original Chinese language sources to examine how comparative education has evolved differently across the four Chinese contexts, and how these differences compare with developments elsewhere. In doing so, this work draws renewed attention to the importance of historical analysis, and challenges much of the existing English language literature by demonstrating the cross-cultural limitations of the generic Western phases formulated to represent the history of the field as a whole. In a related study documenting the research career of Gu Mingyuan Professor of Comparative Education at Beijing Normal University, the post-1949 Chinese traditions reflected in Professor Gu's approach to comparative education thus contrast strongly with the more empirical 'scientific' paradigm that is used to represent the post-World War II period by writers such as Noah and Eckstein. This further emphasises the future potential of work that acknowledges the past and ongoing diversity of the many comparative educations work that, we argue, much enriches this multidisciplinary field.

Looking more directly at the cultural dimension of teaching and learning, research by writers such as E. Thomas; Cummings and Louisy highlights the need for future studies that more systematically explore the influences of culture upon the processes of teaching and learning. Alexander's in-depth study of Culture and Pedagogy in five nations (England, France, India, Russia and the United States) helps to point the way for further work in this respect, by exploring the ways in which children's educational experiences are shaped by multiple levels of contextual, cultural and historical influences. In this he is building on the work of earlier comparative scholars such as Hans and Mallinson and upon the work of more contemporary colleagues. While significant contributions have also been made with reference to *The Chinese Learner*, these advances clearly establish the need for work in a wider range of cultural contexts, and with reference to situations where teaching and learning is carried out with and within cross-cultural groups. Louisy thus maintains that questions about 'whose knowledge' we use and 'for whose benefit' are central to the future of comparative and international education. Arguing for a stronger Caribbean perspective in the establishment of contemporary educational research agendas, she draws upon Creole languages, post-colonial theorising, cultural studies and local conceptions of knowledge. Work informed by such perspectives, Louisy argues, will more effectively contribute to an improved understanding of educational dilemmas within her home state of St. Lucia. In considering the regional implications of globalisation, this work contributes more to the future development of the field by advocating the strengthening of local research capacity, and by calling for Caribbean nationals to play a more central and international role in comparative and international research within the social sciences, across the humanities and beyond. In concluding, Louisy also well demonstrates the creative potential of increased cross-cultural dialogue, and echoes the multi-cultural aspirations for the future of the field that are central to Hayhoe and Pan's edited collection referred to above. Indeed, the designation of 2001 as the 'Year of Dialogue among Civilizations' by the United Nations, helps to reinforce our own commitment to collaborative research, to the bridging of cultures and traditions and to increased dialogue between all stakeholders in both educational research and educational development. These are, however, more methodological issues that we will return to in later chapters. Implications of these emergent trends are, moreover, closely related to ongoing concerns with the relationship between learning and identity and with familiar and ever important equity issues connected to class, race and gender.

Much of the above discussion draws attention to the centrality of power differentials, and the implications of political factors for advances in the future of comparative and international research. This can be seen in the analysis of global influences on educational policy, and in teaching and learning dilemmas related to aspects of culture and identity. Issues of power can also be seen to underpin many questions relating to the contemporary emergence of what has been called the 'knowledge economy'. As Foucault argues 'power is closely related to the ability to control knowledge and meaning'. Comparative and international studies of the impact and implications of the knowledge economy thus have much to offer especially in the light of the enhanced position given to 'knowledge for development' in the re-framing of the World Bank as a knowledge bank. As Gmelin and King point out:

> *... another fashion seems to be sweeping through the agency world, a fascination with knowledge management and knowledge sharing. Again, there is a connection with the World Bank and its sponsorship of a series of 'knowledge projects'. And again, our concern is with the implications for the developing world of the new knowledge architecture being erected in the North.*

While we pay detailed attention to international agency issues in Chapter 6, the implications of the relationship between power and knowledge generate a broader range of issues that warrant future consideration and further attention here. These include the role and impact of information and communications technology in pioneering new forms of teaching and learning, concepts and implications of the 'Network Society', the dilemmas of the 'digital divide' both within and between nations, and the impact of English as the dominant global language to the detriment of the local. To cite Marginson and Mollis, there is an urgent need to recognise power relations within the scope of comparative and international education, and for new research on:

> *... the new geo-political educational structures of power in a globalizing world, to study international education including on-line education, and to consider new forms of governance and identity ... other than the national.*

More disturbingly, many contemporary policy trends potentially heighten the role of education and knowledge in the intensified competition that is being experienced from the global to the individual level. This in itself warrants careful comparative analysis – but if it is combined with increasing global inequalities that can fuel cross-cultural conflict and misunderstandings, the dangers for all in our globally connected world could be further magnified. Re-connecting with the traditional humanitarian concerns of the field of comparative and international education thus emerges, for us, as a major priority for the future. In recognising this dimension of the field, Retamal and Aedo-Richmond draw attention to the deepening of global disparities and the way in which the political optimism generated following the fall of the Berlin Wall has been:

> *... challenged by the appearance of religious, ethnic and nationalistic conflicts witnessing profound inhumanity and viciousness. New and old forms of ideological nihilism and political intolerance have generated uncontrollable explosions of violence around the world.*

This work focuses upon the significance of refugee education, first as a humanitarian response, and secondly with reference to its implications for political transition and national development.

More broadly, we see comparative and international research concerning education's role in national reconstruction in distressing contexts such as Palestine, Afghanistan or Rwanda, as a strategically important contribution to efforts to understand the causes of conflict. In a similar way, this could include future comparative work on the educational implications of national reconciliation initiatives such as those pursued in South Africa, and broader analyses designed to foster improved international understanding and reduced global conflict. In many senses this relates closely to the cross-cultural understanding rationale for comparative and international education articulated most strongly in the post-World War II era, and to the contemporary calls for increased dialogue between cultures that we considered earlier in this chapter. Certainly, comparative and international research is well placed to highlight the nature and extent of global disparities, the dilemmas encountered by marginalised groups and the potential role for education in dealing with such issues.

Pointing to the distinctive dilemmas faced by the world's small states, for example, the March 2002 Commonwealth Heads of Government Meeting (CHOGM) held in Australia reported that:

> *Heads of Government reaffirmed their view that small states are particularly vulnerable to international developments and natural disasters and confront a range of structural challenges to sustainable development. In that context, they endorsed the New Agenda for Commonwealth work on small states, which identified key priorities for the short and medium term. These included notably that the Commonwealth should provide appropriate assistance on trade issues, including working with the international community to strengthen small states representations at the WTO, promote dialogue on the OECD Harmful Tax Initiative and take action to help mitigate the impact on small states of the events of 11 September and their aftermath.*

While this usefully articulates the contemporary problems faced by one marginalised group of nation-states, it also illustrates the importance of the multidisciplinary perspective that enables comparative and international research to develop a holistic analysis of development problems, and of the relationship between education, society and globalisation. The humanitarian dimension of the field also draws attention to education beyond mainstream provision, be it in the form of non-formal provision, adult education, lifelong learning or community development initiatives as emphasised by many NGOs.

In tune with our evolving critique of the field much of the foregoing analysis calls for increased reflexivity in the research process. This, in turn, requires the repeated questioning of many previously taken for granted assumptions by all participants. Given our parallel concern to seek ways of improving the contribution of the field to educational policy and practice, our own research suggests that a more culturally sensitive reconsideration of the concept and use of time, time as a resource, be built into future work on the process of educational reform. As argued elsewhere, the ticking of the 'Western clock' dominates the progress of much international development work often to the detriment of the formation of effective partnerships, collaboration, ownership or, indeed, meaningful dialogue. Unrealistic and culturally insensitive time factors are perhaps most often recognised as a problem by practitioners but, to date, this is an issue that has been given only lip service by policy makers and scant theoretical attention by the research community. What makes it especially significant in the comparative and international arena is the fact that the pace of change is currently intensifying, and different cultures engage with this somewhat invisible resource differently. By way of illustration, the following extract taken from an editorial from the Pakistan daily newspaper, *The News*, usefully reveals differing interpretations and implications of time, both within and between nations:

We in Pakistan fluctuate between several calendars. Most people still begin the day at first light and not at midnight. They fast according to the lunar calendar and celebrate the Eid, which is changeable, according to the cycles of the moon. The offices, which live by the Gregorian calendar, give two days holidays but hardly ever three to cater for the Eid falling after 30 days. The tiller of the soil counts his months from an ancient Hindu calendar which goes back to 1000BC. That is why he still talks of Saun, Bhadon (the months of rain) and Jeth (the month of heat). Modernity has brought the ticking clock but the ordinary Pakistani still lives in the Agrarian, pre-modern mindset. In this mindset the season is important as it is connected with food but arbitrary divisions of it are not. Time, after all, is an unending flow and it becomes a tyrant only when we enter the modern age.

Differences such as these go a long way in explaining cultural resistance to innovation, contrasting responses to reform initiatives, and the barriers faced in translating partnership rhetoric into successful practice. This can be seen to apply not only in the international arena, but also in increasing our understanding of differences in the perceptions and actions of different levels of policy makers and practitioners. Implications for a more thorough, sustained and reflexive critique of the assumed benefits of international development targets represent a further related issue for priority attention. Indeed, as we document in the following chapter, such international targets, and time frames, are repeatedly revised (and renamed) in the light of apparently 'disappointing' experiences in meeting their expectations.

Sustainability thus emerges as a further connected theme that we suggest warrants increased attention in the future and this we relate to many of the issues raised above. It is a dilemma faced by policy makers and practitioners in both the North and the South, and it is an issue that has both practical and theoretical implications. Perhaps more pointedly here, this is an example that demands increased attention to the importance of cultural and contextual sensitivities in both educational research and educational development. Studies of sustainable educational reform or sustainable national development – perhaps focused upon successful practice could benefit greatly from more in-depth cross-cultural analyses, enhanced reflexivity and a more critical and culturally informed consideration of time as both a concept and a resource.

Furthermore, this brief exploration of the centrality of sustainability also well illustrates potential linkages between substantive research issues and research processes. As we have argued elsewhere, much existing comparative and international research suggests that participatory approaches to research, and collaborations between theorists, policy makers and practitioners hold considerable potential for the improved sustainability of innovatory practice in the future. This is characteristic of, for example, Gibbons proposals for a 'transdisciplinary' mode of enquiry that sees research as a socio-cultural process. It is also reflected in Delanty's notion of social science as 'discursive practice' whereby collective problems are democratically identified and defined. Social researchers, Delanty proposes, must mediate between social science and society to enable research to recover its public role. These challenges to contemporary and future comparative and international educational research thus go beyond the choice of substantive issues, and are as much theoretical, methodological and organisational in nature.

To cite Reimers and McGinn:

By recognising that education systems are not machines but are arenas for conflict, and that what education systems do reflects how people construct their roles regarding these systems, researchers can facilitate the development of knowledge and sustained organisational learning. The key guides are democratic dialogue, empowerment, time, persistence, and patience.

They conclude with a cautionary, and comparative, note, however, by adding: 'This is not a panacea, a quick fix, or a magic bullet that will lead to success everywhere'.

SUMMARY

In the light of our emerging critique of the field, we have also identified a number of new issues and priorities that we suggest warrant increased attention in the future. This is not intended in any way to represent a complete and detailed review, or to suggest a comprehensive agenda for the future but it is presented as one purposefully focused contribution to the contemporary advancement of the field. We have, therefore, concentrated upon identifying a select number of substantive issues that best demonstrate the wider significance of our related theoretical and methodological arguments. The chapter is thus designed to engage with contemporary developments in a way that emphasises, in particular, how a diversity of cultural and contextual factors demand increased recognition in the future development and re-orientation of the field of comparative and international research in education.

In undertaking the reviews presented both here and in the following chapter, we recognise that a number of currently dominant issues and priorities will, inevitably, continue to command much research attention in the future. These include, for example, a complex range of issues related to marketisation and the global spread of neo-liberal agendas, privatisation, decentralisation and assessment and accountability. They include the persistence of inequities stemming from issues of class, race and gender; skills development training and socio-economic transition; the quality and outcomes of education; and the international community's prioritisation of basic education reform and the role of education in poverty reduction strategies.

In looking to the future we also acknowledge the emergence of new globally significant priorities relating to issues such as the impact on education of new information technologies, AIDS and other health-related concerns, notions of lifelong learning, especially in societies where people are living longer, as well as the impact of globalisation itself. Our own analysis, however, points more directly to the need for greater critique in such analyses and to the centrality of cultural and context sensitivity within both the educational research and educational development arenas. Our substantive research priorities for the future of the field thus emphasise issues of culture, identity, democracy, power and difference. We highlight the importance of enhanced cross-cultural dialogue; the social, educational and citizenship goals of education; the role of knowledge in development; the cultural dimension of teaching and learning; the new architecture of international development; reflexivity, and culturally informed critiques of the concept of time; the sustainability of educational reform; and the resurgence of the humanitarian dimension of comparative and international research in education.

At the heart of our rationale, however, are questions that relate as much to theory and methodology as they do to the emergence of new substantive issues. This brings us back to the potential of the different cultural contributions to the field of comparative and international research, to the advances that poststructuralist critiques have made across the social sciences and humanities in recent times, and to the importance of more substantial dialogue between all involved in educational research and development. In calling for a more effective bridging of cultures and traditions, we are, therefore, acknowledging the importance of the diversity of comparative educations while, simultaneously, recognising the immense potential for the field that can be gained from the enhanced interchange of ideas, insights and understandings. This requires increased recognition of differing perspectives, mutual respect for alternative positions and a more genuine commitment to the sort of intellectual, professional and multi-level dialogue that is essential for truly multidisciplinary comparative and international research in education.

❑❑❑

4

Conducting Comparative and International Research in Education

INTRODUCTION

Many of these issues relate to fundamental problems faced by all educational and social science researchers concerning epistemological, paradigmatic and broadly methodological dilemmas. Other issues relate more directly to distinctive problems encountered by those working specifically within the field of comparative and international education. Many philosophical and epistemological conceptions of problems encountered in carrying out specifically comparative and international research are closely related to the generic methodological literature, but there are other uniquely comparative dilemmas. To date, however, such work has attracted only somewhat specialist and periodic attention, and where this has been the case, it has stemmed largely from personnel working in the more theoretically-oriented 'comparative' constituency. Pragmatic issues and problems have, nevertheless, been addressed by a wider variety of personnel, and especially by those working in the more 'applied' arenas. Thus, in practice, much of the most accessible literature stemming from the field itself has traditionally conceptualised research problems and difficulties more in terms of the practicalities and logistics of doing comparative and international research.

Writers on such themes draw attention to, for example, problems of conceptual equivalences, the sources and accuracy of statistical data, or the logistics of international fieldwork. Such practicalities are, indeed, of considerable importance in cross-cultural research and they rightly deserve attention, especially in times of rapid change when the value of the cumulative experience of previous generations can easily be overlooked.

We therefore pay initial attention to the more pragmatic and practical conceptions of the problems encountered by researchers working within the field. Consistent with the broader thesis of the book, however, we also go further, to examine the significance of more fundamental theoretical and methodological problems and implications that emerge from this review, as we connect with recent intellectual debates and critical perspectives. Contemporary geopolitical and paradigmatic changes, we argue, make it ever more imperative that comparative and international research more effectively bridges the worlds of theory and practice; and better acknowledges the implications of differing world views, cultural perspectives and values upon the research process. At the heart of this lies the challenge posed by post-structuralist critiques at the meta-theoretical level. Despite their own limitations, such critiques generate insights that demonstrate the theoretical and applied potential of research paradigms and strategies that more effectively acknowledge the significance of cultural differences; recognise the role of power and values in shaping international debates on educational and social policy; prioritise diversity and the dynamic relationship between agency and structure; and challenge the dominance of positivistic notions of the research process itself.

This, we argue, suggests the need for a wider conceptualisation of the nature and scope of the problems to be faced by those carrying out comparative and international research in the future. This, in turn, highlights the significance of the relationship between research methods and research methodologies and draws attention back to the dilemmas generated by the legacy of the division between the more theoretical and applied dimensions of the field itself.

When concluding this chapter we therefore advance this argument further, to explore the implications of reconceptualising our understanding of the difficulties and problems encountered during the conduct of comparative and international research. Moreover, this is done in a way that links directly to the broader arguments for change that are pursued in subsequent chapters. This, we suggest, has implications for the theoretical frameworks we adopt, for the substantive priorities we address, for the ways in which we carry out research, and for the broad nature, organisation and scope of the field. We therefore build upon the arguments that emerge from this initial discussion of difficulties and problems, not only in concluding this chapter, but also throughout the subsequent sections of the volume itself.

PROBLEMS STEMMING FROM COMPLEXITY

In setting the scene here, it is perhaps pertinent to begin on a general note that foreshadows the broader dilemmas faced by all comparative and international researchers in the field of education. To begin with, it has long been recognised that the multidisciplinary nature of the field generates especially significant problems in terms of the organisation and management of potentially vast amounts of information relating to a wide range of cultural contexts. When combined with the equally wide range of disciplinary perspectives and methodological paradigms, the related challenges generate complex problems for the individual researcher. Indeed, the potential conflict or 'jostling' of different perspectives, and the inevitable paradigmatic clashes are clearly visible in our previous account of the historical evolution of the field. A degree of personal specialisation for any individual is therefore necessary to avoid what Foster wisely refers to as 'the bane of the field, the universal expert'.

To some extent the complexities noted above also highlight what some see as an institutional weakness of the field – the absence of tight disciplinary boundaries that can leave it exposed to confusion about its defining characteristics, to the attrition of personnel and to the appropriation of the research agenda.

Perhaps even more pointedly, basic theoretical and methodological debates have repeatedly raised the central problem of how we might best learn from comparative and international research. Can we, for example, legitimately move 'toward a science of comparative education' as advocated by Noah and Eckstein; to what extent can we seek out generalisable statements or universal principles in education and the social sciences; and how can we deal with the potential and limitations of the 'borrowing', 'lending', and 'imposition' on the international transfer of educational theories, policies and practices? These are all distinctive problems that have long been faced by specialists working within the field and they continue to raise new challenges for experienced and new researchers to the present day.

POLITICAL MOTIVATIONS

Even in an age of globalisation, and despite the growth of international and regional organisations, considerable store is still placed by many audiences on national, comparative analyses. Governments like to see their countries in a comparative perspective with other similar, or neighbouring countries – a trend that was encouraged by the early IEA studies in the late 1960s and which has continued to this day. When the comparisons have proved unfavourable, as for example for the USA in the 1980s, they have led not only to national soul-searching as illustrated by the publication of *A Nation at Risk*, but also to ongoing policy changes. Something similar happened in England and Wales in the mid-1970s when the country was adversely compared with other European states in terms of skills training and literacy. This led to the so-called Great Education Debate of the late 1970s and to the major restructuring of the educational system that followed during the 1980s and 1990s.

Traditionally the early 'humanitarian', literary and historical approaches to comparative research ignored all but a few statistical data, partly because they were often unavailable. This was the case even though Marc-Antoine Jullien, who, as we have already noted, as the founder of systematic comparative education had advocated the establishment of a centre for gathering international educational statistics. Not until the establishment of the International Bureau of Education, under the auspices of the old League of Nations, were his ideas realised. The implication, as we explain elsewhere, was that early writers in the field, like Matthew Arnold, Isaac Kandel, Nicholas Hans, Joseph Lauwerys, George Bereday and Vernon Mallinson used remarkably few statistics and other 'hard' data in their analysis of education systems. As a result their comments were often highly personalised and rather sweeping. These authors were mainly concerned with the macro-level of education systems, the use of official government information, and what other data was available, plus, where possible, personal visits.

Following World War II, and more especially from the late 1950s and 1960s as more and more countries gained their independence from colonial powers and placed education high on the national agenda for investment and expansion, the need for improved statistical data for planning purposes increased considerably. This so-called age of optimism or age of expansion coincided with the development of key international bodies, most notably UNESCO and the Organisation for Economic Co-operation and Development (OECD) in Paris, the UNESCO Institute of Education in Hamburg, the World Bank in Washington and the International Institute for Educational Planning (IIEP), also in Paris. As indicated earlier these bodies began systematically to collect education statistics and other data on an international basis and for comparative use. Comparativists and writers in the field of international education, as well as many governments, thus now make much use of this available and influential material.

These developments thus coincided with quite a marked shift in comparative studies from the dominance of the historical, explanatory approach to the more substantial use of statistical information and quantitative data analysis that came to be known as the 'scientific approach'.

Moreover, such are the benefits of attracting international students into higher education, or of undertaking short-term consultancies abroad both, for example, are increasingly seen as avenues for bringing in additional revenue to hard pressed institutions that there are now many involved in comparative and international activities who have little or no background knowledge of the field, or of the theoretical and methodological debates of former years. As Rust have recently observed, many of those engaged in such work who claim to be comparativists are unaware of the key literature, let alone the different research perspectives that have been used. This makes the identification of the many inherent difficulties that have long been recognised increasingly important today.

BIAS AND ACCURACY OF DATA

One of the most frequently acknowledged problems that needs to be recognised by those carrying out comparative and international research is that of bias. This may be based on personal prejudices, implicit values or preconceptions. It may also stem from the ways in which existing data are formally presented. In other words bias can be both personal and 'official'. We are all conditioned by our upbringing, culture, education, environment, our status in society and our perceptions of how others view us, as well as by our political, social and religious values and attitudes. All researchers, but especially those involved in research across cultures or across national boundaries, need to be aware of such potential biases and assumptions, their past 'baggage' if preferred, that they bring with them. Inevitably this will influence how they view the 'other, ' and how they document the similarities and differences that they perceive in different cultures. Such biases are not always easy to recognise, let alone overcome. Attitudes to specific countries in Europe may be influenced by an older generation's views on, say, Germany or France, or by first reactions on visiting one of these countries; there may be deeply held ideological views about Russia and her former territories or there may be an antipathy to American cultural dominance, based either upon experience, or upon others' criticisms. Today, for example, this may be seen in some of the standpoints taken by the critics or supporters of globalisation and America's perceived role in this process.

Questionable assumptions, perhaps, most often influence debate and perceptions about the less developed world, especially relating to Africa, and are as much based on lack of knowledge or selective reading as they are shaped by experience. See, for example, the critique of such misrepresentation presented by Daloz and Chabal in their challenging book titled *Africa Works. Disorder as Political Instrument.* It is difficult enough to overcome potential biases when working in a familiar context; it is even more difficult when the researcher is trying to understand a new cultural context without spending long periods of time in the field observing, listening and trying to get behind the way the society operates on different levels – finding out what is culturally or socially acceptable and what is not. This means that fleeting visits, or brief consultancy trips, do not allow sufficient time to understand, let alone speak with authority on, local contexts. As argued later, here are the seeds of the rationale for working in more depth, alongside local researchers with a knowledge of their own context. Yet too many international initiatives lack an adequate local contextual perspective, precisely because they do not sufficiently appreciate the underlying assumptions upon which that society is based. This is reflected in the earlier critique of Reynolds and Farrell's research on school effectiveness. Another example would be some of the studies commissioned by the United Kingdom's Department for International Development (DFID) which have been strongly criticised by Hoppers for being based too strongly on the agenda of the commissioning agency and biased according to Northern research paradigms.

Bias also works in other ways. Government statistics, publicity brochures and official publications often seek to portray a system, or a country, in the most favourable light. In doing this, figures may be officially massaged if it is perceived that this will be politically advantageous. Recent evidence of this comes from the critique of figures relating to the AIDS epidemic in Uganda. Because both the Ugandan government and the World Bank have tried to show Uganda's battle against AIDS in a positive light, it has been argued that only those figures which do this have been published. While the merits of the various arguments in this case remain open for debate, researchers must clearly guard against the use of official documents as their first, and sometimes only, source of information, and be aware of the need for a cautious 'health warning.' The old Soviet Union was notorious for generating problems such as this. As John Dunstan, a specialist in Soviet affairs, once wrote: 'Facts, figures, information are developed or discarded, changed or falsified, if it is felt that this is beneficial to the cause of the Party' (Dunstan 1978:36). Certainly the old Soviet authorities had few qualms about rewriting the school curriculum as political figures, like Stalin or Kruschev, fell from favour. Other authoritarian regimes have done much the same over time. But it is not only authoritarian governments that seek to massage the figures. The current British government is frequently accused of distorting official statistics in order to show that it is meeting its targets, whether these are related to improvements in the reading and mathematical skills of primary-age pupils, improvements in the treatment of patients in hospitals, success rates in school examinations or the amounts of public funding available to schools, hospitals and universities. Sometimes official agencies have been forced to admit that there are errors; but such discrepancies can often be sidestepped and put down to the technicalities of different ways of collecting data.

More pertinently, in the international arena, if a country is wanting to attract overseas development assistance the state may show the economic or educational picture to be worse than it is; if it is wanting to impress foreign investors or its own electorate it will portray things to be better than they really are. Regarding educational data it also needs to be recognised that this is sometimes difficult to acquire, simply because of a lack of experienced personnel, appropriate infrastructure or effective communications. Information is thus often 'made up' so as not to leave too many blank spaces in formal data columns. This is particularly true in poorly resourced countries, where, for example, head teachers often do not have the time, the staff or the support to find and provide the school enrolment data requested, from which the Ministry of Education will eventually compile an 'authoritative' annual report.

Moreover, in such conditions of austerity, Ministries may not have enough field officers, either at the regional or local levels, to follow up those schools or other agencies which do not respond. On the other hand there are other countries whose data collection is not only exemplary, but is, perhaps, so zealous that it often produces more information than can be used. Getting the balance right between establishing efficient management information systems, and 'filling the gaps' because some participants have not responded to government questionnaires is thus one of the major problems currently facing educational planners throughout the developing world.

Other problems arise where several ministries are involved in providing education; they provide their own databases without necessarily feeding these into the collective education statistics. In several countries the Ministries of Agriculture, Defence, Health, Rural Development and even Sport might be providers of education. As a result, trying to ascertain the educational expenditure of the country as a whole may prove to be very elusive. This used to be a particularly acute problem in the Soviet Union, but it applies just as much to large federal countries such as Brazil, India and Nigeria where regional/ provincial/local governments relate to different ministries that have responsibilities for providing different levels of education.

Thailand provides an interesting example of such overlaps. Some years ago there were as many as 17 government and para-government agencies involved in providing education and development initiatives in the rural areas. At central ministry level different divisions operated as if they ran their own private fiefdoms with little regard for the other divisions. While doing doctoral research in Thailand, one of the present authors thus found significantly different statistical data provided by government ministries, UNESCO and other agencies while all purporting to refer to the same thing. All involved in comparative education studies need to bear these concerns in mind. They also raise the question of the reliability of the conclusions drawn by researchers when they have done little more than look over the official statistical evidence provided by international agencies, without delving into how these figures were arrived at. More disturbingly, both UNESCO and the World Bank are sometimes in danger of decontextualising their own information and extrapolating unrealistic trends from such data.

FOCUS FOR RESEARCH

At the outset of any comparative or international study researchers need to be especially well aware of what they are looking for, and why. Is it for academic interest only? Is it to identify trends? Or is it for the purposes of reforming their own or other systems of education? The latter has long been cited as one of the main justifications for researching comparatively. Or is it to test a set of hypotheses? Unless there is clarity of purpose in this complex, multidisciplinary field, it is likely that much unnecessary material will be collected to the detriment of disciplined enquiry. A clear focus, especially regarding which, moreover, in such conditions of austerity, Ministries may not have enough field officers, either at the regional or local levels, to follow up those schools or other agencies which do not respond. On the other hand, there are other countries whose data collection is not only exemplary, but is, perhaps, so zealous that it often produces more information than can be used. Getting the balance right between establishing efficient management information systems, and 'filling the gaps' because some participants have not responded to government questionnaires is thus one of the major problems currently facing educational planners throughout the developing world.

Other problems arise where several ministries are involved in providing education; they provide their own databases without necessarily feeding these into the collective education statistics. In several countries the Ministries of Agriculture, Defence, Health, Rural Development and even Sport might be providers of education. As a result, trying to ascertain the educational expenditure of the country as a whole may prove to be very elusive. This used to be a particularly acute problem in the Soviet Union, but it applies just as much to large federal countries such as Brazil, India and Nigeria where regional/ provincial/local governments relate to different ministries that have responsibilities for providing different levels of education.

Thailand provides an interesting example of such overlaps. Some years ago there were as many as 17 government and para-government agencies involved in providing education and development initiatives in the rural areas. At central ministry level different divisions operated as if they ran their own private fiefdoms with little regard for the other divisions. While doing doctoral research in Thailand, one of the present authors thus found significantly different statistical data provided by government ministries, UNESCO and other agencies while all purporting to refer to the same thing. All involved in comparative education studies need to bear these concerns in mind. They also raise the question of the reliability of the conclusions drawn by researchers when they have done little more than look over the official statistical evidence provided by international agencies, without delving into how these figures were arrived at. More disturbingly, both UNESCO and the World Bank are sometimes in danger of decontextualising their own information and extrapolating unrealistic trends from such data.

TENSIONS BETWEEN GLOBAL AND LOCAL PRIORITIES

Issues raised in this next section are fundamental to the core spirit of comparative and international research in education. In recent years there has been a growing tendency for policy-makers worldwide to identify global problems and to seek to implement global solutions as if one model fits every situation. Many writers argue that this underpinned much of the approach of the World Bank during the 1990s with its strategies for higher education, proposals for general education below the tertiary level and structural adjustment policies throughout much of the developing world. Critical voices have thus expressed many pertinent and enduring concerns about such approaches. Common problems may exist in different countries but solutions can rarely be found in the application of a common model across different cultures, regions and political regimes regardless of whether the administrative framework or professional expertise or local culture is capable of introducing, or adapting such reforms. While educational reform through school improvement is one area that has been subject to this type of approach and critique, it also applies to much of the literature on decentralisation and local finance as well as that on local community involvement in running and managing schools. Over the years such over-generalised ideas have been advanced by various international organisations without due consideration for local differences. Chapman have shown the fallacy of such strategies with reference to rural Ghana; Cheng in the case of China; and R.C. Riddell with reference to Africa as a whole. Sadly these are just a sample of critiques of global 'solutions' being applied uncritically in diverse local contexts.

To understand an education system other than one's own in real depth ideally requires a long period of time spent within that 'other' context, or at least numerous repeated visits until the researcher has an instinctive feel for what makes that society tick: why decisions are arrived at in the way they are; who the powerbrokers are and so on. As Sadler reminds us, every system of education is shaped by its local, historical, economic, cultural and social context. It cannot truly be understood without this fundamental principle being acknowledged. As Lauwerys argued, only then can the underlying philosophy of an education system be understood. Education, in short, cannot be decontextualised from its local culture, though this is so often the case when less disciplined (but often influential) cross-cultural analyses are carried out across many different countries. UNESCO's World Education Reports have, for example, identified trends in education across many systems, and while they have acknowledged national differences, they have failed to go far in helping us to understand the reasons for the different contextual nuances. For example, the United Kingdom was often compared unfavourably with other European countries because of its low enrolment of children aged three or four, yet these comparisons overlooked the fact that state provision began at age five, and frequently included the rising fives, whereas in much of Europe formal schooling does not begin until six or even seven years of age. More recently there has been a closing of the gap of school provision at an early age across Europe. Similarly, the lower percentage of the age group entering British higher education was often adversely compared with the entry rates to higher education in the USA, France and Germany, with scant regard taken of the fact that the dropout rates in all those countries were far higher than in Britain. If one looked at completion rates instead of entry rates, the gap became very much smaller. With the determination of the United Kingdom's New Labour government to expand both nursery provision and higher education, the differences between enrolments in the different European countries are also becoming less marked. The relatively unstructured school curriculum in England also used to be compared unfavourably with the more centrally controlled national curricula prevailing in most of her continental neighbours; but this has also changed with the development of a National Curriculum for England and Wales, and the paradoxical explorations of less centralised models within Europe, during the 1990s. The continuing importance of understanding the relationship between national culture and the curriculum is, therefore, most appositely demonstrated by writers such as Broadfoot and colleagues in their comparative studies of European education.

The focus of the school curriculum, or the place of the teacher in an education system, can thus only really be understood by an appreciation of the underlying philosophy or purpose of schooling in different societies. This, it has long been argued by comparativists, is best achieved by an extended stay within a country, preferably with a knowledge of the local language(s), or by working alongside local researchers. Unfortunately, an extended timescale for researching and understanding any country, its cultures, social and political interactions, its taboos and customs is a 'luxury' that few can afford. This points to further problems relating to the commissioning of research and to related questions of power and control.

CONFLICTING AGENDAS

Much comparative and international research is now commissioned by governments, international organisations or private educational charities. These each have their own agendas and often want to commission consultants or researchers for their own ends, either to propagate a particular theory or to advance a set of policies. As Preston and Arthur have pointed out, this can often lead to a conflict of interests and professional compromises, especially if the researchers unearth findings that are not acceptable to the commissioning agency or to the host government. Researchers might thus feel compelled to pursue particular lines of inquiry, but be prevented from doing so because of constraints over which they have little control. Consultancy priorities are especially likely to be determined by whoever is pulling the purse strings; or there may be a conflict of interest between the external funding agency, if it is a national or international aid organisation, and the host government. The researchers may then be caught in an ethical dilemma as to which body they should be answerable to. Sometimes researchers may, as a result of undertaking such work, find themselves supporting particular groups against the views of the funder. Dove highlights this in the context of teachers and community schools, especially in rural communities, where teachers might find themselves at odds with the central government over, for example, language or ethnic policy. This, as she demonstrates, can lead to researchers finding themselves aligning with the teachers. Aikman's work with Amazon communities helps to show that these are widespread and ongoing issues. Perhaps the biggest danger stemming from this lies in the way that researchers from the North may become unwitting agents of Northern 'knowledge control' and policy transfer. The main loser in this increasingly common scenario for educational consultancy and research is the academic and professional credibility of the work undertaken.

So much for difficulties facing individual researchers, but few scholars now operate entirely independently. Funding agencies often prefer comparative and international studies to be undertaken in teams, or with counterpart(s) within the countries under study. While such strategies have many advantages, Osborn and Phillips and Economou have highlighted the difficulties encountered in undertaking collaborative research across Europe; Shaw and Ormston have discussed the misunderstandings which occurred in introducing a reform package into Russia; and Lewin and Stuart and Stuart and Lewin touch on the difficulties of conducting a highly complex, interdisciplinary research project across five different developing countries, mainly in Africa but also including the Caribbean.

EQUIVALENCES AND MISCONCEPTIONS

As the above writers note, not only are there 'political' and personality difficulties to be worked through, but language can generate major dilemmas for comparative and international researchers. Even if there is an agreed working language in which the terms being used might appear at face value to be the same, words can have very different meanings in different contexts. The term 'school' has, for example, different meanings in the USA from its use in most European countries. At one level there is a common usage, but at another it is more usual in the USA to talk about students at college or university as going to 'school'. This is not so in Europe. Even defining primary and secondary schools is fraught with potential difficulties because of the differing age ranges involved in the different levels in different countries. Again students 'graduate' from various levels of school in the USA, whereas only university students are seen to 'graduate' in most European and African countries. Familiar terms like 'community', 'participation', 'management', 'decentralisation', and 'professor', also take on subtly distinct meanings in different cultural and political contexts. It is essential, therefore, that all who are involved in any form of collaborative research ensure that they understand what each participant means by the terms being used, even if this might involve hours of careful negotiation before the detailed research gets under-way. This partly explains why it is so dangerous for systems, especially in the developing world, to accept the recommendations of bodies like the World Bank and UNESCO at their face value, because the latter have too often been based on thinking, concepts and rationales largely developed in Western contexts; and which might not be easily adapted into, say, francophone Africa or the Islamic Middle East. Today, even these terms are culturally laden, as we have noted previously.

In concluding here, it is therefore clear that problems of equivalence are both central to comparative and international research and multi-dimensional in nature. Indeed, our own analysis closely parallels Warwick and Osherson's useful categorisation that distinguishes between conceptual equivalence, equivalence of measurement and linguistic equivalence. These are clearly problematic issues that are of enduring significance in comparative research across the social sciences.

LIMITATIONS OF STATISTICAL DATA

Linking back to earlier sections in this chapter, regardless of how official statistical data have been compiled there are a number of additional caveats which need to be carefully recognised in comparative and international research. First, raw statistics ignore the human and cultural dimensions of a society, which for many comparativists, are at the very heart of what they are studying. Raw data do not, as we have seen, reveal the underlying philosophy or rationale of an education system which help to explain anomalies, or reasons for differences with other systems. What they may tell us, for example, are details about enrolments (and even these might be misleading if they provide gross enrolment figures and not the net enrolment figures); or wastage rates (without looking at the underlying causes); or progression from one level to the next (without commenting on the policy on grade retention or annual examinations). These might be helpful but they can also be misleading if they are compared with data from another system where an entirely different set of background information would be needed to explain their figures.

Second, the GNP and per capita income data, that are used by agencies such as the World Bank and UNDP to classify the countries of the world, are typically national data and are essentially aggregated. They therefore ignore regional variations and ethnic and linguistic disparities. Indeed, language differences and problems rarely seem to enter official international data sets, as if these have no bearing on academic performance or economic development or attitudes to education or healthcare. Moreover, any existing data that are used for internal purposes might be significantly different from those that are published by the various international agencies.

Third, much of the above is predicated on the belief that the key data source on population figures – the national census – is accurate. This cannot necessarily be guaranteed. Over a million people did not complete the 1991 British census because, by being unregistered, they could avoid paying the unpopular community charge, or poll tax as it was known. Malawi had no census between 1966 and 1987. China had no census between 1953 and 1983, and even now there are doubts about the accuracy of the country's national census. In many countries, Bangladesh and Pakistan being but two examples, there are no accurate figures for births and deaths, particularly in the remote and rural areas. Nigeria's population figures have been notoriously inaccurate. The 1973 census there had to be abandoned because of irregularities, and the 1983 census was grossly inflated in certain provinces because the larger the population the greater the federal subsidies. These inaccuracies contributed to planning chaos when it came to introducing Universal Primary Education (UPE) in Nigeria. In Ethiopia and several West African countries the census figures have frequently had to be estimated, either because certain areas have proved inaccessible for census officials or, for cultural reasons, people have avoided answering personal or sensitive questions about the numbers in a family or in the village.

If the basic population figures are erroneous, other data which are based on these figures are, at best, questionable, and this poses distinct and significant problems for comparative and international education research in such contexts. As the Nigerian UPE example illustrates, it is also very difficult to plan for the expansion of education provision without an accurate idea of the age group population, its likely growth rate and any understanding of regional density. This is why school mapping has become such an important tool for educational planners in developing countries today. It can be very difficult to calculate the population growth rates accurately, the Gross Domestic Product, the average per capita income, and the percentage of the population engaged in agriculture or in other areas of the economy. Researchers in education, and throughout the social sciences, thus need to recognise where there are elements of uncertainty in the data used. Indeed, some years ago Puryear highlighted the problems of acquiring accurate educational statistics, especially by bodies like UNESCO which rely so heavily on member states providing the organisation with the basic information. At the end of the 1990s Heyneman therefore observed:

> *... in the field of education, UNESCO data must be treated with caution or worse, they must be assumed to be untrustworthy. Consequently, it is possible that the results of research on education and economic development by the World Bank, as well as many academic institutions using UNESCO statistics, are unreliable.*

On a positive note, Heyneman did suggest that the statistical data provided by the Organisation for Economic Cooperation and Development (OECD) were somewhat better because the OECD countries had the resources and infrastructure to ensure greater reliability. Considerable improvements are also now being made to standardise the information being sought, as well as to improve the accuracy of the figures presented. The development of the International Standard Classification of Education (INSCED) should also gradually improve both the access to, and the reliability of, educational data for comparative purposes.

Even so there is still a long way to go. Two of the most notorious areas for acquiring accurate data, whether for comparable purposes or not, are those of literacy and non-formal and adult education. Apart from different interpretations of what constitutes literacy, or a literate person, which varies from country to country, there are problems relating to which language a person might be literate in or in which they function on a daily basis. In Thailand a person is regarded as literate if they have enrolled in primary school for at least two years, whereas in the Philippines a person who is literate has been defined as: 'a good citizen who should be able to read with understanding newspapers, bulletins, advertisements, tax notices and letters and should be able to write an ordinary letter'.

Many countries use school enrolment figures, or examinations data, to arrive at relevant totals but these can prove unreliable if children have dropped out of school before they have reached grades 5 or 6 when there is a possibility of achieving levels of permanent literacy. Even then, as Rogers cogently argues, unless there are materials produced in local languages which can help to sustain that literacy, it does not take many years before there is a lapse into semi-literacy. Samson's study of the situation in Addis Ababa in Ethiopia illustrates this point well. Samson argues that there is ample evidence of semi-literates being classified as literate, whereas she found that many of these individuals were in effect illiterate, and this was only in the area of urban Addis Ababa. The situation in the rural areas may be even more alarming. Wherever there are multilingual situations and the collection of literacy data is in one, or at the most two, languages, figures are likely to be distorted. This was the case in colonial Vietnam. Before the French insisted on teaching and using French for educational purposes the literacy rates in Vietnamese schools were relatively high. However, with the introduction of French medium schooling, many Vietnamese opted out and by the time the French were forced out of the country those rates had dropped significantly. No more than 10 per cent of the population were reported to be literate in French.

In the area of comparative adult and non-formal education the situation has become even more complex, as Carr-Hill have been at pains to explain. Not only has there been continuing uncertainty as to what constitutes non-formal education since the term was first introduced in the early 1970s, but there has been no agreement across countries as to who, or what, should be included in statistical data covering the area of non-formal education, nor where the dividing line between formal and non-formal education should come. The result has been a considerable degree of confusion. Hopefully this will be resolved by further work in the next few years.

There is little room for complacency about the figures for formal school enrolments either. Some international figures for the United Kingdom, for example, refer to the whole country, some to England and Wales, which internally have traditionally been linked together, some to Great Britain, which traditionally has referred to the mainland only, thereby excluding Northern Ireland. If such a situation can arise in a context which has good access to data, how much more problematic must data collection be in large countries such as Brazil, China, India, Nigeria and Indonesia where communication links between the central government and outlying regions are often far from easy. Anyone familiar with Sub-Saharan Africa cannot fail to be aware that while the Ministries of Education have official lists of schools and teachers and pupils, many of these schools do not exist as buildings. Rather they are made up of groups of children sitting in the open air under trees, at least during the dry season! Some of the problems that arise from such situations have been usefully identified by Croft in Malawi as part of her research for the Multi-Site Teacher Education Research Programme (MUSTER) recently co-ordinated by the University of Sussex in the United Kingdom.

Perhaps some of the biggest difficulties in collecting official statistics and using them for international comparative research arise from differences in the length of schooling for different age groups, as argued earlier, and in ensuring that one is comparing like with like. For example UNESCO, World Bank and OECD figures take primary school enrolments as running from ages 6 to 12; secondary enrolments as from 12 to 18; and tertiary enrolments as from 18 to 23. However many countries begin primary school at 5 or 7, secondary at 11, 12 or 13, while tertiary education might begin at 17, 18 or 19 or even later. To arrive at realistic and meaningful data which can accurately be used for comparisons is thus fraught with difficulties.

PROBLEMS RELATED SPECIFICALLY TO RESEARCH IN DEVELOPING COUNTRIES

While many of the above issues have general currency for comparative and international research in education worldwide, there are other problems that apply more specifically to the developing world. These are considered in a little more detail below.

Poorly developed infrastructure

Since many developing countries are located in the equatorial and tropical regions of the world, they experience specific problems of environmental context which are less problematic elsewhere. Many countries in Africa and South Asia suffer from poor soils and scrub vegetation; in South-East Asia and large parts of Latin America there is dense jungle or inhospitable mountain ranges while in the Middle East and North and North-west Africa it is desert that predominates. These environmental features become particularly problematic once the urban areas are left behind. Distances between centres of population may be considerable. Many places are inaccessible by public transport, even when this is fairly reliable. Roads may be badly maintained or even non-existent apart from dirt tracks or laterite highways.

Researchers, whether they be insiders or outsiders, may thus have to travel long distances, in the heat and on foot. Lodgings may lack basic facilities. Access to computers, the internet, telephones or other means of telecommunication may be non-existent because of an absence of electricity. It is revealing to note, for example, that 80 per cent of the world's population has no access to basic infrastructure facilities that are regarded as commonplace in the industrialised world and that there are reported to be more computers in New York alone than in the whole of Africa.

Infrastructure problems might also relate to the postal system, basic administration and law and order throughout the country. All these can hamper researchers in the field on a practical level. Far more problematic, and something that has a direct bearing on the successful development of poverty research and poverty alleviation programmes in many countries, is a weak or poorly developed bureaucratic system. This often means that there are not enough trained personnel on the ground to ensure that government policies are implemented, or that research and evaluation can be actively supported.

Limited levels of public research

Although there are some beacons of successful research initiatives within the South, and there have been successful links established between Northern research institutions and Southern counterparts, it remains true to say that much educational research carried out in developing countries is either done by Northern researchers, or takes place under the aegis of a Northern research consultancy or funding body. In medical research alone barely 10 per cent of funds are spent on those diseases which affect 90 per cent of the world's population. Both Samoff's and Buchert's studies of educational reforms in the South show how these were dictated, or directed, by Northern aid agencies; while Samoff's analysis of the contents, procedures and personnel involved in over 240 educational surveys conducted in Africa between 1990 and 1994, demonstrates that, apart from some nominal representation of local researchers, the work was almost entirely conducted by expatriates. Habte has, therefore, rightly called into question the international community's commitment to developing a viable research capacity in the South. The need for this was advocated as long ago as 1985 in a special issue of the *International Journal of Educational Development*. At the heart of this dilemma are familiar issues relating to funding, resources, human resource development and access to specialist training. However, as we shall argue later, more political questions of dependency, power and control also emerge if any change is to be globally influential and locally sustainable.

Limited funding

While the lack of funding for educational research is a significant problem in most societies, it is particularly acute in developing countries which are desperately short of money for basic system functions. In such contexts research can be seen as a luxury that cannot be afforded. Even in situations where there are active local researchers, they are frequently hampered by their working conditions which place excessive demands on their time so that little is left that might be channelled into productive research. Such situations can fuel sensitivities and political opposition to outsiders receiving support, further limiting the possibilities for positive capacity development.

Language complications

The majority of the world's nations are multi-ethnic and multilingual. This highlights the importance of language skills for cross-cultural researchers. While comparativists have long recognised this principle, it is also clear that few researchers can realistically expect to be fluent in more than one or two of the necessary languages, let alone understand the nuances of the different languages or ethnic groups within a country. It is, therefore, of vital importance that researchers working in such multicultural contexts should, at the very least, recognise the implications of these issues, and familiarise themselves with local customs and aspects of the language which might lead to confusion or misunderstanding. Robinson's studies of language use at the grassroots level in different parts of Africa, for example, well illustrate the problems for aid donors of working at central government level who expect their proposals to be understood by different levels of administrators further down the system. Counterparts at this level might well, and probably do, operate in a local vernacular as opposed to the national language. Certain terms, concepts and ideas familiar to those at the centre who work with, or through, the international community might have entirely different meanings in such different language settings. Thus, while researchers might be able to bypass some of the levels of administration, they are nevertheless confronted with these different linguistic assumptions and understandings the further away they operate from the centre. Chapman and colleagues recently found this while working with local primary school communities in Ghana, and their work could be helpful to others dealing with such issues in the future.

THE CHANGING NATURE OF RESEARCH PROBLEMS AND PRIORITIES

Running throughout the above discussion it can be seen how apparently practical and logistical research problems are so often impossible to disentangle from more substantial issues relating to culture, values, ethics and power. Here it is argued that contemporary changes in geopolitical relations, combined with the implications of the intensification of globalisation, have heightened the significance of such relationships to the extent that the very conceptualisation of problems in comparative and international research is itself in need of fundamental change. Further inspiring this critique is recognition of the challenges raised by the variety of poststructuralist frameworks for the analysis of education. Such thinking points to the need, increasingly acknowledged across the social sciences, for a more critical reconsideration of the relationship between policy and practice, and between theoretical studies and applied research. Too often, as illustrated by the division between the comparative and international dimensions of our own field, the discourses and priorities of academic theorists are pursued in ways that fail to relate effectively and accessibly to matters of educational policy and practice. On the other hand, this hiatus also inhibits policymakers and practitioners from valuing and engaging with potentially helpful theoretical perspectives and insights.

The relevance of these meta-level issues for the reconceptualisation of research problems in comparative and international education is paramount here. As our discussion already demonstrates, underpinning many of what are, at first sight, practical and logistical problems, can be found more substantial dilemmas that existing theoretical work can play a valuable role in understanding. Problems relating to cultural bias, for example, can often be more effectively addressed in the light of theoretical work on the legitimation of educational knowledge, or from the perspective of recent scholarship on cross-cultural knowledge transfer and 'dialogue among civilisations' as demonstrated by Hayhoe and

Pan. Similarly, writers such as Hickling-Hudson usefully demonstrate how post-colonial frameworks can challenge pervasive ethnocentrism that can seriously inhibit very practical efforts to advance genuine research partnerships between the North and the South. Turning the rhetoric of 'partnership', 'collaboration' and 'co-operation' into improved research practice thus has a potentially powerful ally in the arena of theoretical scholarship. For those involved in research capacity building, in the North and the South, this holds much future potential.

To take a different set of priority issues, sensitivity to culture and context also underpins the increasingly successful application of qualitative research strategies in the field of comparative and international education. Case study, action research and critical ethnography, for instance, have all proved helpful in contributing to improved educational policy and practice in developing countries despite the ongoing dominance of positivistic assumptions and paradigms in the agendas of powerful development agencies and government bureaucracies. Much more, however, needs to be done if we are to maximise the benefits of differing perspectives, or, for example, if the applied potential of critical theory, such as that which inspired Freire or Chambers, is not to be limited to the work of 'alternative' pressure groups or the advocacy efforts of non-governmental organisations (NGOs). For the benefits of such theoretical perspectives to be maximised, we argue that the range and the quality of the dialogue across professional cultures must also be improved, and for this to happen the nature and scope of the discourse itself must change.

This brings us back to the primary need to broaden our understanding of the nature of the difficulties and problems that confront contemporary advances in the field of comparative and international education. In doing this, we return to the implications of our argument for more effective bridging between the worlds of theory and practice – the discourses, personnel and cultures in ways that will enhance our understanding of the contemporary problems and priorities that we all face in the twenty-first century. To a significant extent this suggests the need to focus increased critical attention on the ways in which comparative and international research is conducted, by whom, and for whose benefit. The nature of this task thus requires more direct attention to research processes than has hitherto been the case.

Research in the field is sometimes quantitative, often qualitative, sometimes arts-based, sometimes informed by humanities fields, such as philosophy, literary theory, and cultural studies. It is influenced as well by social science fields, such as psychology, political and social theory, and by interdisciplinary fields, such as women's and gender studies and post-colonial studies. The use of the term "research" in the title is intended to emphasize, despite its paradigmatic differences, the field's relative unity in the project of understanding – a term that includes both theoretical and practical interests and initiatives.

For prospective and practicing teachers in the United States and elsewhere, it will contextualize national school reform efforts.

Pressure is increasing on all those involved in education, from teachers to policy-makers, to transform schools as organisations, while continuing to implement effective new approaches to teaching and learning. The demand is not only to reach attained targets, but also to be accountable for teaching methods. Developing Teachers and Teaching Practice brings together a selection of papers given at the ninth conference of the International Study Association of Teachers and Teaching (ISATT). The collection takes as a central theme the issue of education as a key concern within the international rhetoric of globalisation. Developing Teachers and Teaching Practice contains contributions from some of the best-known academics in the field, and will be of great interest to teacher educators and educational researchers around the world.

5

Research Topics in Comparative Education

INTRODUCTION

Communications consist of what people say (oral) and write (printed). Useful oral communications include lectures, speeches, conversations, discussions, debates, criticisms, advice, proposals, and more. Useful printed communications include journal and magazine articles, newspaper stories and editorials, books, encyclopedias, letters, diaries, legal documents, government reports, school board minutes, conference proceedings, and the like.

Problems faced in the daily conduct of education are likewise a fertile origin of research ideas, since dedicated teachers and administrators are continually trying to improve the efficiency of their work. To help with this effort, they either conduct studies themselves or enlist the aid of researchers interested in such issues.

But whatever the immediate stimulus may be, it is usually helpful to have in mind a broad array of possible topics from which to choose. Then, from that array, researchers can select what they wish to compare. The following examples illustrate what I mean by *an array of possible comparisons.* Later in Stage I these matters are discussed in greater detail.

THE ARRAY OF POSSIBLE COMPARISONS

Because there are thousands of potential comparisons, it is useful to know methods of organizing them so they can be surveyed systematically. The following paragraphs describe three such methods a cube display, a set of encyclopedia topics, and a taxonomy of educational objectives.

A CUBE DISPLAY

Figure 5.1 offers a three-dimensional way of exhibiting comparative possibilities. The first dimension is geographical/locational. It contains seven levels: world regions/continents, countries, states/provinces, districts, schools, classrooms, and individuals. This dimension could be expanded by the addition of further intermediate levels. For example, schools within districts could be grouped into clusters, and individual students within a classroom could be placed together in work groups for the study of mathematics, reading, or science.

The second dimension represents nonlocational demographic groupings, with the illustrated groups based on ethnicity, religion, age, gender, socioeconomic status, and an entire population. Further groups could be added, including ones founded on citizenship, language spoken, political affiliation, health condition, tested intelligence, source of family income, educational attainment, and more.

Aspects of the educational enterprise and of society are combined along the third dimension, although it is also possible to cast the education system and society as separate dimensions, thereby producing a four-dimensional model. Only four of a multitude of educational aspects are pictured in the figure-learning objectives, curriculum, teaching methods, and administrative structure. Only four of a host of potential societal variables are portrayed—parents' associations, political change, labour market conditions, and population growth.

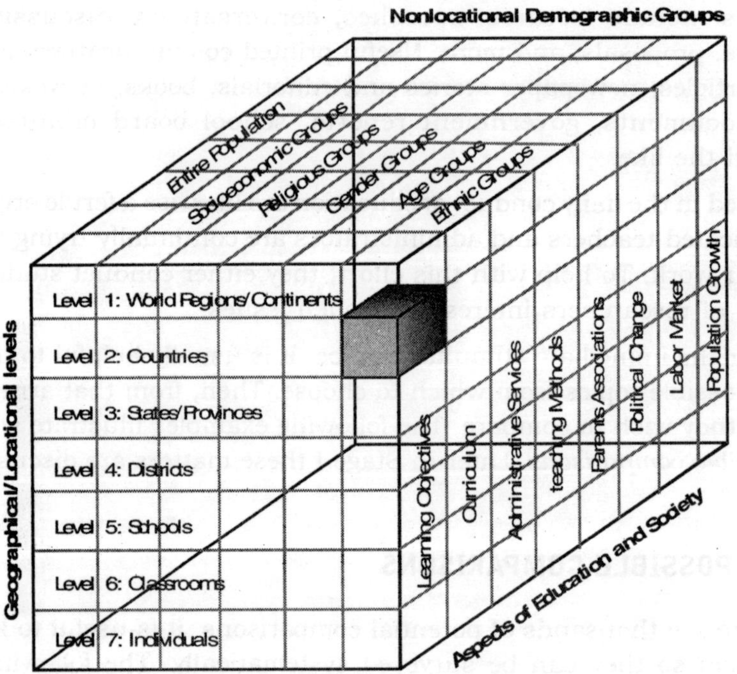

Fig. 5.1. A Framework for Comparative Education Analyses

Every comparative study involves all three dimensions so that a given study can be located in one or more cells in the diagram. For instance, the shaded cell represents a research project comparing learning objectives for ethnic groups in two or more nations.

In summary, the cube suggests a way of looking at possible comparisons, but it does not offer a definitive list of options along each dimension. To expand the options that comprise each dimension, researchers can turn to more specific classification systems. The following example demonstrates one way to extend the aspects of education that are located on the third dimension of Figure 5.1.

SET OF ENCYCLOPEDIA TOPICS

A systematic classification of potential comparisons can be developed by deriving topics from an educational encyclopedia and reassembling them into major categories and subcategories. How this is accomplished can be demonstrated with items drawn from Husén & Post lethwaite *International Encyclopedia of Education.*

The process of organizing such a schema consists of examining the contents of an encyclopedia's index in order to identify suitable topics, then reorganizing the topics into an outline that subsumes more specific items under more general ones. The complete outcome of the process is too lengthy to present here. However, the pattern that the final product may assume can be illustrated with the following segment of a more extensive schema. First, general headings are selected and labelled: (1) social/philosophical foundations, (2) curriculum, (3) teaching/learning activities, (4) characteristics of learners, (5) organization and management (administration), (6) educational personnel, and (7) research techniques. Then, more detailed topics, representing descending tiers of greater specificity, are listed under each heading. Here are the early items in the third general category:

3. Teaching/learning activities	3.2.1.11 Carroll's model
3.1 Learning objectives	3.2.1.12 Freinet method
3.1.1 Types of objectives	3.2.1.13 Herbartian approach
3.1.1.1 Cognitive	3.2.1.14 Montessori's system
3.1.1.2 Psychomotor	3.2.1.15 Rogers' experiential plan
3.1.1.3 Affective/emotional	3.2.1.16 Socratic dialogue
3.1.1.4 Behavioral	3.2.1.17 Wittrock's generative learning
3.1.2 Educational standards	3.2.2 Distance teaching
3.2 Methods of teaching	3.2.2.1 Correspondence
3.2.1 Classroom teaching	3.2.2.2 Radio
3.2.1.1 Lecture	3.2.2.3 Television
3.2.1.2 Demonstration	3.2.2.4 Computer-assisted
3.2.1.3 Discussion	3.2.3 Individualized instruction
3.2.1.4 Group work	3.2.3.1 Tutoring
3.2.1.5 Experimentation	3.2.3.2 Apprenticeship
3.2.1.6 Sociodrama	3.2.3.3 Self instruction
3.2.1.7 Individual projects	3.2.3.4 Dalton plan
3.2.1.8 Mastery-learning	3.2.3.5 Decroly method
3.2.1.9 Ausebel's verbal model	3.2.3.6 Keller plan
3.2.1.10 Bruner's discovery model	

Further second-level headings in the teaching/learning-activities outline can be (3.3) learning materials and equipment and (3.4) evaluating learners' progress. To continue the outline, we would next list subtopics under each of those headings.

In addition to using an encyclopedia to generate topics, we can turn to sources of even more specific issues that fit within the sorts of categories displayed in the above outline. For example, an investigator intending to conduct a study in the realm of learning objectives may profit from inspecting the *Taxonomy of Educational Objectives* that Benjamin Bloom and others devised.

TAXONOMY OF EDUCATIONAL OBJECTIVES

Bloom and his associates first defined three major domains into which instructional objectives could be placed—the cognitive, the affective (emotional), and the psychomotor. Then within each domain, they created categories they believed would accommodate all the types of specific objectives that educational programs are typically designed to pursue. The structure of their taxonomy can be illustrated with an excerpt from the cognitive domain.

The six major classes of objectives are those focusing on knowledge, comprehension, application, analysis, synthesis, and evaluation. The items within each class are ones that could be adapted to any subject-matter field in the curriculum—language arts, mathematics, science, social science, fine arts, vocational subjects, and others. The nature of the subcategories within a major class can be demonstrated by those under the heading *knowledge*. Each item begins with the phrase *Knowledge of*:

1.1 Specifics

1.1.1 Terminology

1.1.2 Specific facts

1.2 Ways and means of dealing with specifics

1.2.1 Conventions

1.2.2 Trends and sequences

1.2.3 Classification and categories

1.2.4 Criteria

1.2.5 Methodology

1.3 Universals and abstractions in a field

1.3.1 Principles and generalizations

1.3.2 Theories and structures.

These generic entries are converted into a form applicable to a specific subject matter area by appending to each entry a phrase identifying the subject-matter field. For instance, for the subject of algebra the resulting statements become:

1.1.1 Knowledge of terminology in algebra,

1.1.2 knowledge of specific algebra facts,

1.3.1 knowledge of algebra principles and generalizations, and so on.

In like manner, each of the other five major classes also subsumes a series of more precise types of objectives. Thus, a person intending to compare instructional objectives may well find Bloom's taxonomy useful in suggesting aspects of objectives to include.

A question can now be asked about why researchers should concern themselves with inspecting a broad array of possible comparisons if they already have in mind a specific issue that interests them? The answer is that considering an extensive range of potential topics can often guide investigators toward improving their project by incorporating aspects that otherwise would have been overlooked. For example, someone planning to compare instructional methods in six classrooms might profit from using the encyclopedia outline for devising the categories into which teachers' methods will be placed. Or, the cube in Figure 5.1 could alert a researcher who is studying student achievement to analyze data at more than one geographical level (state, district, school), so as to reveal differences among states, among districts within states, and among schools within districts.

Finally, almost every research project includes a phase that is typically referred to as "a review of the literature." The review consists of the investigator learning what has been done in the past in relation to (a) defining his or her research topic, (b) selecting methods of data collection, and (c) interpreting the results. Surveying the array of potential comparisons can be one important feature of such a review.

SOURCES OF TOPICS AND RESEARCH-PROJECT AIMS

The following sketches of eight research projects illustrate connections among (a) the source of a topic, (b) the event leading to the choice of the topic, and (c) both the general and specific aims of the project.

The topic source: A professor's research agenda

A university professor interested in the decentralization of educational administration was conducting a series of studies about transferring administrative decision-making responsibilities from the provincial level to the school-district level. In connection with this project, he suggested that one of his doctoral advisees carry out her dissertation research as a segment of thc decentralization program. The topic he recommended to her was: "A comparison of three methods of devolving responsibility for hiring teachers for rural schools."

General aim: Contribute to a broader research project.

Specific aim: Discover the consequences of three methods of assigning local authorities the task of hiring teachers.

The topic source: A speech at an educational conference

While attending a conference, a graduate student doubted the accuracy and wisdom of a conference speaker's declaring that:

> *"In the primary grades, reading instruction for boys should begin later and advance at a slower pace than for girls because (a) girls mature at a faster rate than boys, (b) girls score higher than boys on reading tests, and (c) more boys than girls require remedial reading instruction."*

The student's doubt became the basis of the topic he chose for his master's thesis. He planned to analyze reading-test scores of primary-grade boys and girls, focusing attention on how well individual children succeeded rather than focusing solely on the average score for each sex. On the basis of the results, he recommended that the pacing of reading instruction be founded on each child's reading skills rather than on the conference speaker's generalization about the two sexes.

General aim: Assess a conference speaker's assertion.

Specific aim: Compare the effectiveness of different paces of reading instruction, focusing on individual pupils rather than on girls as a group and boys as a group.

The topic source: Reports of students' interest in studying science

The impetus behind a science educator's decision to conduct a research project came from two published reports that traced a decline over the secondary-school years in students' interest in studying science. In an effort to discover ways to heighten student interest, he studied the effects that a "results-prediction" technique had on learners' attitudes. The technique, used in teaching genetics concepts to high school biology students, consisted of the instructor requiring class members to predict the outcome of genetics experiments before the experiments were actually conducted. The purpose of requiring prediction was to enhance learning "by focusing students' attention on the concepts under consideration and by motivating students to seek verification of their predictions". A comparison of the performance of students under the results-prediction approach with the performance of ones not obliged to offer predictions showed that both groups scored equally well on tests, but the "prediction activities augmented classroom participation, promoted critical analysis, and enhanced student interest in the lesson".

General aim: Evaluate a remedy for an educational problem

Specific aim: Test the instructional effectiveness of having students try to predict the outcome of experiments in the field of genetics.

The topic source: Books about Vygotsky's theory of learning

One definition of theory is: "A set of beliefs that explain why events occur as they do." The label activity theory has been attached to a set of beliefs advanced by a Russian psychologist, Lev Semenovich Vygotsky. Activity theory proposes that learning consists of a sequence of phases in which actions alternate with thought. First, learners take action in a problem situation; then they think about how successful that action has been and they subsequently apply the resultant knowledge the next time they face a similar problem. In effect, action leads to contemplation, which leads to revised action, which then leads to further contemplation, which leads to further revised action, and so on. A team of researchers who had read books about Vygotsky's work applied his activity theory toward discovering when, during the process of learning a new card game, adults' question-asking contributed most to their mastering the game—(a) in the introductory-acquisition phase (acquiring the game rules and strategies) or (b) in the implementation phase (playing the game). From conducting experiments with teaching the game to adults in tutoring sessions, the researchers concluded that "The results confirm the view that questions answered during knowledge implementation more effectively aid comprehension than those answered during acquisition".

General aim: Apply a theory.

Specific aim: Determine when, during the process of learning a card game, the players profit most from asking questions.

The topic source: Articles in professional journals

In American schools, the academic achievement of students from cultural origins other than mainstream American culture is often below average. Some research published in professional journals has identified students' lack of familiarity with the English language as the chief cause of low achievement, whereas other studies have cited a disadvantaged socioeconomic background as a more significant cause. In an effort to cast light on this controversy, Kennedy and Park compared the home language, socio-economic background, and academic records of 1,952 Mexican-American and 1,131 Asian-American eighth-graders. The results of their study suggested that the chief influences on academic success differed between the two ethnic groups.

"Much of the association of home language with academic performance for Mexican-American students could be explained by socio-economic background and social psychological variables [self-concept, cultural variations in oral and written logic, student aspirations]. In contrast, for Asian-American students, speaking a language other than English in school [was more often associated with getting higher course grades but with getting] lower standardized test scores in reading".

General aim: Explore alternative causes.

Specific aim: Discover the extent of association among (a) Mexican-American and Asian-American students' home language, (b) a variety of socio cultural factors in their lives, and (c) the students' grades and reading-test scores.

The topic source: Articles in professional journals

For researchers Anne Cunningham and Keith Stanovich, the impetus to compare ways of teaching young children to spell came from journal articles describing the success of the Simultaneous Oral Spelling method. The method requires that children spell a word by (a) pronouncing the word as presented to them in printed and spoken form, (b) pronouncing the name of each letter while writing the word, and (c) repeating the whole word again. Cunningham and Stanovich sought to learn how important the writing portion of the method was to promoting spelling skill. To do so, they had first-grade children study spelling under three conditions writing words, typing words on a computer, and spelling words by manipulating letter tiles. They discovered that having children write words was the best method, "even under conditions where the post-training spelling assessment was done on the computer and with tiles".

General aim: Compare educational procedures.

Specific aim: Evaluate the effectiveness of three methods of practicing spelling.

The topic source: A computer search of the subject matter of books and articles

The advent of computerized lists of books and articles on educational topics has greatly enhanced the efficiency of searching the professional literature to discover which topics have been studied thoroughly and which have been neglected. When two staff members at the University of Iowa's center for gifted education conducted such a search, they concluded that a category of youths which rarely drew scholars' attention was that of students with extremely high academic talent in particular fields of knowledge (English, mathematics, natural sciences, social studies). To help fill in this knowledge gap, Colangelo and Kerr analyzed the test results of 5,615 students who had achieved a perfect score in one or more academic fields during a nationwide college testing program that included 729,606 participants. The results of the study showed that:

> *"Boys had a higher incidence of perfect scores [than girls] in each subtest except English. Asians and Whites were overrepresented among perfect scorers, and all other ethnic groups were underrepresented. 'Perfection' in one academic area did not assure comparable high performance in other academic areas. Few perfect scorers planned college majors or careers in the disciplines in which they attained perfect scores".*

General aim: Contribute to a neglected area of knowledge.

Specific aim: Among students of very high academic talent, discover the degree of relationship among their test scores across different subject areas by student gender and ethnic background.

The topic source: A college counselor from Indonesia attended a three-month workshop on counselling techniques in the United States. Upon his return to Indonesia, he integrated elements of several techniques to form an approach to diagnosing and treating learning difficulties that seemed compatible with Indonesian culture. To assess the effectiveness of the approach, he devised a continuing research program that involved collecting information from counsellors who adopted his system. He then used the information to change the approach in ways that suited different regions' school facilities, personnel and pupils.

General aim: Transfer an educational practice from one context to another.

Specific aim: Appraise counselling techniques imported from the United States for their suitability in a variety of Indonesian contexts.

The foregoing eight examples illustrate a few of the wide variety of sources of research ideas and suggest aims of the resulting projects. Additional general aims include those of replicating earlier research, refining an educational practice, evaluating instructional materials, assessing traditional procedures or "conventional wisdom," generating a new or revised theory of cause and effect, and more.

CLASSIFYING AIMS OF RESEARCH STUDIES

Developing a convenient framework for surveying aims of research topics can entail (a) dividing investigators' motives into two principal categories (*understanding* and *acting constructively*) and then (b) under each motive, identifying illustrative research topics within the four types of research aims namely description, explanation, prediction, and evaluation. The contents of the following section are assembled on such a framework.

The terms *understanding* and *acting constructively* identify two varieties of research often labelled (a) *basic* or *pure* and (b) *applied* or *practical.*

The concept *understanding* reflects people's need to comprehend how their world operates. In seeking to promote understanding, the researcher's motive is simply to understand life, without intending to apply that knowledge to solving practical problems. This is often the case with studies in atomic physics, astronomy, molecular biology, chemistry, social history, anthropology, sociology, psychology, and the like. In comparative education, basic-research investigators hope to learn the status of educational enterprises and how they function, whether or not such information might be useful for improving the efficiency or quality of those enterprises. They pursue such topics as:

- Educational Effects of Short-Term Military Occupation: Burma and Japan
- The Status of Religious Education in Five Industrialized Societies
- The Relation Between Mothers' Occupational Status and Children's School Success

The concept *acting constructively* reflects people's need to solve problems they face in their lives. Applied-research investigators are driven by a desire to improve the conduct of education through problem solving. The applied nature of their work is often implied in the titles of their studies.

- The Effectiveness of Three Methods of Teaching Logic: Lectures, Debates, and Computers
- When and Where Nationally Adopted Textbooks Work Best

The concepts *understanding* and *acting constructively* are partially linked, in that individuals' attempts to act constructively are based on their beliefs about how the world operates. Thus, a research project may be designed to provide the understanding needed for solving a problem. Such could be the intent of studies entitled:

- Physiological Versus Environmental Causes of Stuttering
- The Effects on School Attendance of Market-Driven Economies and Centrally Planned Economies

DEVISING BASIC AND APPLIED RESEARCH TOPICS

The following section introduces sources of both basic and applied research topics, beginning with the basic-research goal of extending people's knowledge of the world and in the particular case of comparative education—extending people's knowledge of education systems and of the socio-political contexts within which those systems operate.

The Motive Behind Basic Research: To Understand Educational Phenomena

As suggested earlier, research projects that focus on understanding usually have one or more aims—those of describing, explaining, predicting, or evaluating target variables. The principal goals of such studies are often reflected in the projects' titles.

Describing means depicting the status of target variables at two more times or places.

The Increase in Adult-Controlled After school Activities for Children: 1970-1995

The Popularity of the 'Reading Recovery' Plan for Teaching Children Who Have Difficulty Learning to Read: New Zealand, the United Kingdom, and the United States.

Explaining means accounting for how and why the target variables arrived at their particular condition.

The Influence of Language, Culture, and Attitude on Learning Mathematics and Science: A Review of the Literature

Causes of Delinquency: Interactions among Family, School, and Juvenile Offenders

The line of reasoning adduced for explaining educational events is often cast in the form of a theory or model linking causes to effects. Because such theories so often play a critical role in comparative education research.

Predicting means foretelling the future condition of the target variable.

Expected Results of Sex Education in Public Schools

The Impact of Population Growth on Schooling in Subsahara Africa: 2010 and 2050

Evaluating means judging the desirability of the target variables' condition.

Summer Setback: The Drop in Children's Math Skills Over a Long Vacation

Assessing the Effectiveness of Two Speech-Disorder Treatments

The Motive behind Applied Research: To Solve Problems Met in the Conduct of Education

When a researcher's goal is to act constructively for the improvement of some aspect of education, the four general aims assume a slightly different form. *Describing* means establishing the status of the target variable as a foundation for adopting a course of action.

Students' Health Insurance Costs: 1977-1997

High School Dropout Rates by State and School District

Explaining means identifying what, if anything, needs to be changed in order to improve the condition of the target variable.

Effects of Television Violence on Pupils' Moral Values

Sleep, Drugs, and Learning Efficiency

Predicting means estimating the future condition that the target variable will assume if particular actions are taken.

Likely Consequences of Failed School-Bond Elections

Alcohol on the College Campus: Estimating Academic Achievement among Heavy, Moderate, and Light Drinkers

Evaluating means judging how desirable the results of some action have been.

Good News, Bad News: An Appraisal of Single-Subject Research Techniques in Counselling Psychology

Diverse Effects of High-School Tracking

In summary, as researchers formulate their projects, they can profit from deciding the extent to which their aim is to foster understanding of educational events compared to furnishing guidance toward solving educational problems. It is useful as well for investigators to determine the extent to which their project will include description, explanation, prediction, and evaluation.

USING THEORY TO EXPLAIN EDUCATIONAL EVENTS

As mentioned earlier, an important motive behind certain investigators' choice of research topics is their desire to apply, test, or criticize a theory.

The term *theory* can be defined in various ways. One dictionary version is: "A coherent group of general propositions used as principles of explanation for a class of phenomena". Another is: "A more or less verified or established explanation accounting for known facts or phenomena". The word *theory* is also sometimes used as a synonym for such terms as *explanatory scheme, model, paradigm*, or *hypothesis*. However, for present purposes, I have adopted a slightly more detailed rendition. First, I offer a meaning for the word *facts*: "Facts or data are either discrete observations and measurements of people, institutions, or events, or else they are summaries of such observations and measurements." Then *theory* is defined as: "A proposal about (a) which facts are most important for understanding an educational phenomenon and (b) which relationships among facts are most significant for clarifying the causes of the phenomenon."

Dozens of theories in the field of education and in related social sciences we available to researchers to account for educational events. The diversity of those theories can be illustrated with the following 16 examples that represent a limited number drawn from the entire assortment of such schemes. Each example includes a title, the theory's foundational precepts, and typical applications in education.

Structural-Functional Theory

In the social sciences, structural-functional theory proposes that a society has a given structure that is sustained by functions appropriate to that structure—such structural features as a particular style of producing and consuming goods, established roles people play (including their place in a social-class system), and established values and institutions. The task of the education system is to perpetuate the structure. Thus, according to proponents of a structural-functional perspective, the kind of comparative research that is most enlightening consists of studies that clarify the way education supports the form of a society. From cross-cultural research, scholars hope to extract general principles that account for how and why different education systems operate as they do. Typical applications of structural-functional theory are illustrated in McGinn tracing the evolution of the French national education system from the time of Napoleon I to the present day and Kelly analyzing the transfer of that system to France's Southeast Asian colonies in the early 20th century.

Two criticisms directed at structural-functional theory are that (1) it accounts more adequately for social conservatism and stability than for social change and (2) it has not explained adequately why daily teaching in the classroom takes place as it does.

Human-Capital Theory

A human-capital or human-resource perception of education centers on issues of how education contributes to, or detracts from, individuals' economic productivity. The basic assumption of the notion that education is a form of investment in human capital is that education raises the productivity of workers and that the higher earnings of the educated reflect the value of their product". Economists and political scientists are often interested in analyzing educational events from a human-capital, human-resource, or manpower-development point of view. Studies employing human-resource theory bear such titles as *Human Capital: A Theoretical and Empirical Analysis, with Special Reference to Education, Education Finance Reform and Investment in Human Capital: Lessons from California* and "Gender Differences in the Returns to Schooling and in School Enrollment Rates in Indonesia".

Conflict Theory

A conflict view of human affairs focuses on divisions within the society-divisions between individuals, groups, and institutions. From a conflict-theorist's vantage point, dissent and friction are not deviations to be deplored but, instead, are normal conditions that contribute to personal and social change and development. "Conflict turns the wheels of history, because the endpoint of one conflict is a new lineup of resources, which in turn becomes the basis for the formation of new interests and new conflicts".

Conflict theorists seek to discover who belong to groups that are in conflict, what the motives of the dissidents are, what strategies are employed by the antagonists, and how effective the strategies have been. Four convictions that underlie one version of conflict theory are that:

1. Each social resource produces a potential conflict between those who have the resource and those who do not. The basic dimensions of resources and, hence, social conflicts are: (a) economic resources [in the form of) material conditions; (b) power resources, best conceived as positions within control networks; and (c) status or cultural resources [that will provide] control over social rituals [such as education], producing group solidarity and group symbolism".
2. Potential conflicting interests become effective to the extent that they are mobilized relative to the mobilization of opposing interests.
3. Conflict engenders subsequent conflict.
4. Conflicts diminish as resources for mobilization are used up.

Applications of conflict theory for explaining educational change are found in such works as *Schooling in East Asia* and Kravetz analysis of conflicts over bilingual education policies in the United States.

Marxist Theory

A widely influential form of conflict theory is the dialectical-materialism explanation of social systems proposed by a pair of 19th-century German social philosophers, Karl Marx (1818-1882) and Frederich Engels (1820-1895). A basic tenet of Marxist theory is that people's modes of thought and social relations are determined chiefly by the system of producing and distributing goods within their society.

The mode of production in material life determines the general character of the social, political, and spiritual processes of life. It is not the consciousness of men which determines their existence; but, on the contrary, their social existence determines their consciousness.

Marx asserted that societies naturally evolve through three successive stages-feudalism (aristocratic land owners exploit the peasants), capitalism (bourgeois entrepreneurs exploit the workers), and state socialism or communism (all resources of the production and distribution of goods and services in a classless society are controlled by the working masses so that no one is exploited). Marxist doctrine holds that education in each social system is designed to support the production and distribution patterns (political, economic, and cultural practices) of that particular system.

Books in the field of international education that offer Marxist explanations of events include Paulo Freire *Pedagogy of the Oppressed*, Martin Carnoy's *Education and Cultural Imperialism* and Robert Arnove *Education and Revolution in Nicaragua.*

Correspondence Theory

In keeping with a structural-functional viewpoint, correspondence theory proposes that education and work (meaning occupations and the economic system) correspond to each other in structure and content, and that the role of the education system is to maintain the existing social structure. Studies conducted from a correspondence-theory perspective reflect researchers' belief that it is useful to compare educational operations with the world of work.

The bureaucratic organization of schools parallels that found in business; the hierarchical relations among administrators, teachers, and students are similar to the social relations between managers and workers; the lack of control students have over their education and the alienation they often feel as a result reflect a similar lack of control and alienation that workers find in their adult economic lives; and the extrinsic rewards grades, test scores in schools, parallel the use of extrinsic rewards wages found in the workplace.

World-Systems Theory

A world-systems interpretation of educational events proposes that the entire socioeconomic-political-cultural world should be included in any effort to account for the overall condition of modern-day societies, including the effort to explain the operation of a society's educational enterprises. In today's world, socioeconomic conditions of one nation affect the welfare of others. Transnational corporations that locate facilities in multiple regions influence the types of workers employed and the training they receive. Governments that maintain colonial control over dependent societies affect the sorts of education available in those societies.

Chase-Dunn and Grimes credit sociologists with creating the phrases *world economy*, *world market*, and *world system* in the 1970s when a rapidly growing group of social scientists recognized that national "development" could only be understood contextually, as the complex outcome of local interactions with an aggressively expanding European-centered "world" economy. Not only did these scientists perceive the global nature of economic networks but they also saw that many of these networks extend back at least 500 years. Over this time, the people of the globe became linked into one integrated unit: the modern "world system."

Educational studies founded on a world-systems viewpoint include Coombs' *The World Crisis in Education* and Axinn and Sudhaker *Modernizing World Agriculture*. Ways of conducting such analyses are described in Hopkins and Wallerstein *World-Systems Analysis: Theory and Methodology*.

Dependency Theory

The dependency version of world-systems analysis was developed and disseminated during the 1960s to explain how one society relates to others, so that some are at higher levels of socioeconomic development than others, and some must rely on others for their subsistence. One of the progenitors of dependency theory, particularly among Marxist writers, was the concept of imperialism, represented chiefly in the colonial control of most of Africa, Asia, and the Pacific Islands by European and North American powers and by Japan prior to World War II. In Central and South America the imperialism was internal, with a small elite of European heritage controlling the economy and suppressing the culture of native peoples. Since World War II, as so many colonized peoples have attained political independence, their societies have been viewed by dependency theorists as still subservient to the former colonialists.

Among publications that inspect education systems from a dependency perspective are *Education and the Colonial Experience*, *Predicting Development, Dependency, and Conflict in Latin America*, and *Schooling in the Pacific Islands Colonies in Transition*.

Liberation Theory

As a variant of dependency theory, liberation theory adopts a "humanistic approach to questions of development. The underlying assumption is that members of the underdeveloped societies are oppressed by the power holders of their own societies, who control the relevant economic resources such as land, industry, and wealth so the main remedy for overcoming this oppression lies in the education of the oppressed to be aware of their condition. This practice is called *'consientizacao'* by the Brazilian educationist Paulo Freire".

Books reflecting a liberation-theory focus are Freire *The Politics of Education: Culture, Power, and Liberation*, Ivan Illich *Deschooling Society* and David West *Authenticity and Empowerment; A Theory of Liberation.*

Societal-Development Theory

The word *development* identifies one kind of change, the kind that pictures societies progressing, becoming better rather than retrogressing and becoming worse. Development theory is intended to answer such questions as: What are the indicators of societal development? Which conditions promote development and which retard it? How can constructive conditions be fostered and destructive ones be avoided? What part can education play in development?

Among studies featuring development theory are *Social Change and History: Aspects of the Western Theory of Development, Education's Role in National Development Plans* and *Social Transformation: A General Theory of Historical Development.*

Modernization Theory

As one way of looking at societal development, *modernization theory* is employed in studies that focus on the role of education in nations' efforts to adopt increasingly complex forms of technology aimed at enhancing the production and distribution of goods and services. In other words, how does education contribute to, or detract from, the modernization process?

Research that considers how education is related to modernization is found in such sources as *Perspectives on Modernization: Toward a General Theory of Third World Development* and *Gender and Development: Rethinking Modernization and Dependency Theory.*

Information-Integration Theory

The interpretation of human behavior proposed by Norman H. Anderson and his colleagues focuses on how people integrate information in their attempts to derive meaning from their experiences. Integration theory is founded on the conviction that "thought and action typically arise from multiple causes acting together". To explain educational events from an information-integration perspective, a researcher's task includes (a) identifying the kinds of information that contribute toward making a decision in an educational context, (b) determining the sources of the different kinds of information, and (c) estimating the strength of each kind and the role it plays in effecting a decision.

The multiple factors that people weigh in generating their judgments and actions include values, attitudes, moral knowledge, their own and others' motivations, and features of the particular persons and conditions in the present episode. The process of integrating the multiple factors consists of assigning positive and negative weights to each factor (in terms of the goal or goals being pursued), then applying a kind of intuitive algebra to the collection of factors so as to produce a decision about the event at hand. Although people perform the computation automatically, as their intellectual maturity advances they can become at least partially aware of their decision-making process and thereby bring it under greater intentional control.

Representative studies employing information-integration theory are *"Cognitive Algebra of Interpersonal Unfairness"* and *"Moral Algebra of Harm and Recompense"*.

Darwinian Theory

When Charles Darwin in 1859 published *The Origin of Species*, he set the foundation for the dominant present-day conceptions of how biological inheritance affects people's aptitudes and performance in educational settings. From Darwin's fundamental tenets have grown subtheories often grouped under such titles as *ethology* (the study of the behavior of animals including humans in natural environments), *psychobiology* (the study of how body structures relate to behavior), and *sociobiology* (the study of the biological bases of how members of a species act toward one another and toward members of other species).

Examples of educational research that draws heavily on some form of Darwinian theory include Arthur Jensen *Genetics and Education* and *Educability and Group Differences*; G. Stanley Hall classic *Health, Growth, and Heredity*; and S. D. Smith *Genetics and Learning Disabilities*.

Ecological Theory

Whereas Darwinian theory focuses primary attention on people's inherited biological nature, *ecological* or *contextual theory* emphasizes the ways environmental conditions interact with inherited nature to determine the patterns of people's thought and action.

In devising one version of ecological theory, Roger W. Barker at the University of Kansas noted that traditional psychology showed ways in which people differed from one another but failed to trace the great variations in thought, feeling, and action that an individual person experiences during a typical day. He asserted that a large portion of the variation in a single child's life could be accounted for by the environments or *behavior settings* through which that child commonly moves. In effect, ecological theorists contend that a great deal of a child's behavior can be accounted for by the characteristics of the contexts the child encounters. This viewpoint has been illustrated in such studies as *One Boy's Day, Big School, Small School* and *Habitats, Environments, and Human Behavior.*

A more recent variant of ecological theory offered by Urie Bronfenbrenner of Cornell University analyzes environments in terms of how immediately they impinge on an individual's daily life. The most immediate level is the *microsystem*, such as a child's home, school, and peer group that dictate the child's activities, the child's roles, and the quality of the child's interpersonal relations. The next level of analysis is labeled the *mesosystem,* consisting of interactions among home, school, and peers. More distant are *exosystems,* events outside the child's immediate experience but ones that still affect the child (the parents' workplaces, school board decisions, friends of the child's siblings). Each of these systems is set within the general society's cultural milieu that displays a particular pattern of governance, custom, language, and more. Research conducted within this variety of ecological theory is found in *Two Worlds of Childhood: U.S. and U.S.S.R., "Home School Research"* and *Development in Context: Acting and Thinking in Specific Environments.*

Behaviorist Theory

The late Harvard University psychologist B. F. Skinner is perhaps the best known of all the advocates of a behaviorist interpretation of individual and group action. As a theory of learning, behaviorism is founded on the conviction that the consequences which follow a person's actions determine whether that person will act in the same way on similar occasions in the future. If the consequences have been pleasant (rewarding, reinforcing), the tendency to behave in the same way again is strengthened. If the consequences have been unpleasant, then the tendency to behave that way again is weakened. Thus, in Skinnerian behaviorism, the term *learning* refers to the process of people habitually acting the same way when under similar stimulus circumstances because past consequences have been satisfying. Traditional behaviorists, because of their emphasis on the effect of consequences, avoid talking about such unseen entities as *mind* and *thought.* They focus, instead, on people's observable actions and the observable consequences that follow such actions, since behaviorists believe that *teaching* or *guiding people's learning* requires only the manipulation of the consequences that people experience in their lives.

Illustrative studies employing behaviorism as an analytical tool are *"The Shame of American Education", Human Operant Conditioning and Behavior Modification, "Separate and Combined Effects of Methylphenidate and Behavior Modification on Boys with Attention Deficit Hyperactivity Disorder in the Classroom"*, and *"Combining Noncontingent Reinforcement and Differential Reinforcement Schedules as Treatment for Aberrant Behavior".*

Social-Learning Theory

Social-learning theorists, such as Stanford University psychologist Albert Bandura, agree with behaviorism's emphasis on the importance of consequences in forming people's beliefs and habits. However, unlike behaviorists, social-learning proponents are quite willing to talk about such things as *mind* and *thoughts.* They also differ with behaviorists' account of how a person first achieves a new behavior. They contend that most of what people know and do is acquired by imitation (modeling) copying what they see and hear other people do. In other words, most learning is the result of social interaction, either directly (seeing what others do) or vicariously (reading or hearing about what others do).

Research projects that interpret educational events from a social-learning viewpoint include *Juvenile Delinquents, the Martial Arts, and Behavior Modification: An Experimental Study of Social Intervention* and *"Behavior Modeling Training and Generalization: Interaction of Learning Type and Number of Modeling Scenarios"*.

Curriculum and Instructional Theory

Theories of curriculum design and instruction are proposals about how best to organize and purvey educational content. Curriculum designs typically include consideration of the learning objectives to be achieved, the subject-matter content to be used in pursuing the objectives, suitable learning materials, effective instructional methods, and ways of evaluating the learners' progress. Decisions about such matters are founded on curriculum planners' ideas about the abilities of the learners and about the skills and knowledge learners need in order to thrive in their particular society. Studies that employ theories of curriculum design and instruction can be of many kinds, involving comparisons between two or more sets of objectives, types of content, learning materials, methods of instruction, assessment techniques, types of students, types of teachers, or social contexts.

Representative research projects include *Television and the Preschool Child: A Psychological Theory of Instruction and Curriculum Development, The Management of Ignorance: A Political Theory of the Curriculum, Education as a Human Right: A Theory of Curriculum and Pedagogy* and *Radical Curriculum Theory Reconsidered: A Historical Approach.*

Additional Theories

The 16 sorts of theories reviewed in the above paragraphs represent only a portion of the viewpoints that can be used in the design and interpretation of comparative studies. Additional models that can serve those purposes bear such labels as *gender theory, group socialization theory, information theory, interactionist deliquency theory, meaning theory, resistance theory, responsive curriculum theory, reproduction theory, self- efficacy theory, social-class theory, strain theory, value theory* and far more.

SUMMARY

Students and practitioners in the field of education and in allied disciplines (psychology, sociology, anthropology, economics, history) often appear to feel at a loss when they are expected to come up with ideas for research projects. The purpose of this chapter has been to assist them with that task by suggesting a diversity of sources and aims of research topics and by offering examples of topics. Research efforts often include the aim of interpreting events in terms of theories that help dictate the type of data to collect and the kinds of conclusions to draw from data analyses. In this chapter I have illustrated several types of theories that can be adopted to guide the conduct of comparative studies.

❑❑❑

6

Surveying and Studying the Literature of Education

INTRODUCTION

Learning about what other researchers have done can be helpful at each stage of the research process selecting and stating a topic, providing a supporting rationale, choosing methods of data collection, organizing and analyzing the data, interpreting the results, and reporting the outcomes. In searching the literature, an investigator can profit from using these stages as guides for determining what contribution, if any, a given item from the literature can make to the project at hand. A useful aid in the review process is a code sheet that lists the stages, with each stage symbolized by code letters. How code letters are used can be illustrated with an example focusing on a woman's proposed study of violence in schools.

The code sheet she prepared read as follows:

Code	**Research Stage**
TOPIC	Topic statement
DEFINE	Defining key terms
RATION	Rationale—where the topic fits into the field; what the topic contributes
METH	Methods and instruments of data collection
CLASS	Ways of classifying and analyzing data
INTERP	Ways of interpreting data
REPORT	Ways of reporting data

Guided by the key phrase school violence, she then conducted a computer assisted search of journals in university libraries. An article she found in *JAMA, the Journal of the*

American Medical Association, was entitled "Violence-related Attitudes and Behaviors of High School Students." It reported a comparison of students' attitudes in 15 New York City schools. She photocopied the two-page article and wrote code letters in the margin beside four paragraphs at different junctures of the report. She placed the letters RATION beside a paragraph describing the incidence of adolescent homicides in New York City and nationally. She also wrote RATION beside two paragraphs reporting the incidence of violence-related attitudes among the students participating in the study, because she thought those passages might be useful in preparing the supporting rationale for her study. She wrote METH next to a paragraph describing the questionnaire that high school students had filled out to express their attitudes about violence. She had flagged that passage on the chance that she might wish to use a similar type of questionnaire in her own project. In addition to thus marking the margins of photocopied articles, whenever she made handwritten notes about passages from books or articles she also placed relevant code letters in the margins of the note sheets.

By thus coding potentially useful passages, she later could easily find the reference materials she needed at successive stages of the research process without having to reread every photocopied article or set of notes she had collected. For example, in preparing to write her study's rationale, she could quickly gather all photocopies and handwritten notes that displayed RATION in margins. Later, when interpreting her compiled data, she could collect all materials that displayed the INTERP code.

Whenever she reviewed a book or article that yielded nothing helpful for her own study, she copied the author's name and the title of that source onto a note card so she could later recall that she had already inspected the item and had found it of no use.

The code-letter approach is thus a useful method for extracting needed material from the professional literature.

The question now can be asked: Where in the final research report should the results of the literature search be placed? In response, I suggest that the selections extracted from the literature are best distributed throughout the stages of the report relevant to the selections' code letters. This means that in a thesis or dissertation, all of the material taken from the literature review will not be placed in a single chapter. Instead, those selections that help delineate a context for the present research project will be in a *rationale* chapter, those describing data-collection methods will be in a *research-procedures* chapter, those bearing on data analysis will be in a *results* chapter, and so forth. Likewise, in a journal article, citations from the literature are best situated in the sections of the article pertinent to the code letters. Such a practice can be illustrated with segments of representative journal articles.

DEFINING KEY TERMS

In specifying the meaning of key words used in her investigation of students' responses to violence on television, Tulloch adopted a definition employed by another author:

> ***Prosocial aggression** has been defined as aggression 'used in a socially approved way for purposes that are acceptable to the moral standards of the group'.*

PROVIDING A RATIONALE

To furnish a context for their study of alcoholic parents of delinquent youths, McGraha and Leoni wrote:

The relationship between divorce and delinquency has been extensively investigated by researchers. Most of the studies have found that delinquents do come from broken homes significantly more often than do nondelinquents. The Gluecks' classic 1950 study comparing 500 delinquents and 500 nondelinquents found that over 60% of the delinquents came from broken homes as compared to a little over a third of the nondelinquents. More recent studies by Haskell and Yablonsky and others have found clear evidence of the association between delinquency and broken homes. Many researchers, however, have questioned the real importance of the broken home and have focused instead on the quality of the relationships and general atmosphere in the home. Yablonsky and Haskell found that the internal patterns of interaction within the family were more important than the family structure in explaining delinquency. In a study of self-reported delinquency among 500 youth, Hindelang concluded that attachment to parents was inversely related to delinquency, while Cernkovich and Giordano in a survey of 900 youths found that it was the quality of the relationships in the home, not the structure of the family, that was most important.

ADOPTING DATA-COLLECTING METHODS

Kerwin and her associates, in a study of racial identity in biracial children, introduced their research method in this manner:

> *In the present study, we incorporated ethnographic analyses of semi structred interviews with Black/White biracial children and their parents. The purpose of the study was to uncover the important variables for those who are directly involved with biracial identity development Black/White interracially married parents and their biracial offspring. Marshall and Rossman stated that the purposes of exploratory research include the following: "to investigate little-understood phenomena; to identify/discover important variables; [and] to generate hypotheses for future research". In attempting to reach these goals, we used the long interview method articulated by McCracken, who described this method as "one of the most powerful methods in the qualitative armory. It gives us the opportunity to step into the mind of another person, to see and experience the world as they do themselves."*

INTERPRETING RESULTS

As an aid in interpreting the outcomes of their study of delinquent youths' alcoholic parents, McGraha and Leoni prefaced their statistics on runaway adolescents in their sample of delinquents with these references to previous studies:

Family relationships have long been recognized as factors leading to runaway behavior. In contrast to previous theories that characterized runaway children as emotionally disturbed or mentally deficient with poor impulse control, or as a normal part of growing up, the more popular explanation today is that running away is a response to problems and stress in the home. Bennan, Huizinga and Elliott found that runaways are beaten by their parents twice as often as nonrunaways, and that they experience long-term family conflicts. In [our] current study, 30 (83%) juveniles from alcoholic homes reported at least one runaway from their family, while only 13 (45%) of the youth from nonalcoholic homes reported running away.

In Tulloch's interpretation of her students' attitudes toward violence on television, she referred to other researcher's explanations of comparisons between males and females.

The overall shift of older girls to greater endorsement of nonviolent options is in line with the claim of the importance of a principle of nonviolence in mature female morality. While social learning approaches to differences in male and female attitudes to violence have focused on differential pressures on boys and girls to inhibit aggression, the present data have indicated that female students are more rejecting of aggression even when the initial aggression was male.

With the foregoing examples of how references from the professional literature can be incorporated into research projects, we next consider effective ways of performing literature surveys.

CONDUCTING A REVIEW OF THE LITERATURE

Technological innovations in recent decades have revolutionized the task of surveying the research literature. In the mid-20th century, investigators who wished to learn which books had been published in their field of interest were obliged to finger their way through a university's card catalogue and to inspect bibliographies published at the end of the books they found. To locate relevant journal articles, they not only perused bibliographies but also took advantage of such periodicals as *The Education Index, Psychological Abstracts*, and *Sociological Abstracts* which listed articles from a variety of publications and offered brief descriptions of the articles' contents. Once a useful publication was obtained, it became the researcher's task to copy by hand any passages that might prove useful. This process was not only laborious and extremely time consuming, but it resulted in people often failing to find worthwhile materials bearing on their research topic.

By the 1990s, all that had changed. Researchers now enjoyed the advantages of computerized library catalogues, personal computers in the office and home, and modems (modulate-demodulate devices) that linked personal computers into a world-wide network of library holdings via telephone lines and communication satellites. Just as leafing through library card catalogues was a thing of the past, so also was the need to copy by hand everything a researcher wished to extract from a publication. Now it was possible to photocopy passages of a book or of a journal article. As an alternative, it was not even necessary to have the original publication in hand, for it was possible with a home computer to print an abstract or the entire text of a recent newspaper, magazine, or journal article that was stored in a distant library database hundreds or thousands of miles away.

One useful way to view the process of surveying the literature is in relation to the location in which the search is carried out, that is, in a library or from a distance. But in either location, the search is guided by key words drawn from the statement of the research problem and by related terms. Consider, for example, the following research problem cast in the form of three questions.

The underlined words in this example can be combined to furnish terms that direct the search. For example, combining *school finance* with the name of a country such as *school finance in Japan* provides a pertinent phrase to find in the index of a book, in a computerized catalogue of library holdings, or among the titles of journal articles. Related words that may also assist in a literature survey are either synonyms of key terms or else are other words closely associated with the research topic. In our example, useful related terms include educational finance, *school finance, education budgets, education costs, school fees,* and any such terms coupled with a country's name, such as *Philippines school fees.*

The methods of conducting a literature survey within a library itself differ somewhat from those appropriate for conducting a survey from a distance. Consequently, it is useful to inspect the two locations separately.

SEARCHING IN THE LIBRARY

Being physically present in a library enables an investigator directly to examine the contents of books and journals peruse a book's index, scan chapter contents, and copy out useful passages. If the library has an open stacks policy (allowing patrons to wander along the aisles of shelved books and periodicals), people are able to locate the call numbers of publications related to their research topics and then browse among all of the holdings in the section containing those call numbers. Libraries that maintain closed stacks are less convenient, since they require that a patron order a particular volume which then must be found by a library assistant and delivered to the user a process that sometimes takes hours.

Hunting for useful materials in a book store is similar to browsing in an open stacks library. Customers are able to search among books in their field of interest and skim through the tables of contents and indexes to locate key terms.

In recent years, libraries have been changing from a card catalogue system to computerized catalogues. During this transition, patrons have been obliged to hunt for materials by means of both the traditional card drawers and computer terminals. Older library holdings are still listed only on cards, whereas newer ones appear only in the computer bank.

In the past, collections of abstracts of journal articles were available only in paperback report form, with a year's series of these monthly or quarterly periodicals bound together within a hardback cover. However, today such indexes are available in more than one form as computer data banks and/or as compact discs that display their contents on a computer screen.

The easy availability of photocopy machines in libraries saves researchers time by permitting them instantly to reproduce pages of publications rather than copying the material by hand.

SEARCHING FROM AFAR

Surveying the professional literature from a distance assumes two principal forms correspondence through the mails and a computer search by means of a modem that links an investigator's personal computer into libraries via the telephone lines.

The most common form of postal correspondence consists of an investigator writing to an author who has published studies in the investigator's field of interest in order to request a list of relevant bibliographic references or to ask for reprints of the author's articles. The typical way of locating such authors is to find citations of their works in the bibliographies at the end of journal articles or books. Most authors of published studies are associated with higher-education institutions. Their institutional affiliations and mailing addresses can often be found in a footnote attached to their journal articles or book chapters. Or, as another option, authors' addresses may be found in a library's reference volumes, such as in *Who's Who* or in a publication that identifies a nation's higher education faculty members and their locations.

Writing to authors to request lists of their publications often enables a researcher to locate items that would not normally appear among references that accompany the writer's journal articles. Hard-to-find items include speeches, in house reports, unpublished manuscripts, conference presentations, essays in esoteric journals, and works not yet in print. Some researchers make a practice of sending postcard requests to authors for reprint copies of particular articles.

Whereas postal correspondence is of some use, the personal computer is of far greater value for surveying the literature from a remote location. A home computer equipped with a modem that connects to a telephone line enables a researcher to gain access to a range of library holdings in a wide variety of locations—access to the titles of books, journals, newspapers, reports, dissertations, and other publications. A library's catalogue can be reached either via a telephone number specific to that library or by means of a computer network service to which the researcher subscribes. University libraries, in order to limit their users to a reasonable number of individuals, often require that users enter their system with an assigned password. Passwords are ordinarily reserved for faculty members and qualified students of the particular university and for other individuals who make special arrangements with the library to use its facilities.

A few years ago library lists that were accessed from a remote computer offered only the titles of books and articles. Subsequently the lists of articles began to include an abstract of the entries' contents. More recently, the lists have provided complete journal articles for certain entries, enabling an investigator, at home or in the office, to read articles in detail without needing to have the journal itself in hand. It thus has become possible for researchers at home to reproduce with their computer-printer a copy of an entire article or of selected segments.

ADOPTION OF CONTENT STANDARDS

State-level content standards are typically intended to provide the basis for state and local decisions on curriculum, texts, instructional materials, student assessments, teacher preparation and professional development, and other components of programs of instruction CCSSO reported that, by 2000, 49 states had established content standards in mathematics and 46 states had established standards in science. Teachers remain concerned, however, that standards do not always provide clear guidance regarding the goals of instruction and that schools do not yet have access to top-quality curriculum materials aligned with the standards.

STATEWIDE POLICIES ON TEXTBOOKS AND STANDARDS

One way that states can influence the implementation of mathematics and science standards is to select or recommend textbooks and curriculum materials for schools that are aligned with their standards. Fewer than half of the states, however, mandate or recommend particular textbooks and curriculum materials. The Council of Chief State Officers reported that a total of 21 states had a state policy regarding textbooks and curriculum materials for classrooms. Among the total, 11 have a state policy defining state selection of textbooks and materials to be used and another 10 recommend texts or materials to the local districts. In 2000, 20 of the 21 states with a textbook policy use their state content standards to select or recommend curriculum materials, the same as in 1998.

Some examples of state policies on textbooks include California, where content standards and frameworks are used to select the materials that will be adopted by the State Board of Education and recommended to school districts and Tennessee, where the state adopts an approved list of curricular materials from which local schools boards may then choose and receive state funds. These policies contrast with those of Alaska and New Jersey, where textbook selection decisions are left up to the local boards.

STATE ASSESSMENT PROGRAMS IN MATHEMATICS AND SCIENCE

Nearly all states conduct statewide assessments in mathematics, although the grades assessed and the type of test vary widely. Results of the most recent CCSSO Annual Survey of State Student Assessment Programs (for the 1998/99 school year) show that 48 states have a statewide program in one or more subjects. Although many states have administered statewide assessments of student learning since the 1970s, additional states approved policies requiring statewide student testing throughout the 1980s and 1990s, and the number of subjects and grades to be assessed increased. Important factors in the growth of state policies are greater interest in accountability tied to student performance; needs for assessing learning growth related to policies and programs; and federally funded programs linked to state assessments of learning, such as Title I and the Individuals with Disabilities Education Act.

SUMMARY

The purpose of surveying the professional literature is to improve the quality one's own research by discovering what other investigators have done in the area of one's interests. In this chapter I have suggested that literature searches are rendered more efficient if they are guided by code words that identify at which junctures in a research project citations from the literature will be most useful. In recent years, the rapid development of personal computers and of computer networks that provide access to libraries' holdings have greatly enhanced the ease, speed, and comprehensiveness of literature reviews.

In the 1980s, most states approved policies aimed at improving the quality of K-12 education, implementing statewide curriculum guidelines and frameworks as well as assessments. At present, half of the states require students to pass some form of exit examination to graduate from high school, and others report developing such tests, underlying this reform agenda is the assumption that these standards and assessments will lead to higher student achievement. However, assessments and standards are not always tightly linked, and the implied performance incentives for students, teachers, and administrators vary across states. Furthermore, there is concern that some state-level assessments focus too much on facts, even though the associated standards call for complex scientific inquiry. Particular attention is paid to the alignment of these new standards and assessments to student achievement by reviewing recent research in this area.

❑❑❑

7

Approaches for Collecting Data and Its Analysis

INTRODUCTION

It is to describe six popular approaches to data collection in terms of (a) defining characteristics of each approach, (b) the types of research questions the approach is equipped to answer, (c) versions of the approach, including their advantages and limitations, and (d) common problems and their solutions that the approach involves. The six are case studies, historical analyses, ethnographies, surveys, correlational comparisons, and experiments. As will be demonstrated, these six are not mutually exclusive. A given research project may utilize more than one of them.

CASE STUDIES

A case study is an in depth analysis of a single entity. That entity may be a person, a group, an organization, a system, a method, or an event. Such studies assume a comparative character when two or more cases are considered in relation to each other or when the study of a single entity encompasses several time periods that are compared. Typical titles of case studies featuring description, explanation, evaluation, and prediction are:

Description — *The Education of Theodore Roosevelt*

Model English Universities: Oxford and Cambridge

A Day in Three Classrooms

Explanation — *Alternative Causes of Autism*

Environments and Genius: Einstein, Mozart, Michaelangelo

Contrasts in Teachers' Influences: Adolf Hitler's School Days

Evaluation — *The Quality of Child Rearing in Three Innercity Families*

Comparing Reinforcement Schedules in Four Cases of Attention Deficit

The Success of Two Counseling Techniques with Four Pakistani Immigrants

Prediction — *School Budget Projections: A Rich District and Its Poor Neighbor*

University Enrolment Prospects: Belgium and the Netherlands

Dim Future: Family-Planning Education in the Sudan, Uganda, and Zaire

The greatest advantage of a case study is that it permits a researcher to reveal the way a multiplicity of factors have interacted to produce the unique character of the entity that is the subject of study. If we can assume that every person, group, institution, or event is unique unlike every other in at least some details then the case study becomes the most suitable approach for delineating that uniqueness. An important limitation of the case approach is that generalizations or principles drawn from one case can be applied to other cases only at great risk of error. Users of research studies are usually not interested in learning only the outcomes of a particular investigation; instead, they are interested in finding how a given case can help them understand other similar people, institutions, or events. The question they ask is: What knowledge derived from the present instance can validly be applied to explaining a broader collection of cases? This risk of error in assuming that other cases will somehow be the same as the one at hand can be reduced by studying more than one case in order to identify their likenesses and differences and thereby better recognize the level of confidence that can be placed in conclusions drawn about such phenomena. However, researchers are not always hoping to generalize the results of a particular case to other situations. For instance, a teacher may study her pupils' use of the PLATO computer program for learning mathematics simply so she can better understand those children's motivations, skill improvement, social interaction patterns, and attitudes toward computers. Case studies can also serve to introduce readers to new ways of perceiving educational events, as in studies entitled:

- The Role of Unstated Behavior Rules in Four High-School Classrooms
- The Effect Over Time of Placing an Epileptic Child in a Fifth-Grade Class
- Two Afro-American Teachers' Experiences in an All White School

Finally, it may be the methodology of a particular case study, rather than principles derived from its results, that people find most useful, as when researchers who read a case adopt the methods of that study for conducting their own investigations.

In planning a case study, a researcher can profitably begin with the questions, problems, or hypotheses that define the target variable. The research then becomes an investigation of the system of factors and the patterning of their transactions that explain how and why the target variable behaves as it does. The target definition is then analyzed to yield specific guide questions that identify the kinds of information to be sought, feasible sources of such information, and methods of collecting it. The set of guide questions, in effect, defines the case study's structure and content. It identifies the perspective from which the participants in the case are viewed.

The following examples illustrate the kinds of questions guiding the conduct of three quite different cases. The first example compares a successful publication project with a failed project, the second focuses on the politics of a nursery school over time, and the third compares the educational backgrounds two historical figures.

PUBLISHING VENTURES: ONE SUCCEEDED, ONE FAILED

In the Pacific island territory of American Samoa, a consultant was hired by the government's department of education to suggest methods of discovering the islanders' most pressing educational needs. After considering a variety of options, education officials adopted three approaches: (a) testing pupils' academic and psychomotor achievement, (b) collecting community members' opinions, and (c) surveying classroom problems. Over the following months, the three approaches were successfully implemented, the resulting data were analyzed and reports were published.

One unmet need discovered during the project was the lack of traditional Samoan cultural elements in the schools' curricula at all levels of the educational ladder. As the research team considered which aspects of culture might best be added to the course of study, it became apparent that a wide range of traditional forms of recreation games, sporting events, amusements were pursued in Samoans' daily life, but none of them were in written form. They existed only in people's memories. As older Samoans passed away, these elements of culture were gradually being lost. Thus, the research consultant suggested that the department of education sponsor a project aimed at collecting descriptions of types of recreation and publishing them in book form so they might be preserved and taught in school. The department's leaders agreed to the plan and assigned two seasoned Samoan educators to interview members of the community in order to collect the information required for the book. The consultant and the two Samoan staff members devised an interview guide sheet to ensure that complete information would systematically be gathered about each pastime. Then the consultant left the islands to return to his own institution, scheduled to come back to Samoa at the end of six months to aid with the final preparation of the book. When he did return, he learned that nothing had been done about the project during his absence. In effect, the envisioned publishing effort had died, and there were no plans to revive it.

These two events the successful publication of unmet educational needs and the unsuccessful attempt to publish traditional island pastimes set the stage for a comparative case study aimed at explaining why one project had succeeded and the other had failed. Here, then, are the central questions to be answered by the case study and the specific guide questions that delineated the domain of the study by identifying the sorts of information needed, likely sources of the information, and methods of collecting it.

- The target variable: What were the factors that caused the needs-study project to succeed and the recreational-activities project to fail?
- Guide questions defining the domain of the case: How did the people in List A view the issues in List B?

List A:

- The director of the department of education
- The assistant director of the department
- The director of curriculum development
- The head of the unmet-educational-needs project
- The head of the Samoan-language-and-culture program
- The two staff members assigned to the traditional-recreation project
- The off-island research consultant

List B:

- What was the importance of the unmet-needs study as compared to the traditional-recreation project? If one was more important than the other, what made it so?
- Is the curriculum content derived from Western civilization, which has dominated the school program, more important than traditional Polynesian cultural content? How desirable or necessary is it that descriptions of traditional culture be recorded in written form? (This question is posed in view of the fact that there was no written version of the Samoan language prior to the arrival of Christian missionaries in the islands in 1830, so records of Samoan culture were traditionally transmitted only in oral form.)
- How might Samoan social traditions have influenced the behavior of the department of education's decision makers and the staff members' commitment to the two projects? In other words, did Samoan social etiquette affect the enthusiasm and sincerity with which individuals embraced the unmet-needs program compared with the forms-of-recreation project?
- What professional or personal interests or commitments competed for the time and energy of the particular staff members assigned to implement the two projects? To what extent did those staff members command the skills needed to carry out their assignments? If the staff members needed help with performing their duties, was that help readily available?
- What administrative machinery was available to ensure the continuing operation and monitoring of each project? If such machinery was not available, then why? If it was available but did not function, then why?
- What would be the consequences expected from the success or failure of the unmet-needs study as compared to consequences expected from the success or failure of the forms-of-recreation project?
- Sources of answers to the guide questions: The individuals in List A. Written communications regarding the two projects, including minutes of meetings, written directives, and progress reports.
- Methods of collecting answers: Interviews with the people in List A. Content analysis of written communications about each of the projects.

POWER STRUGGLES IN A NURSERY SCHOOL

Early childhood education was the major field of interest of a university graduate student who was the mother of a three-year-old daughter enrolled in a nursery school that was partially associated with the university's department of education. As a master's degree research project, the student chose to analyze the political maneuvers of competing groups that sought to control the operation of the nursery school. The study was carried out from the vantage point of a participant-observer, since the student herself was a member of one of the competing groups. Thus, one challenge she faced in conducting the study was that of maintaining some measure of objectivity in collecting and interpreting data.

The study assumed the form of a time series, since the researcher analyzed the pattern of relationships among participating groups at four junctures during a six month period. Each juncture represented an event that marked significant change in the power relationships among the rival groups.

The primary groups consisted of (A) the woman who directed the school and her supporters in the form of two assistant teachers and a few mothers of children enrolled in the school and (B) several mothers of nursery-school children. Each of these primary groups was loosely linked to background supporters. Group A counted on the support of the university's director of business services who provided part of the nursery school's funds. Group B counted on the backing of the head of the education department's early-childhood-education program.

The publicly visible issues at the heart of the struggle were the charges by Group B that the school's quarters were not kept clean, food was prepared in an unsanitary fashion, university students who visited the school were not properly supervised, and conflicts among children were handled badly. However, observers of the case noted that behind these stated issues were the political motives of strong-willed individuals vying for decision-making control of the school.

The question that identified the target variable and the constituent questions delineating the study's domain were as follows:

- The target variable: At key transition points in the struggle for control of the nursery school, what was the composition of the rival groups, what were their goals, what were their strategies, how effective were their efforts, and what were the causes of their success or failure?
- Guide questions defining the domain of the case : At each of the four critical junctures in the struggle for control:

What contending groups or factions could be identified? Who were the members of each faction (core members and supporters)? What factors bound the group members together? What role did each member play in a group's activities; what were the relationships of power and position within each group? How cohesive was each group in the sense of how much the group's members agreed with each other? What were the stated aims of each group? What unstated aims or motives did each group appear to harbor? What strategies did each faction adopt to achieve its goals? What was the nature and outcome of confrontations between the factions? How well did each faction achieve its stated and unstated aims?

Sources of answers to the guide questions: Members of each group. Outside observers who did not participate in the struggles between factions. Meetings conducted within a faction or conferences between individual members of a faction. Meetings between groups or between individual members of rival factions. Such documents as reports submitted by the nursery-school director to the university's head of business services, correspondence between groups, correspondence of individuals or groups with the head of business services or with the head of the university's early childhood-education program.

Methods of collecting answers: Interviews with members of the rival factions. Observations of meetings about the nursery-school's affairs. Observations of conversations and discussions among members of a faction and between members of rival factions. Content analysis of documents.

After collecting answers to the guide questions at each of the four transition points in the six-month struggle for control of the school, the researcher compared the results at one point with the results at subsequent points in order to identify the dynamics of change that the case involved.

MORAL EDUCATION: NIGHTINGALE AND FRANKLIN

Two historical figures often Lauded for their moral convictions are : (a) the English woman recognized as the inspiring pioneer of nursing education, Florence Nightingale, and (b) the American colonial publisher, inventor, and political luminary, Benjamin Franklin. The foci of interest for a comparative case study were the educational foundations of these two individual's moral development.

The target variable: What were significant causal factors in Florence Nightingale's and Benjamin Franklin's moral development?

Guide questions defining the domain of the case: Within what social environments did the central figure's early moral training take place? Who were important people in these contexts? What roles did each of those people play in the central figure's moral education? How was that influence exerted? In other words, what was the nature of each person's interaction with the central figure? What were the apparent moral effects of each of those persons' influence? What was the central figure's moral self-identity? In other words, how did the central figure perceive herself or himself as a moral being?

With the passing years, what new people or communication media (reading matter) affected the central figure's moral education? In what ways did these new experiences influence that individual's moral principles and behavior? To what extent did the central figure implement her or his own moral education, and how was this done? What were the central figure's apparent motives that directed her or him toward the moral commitments that she or he adopted? Did the individual's moral self-identity change over time; and if so, how and why?

In what ways were Florence Nightingale's and Benjamin Franklin's moral upbringing alike and different? How have Florence Nightingale's and Benjamin Franklin's moral natures been judged by historians?

Sources of answers to the guide questions: Biographies of Nightingale and of Franklin, Benjamin Franklin's autobiography, Florence Nightingale's collected letters and selected Nightingale publications.

Methods of collecting answers: Content analysis of the published documents.

SUMMARY

The principal contents of case studies are determined by the guide questions that establish the investigator's focus at the outset of the study, researchers should take advantage of unexpected types of information that were not foreseen but are nevertheless valuable additions to the case. For instance, in the nursery-school study, a casual conversation with a homeowner whose property was adjacent to the nursery school might yield pertinent data. Or from reading biographies of Florence Nightingale and Benjamin Franklin, an investigator may be moved to add the following pair of guide questions to the original list: How may accidental events as compared to planned events affect a person's moral development? How may the places to which an individual travels influence that person's moral education?

HISTORICAL ANALYSES

Historical investigations often assume the form of case studies traced over time or located within a particular era of the past. The focus of historical accounts can be individual persons, groups (team, religious denomination, ethnic entity), segments of society (the aristocracy, the middle class, the homeless), institutions (schools, museums, philanthropic foundations), geographic units (cities, nations, regions), educational philosophies (Deweyism, Hinduism, Marxism), educational practices (lecturing, field trips, aptitude testing), events (the establishment of schools, the passage of education laws, the appointment of ministers of education), and more. As noted earlier, descriptive accounts tell what occurred on particular occasions or else they trace the progression of successive events. Explanatory studies not only describe events, but also seek to explain why they happened as they did. Evaluative histories assess the desirability of the events.

Representative titles include:

Description — *A Chronicle of Early Childhood Education in Japan*
A History of the Montessori School Movement
The Sorbonne 1259-1959

Explanation — *Educating the James Brothers: Henry and William*
The Sources of Jesuit Educational Goals and Practices
Social Forces and Curriculum Change in Spain: 1898-1998

Evaluation — *Consequences of a Civil-Service Examination System: The Ch'ing Dynasty*
The Quality of Parents' Assessments of New York City Schools: 1930, 1960, 1990

Four interacting variables that determine the nature of a historical study are: (a) the time span encompassed, (b) the aspects of education and/or of the society to be included and emphasized, (c) the theoretical vantage point from which those aspects are viewed, and (d) the availability of relevant historical information. Researchers can profitably have these four factors in mind as they plan their historical accounts.

THE TIME SPAN

The chosen time span can be either continuous or segmented. It is continuous when the historian traces the gradual development of an aspect of education or the society, as in *The Evolution of the Malaysian Ministry of Education—1965-1995 or A History of Los Osos Middle School.*

The time span is segmented when the target variable is inspected at more than one discrete point in time: *Costs of a University Education—1940 and 1990.*

ASPECTS OF EDUCATION AND OF THE SOCIETY

As noted earlier, educational research can focus on some aspect of the process of education or on interactions of education with aspects of the surrounding society. Because both education and society in their entirety are far too complex to manage within a single historical account, investigators are obliged to select which facets of education and society they intend to include—and among the facets, which are to be emphasized. By making this selection, historians establish the boundary lines of their studies and identify the types of information needed to answer their projects' guide questions. The aspects to be emphasized in a study are usually featured in the statement of the target variable and oftentimes in the title of the work.

- *A History of Main Street School's Parent-Teacher Association*
- *Political Party Influence on Moral-Education Legislation in Ohio and Florida*
- *The Changing Goals of Village Primary Schools in Wales*
- *Portrayals of Nationalism in Burmese Textbooks: 1930-1990*

THEORETICAL VIEWPOINTS

Just as three-dimensional objects in space cannot be seen from all sides at the same time, so also aspects of education and society are usually inspected from selected vantage points in the form of theoretical perspectives. A historian's theoretical stance affects which happenings from the past will be chosen as significant and what interpretation will be placed on those events.

For instance, a researcher using *conflict theory* to interpret the development of schooling in post-independence Tanzania (1961- 1998) could be expected to collect data that reveal: (a) which factions in the society were in competition with each other for control of the schools, (b) the overt and covert goals held by each faction, (c) the source of each faction's power, (d) the strategies each adopted to achieve its ends, and (e) how successful those techniques proved to be. In contrast, an advocate of *neo-colonialist theory* would more likely collect information about: (a) the nature of schooling when Tanzania was under British colonial administration, (b) the colonial schooling background of Julius K. Nyerere, who became the most influential political figure in post-independent Tanzania, (c) sources of the educational structure planned by the new government so that the society might achieve self-reliance, and (d) vestiges of colonial education that forced adjustments in the government's plan.

RELEVANT HISTORICAL RESOURCES

One of the greatest challenges authors of historical studies face is that of ensuring that the account they write is an accurate portrayal of what occurred. The challenge derives from the fact that historians are limited to the particular chronicle of the past that they happen to find. And how authentically those materials represent the events they depict is often open to serious question. Furthermore, the farther back in historical time the events occurred, the greater the question about the validity of the records that remain. For example, heated controversies continue today over the issue of who wrote the Jewish Torah and Christian Bible and about the authenticity of those books' contents.

A variety of factors in the past have contributed to the distortion and loss of historical records. Over the centuries, valuable books and letters have been destroyed by fire and flood. In wartime, armies intentionally demolish the libraries and archives of the vanquished. The victors in revolutions and political elections replace the defeated forces' accounts of events with their own version of what took place. Manuscripts, letters, books, and newspapers are lost through the carelessness, neglect, or ignorance of people who fail to recognize the potential future importance of those materials. In addition, some significant social developments were never cast in written form for any of several reasons-the particular society had only a spoken form of language, or the developments occurred within a segment of the population that was illiterate, or those people who might have recorded the events did not consider them worth writing about. Hence, no documentation of such developments became available.

Finally, researchers themselves may be to blame for presenting an erroneous view of the past. They distort reality either because they have been incomplete in their search for source materials or else because they bring to their work a bias (religious, philosophical, ethnic, political, social-class) that predisposes them to favor certain materials and discount others.

In view of these risks to the authenticity and balance of knowledge about the past, conscientious historians adopt several safeguards to promote the accuracy of their work. One way is to obtain multiple accounts of a particular event or of a document in order to determine how closely different versions match. For instance, the minutes of a school board meeting can be checked against a newspaper report of the event or against a letter found in the effects of a participant in the meeting. Where there are contradictions between accounts of an episode, the researcher may choose to present both versions to readers, then offer arguments in support of each version or else adduce a line of logic that favors one account over the other.

Another method of testing the accuracy of a historical account is to locate the account within the socio-political atmosphere of its day. The historian attempts to find convincing evidence that a given description of an incident reasonably reflects what would be expected to occur in the context of those times.

A third avenue for judging the trustworthiness of historical records is through estimating the reliability of a source by its status as an official document or by the reputation of its author. A copy of an education law bearing a government seal is usually more to be trusted than a newspaper editorial about the law. The description of a controversial event by a political office holder or spokesperson for a government department is likely to be questioned more than a description of the episode by an ostensibly objective scholar whose professional fate does not depend on political approval.

To compensate somewhat for the risk of inaccuracy inherent in historical studies, the historical approach has much to offer for explaining the causes of educational conditions. That is, a traditional and much-practiced way to conceive of causation has been in terms of the chronology of events. Earlier happenings are seen as the well-springs of later ones. Past episodes are viewed as the causes of present effects. In like manner, present effects themselves will be the causes of future outcomes. Thus, the task faced by the historian who seeks to explain cause is that of: (a) identifying which factors from the past have contributed to the present state of affairs, (b) calculating how much influence each of the factors exerted, and (c) proposing how the factors blended together to bring about such a result.

PLANNING A HISTORICAL STUDY

As with case studies, planning historical research can profitably start with a statement of the target variable, then continue (a) with guide questions defining the realm of that variable, (b) with sources of answers to those questions, and (c) with methods to be used in searching through those sources. The following examples illustrate the planning that can be inferred from the contents of two representative historical accounts.

The first study describes the competition between Protestants and Catholics to determine the nature of schooling for American Indians during the quarter century 1888-1912. The second study analyzes the fate of progressive education in the Midwestern United States between 1930 and 1960. The analysis includes comparisons between traditional schools and their progressive-education counterparts.

PROTESTANTS, CATHOLICS, AND AMERICAN INDIANS

The Churches and the Indian Schools, 1888–1912, is a detailed study written by a Jesuit priest, Francis Paul Prucha, to explain the tension and conflict between Protestants and

Catholics over Indian mission schools at the end of the nineteenth century and the beginning of the Twentieth. This account grows out of an earlier study of the Protestant humanitarian reform organizations that dominated American Indian policy in the late Nineteenth century. The goal of those reformers was to Americanize the Indians, to destroy tribalism with its communal base, and to substitute the individualism which marked white society. Since the Americanism that they sought to impose upon the Indians was conceived in terms of the evangelical Protestant heritage of America from which the reformers came, the Catholic missionaries did not fit well into the proposed patterns.

The conflict between the two religious groups was perhaps inevitable and unavoidable, for the fundamental expectations of each of the antagonists clashed sharply with those of the other. There was no disagreement about the absolute necessity of religious (specifically Christian) influence upon the civilization of the Indians as they were prepared for assimilation into the white man's society.

The conflict rose, rather, over differing Protestant and Catholic views about the place of each other within American society.

The contents of Prucha's book suggest that his research plan included the following elements:

The target variable: Over the quarter century 1888–1912, what were the issues involving Indian schools that Protestants and Catholics fought about, what were the aims that each of the combatants hoped to achieve, and how was the conflict ultimately resolved?

Guide questions defining the domain of the study: What was the condition of the Indian tribes in the latter 19th century; how and why did they arrive in such a condition? What provisions were made for Indian children's education? Who made such provisions and why? What religious practices did the Indians follow; what influences determined which practices they would adopt? What roles did Protestant and Catholic groups play in determining the curriculum and control of the Indian schools? What issues involving Indian schools produced conflicts between Protestants and Catholics, and why? What key events occurred in the struggles over those issues? What agencies and individuals played key roles in the events? What part did Indians play in the conflict? By 1912, how was the conflict resolved?

Sources of answers to the guide questions: Records of the Bureau of Catholic Indian Missions, the Indian Rights Association Papers in the Historical Society of Pennsylvania, and records of the U.S. government kept in the National Archives. Papers of individuals who participated in the controversy. Printed documents from all three branches of the federal government (administrative, legislative, judicial). Newspaper and periodical articles.

Methods of collecting answers: Content analysis of the sources as directed by the guide questions.

PROGRESSIVE EDUCATION'S RISE AND DEMISE

Zilversmit book-length account of the progressive education movement in the United States is titled *Changing Schools: Progressive Education Theory and Practice, 1930–1960.*

The target variable: When, where, and how have principles of progressive education been applied in representatives schools in the Midwestern United States?

Guide questions defining the domain of the study: How and when did the progressive education movement start? What were the key principles of the movement? In what ways were those principles similar to and different from traditional educational principles over the years 1930–1960? In representative schools in the Midwestern United States, when, where, and why were progressive methods applied in classrooms? How did progressive practices compare with procedures found in traditional classrooms? What sorts of evidence have been used by different authors to assess the impact of progressive philosophy on classroom practice? What were the historical trends in the adoption of progressive methods? What vestiges of the progressive movement could be found in classrooms in the 1990s, and how and why did those remnants become part of school practice near the end of the 20th century? What does the analysis of the rise and decline of progressive education suggest about the process of school reform?

Sources of answers to the guide questions: Books and journal articles about the history of American education, about progressive education, and about educational reform movements. Archives of records from progressive schools (minutes of meetings, curriculum guides, teachers' manuals, regulations, speeches). Newspaper accounts of educational developments during the 1930–1960 period. People who were personally involved with progressive education or with competing educational movements. Scholars who have studied progressive education and other reform efforts.

Methods of collecting answers: Content analysis of books, journal articles, newspaper accounts, and archival materials. Interviews and written correspondence with people who were involved in the progressive education movement or with competing movements, or ones who have studied such matters.

The theoretical position from which Zilversmit's analyzed progressivism includes at least three perspectives, those of: (a) *reformation theory* in which a philosophical ideal (John Dewey's child-centered school) is translated into classroom practices that are disseminated through books, professional journals, educational conventions, and teacher-education programs, (b) *conflict theory* in which innovators vie with conservatives for control of classroom practices, and (c) *inertia theory* in which traditional patterns of behavior within a massive social system, and the shortage of facilities and funding to achieve required alterations, prevent reform movements from effecting significant change in the majority of the system's components.

Despite the impassioned discussions of progressive education in the 1920s and 1930s, despite the marked progressivism of a few school districts and the increasing importance of progressive ideas in state education departments and teachers' colleges, it is clear that by 1940 progressive education had not significantly altered the broad pattern of American education. The call for a child-centered school had, for the most part, been ignored.

ETHNOGRAPHIES

Ethnography is the chief investigative approach employed by cultural anthropologists. Here are three typical ways ethnography is defined.

Ethnography [is the] descriptive study of a particular human society or the process of making such a study. Contemporary ethnography is based almost entirely on fieldwork and requires the complete immersion of the anthropologist in the culture and everyday life of the people who are the subject of the study.

Ethnography means, literally, a picture of the "way of life" of some identifiable group of people. Conceivably, those people could be any culture-bearing group, in any time and place. Particular individuals, customs, institutions, or events are of anthropological interest as they relate to a generalized description of the life-way of a socially interacting group. Ordinarily an outsider to the group being studied, the ethnographer tries hard to know more about the cultural system he or she is studying than any individual who is a natural participant in it, at once advantaged by the outsider's broad and analytical perspective but, by reason of that same detachment, unlikely ever totally to comprehend the insider's point of view. The ethnographer walks a fine line. With too much distance and perspective, one is labeled aloof, remote, insensitive, superficial; with too much familiarity, empathy, and identification, one is suspected of having "gone native."

Ethnography is that form of inquiry and writing that produces descriptions and accounts about the ways of life of the writer and those written about.

In educational research, the societies on which ethnographies focus include those found within a classroom, a school, a community, an ethnic group, a neighborhood, a department in a university, a team, a club, a teachers' union, a school board, an administrators' organization, a ministry of education, or the like. Donning the analytical lenses of a cultural anthropologist, the investigator enters the society for an extended period of time to study how it functions. For instance, a graduate student assumes the position of a teaching aide in a primary school classroom, thereby equipped to experience classroom activities from an assistant teacher's vantage point and to mingle with the children on the playfield and in the lunchroom. Or a researcher joins a teachers' union, attends its meetings, and talks with fellow members about union activities. Or an educator lives for a period of time in a foreign country to analyze mass communication media (television, radio, newspapers, magazines) that exert an educational influence on the populace and to observe ways members of the society respond to the media.

Since the purpose of ethnographic research is to depict a group's culture, it is important that investigators have a clear notion of what the term *culture* is intended to imply for their work. Not everyone defines *culture* in quite the same manner. However, most popular definitions contain similar core meanings, as indicated in these examples.

Culture or civilization, taken in its wide ethnographic sense, is that complex whole which includes knowledge, belief, art, morals, law, custom, and any other capabilities and habits acquired by man as a member of society.

Culture—the integrated pattern of human knowledge, belief, and behavior. Culture, thus defined, consists of language, ideas, beliefs, customs, taboos, codes, institutions, tools, techniques, works of art, rituals, ceremonies, and other related components.

The culture of any society is made up of the concepts, beliefs, and principles of action and organization that an ethnographer has found could be attributed successfully to the members of that society in the context of his dealings with them.

Whereas case studies are intended to reveal the individualistic attributes of a particular person or institution, the purpose of ethnographies is to identify beliefs and customs shared by members of a social system. In effect, case studies emphasize features that make one person or organization different from others, while ethnographies emphasize the commonalities that unify members of a society.

No society—whatever its size is sufficiently simple to be analyzed completely within a single research project. Thus, as with historical research, it is necessary for an investigator to select the aspects of culture that will be the focus of the ethnography at hand. Those aspects in a particular project can be identified by questions that serve as guides to data collection. This point can be illustrated with three examples. In the first, attention centers on religious education in two widely separated cultural settings a Navajo Indian community in the Southwestern United States and the island of Okinawa in the Western Pacific. The second example analyzes students' responses to teachers' classroom management techniques in an American high school. The third compares the role of physical punishment as a child-rearing tactic in the South Seas nation of Tonga with the role of physical punishment in Australia.

NAVAJO AND OKINAWAN RELIGIOUS EDUCATION

In this research effort, separate ethnographic field studies of life in Navajo and Okinawan societies provided the data for comparing the transmission of religious beliefs from one generation to the next in the two settings. The guide questions identify the portions of those studies which provide material for the comparison.

The target variable: What are the important components of each of the two societies' religions, what means are used to propagate religion from one generation to the next, and in what ways are the two societies' religions and methods of religious education alike and different?

Guide questions defining the domain of the case: Answer these questions about the traditional religion in each of the two societies: What is the purpose of human life? What natural and/or supernatural forces control events in the physical and social universe? By what means, and to what extent, can people influence those forces? What rites and rituals are practiced? What are the purposes of those rites and rituals? What material objects are part of religious practices, and what are the functions of those objects? What moral rules or values should guide people's behavior? What are the sources of those values? What consequences can result from abiding by or from violating moral rules? What are the sources of such consequences? To what extent is there agreement within the society about the purpose of life, the forces affecting events in the universe, the means of influencing the forces, proper moral values, and the consequences of abiding by or violating moral rules? What controversies arise over the foregoing beliefs, and how do those controversies affect people's lives?

In each of the two societies, who teaches the foregoing religious beliefs and practices? In what settings does such instruction take place? At what times in people's lives are the beliefs and practices taught, and why at these times? What instructional methods and materials are used? How is the success of religious education evaluated?

In regard to the above aspects of religious education, how are Navajo and Okinawan religious beliefs and practices similar to and different from each other? What are likely reasons for these similarities and differences?

Sources of answers to the guide questions: Members of the society who occupy different positions in the political authority structure, in the social class system, and in the religious hierarchy including informants of different ages and of both genders. Published histories, anthropological accounts, and sociological studies of each society.

Methods of collecting answers: Interviews with members of the society, observations of events bearing on religious matters, content analysis of published materials.

STUDENTS' PERSPECTIVES, GOALS, AND STRATEGIES

A doctoral candidate in a university's department of education obtained permission from the principal of a nearby high school to attend high school classes for a semester in order to study how students perceived teachers' techniques of classroom management, particularly the teachers' ways of directing learning activities and maintaining order. The project included a description of students' academic and social goals, the strategies class members adopted for pursuing those goals, and how teachers responded to such strategies. The comparisons drawn in this research were between classes in different subject areas, between teachers, and between students who differed in their perceptions, goals, and strategies.

The target variables: What techniques of classroom management do teachers use, how do students interpret those techniques, what goals do students hope to achieve by their responses to teachers' management efforts, and what strategies do students adopt for pursuing those goals?

Guide questions defining the domain of the case: What tasks of classroom management do the teachers face? How do these tasks vary from one class to another? What techniques of classroom management do different teachers adopt? How successfully do these techniques achieve the teachers' apparent goals? What do students believe are the teachers' motives behind the management techniques? What strategies do students adopt for responding to those techniques? What goals do students hope to achieve by their strategies? How successful are the students' strategies for achieving their goals, and why? Which of the teachers' techniques are most successful in achieving the teachers' goals, and why?

How does the particular mixture of students in a given class influence the management tasks the teacher faces, the techniques the teacher employs, and the success of those techniques in achieving the teacher's goals? How does the mixture of students influence students' interpretation of the teacher's motives and management techniques, the strategies students adopt, the goals at which those strategies are directed, and the effectiveness of the strategies in attaining such goals?

In what ways do teachers vary in their goals and their management methods? In what ways do students vary in their interpretations of teachers' management techniques, in their own goals, and in the strategies they employ for pursuing those goals?

Sources of answers to the guide questions: Class sessions, Teachers' opinions, Students' opinions. Records of disciplinary actions relating to the classes, teachers, and students who are the subjects of the research.

Methods of collecting answers: Daily observations of class sessions. Informal observations of students' conversations outside of class. Interviews with teachers. Interviews with students. Content analysis of records of disciplinary actions.

CHILD PUNISHMENT AS A TEACHING DEVICE

In a journal article entitled "Dealing with the Dark Side in the Ethnography of Childhood: Child Punishment in Tonga," Helen Kapavalu described the role of physical discipline as an instructional device in contemporary Tongan society. The article also included occasional comparisons between Tonga and a typical Australian community. The content of Kapavalu's description implies that the following kinds of questions guided her research.

The target variable: What role does physical punishment play in traditional Tongan child rearing, on what rationale is such punishment founded, and what consequences result from that practice?

Guide questions defining the domain of the case: What is the authority structure (the system of controllers and the controlled) in Tongan society? How is this structure reflected in the broader community, the family, and the school? What characteristics determine a person's place in the authority hierarchies? What personal-social qualities are valued in Tongan culture? What methods are used by authority figures to foster those qualities in children and youth? Upon what rationale and perception of child nature are these methods founded? How do children and youths respond to such methods, particularly to the use of physical punishment? What significant consequences appear to result from physical punishment consequences for individuals and for the conduct of Tongan society? What changes, if any, are occurring in the techniques used for socializing the young; what are the likely causes of those changes; and what are the probable consequences of such changes for the welfare of individuals and for the traditional Tongan social system?

How does the role of physical punishment as a child rearing device in Tonga compare with its role in a typical Australian community? What problems can occur for people from a Tongan background when they enter Australian society, and vice versa?

Sources of answers to the guide questions: Incidents of punishment in the daily routine of life in Tongan homes, schools, church sessions, markets, playgrounds, recreational events, and work sites. Tongans living in Tonga and ones living in Australia. Ethnographies and accounts of life in Tonga written over past decades by missionaries, anthropologists, and visitors to the islands. Descriptions of child rearing and of child abuse in Australia.

Methods of collecting answers: Observations of child-rearing practices in Tongan settings. Interviews with Tongans in Tonga to learn their perceptions of physical punishment as an instrument of child socialization. Interviews with non-Tongan observers of life in Tonga to gather incidents of physical punishment and the observers' assessments of the desirability of such punishment. Interviews of Tongans who have emigrated to Australia, with the interviews directed at discovering immigrants' views of the physical punishment of children. Content analysis of published accounts of Tongan culture and of child rearing practices in Australia.

SURVEYS

The purpose of survey research is to describe specific characteristics of a large group of persons, objects, policies, practices, institutions, or events. The process of conducting a survey involves *gathering information* about some *target variable* from a quantity of *sources of the same type*, then summarizing the information in a readily comprehended form. By analyzing each of the italicized items in this description, we can illustrate the multifaceted nature of surveys and the contributions they can make in comparative research.

TARGET VARIABLES

Target variables are of many kinds, as demonstrated by the titles of studies focusing on the following dozen types of variables:

Knowledge	—	*Mathematics Achievement among Nine-Year-Olds in 32 Nations*
		Pupils' Misconceptions of Historical Events
Skills	—	*Computer Keyboarding: Speed and Accuracy at Four Stages of Training*
		Kinds of Practice Routines among Distance Runners
Habits	—	*Girls' and Boys' Use of Leisure Time*
		Health Effects of Four Weight-Reducing Diets
Attitudes,	—	*Parents' Expectations for Children's Academic Success*
Opinion		*University Students' Opinions of Fee Increases*
Evaluations,	—	*How Teachers Rationalize Their Methods of Discipline*
Judgments		*Ratings of Teachers by Good and Poor Students*
Objectives	—	*What is Worth Learning? Humanists versus Pragmatists*
		The Aims of Canadian Education, 1850, 1900, 1950, 1998

Policies —	*Legal Control of Private Universities in China and Japan*
	Compulsory Schooling Regulations in Developing Nations
Practices —	*Changing Roles for School Inspectors in Remote Rural Regions*
	Who Pays for the Village School? A Study of Sub-Saharan Africa
Teaching —	*The Classroom Use of Computers in London and Paris*
Methods	*The Popularity of Chalk-and-Talk versus Class Discussion*
Equipment —	*The Availability of Textbooks in Saudi Arabia's Primary Schools*
	Facilities for Preparing School Lunches in Small and Large Schools
Communication —	*Linking Violence on Television with Student Misbehavior*
Media	*Evidence of Racial Prejudice in Secondary-School History Books*
Educational —	*Population Density and Achievement Test Scores*
Contexts	*Home Languages of Bilingual Students in Southern France*

It should be apparent that this list of target variables is far from definitive. Among many additional types are: educational philosophies, teacher characteristics, student characteristics, curriculum designs, types of schools, community resources, administrative structures, laws and regulations, and sources of funds.

The titles of studies in the above list represent two general classes of surveys—the cross-sectional and the longitudinal. In cross-sectional studies, information about the status of the target variable is collected for one particular time. In longitudinal studies, information is gathered at successive periods of time as reflected in such entries as *"Changing Roles for School Inspectors"* and *"Aims of Canadian Education, 1850, 1900, 1950, 1998."*

In preparing to conduct a survey, an investigator can usefully begin with the research question that defines the target variables and then identify sources of information about those variables.

SOURCES OF INFORMATION

The phrase *sources of the same type* refers to the kinds of entities from which data are to be collected. As a further example, in a study of parents' opinions of a city's schools, the source-type is comprised of adults who have children currently attending those schools. In a project focusing on the legal control of private universities, the type includes printed laws and regulations as well as records of court cases and government directives related to violations of rules. Specifying the types of sources from which information is to be collected guides the researcher in selecting the methods and instruments to used for collecting the data.

GATHERING INFORMATION

The following five examples illustrate typical options available for collecting information from the identified sources. From among the options, investigators select one or more that are feasible in the circumstances under which they are obliged to work.

Topic —*A Nationwide Survey of Twelve-year-olds' Reading Skills*

Source —12-year-old pupils

Data-gathering options —(a) Paper-pencil testing or (b) computerized testing in which pupils read passages silently, then offer answers to questions that assess how well they comprehended the passages. (c) Individual interview sessions in which a pupil reads a passage aloud, then orally answers questions about the content of the passage.

Topic —*Changing Curriculum Patterns in Five Cities' Primary Schools*

Sources —(a) *Printed materials:* Curriculum guidebooks, courses of study, teachers' instructional manuals, records of curriculum-planning sessions, newspaper articles, minutes of legislative hearings, school laws, and administrative directives. (b) *People:* school principals, curriculum planners, teachers.

Data-gathering options —(a) Content analyses of printed materials as guided by research questions and rating devices. (b) Interviews with people engaged in curriculum planning or implementation, or (c) questionnaires filled out by such people.

Topic —*Types and Incidence of Behavior Problems in Representative Urban, Suburban, and Rural Secondary Schools*

Sources —(a) *Printed materials:* Schools' records of student disciplinary cases, individual students' cumulative record folders, juvenile-court records. (b) *People:* Such school personnel as teachers, school counselors, school principals, and truant officers.

Data-gathering options —(a) Content analyses of printed materials, with the results compiled as anecdotal records, checklists, or rating scales. (b) Interviews with school personnel or questionnaires that personnel complete.

Topic —*College Instructors' Distracting Mannerisms*

Sources —(a) classroom observations and (b) students' responses.

Data-gathering options —(a) *Classroom observations:* Trained observers attend college classes to record (anecdotal record, checklist, rating scale) instructor mannerisms that distract learners from the content of the instruction; or a video camera records instructor behavior that is later analyzed by researchers to identify distracting mannerisms. (b) Students' responses: By means of individual or group interview sessions or else by means of written questionnaires, students report instructor mannerisms that divert attention from the content of the lesson.

Topic—*Students' Opinions of Vocational and College-Preparatory Curriculum Tracks*

Source —Secondary-school students

Data-gathering options —(a) individual interviews, (b) group interviews, (c) printed opinionnaires.

Researchers can choose the data-gathering methods they will use by (1) inspecting the options, (2) estimating how accurate the information will be, and (3) weighing the accuracy of data against the feasibility of the data-gathering process to arrive at the method of collecting needed information.

THE MATTER OF SAMPLING

In some instances researchers intend the conclusions derived from their surveys to apply only to their sources of information (people, documents, events) that participated in the survey. For example, the headmaster of a secondary school canvassed all members of the student body to learn how many students wished to study a foreign language during the coming school year and which languages they would prefer to learn. As a second instance, a teacher solicited the opinions of her class members' parents about the disciplinary policy she intended to adopt as a means of encouraging more students to complete homework assignments. Another investigator analyzed the minutes of every meeting of a city's school board for the previous five years to learn which members of the board most often supported measures to increase services to the handicapped and which members failed to support such measures.

Although some researchers thus wish to draw generalizations only about the participants in their survey, far more wish to extend their survey conclusions beyond those participants. In effect, the survey's subjects are considered to be only a portion no more than a sample of the population to which the research conclusions will be applied. To illustrate, on the basis of testing the mathematics skills of 1,500 12-year-olds, researchers may draw conclusions about all of a province's 127,000 12-year-olds. From a review of 130 cases of students dismissed from school for breaking the law, investigators can extract generalizations that they assume are valid for the entire population of 1,600 such cases in juvenile-court files. If researchers are to make extensions of survey results convincing, they need to furnish evidence that the sample of people, documents, or events accurately reflects key characteristics of the population which the sample is supposed to depict. It is thus important that researchers recognize the advantages and limitations of various methods of drawing samples and that they understand statistical procedures for estimating how faithfully samples of different sizes represent their envisioned populations.

CORRELATIONAL COMPARISONS

A substantial proportion of comparative studies involve correlational analyses. In such studies, the investigator is interested in discovering the extent to which a change in one variable is accompanied by some degree of change in another. Consider, for example, the relationship between these variables:

- **School size and students' extracurricular participation**: Does the average student in large schools engage in more types of extracurricular activities than the average student in small schools?
- **Teachers' reading habits and pupils' reading skills:** Do pupils whose teachers read extensively score higher on reading tests than pupils whose teachers spend little time reading?
- **Age and the motive of revenge:** Does revenge as a motive for punishing wrongdoers increase between late childhood and young adulthood?

Correlations can be either positive or negative. In positive correlations, an increase in one variable parallels an increase in the other. To illustrate, children in the United States have been found to be better readers if they attend schools that have more books per student, provide more hours of reading instruction, and have teachers with more years of teaching experience. As a second example, research on science instruction among 200,000 students in 23 countries revealed that:

> *In nearly all countries, 10-year-old and 14-year-old children from [socio economically] higher status homes, from homes with more reading resources, and from homes with parents with more years of education performed better on science tests than children from poorer homes with respect to these characteristics. The length of time students spent on homework also had a positive effect on achievement.*

In the case of negative correlations, an increase in one variable is accompanied by a decrease in the other variable, as in the above references to (a) school size and extracurricular participation and (b) age and the motive of revenge.

If, when one variable changes, nothing happens to the other, then the two are not correlated. For instance, the investigators conducting the 23-nation study of science instruction found that, on the average, neither the size of a school or of a class, nor the number of different subjects that students studied in their final year of secondary school, was related to how well students performed on standardized science tests.

Obviously, not all variables are related to each other in the same degree. At the highest level of correlation, the extent of change in one variable is accompanied by the same extent of change in the other variable. In contrast, at the opposite extreme of correlation, change in one variable is associated with no change at all in the other. There are many methods of expressing degrees of relationship. One popular method, applied when the variables are expressed in quantities, is Pearson's product-moment correlation coefficient. In the Pearson system, the highest level of correlation is labelled 1.00, indicating that any change in one variable is always attended by the same extent of change in the other. The lowest level of correlation is labelled .00, meaning that change in one factor is never attended by any change in the other. In between these two extremes are graduated levels of relationship. For instance, the following are product-moment correlations reported for various sorts of comparison.

The relationship between:

Fourth-graders' scores on a standardized reading test and their scores on a mathematics test = +.82.

High-school students' fear of failure and their fear of how their parents' would react to the students' failure = +.52.

General intelligence and extroversion in girls = +.19 and in boys = +.21.

School achievement and self concept = +.32.

Amount of psychotherapy and amount of patient improvement = +.32.

Class size and amount of bullying among students in a group of English secondary schools = +.62.

Affluence of a community and the frequency of bullying in the community's secondary schools = -.32.

Family size and Spanish-language achievement of secondary-school applicants in Mexico = -.16.

Frequently correlations are offered in verbal rather than numerical form. This is particularly the case in historical studies where authors postulate relationships. Consider three examples. In the first, the proposed relationship is between (a) how nation-states were created and (b) European and African socio-cultural settings. In effect, the author proposes that the way nations were formed differed between Europe and Africa.

In Europe, the acknowledgement by ethnic communities of their common history and cultural identities served as a basis for the creation of nation-states. In certain cases, like the Italy of Cavour or Germany of Bismarck, unity was strenuously sought when there was sufficient conviction that a cultural nation already existed.

In Africa, however, this process was inverted and essentially diachronic. Colonial states were created within artificial boundaries which hardly coincided with the limits of traditional politics. Irrespective of their historical past, social affinities, or long-standing feuds, various communities whose cultures, traditions, and languages differed considerably were brought together for the purpose of facilitating colonial administration. Under such circumstances, the colonial state can be seen as a "proto state" within the limits of which Africans had to forge a new sense of solidarity and belonging, [an assignment borne by education systems].

Researchers sometimes offer examples intended to suggest the intensity of a correlation. Here is a case in which the relationship is between (a) the extent of pain or inconvenience parents are willing to suffer to have their children succeed with school examinations and (b) the amount of assistance that parents hope the gods will provide for their children at examination time. The link between variables a and b is the religious ritual that many Japanese or Korean parents perform.

The most desperate manifestation of Shinto devotion to exams is probably the "one-hundred-time homage" (*ohyakudo-airi*), which aims to win sympathy from the deity through self-inflicted torment. To perform *ohyakudo-airi*, parents or students climb stone steps leading to the shrine, pass through an archway representing the division between the secular and divine worlds, ring a bell that announces their visit to the god, and then pray. To fulfil this ritual, the procedure is repeated a hundred times. In Korea mothers at a Buddhist temple bow 3,000 times a night for their children's success on exams.

Correlations are extremely important in explanatory research, because all statements about causation are statements about correlations among variables. However, the fact that two variables are correlated does not necessarily mean that one contributed at all to the outcome of the other. Thus, it is critical that researchers recognize the difference between *casual* or *incidental* correlations and *causal* or *determining* correlations. An anecdote used to illustrate this distinction focuses on the relationship between the numbers of storks in communities of the lowland countries of Western Europe and the number of babies born there. Observers noted that communities which had larger numbers of storks also had more babies born. This correlation might then be cited in support of the theory that storks bring (are causes of) babies. However, doubters could contend that the positive relationship was no more than casual, derived from the fact that storks happened to prefer living in villages rather than in cities and that villagers traditionally bore more children than did urbanites. The relationship, according to skeptics, is incidental rather than causal.

Thus, simply demonstrating a positive or negative correlation is not sufficient evidence of cause. What is also needed is a convincing line of logic demonstrating that one variable was at least partially the result of the other variable's presence. Frequently the line of reasoning is designed to show that one variable (the cause) preceded the other (the effect) and that the two could not have occurred in the reverse order. Constructing a persuasive argument that links two variables in a causal relationship often entails proposing how the relationship is mediated by a chain of factors.

EXPERIMENTS

An experiment usually consists of applying one or more specified treatments to an individual, group, or institution, then assessing what effects those treatments had (this is the step of description) and estimating why such effects occurred (this is the step of explanation). A key assumption underlying experiments is that events are the result of one or more causal factors. The purpose of an experiment is to manipulate the potential factors in a manner that reveals (a) which of them have indeed caused an event, and (b) how much each factor contributed to the outcome.

Designs of experiments can assume a variety of forms that vary from the extremely simple to the highly complex, with each form bearing particular advantages and limitations. The simpler the design, the easier it is to carry out the research. The more complex the design, the better the experiment accounts for variables that affect the outcome and, as a result, the greater the confidence a researcher can place in the conclusions drawn from the results. In brief, ease and feasibility of application are bought at the expense of insecurity regarding conclusions drawn about cause. Confidence in conclusions is paid for by greater difficulty, time, and bother.

The following overview of experimental designs advances from the simple to the complex. The final matter addressed in the discussion is the question of which features of a design researchers can profitably consider when choosing the design most suitable for guiding a particular educational decision.

EX POST FACTO

The most elementary design involves (a) applying a treatment to an entity, (b) assessing how well the entity performs following the treatment, and (c) estimating how much the treatment contributed to that performance. For example, a secondary-school science teacher used a new biology textbook with her class. At the close of a three week unit of study on genetics, she gave a final test to discover how much the students then knew about genetic inheritance. If the students received high scores on the test, the teacher might conclude that the textbook was a very efficient learning aid. If they received low scores, she might decide that the book were poorly suited to her class's needs and abilities.

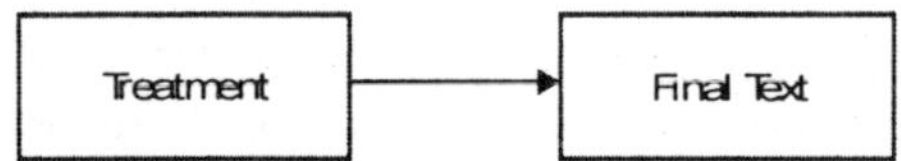

This form of experiment can be labelled *ex post facto* or *after the fact* because the teacher has drawn conclusions about the effect of the treatment the effect of the particular textbook—solely on the basis of evaluating students after they had experienced the treatment. The main advantage of the *ex post facto* model is that it's easy to use. It involves little bother on the part of the experimenter. But it also leaves unanswered important questions about which factors contributed to the students' test performance. In particular, we know nothing about how much the students already understood about genetics before they read the book. It is even conceivable that some students had a more accurate knowledge of genetics before they studied the text, and that the text explained things in such a muddled fashion that it confused the readers, causing them to doubt what they already knew. Further, we do not know what other sources of information the students may have used during the three week unit of study. And we are left wondering whether the class learned more using the new textbook than they would have learned from some other book or from the teacher's lectures.

PRETEST-TREATMENT-POSTTEST

To provide a more convincing foundation for estimating the influence of the biology textbook, the teacher could replace her *ex post facto* plan with a pre test treatment-post-test design. In this case, at the outset of the study unit on genetics, she would have the students take a test (pretest) about genetics before she even discussed genetics or assigned the class members to read the genetics section of the text. Then, after the class members had completed the three week study of the book (treatment), she would test (posttest) their command of the material. In order to estimate how much the textbook had added to the learners' knowledge, she would subtract the students' pretest scores from their posttest scores and conclude that the obtained difference represented the contribution made by the book. In other words, the teacher's judgment would be based, not on the final test scores, but on the extent of change from pretest to posttest.

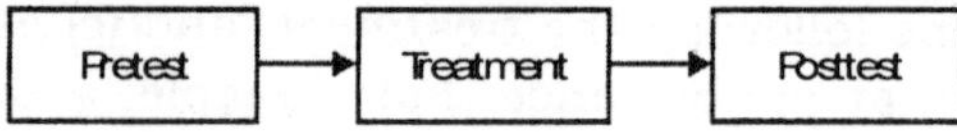

COMPARED TREATMENTS

Although the pretest-treatment-posttest design clears up some questions that the *ex post facto* plan failed to answer, it leaves in doubt several other matters. Is the new textbook better than the old one? Would students have learned more by working on problems involving genetic inheritance? Would they have succeeded as well if the teacher had presented the material in the form of illustrated lectures or a series of videotaped television programs?

In an effort to answer such queries, the teacher could divide the class into two equal groups. One group would use the old textbook and the other group the new book. Or one group would study the new text while the other group viewed videotaped programs. But if the teacher arbitrarily assigned students to the two groups, it is possible that one group would end up with more adept science students than the other group. Subsequently, if the higher-ability group succeeded better than lower-ability group on the posttest, it would not be clear how much of their success should be credited to their greater aptitude and how much to the particular treatment they received. One way the experimenter could cope with this problem would be to pretest the students before assigning them to treatment groups, then pair up the students so that both members of each pair had nearly identical scores. One member of each of the matched pairs would be assigned to Treatment A and the other member to Treatment B. This process would help ensure that at the outset of the genetics unit the two groups were evenly matched in terms of their entry knowledge of genetics. When change scores were later computed between the pretest and posttest results, the researcher could be more confident that the treatment, and just the treatment, rather than variations in the individuals' prior knowledge, was the greater cause of any of the difference found between the groups' levels of success.

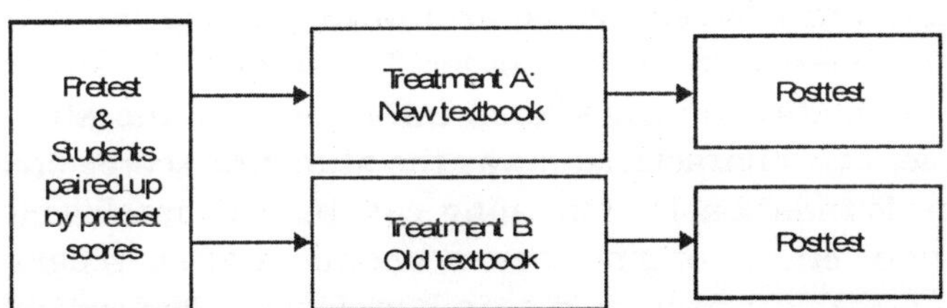

This compared treatments design could be expanded to include more than two treatment options. The experimenter could divide the biology class into three groups so as to permit comparisons among the new-textbook, old-textbook, and illustrated-lecture approaches. As a further step, a videotape-program approach could be included by dividing the class into four groups. However, adopting more treatment alternatives creates problems of sample size and logistical feasibility.

It is apparent that every additional division of the class reduces the size of each group. In a class of 32 students, the average final-test score in a simple pre-test treatment-posttest plan is based on 32 participants. In contrast, each group's average score in a four-treatment comparison is based on only eight students. Obviously, the greater the number of students on which an average is founded, the more likely the average score will accurately represent the performance of a typical student. In effect, small samples of participants are highly subject to the influence of a few deviant individual scores which may happen to be included in a sample, with such participants contributing to a distorted picture of the typical effectiveness of the treatment they experienced. But in samples composed of large numbers of participants, the influence of individual deviant scores is diminished by the presence of far more scores from more typical participants.

In addition to causing problems of sample size, adding treatment options increases experimenters' logistical difficulties. How can the biology teacher reasonably manage a class of students who are divided into groups that simultaneously study genetics via four different approaches? Thus, the advantages of adopting increasingly complex compared-treatments designs must be paid for in reduced feasibility. One obvious way to solve the problem of unduly small samples is to solicit larger numbers of participants. In our present illustration, that would mean engaging more biology classes from more schools in the genetics-instruction experiment. However, doing so would raise costs and increase the difficulty of coordinating and monitoring the study. It would also add to the number of uncontrolled variables that could affect the test results, such variables as having more teachers with different levels of instructional skill and more students from diverse socio-economic backgrounds. As a result, investigators are obliged to choose an acceptable compromise between complexity of experimental design and the practical demands of their research setting.

ASSIGNING PARTICIPANTS TO TREATMENTS

We have already inspected two ways of assigning people to different treatments. The first and easiest way is to allocate people arbitrarily, paying no attention to how they might be similar to, or different from, each other. The second way is to match participants according to some characteristic considered influential for the study at hand. In our biology-class example, that characteristic was the students' scores on a genetics pretest. In other studies the foundation for matching can be age, intelligence, language skill, muscular coordination, ethnic origin, socio-economic status, religious affiliation, and the like, depending on the nature of the research project's target variable. As noted above, the problem of achieving a good match between participants increases with the number of treatment groups that the particular experiment involves. Pairing up students on the basis of similar intelligence-test scores for a two treatment study is easier than matching them in quartets in a four-treatment design.

A third method of assigning subjects to treatment groups is by random selection. One popular way of carrying out the random-assignment method consists of a series of steps that can be illustrated with the case of a two treatment experiment. First, each participant is assigned a number, which is written on a slip of paper. Second, all of the numbered slips are placed in a hat or bowl and thoroughly stirred around. Third, one slip is drawn randomly from the hat, and the person belonging to that number is assigned to Treatment A. Another slip is then drawn, with the person bearing that number assigned to Treatment

B. This process is then continued, with the odd-drawn individuals relegated to Treatment A and the even-drawn to Treatment B, until the entire collection of slips has been exhausted.

As an alternative to the slips-in-the-hat procedure, the experimenter can assign each participant a number, then use a table of random numbers from a statistics textbook or a series of random numbers generated by a computer program to place the participants in their treatment groups.

The random-assignment method is based on the assumption that unrecognized factors which could inadvertently affect the outcome of the experiment will be distributed equally between the treatment groups. Therefore, if those factors do, indeed, influence the results of the experiment, the influence will be the same within each treatment group. In other words, the unrecognized factors in one group cancel out the same factors in the other group in their effect on the final results. It is thus assumed that any differences found between the groups in the final testing will be solely the consequence of the differences between the two treatments and not a result of extraneous variables.

The following example illustrates an experimental design for which the random assignment of learners to different treatments is especially appropriate. Imagine that a researcher wishes to discover the comparative effectiveness of two self-instruction methods of teaching introductory economics. The information gained from this experiment will help administrators of an open university decide which method they should adopt in their distance-learning program for students who are taking economics courses by correspondence. One of the methods employs a series of workbooks in which students solve problems. The other method utilizes step-by-step lessons provided on personal-computer diskettes.

A special feature of the researcher's experimental design is its provision for revealing a potential reactive effect. As Ball explains, Reactive effects in measurement occur when the behavior elicited by the measurement procedures is not characteristic of the behavior that would have occurred in the absence of the measurement procedure.

Aware of the possibility of reactive effects, the researcher planning the introductory-economics experiment suspects that if students were given a pretest to show what they already knew before studying the workbook or computer program, the pretest itself might function as a type of treatment. In other words, students might learn something about economics during the process of taking the pretest, and that knowledge would later serve to improve their posttest scores. Hence, the posttest might not accurately reveal what students gained solely from the workbook or computerized lessons, because the students' scores could be a mixture of knowledge derived from both the pretest experience and the intended treatments. In an effort to determine the influence of these two sources of knowledge the pretest and the planned treatments the investigator randomly distributes the experiment's participants among four groups. Two groups—A and B will study from workbooks and two C and D from computer programs. Group A will take a pretest before starting the workbook, while Group B will begin the lessons without having taken the pretest. In like manner, Group C will be pre-tested but Group D will not.

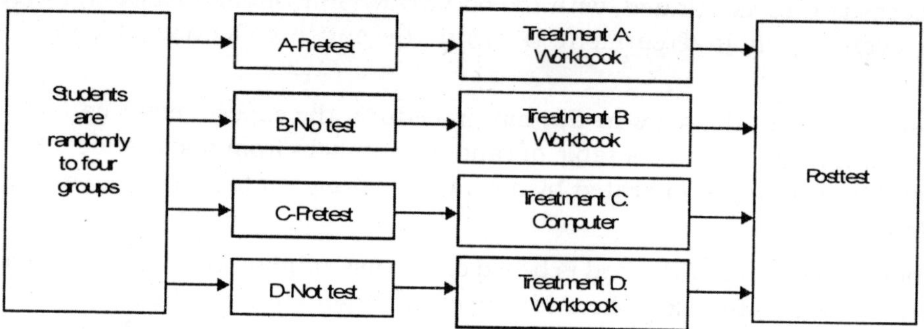

Let us now assume that 600 university students took part in the experiment so that there were 150 in each group. Finally, on the 100-item posttest, the groups' average scores were:

Group A = 84; Group B = 74; Group C = 92; Group D = 83

On the basis of these results, it would appear that the pretest did indeed function as a kind of treatment, since students who took the pretest in either a workbook or computer group earned scores about 10 points higher than students who were not pretested. It would also appear that the computer version of the economics course was somewhat more effective than the workbook version, since scores in groups C and D were higher those of students under the comparable A and B treatments.

It is useful to recognize that reactive effects may result not only from pretesting but also from a variety of conditions related to assessment situations. For instance, the presence of an observer taking notes in the back of a classroom may change the pupils' or teacher's behavior so that the events the observer records are not typical for that classroom. Likewise, the age, gender, or ethnicity of an interviewer may cause interviewees to respond in ways that are less than candid.

In the field of education and in other social-science disciplines, patterns of experiments are often referred to *quasi-experimental designs* to distinguish them from *authentic experimental designs* employed in the physical sciences. The term *authentic* in this context refers to the practice of randomly assigning people to different treatments. However, random assignment is often impossible in educational settings. Such is the case when a teacher must, for practical reasons, apply a particular teaching method to an entire class of students. Or a researcher must include all of the schools within a district in a study of a method of budgeting, because all of the schools are legally obligated to use that method. And the budgeting method is then compared to a different method used in another school district. Or an investigator is obliged to depend on those parents who are willing to be interviewed about their child-rearing methods, thereby leaving out all parents who are unwilling to be interviewed. In these instances, since the resulting experiments lack the randomization feature, they do not qualify as true or authentic experiments. However, since in all other respects they are indeed experiments, their designs can be deemed at least *quasi-experimental.*

TIME SERIES

In addition to the designs described above, many others are available, each incorporating characteristics required for solving particular research problems. For example, when investigators study a teaching method, they often wish to know not only the immediate effects of that method but also how stable those effects will be with the passage of time. In other words, after a few weeks or months, how much have students forgotten of what they learned from the method? Has their long-term memory of the lesson contents been distorted in any way? To answer such questions, one or more posttests can be added to the experimental design.

However, some people are not content with knowing the condition of the target variable only at periodic intervals following the application of a treatment. They also want to know the variable's condition over a period of time leading up to the treatment's intervention. Their purpose is to learn whether the apparent change at the point of intervention was actually caused by the treatment or, in contrast, was no more than a segment of a trend that had been going on for some time prior to the intervention. The research design necessary to fulfil this requirement is one that involves the periodic collection of data substantially before and after the treatment's initial application. The trend line established by the periodic measurements reveals what effect the treatment apparently exerted on the target variable. To illustrate what such a design can reveal, let us assume that a high school mathematics teacher institutes an incentives plan aimed a stimulating students to better performance on weekly algebra tests. The teacher's plan consists of awarding students points for improving their test scores. When students have accumulated enough points, they can exchange the points for ice cream at the school cafeteria, for tickets to a nearby theater, or for reduced prices on tape cassettes at a local music store.

Next, assume that the teacher instituted this plan last February. It is now May, so the scores students have earned on weekly tests over several months can suggest how well the incentive program achieved its purpose. Our attention focuses on the performance of three students—Albert, Bart, and Candice. First, consider some simple pretest-treatment-posttest data from February. The test given the week before the incentive-plan was introduced serves as the pretest. The test given two weeks after the plan appeared acts as the posttest. Figure 7.1 displays the three students' scores on these occasions.

From these results, it appears that the incentive plan worked very well indeed for Bart, had slight effect on Albert, and had very little, if any, influence on Candice. However, when these results are cast within a time series extending from September to May, our conclusion about the effect of the incentive program can be quite different. Figure 7.2 represents the trend line drawn from the students' test scores, September through May, with the T in the graphs indicating the point at which the incentive plan was introduced.

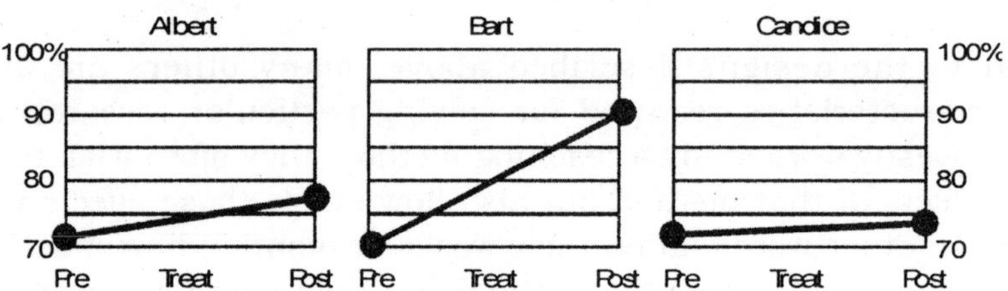

Figure 7.1. Pretest-Treatment-Posttest Design

It is apparent that the three time-series in Figure 7.2 furnish a more complete foundation for estimating the effect of the incentive program than do the simpler pretest-treatment-posttest data in Figure 7.1. In Albert's case, there is a question of whether the program actually did interrupt the time series reflected in his performance, since the gain during the initial weeks of the incentive plan could well be no more than a continuation of an improvement trend that had begun some months earlier, a trend due to factors other than the enticement of the new incentives. .

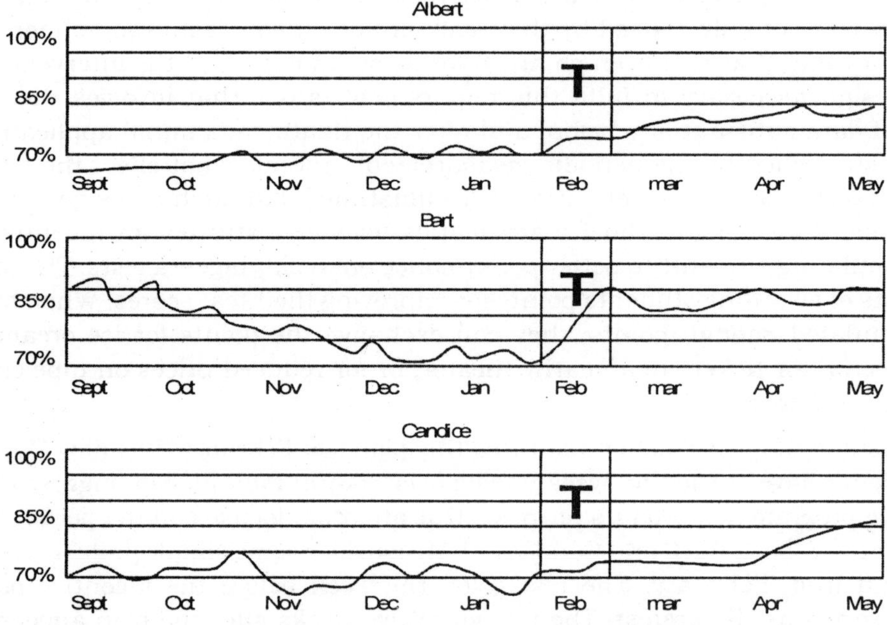

Figure 7.2. Interrupted-Time-Series Design

For Bart, the incentive program may well have aided in getting him back on track after his test scores had been slumping over the past several months. The pattern of Candice's scores brings up the question of whether the incentives had no effect on her performance or, on the other hand, the effect was substantial but was delayed. To settle this question, we might ask Candice how she accounted for her improvement in April and May. Perhaps she would say, "A few weeks after the teacher was giving prizes for doing better on tests, I decided I'd like to get some prizes too, so I started working harder on my homework." Such a response would support our *delayed-effect* hypothesis. However, assume that instead she says, "In April I got my new reading glasses, and that made it easier for me to do my written work." On the basis of this information, we might conclude that the incentives did not alter Candice's achievement in algebra class.

In summary, time series are useful in revealing the role that a treatment apparently has played in the behavior of individuals or groups by showing how the intervention fits into, or interrupts, an extended pattern of behavior. The time-series design is particularly useful when the researcher has only one or two individuals to study rather than a large group. The simple logic of the time series experiment is this: if the graph of the dependent variable shows an abrupt shift in level or direction precisely at the point of intervention, then the intervention is a cause of the effect on the dependent [target] variable". However, a considerable amount of subjective judgment is involved in deciding how much of a change in a trend line warrants a conclusion that a treatment has indeed been an effective cause of an individual's or group's performance.

CHOOSING AMONG EXPERIMENTAL DESIGNS

The foregoing overview of experimental designs has introduced some of the most common types but certainly has not exhausted the options.

The task of selecting a suitable design for a particular study involves at least three steps:

(1) considering the characteristics of the available experimental designs,

(2) deciding whether an experiment will be the most appropriate mode of investigation to answer the research question (or will some other form–historical, ethnographic, correlational—be more appropriate), and

(3) selecting a design that will produce the most convincing evidence within the context of the study at hand. Significant features of "the context of the study at hand" include:

   (a) the magnitude of the educational consequences that can potentially result from the outcome of the study,

   (b) how much the experiment will interfere with normal events, and

   (c) the availability of the time, funds, facilities, and participants that the experiment requires.

When judging the likely magnitude of consequences, researchers can consider how greatly decisions derived from an experiment will influence people's welfare and how many people will be affected. A way of arriving at this judgment can be illustrated with two kinds of decisions, the first involving science videotapes and the second involving drug treatments for hyperactive pupils.

In the first example, a high school teacher wishes to assess the comparative effectiveness of two introduction-to-geology videotapes as the basis for deciding which tape the school should purchase. He intends to derive his assessment from an experiment in which one group of students views Tape-A and the other group views Tape-B. In terms of the welfare of students, it likely makes relatively little difference which tape is judged more effective. In other words, one tape will probably not have much more impact on the students' academic progress than the other. Furthermore, a relatively small number of people will be affected by whichever tape is chosen as the better one, for the number will be limited to students who enroll in that particular school's geology classes over the next few years. Thus, the teacher is not taking a great risk with students' lives if he adopts a simple, rather than complex, experimental design. Probably a two-group pretest-treatment-posttest form will be sufficient to suggest which tape is the preferred instructional tool. It is true that such a design will fail to account for a number of variables that might influence students' test scores— such as sample size (the two groups to be compared will be relatively small), distractions during the videotape viewing, and memory loss over coming weeks. However, adopting a design that would accommodate all such variables would entail more bother and expense than the choice between tapes is worth. The simple pretest-treatment-posttest seems to represent an acceptable compromise between feasibility and precision. The results of the experiment will not be foolproof, yet they should be sufficient for the teacher's rather modest purpose.

In the second example a psychiatrist from a university's medical college is cooperating with a large city's schools in studying the effects of three drugs in the treatment of hyperactive elementary-school pupils. The aim of the study is to determine which of the drugs reduces distractibility in pupils, enabling them to concentrate on their school work without suffering such undesirable side effects as drug addiction, lethargy, depression, and long-term memory deterioration. The research team intends to conduct an experiment that can reveal which of the three drugs is best. In this case, the choice of a research design is far more crucial than in the case of the geology videotapes. The final decision about which drug, if any, should be administered to hyperactive pupils could critically affect the academic success and general health of large numbers of children—not only children in this one city's schools, but hyperactive pupils throughout the nation if the experiment's results are widely disseminated. Hence, it will not suffice to employ a simple pretest-treatment-posttest design that includes four groups of hyperactive pupils (one group taking no medication and each of the other groups taking one of the three drugs). It will be more appropriate to adopt a time-series design that includes large numbers of participants that are randomly assigned to the treatments. Adequately assessing the outcome of the experiment will also require a far more complex evaluation system than the one called for in the videotape study. Whereas the science teacher's pretest and posttest instruments could reasonably consist solely of paper-pencil tests of the content of the videotapes, the psychiatrist's drug study requires a variety of measures, including appraisals of hyperactivity (types and levels), pupils' concentration skills, conditions of distractibility, mood (depression, optimism, self-confidence), speed and accuracy in acquiring knowledge, study habits, and long-term memory.

In summary, there is no experimental design that is superior to all others for all research situations. The choice of a design requires balancing costs (time, energy, participants, facilities, funds, bother, undesirable side effects), the gravity of decisions that are based on the outcome of the experiment, and the benefits that could derive from the research results.

SUMMARY

The approaches to data collection reviewed in this chapter have been presented as six separate types. However, it is clear that in practice those types are not mutually exclusive. One type often merges with another. A case study conducted over an extended period of time becomes historical research. Most ethnographies are essentially case studies. And correlational information, survey results, and experiments can be embedded in a historical account.

Qualitative researchers may use different approaches in collecting data, such as the grounded theory practice, narratology, storytelling, classical ethnography, or shadowing. Qualitative methods are also loosely present in other methodological approaches, such as action research or actor-network theory. Forms of the data collected can include interviews and group discussions, observation and reflection field notes, various texts, pictures and other materials.

Qualitative research often categorizes data into patterns as the primary basis for organizing and reporting results. Qualitative researchers typically rely on the following methods for gathering information: Participant Observation, Non-participant Observation, Field Notes, Reflexive Journals, Structured Interview, Semi-structured Interview, Unstructured Interview, and Analysis of documents and materials.

The ways of participating and observing can vary widely from setting to setting. Participant observation is a strategy of reflexive learning, not a single method of observing. In participant observation researchers typically become members of a culture, group, or setting, and adopt roles to conform to that setting. In doing so, the aim is for the researcher to gain a closer insight into the culture's practices, motivations and emotions. It is argued that the researchers' ability to understand the experiences of the culture may be inhibited if they observe without participating.

Some distinctive qualitative methods are the use of focus groups and key informant interviews. The focus group technique involves a moderator facilitating a small group discussion between selected individuals on a particular topic. This is a particularly popular method in market research and testing new initiatives with users/workers.

One traditional and specialized form of qualitative research is called cognitive testing or pilot testing which is used in the development of quantitative survey items. Survey items are piloted on study participants to test the reliability and validity of the items.

In the academic social sciences the most frequently used qualitative research approaches include the following:

1. *Ethnographic Research*, used for investigating cultures by collecting and describing data that is intended to help in the development of a theory. This method is also called "ethnomethodology" or "methodology of the people". An example of applied

ethnographic research, is the study of a particular culture and their understanding of the role of a particular disease in their cultural framework.

2. *Critical Social Research*, used by a researcher to understand how people communicate and develop symbolic meanings.
3. *Ethical Inquiry*, an intellectual analysis of ethical problems. It includes the study of ethics as related to obligation, rights, duty, right and wrong, choice etc.
4. *Foundational Research*, examines the foundations for a science, analyses the beliefs and develops ways to specify how a knowledge base should change in light of new information.
5. *Historical Research*, allows one to discuss past and present events in the context of the present condition, and allows one to reflect and provide possible answers to current issues and problems. Historical research helps us in answering questions such as: Where have we come from, where are we, who are we now and where are we going?
6. *Grounded Theory*, is an inductive type of research, based or "grounded" in the observations or data from which it was developed; it uses a variety of data sources, including quantitative data, review of records, interviews, observation and surveys.
7. *Phenomenology*, describes the "subjective reality" of an event, as perceived by the study population; it is the study of a phenomenon.
8. *Philosophical Research*, is conducted by field experts within the boundaries of a specific field of study or profession, the best qualified individual in any field of study to use an intellectual analyses, in order to clarify definitions, identify ethics, or make a value judgment concerning an issue in their field of study.

8

Classifying Data in Education

INTRODUCTION

One of the most fundamental attributes of human thought is people's propensity to arrange their experiences in terms of categories or classes. By assigning happenings to categories, we render events comprehensible by revealing how they are similar to, and different from, other events. Classifying people, objects, and incidents enables people to compare and contrast experiences and thereby construct an orderly mental map of reality that assists them in coping with the demands of their lives. And certainly classification is the essence of comparative education.

The tendency indeed, the necessity for people to classify experiences derives at least partly from the limited capacity of the human mind to simultaneously contemplate a multitudc of variables.

How many comparisons can be assimilated by those who seek an understanding of the patterns of comparisons? Writers on psychology such as Nobel laureate Herbert Simon believe that humans can simultaneously consider only a few items of information, perhaps fewer than four (depending partly on [how much is compressed into a comprehensible "chunk" of information]). For this reason, humans employ categorical ideas to think efficiently about what would be overly complex.

It appears that most of the classifying people do is automatic and subliminal rather than conscious and intentional. In other words, the act of relegating the content of events to mental categories usually is performed below the threshold of consciousness. However, as children grow up, and especially as they pursue formal education, the task of classifying becomes increasingly deliberate. Formal education to a great degree consists of teaching diverse styles of classifying so that happenings can be compared in useful ways.

Every comparative-education study involves classes, whether intuitive and perhaps hardly recognized as classes by the researcher or intentionally designed. Intentionally designed categories are much to be preferred, since they are under the investigator's conscious control. In contrast to intuitive and unrecognized categories, intentional classes can be precisely defined, the nature of the categories can be readily explained to the researcher's audience, and a system can be devised for accurately determining what sorts of data should be placed in which categories.

The practice of mentally categorizing observations has apparently been a natural human function from earliest times. However, the business of rationally devising formal systems for classifying events is of more recent vintage. The science of classification, often called *taxonomy* or *systematics*, probably originated with the ancient Greeks, brought to fruition during the fourth century B.C.E. in the works of Plato and his student Aristotle. The product of systematics can be referred to as a *taxonomy* or, alternatively, as a *typology, classification scheme*, or *codification system*. In the field of biology, the theory of evolution proposed by Charles Darwin (1809–1892) is a taxonomy for codifying the patterns in which the earth's multitude of life forms descended from common beginnings over eons of time. In chemistry, Dimitri Mendeleyev (1834–1907) created the periodic table, a taxonomic system that not only equips chemists to classify known chemical elements but also to predict properties of as-yet-undiscovered elements. In education, the taxonomy of educational objectives described in this book's opening chapter allows researchers to compare educational aims in terms of selected distinguishing features (Bloom, 1956). The cube introduced enables people to classify any educational research proposal in terms of its geographical/locational level, non locational demographic features, and influential aspects of the education system and of the society.

Three characteristics of classification systems discussed in the following pages include (a) their sources, (b) decisions about when to establish classes, and (c) assigning data to categories.

SOURCES OF TYPOLOGIES

The sources of a researcher's classification scheme can be (a) someone else's theory or typology, (b) someone else's scheme as modified by the researcher, or (c) a system created entirely by the researcher herself or himself.

ADOPTING SOMEONE ELSE'S SCHEME

The taxonomy of children's stages of intellectual development proposed by the Swiss psychologist, Jean Piaget, is an example of a classification scheme subsequently applied by scores of other researchers. Piaget identified four major stages of mental growth between early infancy and later adolescence-sensorimotor period (birth to age 2), preoperational-thought period (ages 2-7), concrete-operations period (ages 7-11), and formal-operations period (ages 11-15). He also located substages within certain periods. A host of other researchers have found Piaget's system useful for classifying the intellectual performance of diverse kinds of children in different societies, on different tasks, and under various experimental conditions.

MODIFYING A SCHEME

Frequently an investigator alters an existing taxonomic system to suit the needs of a particular research question or population of subjects. For instance, Piaget's four-stage classification system was changed in several ways by Case by Fischer, and by Mounoud as they analyzed children's performance on the tasks posed in those three authors' own studies.

An even more radical alteration of Piaget's development hierarchy was introduced by Kohlberg when he created a taxonomy of the development of moral reasoning among children and adolescents. In Kohlberg's typology, three major stages of development were each divided into a pair of substages so as to form a six-step hierarchy. The steps ranged from reasoning at the lowest stage (as founded on self-centered hedonism) to reasoning at the highest stage (as founded on principles of objective, even-handed justice).

CREATING A NEW SCHEME

Investigators can devise their own classification plan if they fail to find an existing system that fits the requirements of their research question. An example is the taxonomy created to guide the selection of curriculum content regarding indigenous Samoan culture for use in the schools of American Samoa. The research question was: What will be the most appropriate curriculum contents for teaching Samoan culture to Samoan children and youths in a school system that has focused mainly on curricula imported from the United States? To answer this question, a team of seven Samoan educators and a research consultant from the United States pored over books about Samoan culture and discussed daily life in Samoan villages. From their analysis of the resulting material, they extracted eleven categories of culture that they believed would provide students with a multifaceted view of traditional Samoan life. The eleven concerned:

(1) the society's long-established, chieftain-centered social system,
(2) methods of governance in the islands over the past two centuries,
(3) material culture (housing, tools, boats, etc.),
(4) occupations,
(5) the oral arts, music, and dance,
(6) religious beliefs and practices,
(7) ceremonies,
(8) games, sports, recreation, entertainment,
(9) land animals, birds, fish, sea animals,
(10) plant life, and

(11) significant non-living elements of the environment (the ocean, mountains, rain, etc.).

Within each of these major classes, three principal subcategories were defined: (a) types of products or activities under a particular major class, (b) significant characteristics of each of those types, and (c) how the types changed with the passing of time. As a further substep, significant types were identified. The form of the resulting scheme can be illustrated with the items under major category 5: oral arts, music, and dance.

Types of Artistic Expression

- Stories and legends
- Poems
- Songs
- Proverbs
- Riddles
- Recitations of chieftain-title lineage (*faalupega*)
- Instrumental music
- Dances

The following characteristics of each type listed below :

- Its name and varieties
- Its likely origins
- Its function in Samoan society and in the lives of individuals
- Who created it
- Occasions on which it was performed
- Who performed it, and how performers obtained their training
- What standards were used to determine the:
  - Structure or form of the particular type
  - Quality of such an art work or its performance (For example, what characteristics cause a story to be judged excellent or of poor quality?)

WHEN TO ESTABLISH CLASSES

For convenience of presentation, I have located this chapter on codification systems to follow the data-collection chapters. However, it should be apparent that the choice of classes can also occur at other stages of the research process. In fact, class selection begins with the initial statement of the research question when the investigator delineates the phenomena that come within the purview of the intended study. Proposing to compare methods of financing education in France, Germany, and Italy implies that those three nations will form one set of classes, and alternative methods of finance will comprise a second cluster that interacts with the three nation categories. In addition, a further set of classes focusing on causes is implied if the research question is stated as: What are the similarities and differences in the methods of financing education in

France, Germany, and Italy, and what factors account for such similarities and differences?

Whereas certain ways that data will be codified can be specified in the early stages of a project, others will not be identified until during or after the data have been collected. Consider, for instance, Johnston investigation of the moral reasoning of adolescents who were asked to offer solutions to the central problems in two of Aesop fables. The intent of the study was to gather evidence for assessing the validity of Gilligan's contention that Kohlberg's six-stage hierarchy of moral development, which focuses on *justice* as the basis for moral decisions, is appropriate for males but not for females. Gilligan research had led her to conclude that while males tend to base their moral decisions on concepts of *justice*, females tend to found their judgments on concepts of *compassionate caring*. Kohlberg's justice-and-rights orientation holds that everyone should be treated the same under the law. Gilligan's care-and-response orientation holds that feelings of compassion for the plight of the people involved in moral conflicts should take precedence over even-handed justice in solving moral dilemmas. As Johnston prepared to test Gilligan's proposal, she already had two sets of classes into which adolescents' responses to the fables would be placed: (a) the two gender categories (girl/boy) and (b) the two moral-orientation categories (justice/care). Then, to obtain 60 adolescents to participate in her study, she recruited a group of volunteers from the sixth grade of two elementary schools and another group from the sophomore class of a high school. Thus, she had now added two age categories (11-year-olds and 15-year-olds) to her classification system. Subsequently, after collecting all 60 students' solutions to the fables' dilemmas, Johnston discovered that not all of the participants' answers fit neatly into either the justice category or the caring category. Some answers included an equal measure of justice and caring, so Johnston created a new category to accommodate answers focusing on both justice and caring. Furthermore, a few responses failed to fit any of the three categories, so those answers were relegated to another class entitled uncodable, "which meant the answer did not clearly represent any identified logic".

So it is that decisions about how to classify information can be made at various junctures of the research process, from the very beginning through the act of placing the collected data into appropriate categories.

ASSIGNING DATA TO CATEGORIES

If the research outcomes are to provide accurate answers to research questions, then the classification categories must be defined precisely enough to enable any reasonably-informed judge to place data in their proper locations. Some types of categories are easy to define and recognize. Such is the case with divisions based on gender, age, time interval (year, decade, century), place (school, city, nation), and measures that result in definite quantities (heights, test scores, days absent from school). Any errors made in placing data in their proper categories are the result of carelessness of the people doing the placing, not the result of imprecise definitions.

However, the distinctions among categories designed for certain other variables are not so obvious, so that codifiers are quite apt to disagree about where a particular response or observation deserves to be located. Consider, for example, the task of assigning students' answers to the justice and caring categories in Johnston's Aesop's fables study. When students were asked about the moral problem embedded in each fable, they could reply in any way they chose. It then became the researcher's task to extract from students' replies (some of which were quite complex) the portions that seemed to reflect either a justice attitude or a caring viewpoint or both, or neither. Such judgments on the part of the researcher could involve a substantial measure of subjectivity which might result in one person coding data into different categories than did another. The greater the amount of subjective opinion involved in the coding process, the less trustworthy are the reported outcomes of the research. Three of the ways investigators seek to increase the accuracy of assigning data to categories are those of (a) defining each class in a manner that clearly distinguishes it from any other class, (b) accompanying each definition with examples of the sorts of data (such as the students' replies in the Johnston study) that belong in that category, and (c) conducting training sessions for the people who will do the coding.

Thus, just as researchers should be concerned about the reliability of tests (internal, split-half, alternate-form consistency), so also they should be concerned about consistency in classifying data. The issue of interest here is reflected in two questions.

The first question concerns the successive-judgments reliability of researcher decisions. Specifically, to what extent does the researcher place a particular kind of observation or response consistently in the same category? Imagine that a teacher is judging how logically students' argue their case in essays they have written about human rights. The teacher has established five categories of logic in which to locate students' arguments *superior, above average, moderate, below average*, and *very poor.* Her appraisal technique is deemed perfect in terms of successive-judgments reliability if, when she reevaluates the essays this week, she gives each one exactly the same rating that she gave it last week. In effect, her method is 100% reliable. However, such an outcome would be quite unusual. Studies of such matters have shown that raters' successive judgments of narrative data (essays, letters, descriptive oral responses, and the like) are often quite inconsistent.

The second question concerns *interrater reliability*: To what extent do two or more judges agree on where to locate a particular observation or response? If multiple judges are in substantial agreement about the placement of data, then the definitions of categories and the training of judges are considered trustworthy. A typical way to assess interrater reliability is to have two or more raters independently classify the same data (narrative answers to questions) into the study's categories. The interrater reliability is then reported as the percent of times the coders' judgments matched. In the Aesop's fables project, Johnston reported intercoder reliability for two raters as 100% agreement on coding students' solutions to *The Dog in the Manger* story and of 90% agreement on coding solutions to *The Porcupine and the Moles* fable.

We would hope that when Johnston's coders received copies of students' responses, the copies did not include information about each student's gender, because providing gender information could conceivably bias the raters' judgments. It seems likely that when Johnston launched her project, she was already favorably disposed to Gilligan's hypothesis about differences between females and males, for Johnston conducted her project in Boston, adjacent to Gilligan's academic base and Johnston's study was published in a book edited by Gilligan and associates. Hence, if Johnston's coders did know the gender of a student whose protocol they were judging, they could be inclined intentionally or not to make the coding of answers support the Gilligan hypothesis. Consequently, if raters' assignment of data to classes is to be not only reliable but also valid, it is important that the raters be obliged to make "blind" judgments, that is, to reach decisions unmarred by information that could compromise the objectivity of those decisions.

ILLUSTRATIVE CATEGORIES

The purpose of this second section of the chapter is to identify diverse modes of classifying information found in representative studies. The studies illustrate seven different bases for classifying data. It should be clear that these seven represent only a few among many classification systems that researchers have used.

To render the studies convenient to compare, I have described each in terms of its central theme, sources of data, types of data collected, and classification scheme.

CHRONOLOGICAL CATEGORIES

The most common way of ordering information in historical studies is by successive time periods; and within each period, subcategories may be identified. Sometimes the subcategories are identical from one epoch to another. For example, within each period an author may provide data on the numbers and types of schools, their enrolments, their sponsoring organizations, and relevant economic and political conditions in the society. In other instances, the subcategories in one era will differ somewhat from those in others. One period may feature the effect on education of a current war and economic problems whereas another may stress student unrest and new curricula in the schools.

In the first of two illustrative cases, each chronological period focuses on key people and events in the development of international comparisons of educational achievement. In the second example, values education in Russia is described for two time periods: (a) the 70-year era of communist hegemony, and (b) the recent period following the introduction of perestroika.

CASE 1: The opening chapter of a volume entitled *Monitoring the Standards of Education* furnishes a historical background against which the contents of the remainder of the book can be viewed.

Sources of data: (a) Content analyses of books, journal articles, and government reports of international assessments of educational achievement and (b) the authors' personal recollections as participants in international evaluation projects.

Types of data: Names and contributions of individuals, groups, and organizations that played key roles in the development of international evaluation activities from the 1930s into the 1990s.

Classification scheme: The five major categories are labelled "the early days", "the 1960s," "the 1970s," "the 1980s," and "prospects for the 1990s and beyond."

CASE 2: In a journal article entitled "Russian Education after Perestroika: The Search for New Values," the vice-president of the Russian Academy of Education, Nikolai D. Nikandrov, described changes in values education before and after the demise of the USSR's communist regime.

Sources of data: (a) Content analyses of newspaper articles, history books, and government directives bearing on education, (b) public opinion surveys, and (b) the author's direct observations of events from his key position in the Russian education system.

Types of data: Educational policies regarding the aims and methods of values education, the political sources of such policies, the effects of those policies on students' learning, changes in people's attitudes since the end of the USSR, and effects of such changes on enrollments in different types of higher education.

Classification scheme: The author divided his presentation of data into three categories: (a) the historical background of values and education in the USSR—1920-1989, (b) changes in value commitments in Russia during and following the period of perestroika introduced by Mikhail Gorbachev in 1989, and (c) post-1989 attitude changes in Russian society along with educational implications of those changes.

PROCESS CATEGORIES

The process through which an educational activity or social event progresses can provide categories into which data are placed.

In *Monitoring the Standards of Education*, one chapter inspected ways of checking on the performance of education systems in a variety of nations.

Sources of data: (a) Personal observations as a consultant to diverse nations' ministries of education and (b) content analyses of journal articles and books reporting evaluations of education systems in different countries.

Types of data: Reports of methods used in periodic assessments of how well nations' schools and their students have met performance criteria.

Classification scheme: The researcher divided the schooling process into three phases: (a) inputs into schools, (b) processes in schools, and (c) outcomes and outputs. Each of these major categories was defined in terms of its constituent subcategories. For example, the subcategories under "processes in schools" were: teacher time (teacher work load or time spent in class), curriculum, opportunity for students to learn, time allocation (number of hours each week devoted to each subject), how the school is organized, and methods of school inspection (supervision).

STAGE CATEGORIES

The development of people, institutions, and social movements is often conceived as a series of progressive stages to be used in classifying individuals, institutions, social movements, or socio-political systems. Piaget's portrayal of children's intellectual growth and Kohlberg's version of moral-reasoning styles are both ways of categorizing human development. Karl Marx proposed a three stage scheme for classifying the evolution of societies' political-economic systems (feudalism, capitalism, state socialism) and of those systems' educational institutions. Walberg, Zhang and Daniel performed a complex statistical analysis of 139 variables "world education indicators" for 164 countries in order to generate a taxonomy that permits nations' education systems to be "parsimoniously and discretely clustered into three major groups" that reflect stages in societies' socio-political development.

Group A consists of 49 underdeveloped countries, largely in Africa.

Group B is composed of 79 functional democracies, mostly in Asia, Europe, Oceania, and North and South America.

Group C includes 36 post-industrial democracies in Northern Europe and North America.

A further development example is Beeby's evolutionary taxonomy for analyzing the nature of change in education systems:

In *The Quality of Education in Developing Countries*, Beeby asserted that school systems pass through four discrete qualitative stages whose identifying characteristics are determined to a great extent by teachers' levels of general education and by their professional training.

Sources of data: (a) The analysis of books and journal articles that describe education in developing nations and (b) the author's direct observations of educational practices in a variety of nations in which he conducted research and served as a consultant on educational matters.

Types of data: Descriptions of teaching practices in the schools of developing societies, analyses of change processes in such schools, and information about the levels of teachers' general education and professional training.

Classification scheme: Four stages of development and the teacher and school system characteristics that Beeby identified are summarized in Table 8.1.

PROBLEM-CENTERED CATEGORIES

In problem-centered research, the chief classes of data are the problems the author has identified. Frequently the problem categories are accompanied by solution categories, as in the following example.

The book *Lives in the Balance—Youth, Poverty, and Education in Watts* describes the living conditions and educational experiences of students in a Los Angeles inner-city high school.

Sources of data: (a) Observations of students and their living conditions, (b) interviews with students and school personnel, and (c) content analyses of books, journal articles, newspapers, and television news reports.

Types of data: The author, a high school teacher and counsellor, assumed the role of participant-observer as she witnessed her students' behavior, talked with them about events in their lives, and maintained a log of what she learned from those encounters. From her notes she extracted a series of problem conditions that seemed to contribute to adolescents' academic and personal social difficulties. To provide a comparative context within which to interpret her observations, she analyzed the contents of books and journal articles bearing on the identified problem conditions.

Table 8.1. Stages in the Evolution of Schools' Approaches to Instruction

Stage Title	Instructional Mode	Teachers' Characteristics
Dame school	Unorganized, meaningless symbols, very narrow subject content, very low achievement standards	Limited education, no training in teaching methods
Formalist School	Highly structured, symbols with limited meaning, rigid syllabus, rote memorization	Limited education, but some training in teaching techniques
Transition school	Highly organized, less restrictive syllabi and textbooks, more emphasis on meaning	Better general education, more training in methods of teaching
Meaningful teaching	Stress on meaning and understanding, richer curriculum offerings, wider range of methods, problem solving and creativity emphasized	Good general education, well trained in teaching methods

Classification scheme: The author adopted two sorts of categories problems and potential solutions. The problem categories into which she fitted data (events from students' lives) were: academic performance, family life, street gangs, substance abuse, malnutrition, and unsanitary and unsafe environments. The solutions categories were similar: academic performance, family life, gangs, substance abuse, stress, premature mortality, joblessness, and needed services.

PAIRED-CONTRASTS CATEGORIES

Researchers frequently classify data in terms of two contrasting attributes–male/ female, public/private, urban/rural, developed nation/developing nation, and such. Sometimes more than one pair of contrasting viewpoints are adopted by an author, as demonstrated in Ishumi choosing two pairs of opposing viewpoints for organizing his analysis of ethnocentrism in African schools.

The book chapter entitled "Colonial Forces and Ethnic Resistance in African Education" is a historical study of conceptions of culture in colonial and post-colonial Africa.

Sources of data: Content analyses of selected historical accounts from the 19th century through most of the 20th century.

Types of data: Historical materials reflecting different authors' perceptions of indigenous African culture.

Classification scheme: The chapter's first pair of categories contrasts (a) opinions about African culture as drawn from an outsider's (European) perspective and (b) opinions drawn from an insider's perspective (African's or sympathetic Muslim scholar's view). The second pair examines ethnocentrism as displayed (a) within African schools and (b) outside the schools.

CAUSAL CATEGORIES

Often the classes that researchers employ represent potential causes of the study's target variable. The purpose of such research is to determine if, and to what degree, the characteristics represented by the categories have likely contributed to the target variable, as determined by computing correlations between the characteristics and the target variable. Sometimes only one or two such categories are identified, in the belief that the characteristics of the target are the result entirely or mainly of the operation of one or two causes. Other times a large number of potential causes are cited, under the impression that the condition of the target variable could be the consequence of multiple components. Such is the case in the following example in which the target was students' tested reading skills and the categories of potential causes were characteristics of teachers and of the teaching context. The study involved 93,049 nine-year-olds and 100,365 fourteen-year-olds in 32 countries as well as the 4,992 teachers of the nine-year-olds and 5,526 teachers of the fourteen-year olds.

In their book *Teaching Reading Around the World*, Lundberg and Linnakyla reported correlations between students' tested reading skills and 17 variables estimated to be possible contributors to reading competence.

Sources of data: (a) Achievement tests of students' reading skills. (b) Questionnaires completed by teachers and by students.

Types of data: (a) Test scores reflecting students' ability to comprehend narratives, documents, and expository writing. (b) Student-completed questionnaires reflecting students' voluntary reading habits. (c) Teacher completed questionnaires reflecting teachers' characteristics, their teaching methods, and the context in which they taught reading.

Classification scheme: Three clusters of categories offered information about 17 input variables, while a fourth cluster focused on students' reading abilities and habits.

Three sets containing a total of 17 input (likely causal) variables:

Cluster I: Teacher characteristics:

(1) education,

(2) experience,

(3) gender,

(4) readership (amount and type of reading done by teacher),

(5) teacher's aims in reading instruction.

Cluster II: Teaching strategies:

(1) time allocation,

(2) assignment of homework,

(3) skill orientation,

(4) strategy orientation,

(5) literature orientation,

(6) functional orientation (practical use of reading),

(7) assessment for accountability (providing reports for the school's administrators),

(8) assessment for instruction (providing information to improve teaching methods).

Cluster III: Proximal teaching conditions:

(1) class size,

(2) instructional time,

(3) percentage of students speaking a language other than the reading test language,

(4) number of textbooks per student.

One set of four categories offered information about the target variable—that is, the output variable of pupils' reading competence:

Cluster IV: Students' reading skills and habits:

(1) narrative comprehension,

(2) expository comprehension,

(3) document comprehension,

(4) frequency and types of voluntary reading.

LINE-OF-LOGIC CATEGORIES

Many research reports are organized as a sequence of categories representing what authors believe forms a line of reasoning that readers will find comprehensible and convincing. The following instance illustrates the set of categories adopted by a coalition of researchers to depict the legislative and policy environments of adult education in ten nations.

A special issue of the *International Review of Education* featured articles designed to account for the legal status of adult education in Australia, Brazil, England and Wales, the Ivory Coast, Hungary, India, Morocco, the Philippines, Switzerland, and the United States.

Sources of data: Content analyses of national-history books, of legal documents bearing on educational opportunities for adults, of government publications focusing on adult education and employment, and of critiques of the nation's educational provisions.

Types of data: Historical background and demographic information about levels of literacy and education in the society, legal provisions and policies relating to education for adults, descriptions of adult-education programs, and analyses of the strengths and weaknesses of adult-education provisions.

Classification scheme: The five principal categories adopted by the authors were ordered in this sequence: (a) the historical background of adult education, (b) the legislative and policy framework, (c) the structure and amount of adult education, (d) current contextual problems, and (e) trends in providing adult education. Within each main category, authors were free to define subcategories that would accommodate special conditions in the nation whose adult-education system they described.

Qualitative means a non-numerical data collection or explanation based on the attributes of the graph or source of data. For example, if you are asked to explain in qualitative terms a thermal image displayed in multiple colours, then you would explain the colour differences rather than the heat's numerical value.

First, cases can be selected purposefully, according to whether or not they typify certain characteristics or contextual locations. Secondly, the role or position of the researcher is given greater critical attention. This is because in qualitative research the possibility of the researcher taking a 'neutral' or transcendental position is seen as more problematic in practical and/or philosophical terms. Hence qualitative researchers are often exhorted to reflect on their role in the research process and make this clear in the analysis. Thirdly, while qualitative data analysis can take a wide variety of forms it tends to differ from quantitative research in the focus on language, signs and meaning as well as approaches to analysis that are holistic and contextual, rather than reductionist and isolationist. Nevertheless, systematic and transparent approaches to analysis are almost always regarded as essential for rigor. For example, many qualitative methods require researchers to carefully code data and discern and document themes in a consistent and reliable way.

Perhaps the most traditional division in the way qualitative and quantitative research have been used in the social sciences is for qualitative methods to be used for exploratory (i.e., hypothesis-generating) purposes or explaining puzzling quantitative results, while quantitative methods are used to test hypotheses. This is because establishing content validity do measures measure what a researcher thinks they measure? is seen as one of the strengths of qualitative research. While quantitative methods are seen as providing more representative, reliable and precise measures through focused hypotheses, measurement tools and applied mathematics. By contrast, qualitative data is usually difficult to graph or display in mathematical terms.

Qualitative research is often used for policy and program evaluation research since it can answer certain important questions more efficiently and effectively than quantitative approaches. This is particularly the case for understanding how and why certain outcomes were achieved (not just what was achieved) but also answering important questions about relevance, unintended effects and impact of programs such as: Were expectations reasonable? Did processes operate as expected? Were key players able to carry out their duties? Were there any unintended effects of the program? Qualitative approaches have the advantage of allowing for more diversity in responses as well as the capacity to adapt to new developments or issues during the research process itself. While qualitative research can be expensive and time-consuming to conduct, many fields of research employ qualitative techniques that have been specifically developed to provide more succinct, cost-efficient and timely results. Rapid Rural Appraisal is one formalised example of these adaptations but there are many others.

9

Content Analyses and Description in Education

INTRODUCTION

Researchers can offer various meanings of documents. The kinds illustrated in the following paragraphs are not intended to represent an exhaustive list but merely to show that a number of different meanings can be constructed from the results of descriptive analyses. The first three represent attempts of authors to express the essence of communications. The next three involve researchers' efforts to identify causes of depicted events. The final three perform confirmative, hortatory, and evaluative functions. As the discussion progresses, it will become apparent that the types are not mutually exclusive. Frequently, two or more modes are combined.

EXPRESSING THE ESSENCE OF COMMUNICATIONS

Three ways researchers attempt to portray the essential nature of messages are by suggesting the documents' key themes, identifying personal qualities of the communications' subjects, or offering synopses of the documents' contents.

KEY THEMES INTERPRETATION

In this variety, the investigator tries to capture in a few phrases the essence of a communication in respect to the themes it treats. The question guiding this effort is: What core ideas does the document contain? The task of interpretation assumes a comparative form when it sets the themes of one document or one set of documents against the themes of another, as in Gerbert's comparison of Japanese and American elementary-school reading books.

Cultural diversity, so absent in the Japanese reader, is everywhere present in the American reader. So varied are the characters and experiences depicted in [American books] that one is often left wondering what nation their audiences might be living in. By contrasting the Japanese textbooks with American textbooks, I hope to show how Japanese materials are designed to create a common singular consciousness in their youth, a sense of belonging to the Japanese nation.

An example from a more distant historical setting is Boorstin view of the contrasting purposes of higher education in Thomas Jefferson's writings and in the Harvard University curriculum of Jefferson's day.

Boorstin points out in his book *The Lost World of Thomas Jefferson* that Jefferson's notions of modernity and usefulness tended to leave an educational legacy that was essentially "uncritical and conservative," whereas Harvard's more traditional emphasis on metaphysics and pure science made it "a center of intellectual ferment, a breeding ground for potent and revolutionary ideas, for new and pregnant systems of philosophy".

Extracting key themes is not simply an objective act. As with all interpretation, it involves a substantial measure of personal judgment. In an effort to convince their audience, key-theme analysts may describe in some detail the line of reasoning that led to the themes they put forth. However, this effort may still leave some doubt in the reader's mind, as implied by Bailey's slightly guarded reaction to Boorstin's conception of the themes embedded in Jefferson's writings and the Harvard curriculum.

Whether Boorstin is right or wrong, Jefferson's notion of educational utility was far removed from the emerging concepts of educational utility today.

PERSONAL QUALITIES INTERPRETATION

Often an analyst endeavours to abstract from documents prominent features of an individual's or a group's personality. The documents that frequently serve this purpose are biographies, letters, speeches, and regulations that the individual or group has formulated. The question guiding such inquiry is: What characteristics typify this individual's or group's thought and behavior?

One variety of this sort of interpretation consists of a researcher comparing the personal qualities of different individuals who interact in an educational context. A case in point is Kyle's examination of the life of Cara Mallet, an Englishwoman who served in Australia as principal of a teacher-training college for women over the period 1883-1885. In her synthesis of information from a variety of archival materials, Kyle characterized Mallet and three other women who succeeded her as:

> *well-educated, interested in promoting academic excellence for female trainees, and active in pursuing curriculum change and new teaching practices. They were ambitious and adventurous, and they actively pursued professional gains and better training within the real constraints of the times. They were also the first tertiary-trained women professionals in Australia. This characteristic alone marks them out as especially interesting compared to their contemporaries.*

In contrast, a male principal of another institution, who took offense at Ms. Mallet's criticism of the way he taught English literature, was pictured in Kyle's analysis as having "penned a bitter response" to Ms. Mallet's reproach; "his apologia for his program proved less than convincing" and he "scorned her suggestion that studying 'two books' would be more appropriate." He stated that "'we are not disposed to commend any departure'" from his traditional mode of instruction. Kyle's analysis then continued with:

One wonders at his use of the royal "we"! Perhaps he felt he was speaking for the department and other male teachers and administrators. Nonetheless, his use of the word "safe" is illustrative of his caution and opposition to change.

SYNOPTIC INTERPRETATION

In synoptic interpretation, the analyst endeavours to provide a concise version of a longer communication. The analysis is guided by the question: How can I best prepare a brief version that is true to the spirit and content of the original document?

A synopsis goes beyond just identifying key themes in that it provides considerable detail, and in some cases it attempts to maintain a sense of the original author's writing style. In the comparative form of synoptic interpretation, summaries of two or more communications are placed side by side, with the analyst usually pointing out what could be regarded as significant similarities and differences. An example is the book *Models of Moral Education* in which each chapter represents an abridged version of a particular theorist's moral-education program—Shaver's rationale-building model, McPhail's consideration model, Raths' values-clarification model, Kohlberg's cognitive–moral development model, and more.

The researcher's challenge in synoptic interpretation is to decide what to take from the original documents and what to leave out. To do this properly, the investigator needs to be guided by selection criteria which identify comparable features to be derived from each document. For instance, the team of analysts who wrote the book *Oriental Theories of Human Development* used a series of questions to determine what they would distill from authoritative writings of five philosophical/religious traditions Buddhism, Confucianism, Hinduism, Islam, and Shinto. The questions concerned such issues as (1) the origin of the human species, (2) the goals of development, (3) causes of development, (4) the structure of human personality, and (5) implications of the theory for child rearing and education. Each religion's answers to the questions formed the content of the particular chapter of the book focusing on that philosophical tradition.

CAUSAL INTERPRETATIONS

The process of causal analysis involves two steps: (1) identifying a correlation between two or more phenomena and (2) providing a line of logic which suggests that one of those phenomena is the result at least partially of the other. The first step demonstrating a correlation is descriptive; it consists of showing that as one factor changed, the other also changed, at least to some degree. The second step establishing a causal link—is speculative, representing the analyst's estimate of how one of the factors has caused, or could cause, a related one. Three versions of causal interpretation can be called the explanatory, the predictive, and the implicative.

EXPLANATORY INTERPRETATION

Explanatory analysis is concerned with the past, focusing on events that have already occurred. In one form of explanation, the researcher's purpose is to detect the influence of earlier documents (the antecedent or independent variable) on subsequent events (the outcome or dependent variable). The connection the analyst is seeking to establish can be expressed as a question.

- In what ways did changes in the university's sexual harassment rules alter faculty-student relationships?
- In terms of compulsory-education regulations, what differences are found among the Thai, Singaporean, and Malaysian school systems, and how have these differences affected school enrolments?

Another form of explanatory interpretation reverses the order of documents and events. Past events are viewed as responsible for the characteristics of subsequent documents. A familiar version of this approach involves an analyst identifying differences between an earlier document and its later counterpart, then proposing that particular events occurring in the time between the two publications are responsible for those differences. A case of Japanese school books illustrates this point. In 1993, new history textbooks approved by Japan's ministry of education replaced existing texts in the nation's schools. Observers noted that a significant difference between the old and new books was their description of Japan's occupation of Korea and invasion of China. According to Greenlees:

> *The ministry has traditionally preferred to overlook some of the uncomfortable facts of Japan's wartime history. Details of atrocities such as the notorious massacre of Nanking in 1937, when the Japanese army raped and murdered thousands of Chinese civilians, have repeatedly been deleted from school textbooks. Existing history texts describe the 1937 invasion of China as "an advance" and largely ignore unpalatable events such as the infamous Bataan Death March [in the Philippines]. The new textbooks are intended to provide a more honest picture of Japan at war.*

To account for the reasons behind such changes, Greenlees proposed that:

> *The whole revision of history texts, the first in 12 years, is partly a response to the barrage of complaints from South Korea, China, and other East Asian states about the way Japanese children are presented with "sanitised" versions of their country's wartime history.*

As support for his analysis, Greenlees noted: "In a recent statement, the Japanese ministry of education agreed that consideration must be given to events in modern history that concern both Japan and its neighbours." He then provided his own estimate of motives behind the ministry's move.

The Japanese hope that a fairer, franker account will lead to improved political and economic relations between Japan and its neighbours. The South Korean embassy in Tokyo has already welcomed the acknowledgement of the forced use of Korean women as "comfort women."

In contrast to the people who analyze documents to explain causal influences, there are critics who play the role of debunkers, disputing the validity of such analyses. Debunkers operate either by doubting that the investigator truly understood the documents or by disputing the line of logic with which the investigator has connected the contents of documents to events. An example is Walford's quarreling with the argument put forward in a book focusing on connections between education and poverty.

The authors claim that the first of [their] chapters uses data from up to 40 countries to investigate the effect of education on reducing poverty. What the chapter actually does is provide some interesting correlations between various factors for the countries selected. But it is positively misleading for the authors to infer causation from correlation in that they do not overcome the simple problem of untangling whether, for example, more equitable income distributions are caused by improvements in education or vice versa. The reality is probably a lot more complex than either possibility.

PREDICTIVE INTERPRETATION

Predictive analysis addresses the future. Its aim is to estimate the influence that presently existing or newly proposed communications will exert on events in the days or years ahead. A predictive interpretation is essentially an inference about a likely causal connection between particular communications and specified future events. As in the case of explanatory interpretations, the connection the analyst is postulating can be expressed as a question. Here are three examples:

- Will the newly proposed school-attendance voucher system result in higher levels of student performance than the levels found under present school funding policies?
- What changes can be expected in the contents of science textbooks if religious groups' criticisms of humanistic secularism replace prevailing publishing guidelines?
- Will statistics on immigration trends affect regulations governing the language of instruction to be used in schools?

IMPLICATIVE INTERPRETATION

Implicative analysis is similar to the predictive variety in the sense that both of them focus on the future. However, the two differ in their emphasis. Predictive interpretation consists of speculating about what *will likely occur* as a consequence of a communication, whereas implicative interpretation concerns *potential applications* of a communication. Two subtypes of implicative interpretation involve comparing (1) different analysts' educational applications of the same document and (2) an analyst's proposing applications of two different documents.

Same Author, Different Analysts. Although the Swiss psychologist Jean Piaget wrote voluminously about child development, he seldom proposed educational implications of his theories. That job was left to his host of disciples, whose opinions sometimes differed regarding the types of applications that should reasonably derive from Piaget's writings.

Same Analyst, Different Authors. Whenever a single researcher infers educational practices from documents deriving from different authors, the results of this inquiry may form the contents of a book bearing such a title as *Models of Moral Education.*

CONFIRMATIVE INTERPRETATION

Content analysis performs a confirmative function whenever the comparison of communications is intended to corroborate a belief the analyst wishes to advance. One sort of confirmative analysis is the manifold-support type, guided by the question: How much documentary evidence can I compile in support of my position? Another is the conflicting-version variety, derived from answering the question: Which of several contradictory accounts of an event is most convincing?

In the manifold-support type, multiple documents are interpreted as all substantiating the hypothesis, viewpoint, policy, or practice the analyst is advocating. In other words, the analyst seeks to convince others of the soundness of his or her stance by offering not just one, but a multitude of materials in support of that position. In way of illustration, Cremin cites 12 "recent works" that represent the "serious and systematic study of characteristic family life" on which he based his own rendition of family influences on education in colonial America.

In the conflicting-version mode, a researcher compares two or more contradictory accounts of a policy or an event, then offers a line of argument to show that the particular account which supports his or her position is the most logical of the lot or, perhaps, is the one best supported by empirical evidence. For instance, Walberg compared policies urging school district consolidation with more recent studies of school district size and proposed that:

> *the consolidation of districts into larger units that has been taking place for the past half century may have been a move in the wrong direction. Generally, it appears that the smaller the district, the higher the [student] achievement when the socioeconomic status and per-student expenditures are taken into account. Why? Superintendent and central staff awareness of citizen and parent preferences, the absence of bureaucratic layers and administrative complexity, teacher involvement in decision making, and close home-school relations these may account for the apparent efficiency of small districts in North America.*

HORTATORY INTERPRETATION

A central motive behind this kind of analysis is to use the comparison of communications as a means of urging a reading audience to act in support of a particular educational philosophy, policy, organization, or set of practices. It is a form of advocacy research. An illustration is Ross essay reviewing five books treating feminist themes. The advocacy nature of the essay is reflected in such observations as:

further research on gender and education must not only reflect the complexity of the relationship between gender and education but analyze the sociopolitical contexts in which these relationships are forged. The subversive challenge of such a "morally engaged" enterprise "means facing questions of power and conflict that disrupt a comfortable academic world still heavily influenced by the myths of harmony and meritocracy". These books suggest the possibilities for creating new knowledge from our educational disorder.

EVALUATIVE INTERPRETATION

Evaluative analysis is concerned with judging whether one communication is better or worse than others in terms of specified characteristics, such as cost, social equity, clarity, user convenience, functional efficiency, aesthetic appeal, and far more. For example, several colleges' student-admission policies can be compared in terms of both cost and racial-group equity. Or two versions of a regulation governing the treatment of experimental animals in university psychology laboratories can be analyzed for the documents' clarity of explanation and provisions for protecting the experimental subjects' welfare. Alternative landscape-architecture plans for a high school can be reviewed for their visual charm and their efficiency in routing student traffic. Descriptions of several teacher-education programs can be examined for their balance between theoretical studies and practical classroom experiences.

Oftentimes the comparison is not based on a single document that is intended to represent a given educational practice but, rather, is founded on a series of related documents. This is illustrated in Castro comparison of five models of vocational education that have been associated with four nations and one region—France, Germany, Japan, the United States, and Latin America. From a variety of materials describing vocational education in these countries, Castro extracted "defining characteristics" of each model. He used the resulting characteristics for assessing the models along several dimensions–cost, how well they suited their nation's socio-cultural traditions, the extent of labor mobility in the nation, the coordination of schooling with work experience, and the balance between academic and vocational studies.

HERMENEUTICS

Hermeneutics, in its most general sense, can be broadly defined as the art or science of interpretation. Although the word *hermeneutics* has been around for centuries, its present-day heightened popularity in education and in the humanities and social sciences is of rather recent origin, dating principally from the early 1960s. Along with this heightened interest has come a fair amount of puzzlement arising from a lack of consensus among writers about precisely what the aim and methods of hermeneutics are. This lack of agreement even extends to the pronunciation of the term itself. (Is it best as *her-me-NOO-tics*, *her-me-NYOO-tics*, or *her-me-NOY-tics*?) One result of the confusion is that potential users of hermeneutics fail to understand when or how to apply its methods.

A search of the literature on hermeneutics to learn how the procedure is defined yields a harvest of mixed worth. Wilhelm Dilthey, the German philosopher most often credited with stimulating the modern-day movement, defined hermeneutics as "understanding social phenomena in terms of the motives of the participants and the meanings [that such motives] give to institutions and events".

Less clear than Dilthey's statement is Bubner's assertion that: "For hermeneutics, understanding means a fundamental apprehension of truth which takes place in inter-subjective processes of communication and in the mediation through history".

Equally elusive seems the meaning Giddens intended when writing that hermeneutics involves "grasping frames of meaning contextually as elements of the practice of particular forms of life and not only consistencies with frames, but also inconsistencies and disputed or contested meanings".

In view of this murky condition of much of the discourse about hermeneutics, my problem in composing the following presentation was that of determining more precisely what roles hermeneutics might perform in educational research. I attacked the problem by reviewing key writings bearing on document interpretation in various disciplines, then extracting from those writings six functions that might reasonably qualify as hermeneutic activities applicable to educational research. The six functions are those of *contextual interpretation, verification interpretation; data accuracy interpretation, alternative interpretation, clarifying interpretation*, and *symbolism interpretation.*

CONTEXTUAL INTERPRETATION

In content analysis, *contextual interpretation* most often refers to how a document's meaning is affected by the historical or socio-cultural context within which the document was composed. An example is Bailey's comparing the socio-cultural environment of Thomas Jefferson's time with Bailey's own late 20th-century environment, implying that if Jefferson were living today he would likely offer quite different educational proposals.

Most of Jefferson's specific educational assumptions and recommendations are, if taken in their appropriate historical context, starkly irrelevant to our present age. His task was to design an education system to undergird political freedom in a wilderness. Ours is to design an education system to preserve political freedom in a wildly elaborated technology. His task was to fashion an education suitable for national independence. Ours is to fashion an education suitable for a condition of global interdependence. His task was to construct an educational curriculum that would assist citizens in unlocking and exploiting natural resources. Ours is to remind citizens, through education, that, first, our natural resources are precious gifts that need prudent conservation, and, second, that we must live not as exploiters of nature, but in loving symbiosis with other life and with nature generally.

VERIFICATION INTERPRETATION

Verification analysis is aimed at determining the authenticity of a communication. The purpose is to help the analyst decide whether a communication is actually what it is purported to be. Verification interpretation, in its comparative version, usually involves ascertaining which of two or more communications is the most authentic. This mode of analysis can result in such appraisals as Cremin's conclusion that "The literature on Horatio Alger, Jr., is replete with legend and even some fraudulent biography based on a nonexistent diary. Edwin P. Hoyt, *Horatio's Boys: The Life and Works of Horatio Alger, Jr.* appears to be authoritative". Perhaps the most common sort of verification analysis is reflected in the question: When there are two somewhat contradictory accounts of an event, which account is the more accurate? In attempting to answer this question, the experienced investigator will typically depend on both internal and external sources of evidence. The word *internal* refers to characteristics of the documents themselves, such things as factual consistency, completeness of presentation, chronological accuracy, and writing style. The word *external* refers to evidence from outside the document that either corroborates the account or casts doubt on it. External evidence usually consists of information about the same events as provided by other documents or witnesses.

DATA-ACCURACY INTERPRETATION

Sometimes an investigator wonders whether the data and portrayal of events in a document are accurate. The researcher's guide questions become: To what extent are the episodes or information in the document complete, or at least representative of conditions at the time? What other information should have been included in the document to ensure that the data were accurate? Techniques for answering such queries include:

1. Reviewing the apparent sources of the original author's data to estimate whether the author had extracted from them a balanced description of conditions at the time.
2. Searching for new sources of information so as to check the contents of these new sources against the contents of the original author's work to learn whether adding the new information warrants changing the conclusions drawn in the original work.

Estimating reasons for any data inaccuracies that have been discovered in the communication.

ALTERNATIVE INTERPRETATION

Frequently a critical reader will accept at face value a document's descriptive content but will question the author's interpretation of the material and then will suggest a different meaning for the data. Thus, the comparison the reader draws is between the existing document and an alternative version that the reader either has in mind or actually produces. A case in point is Shields' reaction to Schoppa book *Education Reform in Japan.*

The data Schoppa presents, however, do not provide a totally convincing case for *immobilist* politics. The reform agenda he explores appears to originate more from players on the margins of the educational policy process than from the government in its fullest definition. Also, a contrary argument could be made that the government has dynamically moved away from many U.S. occupation democratic reforms toward more historically conservative Japanese practices. The strength of the Schoppa book is the root of its weakness. His data are so comprehensive that it is difficult to find theoretical constructs to give his descriptive detail coherent explanatory power. An obvious first step for Schoppa to consider for dealing with this challenge in future work is to develop more rigorous definitions of such key terms used in his arguments as: *conservative, policy process, immobilist, and government.*

The researcher's guide questions for conducting such a reappraisal can be: What is the political, moral, social-class, ethnic, or gender vantage point from which the original author viewed the events depicted in this document? To cast the issue in a comparative form, the investigator asks: How might the account have been different if the author had assumed a different vantage point?

This type has been most prominent in recent decades in formerly colonized nations whose people have sought to revise, from their own viewpoint rather than from that of the colonialists, the history of education during colonial times. But such revisionism is not limited to cases of newly independent peoples. It can occur as readily whenever the political control of a state falls into new hands, and the leaders of the new regime choose to recast historical accounts by reinterpreting the previously presented evidence. The resulting revised interpretation typically attributes ignoble motives to the people involved in the original account or else suggests that the educational practices of those earlier times produced different consequences than the ones described in the original document.

The researcher's methods for determining the accuracy of a work's interpretation can involve:

1. Estimating the way political, economic, and social motives of various groups in the society would likely have influenced their explanation of the educational events depicted in the original document, then
2. Comparing the analysis found in the document with the explanation that might derive from each groups' motives in order to determine whether the document's interpretation was biased or else was a balanced representation of different groups' viewpoints.

What often stimulates a scholar to initiate an alternative interpretation is the philosophical or theoretical persuasion to which the scholar subscribes, a persuasion different from that of the original author of the documents under question. For example, Marxist theory may be used for reinterpreting an account of 19th-century schooling in the Pacific Islands that had been written by a Christian missionary who founded schools there. Or conflict theory may be used to reassess changes in Eastern German education as described by a Russian historian after the Soviet Union took political control of Eastern Germany after World War II. When researchers thus intentionally bring a different theoretical perspective to interpreting a communication, they add further items to their list of guide questions: What were the philosophical assumptions and investigative methods of the original author, and how do those compare with the ones I bring to the reinterpretation of the work? What additional kinds of information do I require for my reappraisal, and why are these new kinds needed?

CLARIFYING INTERPRETATION

The aim of this type is to render the meaning of a communication more easily understood than it was in its original form. In attempting to create a more lucid version of a work, the analyst is essentially saying, "What the author really meant was this." The rationale behind producing a clarifying interpretation is that the original version would be inordinately abstruse for potential readers. In other words, phrasings and concepts in the original work would be unduly archaic, foreign, technical, or ambiguous for the audience that the analyst hopes to reach. Examples of clarifying versions are Wadsworth book *Piaget's Theory of Cognitive and Affective Development* and the critical reviews that comprise Cahn edited volume *New Studies in the Philosophy of John Dewey.*

SYMBOLISM INTERPRETATION

Much of language is symbolic, in the sense of words being used to convey meanings that differ from the literal meanings originally attached to those words. For example, the sequence of levels through which children advance in school have been called "the schooling ladder." A politician who wildly launches irrational accusations at a school system may be deemed "a loose cannon." A secondary school teacher whose mode of leading class discussions is reminiscent of Plato's dialogues may be referred to as "the Socrates of the tenth grade."

Not only do authors use individual words and phrases symbolically, but they sometimes speak in parables, describing an event or telling a tale whose meaning is not to be accepted literally but, rather, viewed symbolically as a representation of similar conditions at a different time or place. One of the best known parables in modern-day educational literature is Harold Benjamin small book entitled *The Sabertooth Curriculum,* which ostensibly describes educational practices in prehistoric times but actually is a parody intended to convey Benjamin's observations of how curriculum change operates in modern times. Jonathan Swift *Gulliver's Travels* is one of the best known parables from the past that holds implications for educational practice. Jean Jacques Rousseau's *Emile,* although cast as a novel, is a broad ranging treatise on child rearing and education.

We can thus suggest that when researchers hunt for a communication's symbols and seek to interpret them, they can be led by such questions as: Is the entire document symbolic a fable, parable, or analog, so that its literal meaning is not the one intended by the writer? Or does the document offer two meanings, one literal and the other symbolic? Is most of the meaning of the document intended to be direct and literal, but within the work there are symbolic meanings found in proverbs, aphorisms, or allusions? How can a researcher recognize symbolic contents?

The investigator can seek answers for these queries through the use of such tools as dictionaries that trace word etymology, collections of proverbs, and literary and professional-education works from the time the document was written. In societies that have depended more on oral rather than written history and literature, clues to symbolic meanings may be sought through interviewing elderly members of the society. Essays, letters, or diaries that the original author produced may address themselves to matters of writing style, including how symbols are employed. If the document under consideration is a translation of a work originally produced in another language, then bilingual dictionaries can prove useful.

SUMMARY

The varieties of interpretation described in this chapter are no more than a sample of the diverse sorts of analysis authors can apply to the contents of communications. It should be apparent that the types reviewed are not entirely separate but, rather, are intertwined. For instance, the tasks of verifying the authorship of a document and of interpreting a writer's use of symbols are both related to understanding something of the author's motives and the social and intellectual climate of the author's time and place.

It is also clear that content-analysis interpretations may be appropriate at several junctures of a research program. As authors review the published literature related to their research topic, they may summarize the results and significance of previous research in the form of a *synopsis* or identification of *key themes*. In the methods section of a research report, a writer may explain how the present-day social or technological *context* calls for different methods than those used in similar studies of the past. In the interpretation portion of a report, an author may explain how his or her theoretical stance requires an alternative to the interpretation offered by the producer of an earlier document.

❑❑❑

10

Observations of Groups in Comparative Education

INTRODUCTION

The dual purpose is to suggest something of the diversity of available approaches and to illustrate the approaches with examples of specific educational investigations. The approaches are offered under the following topics:

(a) behavior summaries,

(b) inferred constructs,

(c) learning environments,

(d) person-context interactions,

(e) instrument validation,

(f) alternative cause estimates, and

(g) behavior and attitude explorations.

BEHAVIOR SUMMARIES

At the outset, we can usefully examine the distinction drawn in the following pages between behavior summaries and inferred constructs.

A *behavior summary* is a concise description of some aspect of one or more observations. Consider, for example, an interpretation drawn about a four-year old girl's ability to follow simple directions. The researcher makes the following three-part request, then observes the child's behavior.

Marsha, would you please do this? Pick up the flower that's on the table, put the flower in that glass, then bring me the book that has the picture of the cat on it.

After the child does indeed perform the three steps in the desired sequence, the observer interprets her behavior as reflecting a form of language competence–that of remembering and executing in proper order three requests of the type issued on this occasion. Behavior summaries are thus essentially non debatable, since they are conclusions any reasonable person would reach. They are instances of "what you see is what you get." In contrast, *inferred constructs* are often debatable, for they consist of interpretations an observer makes about unobservable abilities, traits, attitudes, values, or motives that are assumed to underlie the observed behavior. The overt behavior, in effect, is interpreted as signifying a general feature of the observed individual's personality. For instance, a spectator watching an informal basketball game on a school playground draws interpretations not only about which participants are the most skillful players (summaries of players' dribbling, passing, and shooting behavior) but also about personality characteristics that presumably underlie certain of their actions, such characteristics as *sense of fair play, desire to win*, and *team spirit*. None of these characteristics consists of observable actions. Instead, each is a psychological construct inferred from what was seen and heard. The four types of behavior summaries reviewed below are those of specific competencies, likenesses/differences, trends, and time allotments.

SPECIFIC COMPETENCIES

To decide whether the subjects of a research project command particular types of knowledge or skill, an investigator can observe and summarize how well:

- each kindergarten child skips, hops on one foot, hops on two feet, jumps over a six-inch barrier, and plays a game of hopscotch according to the rules;
- each student in a high school choir sings in tune, keeps in time with the music, and sight-reads a simple song.
- each pupil from an inner-city junior high school exhibits standard American language usage when in conversation (a) with an agemate, (b) with a parent, and (c) with a teacher.
- each basketball player accepts referees' decisions without complaint.

LIKENESSES AND DIFFERENCES

Frequently researchers interpret data in terms of likenesses and differences among individuals or groups. For instance, observers recorded the contents of the humorous remarks and messages of 208 children ranging from age three to age 14. Children between ages three and eight were alike in producing mostly prosocial humor, that is, "courteous" or "clean" jokes and comments that conformed to decorum and politeness. From around age nine to age 14, children tended to be alike in producing proportionately more antisocial than prosocial humor, with antisocial jokes and remarks featuring mutilation, scatology, "dirty" sexual messages, and disparagement of people's appearance, gender, race, and social class. As for differences between groups' humor productions, boys indulged in more antisocial humor than did girls, and boys expressed more antisocial humor among their friends than in the presence of their teachers.

TRENDS

A series of behavior episodes that change gradually in a given direction can be interpreted as representing a trend. To be considered a trend, the series need not involve each succeeding episode progressing another step toward an identified end state. In other words, on some days there may be no advance or the behavior may actually regress. For example, when people are learning a skill, the chart of their improvement typically forms a jagged line of progress, a line reflecting periodic starts and stops, advances and retrogressions rather than continuous, smooth progress. Thus, to qualify as a trend, only the general pattern across the entire series need progress in the identified direction.

Researchers often depict trends by contrasting the past and present conditions of an event or institution by means of a narrative that focuses on qualitative rather than quantitative change. Consider, for instance, the annual children's parade in Aracana, a small town in the Andalusian region of Spain. In the past, following the adults' yearly Holy Week processions, boys and girls ages six through 12 would conduct their own spontaneous parades over a period of several days.

In constructing their *pasos* (floats), the children would begin with old tables or cardboard boxes, cover each with a cloth that extended to the ground, mount their favorite possessions on top with GI Joe, for example, pressed into services as Christ and with Barbie assuming the role of Virgin Mary and surround the images with wild flowers.

Thanks to the recent efforts of the teachers, however, the *pasos de los niños* have lost their character as an autonomous children's activity. Prizes are awarded for the best *paso*, the best procession, and so forth. In addition, parents are enlisted to help their children construct permanent and much more elaborate *pasos* and to sew the traditional costumes of penitents, clergy, and matrons, which many of the children now wear instead of ordinary street clothes. In sum, the processions have been largely taken out of the children's hands and turned into a well-disciplined and competitive event.

TIME ALLOTMENTS

Observations of how much time a person spends in different activities are useful in suggesting the amount of experience a person has with assigned tasks or the amount of attention a person dedicates to different interests.

The matter of task experience is illustrated in a study comparing the effectiveness of four methods of improving the reading performance of first-grade pupils who lagged behind their classmates in reading skill. One of the methods, labelled the *reading recovery* approach, was of particular interest to the researchers who wanted to discover how closely teachers adhered to the recommended time allotments for this mode of instruction and, consequently, how much experience children had with each task. Teachers' time-allotment behavior was summarized in the following manner:

> *A total of 18 RR [reading recovery] lessons were videotaped (2 lessons for nine teachers). Lessons in RR averaged 33 minutes, 21 seconds (slightly more than the 30 minutes designated for the instruction, indicating that the teachers exceeded allotted time). Average proportion of time devoted to reading was 60.2%. The lesson activities also included 25.3% of time spent on writing and 14.5% of time spent on the category called "other." The 14.5% "other" can be further broken down into: talk about books (63.2%); letter-sound work, or phonics (15.0%); word fluency practice (12.4%); letter identification work (3.9%); teacher reading to the child (3.5%); and general (2.0%). It can be seen that the greatest proportion of the "other" category involved teachers and children talking about the books read.*

INFERRED CONSTRUCTS

The four varieties of inferred constructs addressed in the following paragraphs concern cognitive functions, attitudes, estimated meanings, and social interaction styles.

Cognitive Functions

The task attempted by researchers is often that of identifying types of thinking in which people engage in educational settings. The teacher who asks a student to "Think out loud as you work the next problem" is interested in understanding the student's cognitive functions, as is the counsellor who asks, "What did you think would happen if you got caught driving after drinking?"

The matter of inferring cognitive functions is illustrated in a study by Dufresne-Tasse and Lefebvre designed to answer the question "What do people think as they view exhibits in a museum?" To gather data for the investigation, a member of the research team, equipped with an audiotape recorder, accompanied each of 45 visitors through a set of museum exhibits with the request that: "As you walk along, I would like you to communicate to me what you see, what you think, what you feel, and what you imagine, in short, everything that happens to you". Later, as the researchers listened to the tapes, they assigned each of a visitor's remarks to a cognitive-function category within their system of categories that bore such labels as *expressing, taking note of, identifying, comparing, explaining, justifying, solving, modifying, suggesting, anticipating, verifying, and judging.*

Attitudes

The term *attitudes*, as intended here, refers to ways a person perceives life events, ways that influence how the person will behave. An attitude, in effect, functions as a mental lens that colors how individuals interpret, and react to, their encounters with the environments they inhabit. Thus, a person's attitude is not something that others see directly but, instead, it is a construct inferred from observing what the person says and does. For convenience of communication, people assign labels to these assumed propensities to act, and researchers often employ the notion of attitudes in their studies of educational phenomena. The following two examples illustrate attitudes deduced from researchers' observations of people's behavior in educational settings.

In the nation of Malawi, Davison and Kanyuka saw a contrast between the ways parents and teachers treated girls and the ways they treated boys. Their observation led them to apply the labels *gender structuring* and *gender bias* to the attitudes they assumed underlay such differential treatments. The concept *gender structuring* referred to "Culturally determined ways of defining women and men and their roles in a given society at a particular historical time period [to] shape gender-specific opportunities and constraints". *Gender bias* referred to people's tendency to provide more favorable educational opportunities to boys than to girls. After the authors described a host of observed behaviors that they interpreted as indicators of gender structuring and bias, they reflected their own attitudes toward such treatment in their proposal about what activists in Malawi society should do to alter conceptions of gender.

Changing societal attitudes is not an easy task, particularly in rural areas where traditional gender beliefs and norms persist. However, an active campaign to change stereotypes about females, through the use of media at the national level, can provide a beginning. Similarly, institutional interventions to guarantee that girls showing academic promise be assured financial support possibly through a government affirmative action program will increase [girls'] staying in school.

The second instance of attitudes inferred from observed behavior appears in Resnick's analysis of the failure of an educational program in Israel. In the early 1990s, the Israeli ministry of education's ability to finance schools diminished, resulting in a reduction of the variety of subjects in the curriculum. To counter this trend of curtailed learning opportunities, parents in one public school (grades one through eight) introduced an after-school curriculum enrichment program (CEP) that students could attend following the close of the regular school session at noon. Enrolment in the range of subject fields in the afternoon was voluntary and paid for by parents. However, the program barely lasted one year, its death due to a host of problems that included a student drop-out rate of 44%, disorderly learners, teachers often late to class, inadequate supervision by part time administrators, a shortage of funds for supplies, and more. According to Resnick's analysis, much of the cause of the program's failure could be attributed to the contrast in attitudes that participants (students, teachers, administrators, parents) held about the regular school and the CEP. Resnick labelled this contrast the *Jekyll/ Hyde syndrome*.

What was "wrong" with CEP is that it took "Dr. Jekylls" from the morning classes, mostly well-behaved, achieving students, and turned them into afternoon "Hydes": unruly, dissatisfied children who did things in CEP in the afternoon, like cutting classes, that they would never consider doing even for the worst subjects in the morning hours.

What had changed was the cultural context of CEP—the unarticulated "rules of the game." The essence of the school climate literature points precisely to the cultural variables of the school peer norms, the level of expectation of academic behavior, and consensus about expectations and discipline as determining, to a large degree, the success of the school. These were precisely the dimensions on which there was a reasonable degree of clarity and consistency in the mornings at the school, but which evaporated with the arrival of CEP in the afternoons.

Thus, in his interpretation, the researcher inferred three sorts of constructs. The first focused on the elements of the school program, a construct that Resnick labelled *cultural context* or *school climate*. The second focused on attitudes implied in the description of students' behavior (obedient versus disobedient, responsible versus irresponsible, serious versus frivolous). The third reflected the connection between the first two constructs by means of a literary analogy the *Jekyll/ Hyde syndrome*.

Estimated Meanings

Researchers often speculate about what observed events mean to the people engaged in those events. An example is Mcguire's study of fifth-and-sixth-grade. Canadian pupils who were under the tutelage of two teachers who employed different pedagogical approaches. After Mcguire systematically observed children's story-writing lessons in the two teachers' classrooms, she first inferred the intentions on which each teacher seemed to found her instructional approach. She then inferred the meaning that pupils would derive from their experiences under those approaches. In effect, Mcguire abstracted two estimates from her observations—one estimate of the teachers' conceptions of suitable writing lessons and another of the pupils' interpretations of those lessons.

Although both teachers appeared to value literacy and story writing as a set of social practices and to set up collaborative writing environments, they had different ideological views about the functions of literacy events and stories in their classrooms. Mrs. G. was more an enabler and responder to children's ongoing efforts; [Ms. M. J.] was more a linguistic resource for the children to draw on for vocabulary and spelling and a corrector of their written texts after a story-writing event. Consequently, the children are caught somewhere among [1] perceiving story making as a constraint; a school chore of writing something down; reporting how things are for someone who "already knows how things are"; and [2] perceiving it as a playful symbolic act a free play of language and consciousness.

Mcguire also speculated about the meanings children attached to storytelling as influenced by the cultural context in which they were raised within a bilingual society (Quebec). She then bolstered her interpretations with detailed descriptions of two particular children's writing activities and of the children's comments about their work.

Social-Interaction Styles

A series of observations of people in social situations can lead a researcher to propose styles of social interaction exemplified by the behavior, to label each style, and to estimate the attitudes or motives underlying such actions. For example, from observing classrooms in South Korea, Sorenson concluded:

In the elementary grades I would characterize the student-teacher relationship as one of "warm authoritarianism" demanding respect and compliance from students but at the same time convincing them that they care about them as human beings and have their best interests at heart. Such authoritarianism is not punitive, though later on, in middle and high school, less warm and more punitive forms are common. Almost half of middle and high school students, for example, report having received corporal punishment.

LEARNING ENVIRONMENTS

Recent decades have witnessed increasing attention to the way characteristics of environments affect individuals' behavior. Such labels as *ecological psychology* and *contextualism* reflect viewpoints about how environmental conditions influence learning that takes place under particular environmental conditions. The following three studies illustrate alternative ways scholars used their observations to infer how environments affect learning outcomes. In the first example the environment is a mother's style of teaching her child, in the second it is the presence of deviant students in a classroom, and in the third it is the assortment of sounds in a classroom.

MOTHERS' INSTRUCTIONAL STYLES

To investigate how parents' styles of instructing their children might affect children's intellectual development, Portes observed sessions in which each mother taught her elementary-school child an assigned learning task. The observations were guided by a style sheet that divided mothers' actions into a variety of types, such as (a) mother asks open-ended question or prompts child, (b) mother uses positive reinforcement, encourages, agrees with child, (c) mother interrupts child, (d) mother influences the child's response with obvious cue or statement, and (e) general comments not related to task. Different patterns of parental teaching styles were then correlated with the children's tested achievement in reading, language skills, mathematics, and ability to use reference sources. Correlations were also computed between children's academic performance and their gender, race, parental marital and socio-economic status, and parental expectations for the child. By means of factor analysis, Portes was able to identify a cluster of parents' teaching behaviors that appeared to be the most important of the inspected variables in accounting for the differences among the children in achievement particularly achievement in math and reference skills. He envisioned this cluster as a construct that could be labelled *the maternal verbal guidance factor* (MVG).

The mother's use of positive reinforcement, encouragement, and agreement with the child is important. However, she also provides guidance by asking open questions and [offering] statements without giving obvious information to the child. Sex, race, and parental marital differences were analyzed and not found to be significant for this factor. The MVG factor may represent an active ingredient of the home environment that supports children's development in general, and perhaps more in some zones of development [such as math and reference skills] than others.

DEVIANT STUDENTS IN THE CLASSROOM

Over a four-year period, Stevenson observed two dozen first-grade classrooms in order to discover the functions of deviant pupils within a classroom society. Most studies of classroom behavior problems have focused either on teachers' methods of maintaining order or on individual children's characteristics. In contrast, Stevenson adopted the construct *collective-resource perspective*, a viewpoint from which he sought to identify functions that deviant students (ones who test and break rules) perform as an aggregation.

Even though deviant students are often viewed as disruptive and as challenging the teacher's authority, they also may promote order in the class in several indirect ways. One way is to clarify the rules and procedures of the classroom. The constant struggle between teachers and deviant students serves to articulate publicly the classroom rules and procedures and their spheres of jurisdiction. Furthermore, deviant students make the distribution of rewards more meaningful, since it is the constant contrast between the rewarded and unrewarded that gives value to being rewarded.

One finding of this investigation was that the size of the collection of deviant students in a class was established early in the school year and remained stable throughout the year. Stevenson then used his data to test two competing interpretations of such stability: (a) a particular teacher's methods of classroom management determined the size of the collection of deviants, or (b) certain characteristics of students (cognitive and emotional skills or such social identities as "class clown") accounted for the size of the deviant group. However, he was obliged to reject both of these explanations because (a) the size of the cluster of deviants in a given teacher's classroom varied from one year to the next, and (b) the membership in the cluster changed somewhat during the year. In other words, pupils who qualified as deviant during one period of time did not qualify at another time but were replaced by classmates who were newly considered deviant. Thus, the cause of the size stability of the ranks of deviant students required a different interpretation from either the teacher-method or student-characteristic explanation. Perhaps, Stevenson implied, the stability resulted from a complex of factors as yet unknown, so that more research would be necessary to reveal how the ranks of deviant students are established, how the ranks are maintained, and how deviant students contribute to keeping order in the classroom.

In summary, the researcher inferred that students who tested and broke class regulations formed an aggregation that qualified as a collective resource in promoting the operation of a classroom. Observations of 96 first-grade classrooms appeared to support this inference. The observations also revealed that the size of a deviant collectivity remained stable over the school year, but two possible interpretations of this stability (teacher-method, student-characteristic) were not supported by the data.

CLASSROOM SOUNDS

In comparing kindergartens in Israel with some in West Germany, Kalekin-Fishman inferred that a teacher's conception of what constitutes good teaching will determine many of the sounds heard in the teacher's class, and that a particular pattern of sounds will affect what pupils learn.

To gather data, the researcher interviewed teachers and observed the sounds heard during kindergarten sessions. Her interviews were designed to discover the learning goals that teachers held for their children and the classroom-management methods teachers believed would best foster those goals. Her system for charting the sources, types, and quantities of kindergarten sounds enabled her to "map patterns of kindergarten events, as well as to characterize the environment". She concluded that the patterns of sounds differed significantly between the two countries' kindergartens, and she inferred that this difference was the result of the different conceptions of what constituted good teaching that the teachers in the two countries expressed.

In Haifa, the teachers pressed for achievement and group solidarity by enforcing a crowded schedule with a relatively strict time framework and an authoritarian distribution of activities. The focus of their messages was on naming activities and imposing recipes of behavior to induce socialization. This focus was reflected in the acoustical environment; sounds produced by different sources were highly differentiated, and teachers' sounds were often dominant.

Interviewees in Konstanz asserted that their aim was to help the children develop their unique personalities. The teachers were guided by the notion that if they avoided putting pressure on the children, they were helping the children develop self-confidence and autonomy. The acoustical environment reflected their intentions. In these kindergartens, there was a flow of relatively undifferentiated "white noise" throughout the sessions.

To interpret what the contrasting sound environments could mean for children's learning, Kalekin-Fishman adopted a strategy sometimes used by researchers as they seek to support the educational implications they draw from their studies. That is, she did not evaluate what children actually learned in the two sets of kindergartens. Instead, she depended on other people's studies for identifying the learning outcomes that she would expect to result from the acoustical environments she found in her investigation. To identify the learning consequences that she believed would derive from the Israeli teachers' methods, Kalekin-Fishman cited "findings from laboratory experiments" which showed that:

> Frequent variations of sounds and frequent cuts in the flow of sound (as in the salient teachers' talk) promote alertness, concentration, persistence, and success in learning.

She also referred to others' studies to support her belief that the kind of "white noise" observed in the German kindergartens worked against children's reaching the self-confidence and autonomy goals to which the German teachers subscribed.

> Exposure to constant noise has been shown to lead to increased aggression or anger, as well as to learned helplessness and passivity. It detracts from sensitivity and contributes to a reduction of sociability and helping behavior.

It should be apparent that the practice of using other people's theories and research findings as the sole basis for drawing implications from one's own findings can involve a considerable risk of error. Researchers who adopt such a strategy can properly caution their readers about the tentative and disputable nature of those interpretations. In Kalekin-Fishman's study, direct assessment of changes in the children's self-confidence, autonomy, alertness, concentration, persistence, and improvement in cognitive, social, and physical skills would have been a far sounder basis for her interpretation of the learning effects of acoustical environments than was her extrapolating implications from others' investigations.

PERSON/CONTEXT INTERACTIONS

Whereas such theoretical positions as environmentalism, ecological psychology, and contextualism have usually emphasized how environments affect people's behavior, the concept *interactionism* has been used to focus attention on the reciprocal influence of person and of context. Hence, research from an interactionist perspective goes beyond estimating the effects of environments on learning by giving attention as well to how learners influence the settings they occupy. A notable example of interactionist interpretation is the substantial body of *interpersonal-expectations* and *self-fulfilling-prophecy* research produced since the publication of Rosenthal and Jacobson's pioneering book, *Pygmalion in the Classroom.* In the typical classroom case of interpersonal expectations, the mutual influence between person and context:

(a) Begins with observable characteristics of a student, such as racial or gender indicators, influencing the teacher (as a component of the student's environment) to assume that those characteristics are necessarily accompanied by certain personality, attitude, aptitude, or behavior attributes. Thus, the student's skin color or facial expression may be connected, in the teacher's opinion, with either inferior intelligence or superior intelligence, with either eagerness to learn or disinterest, with a propensity either to violence or to submissiveness, or the like. Other observable features such as a student's grooming, dress style, posture, or use of language may likewise be interpreted by the teacher as indicative of character or ability. Consequently, according to *interpersonal-expectations theory*, the teacher will likely treat the student as if those assumed attributes were true.

(b) The student, in response to the teacher's treatment, may accept the teacher's appraisal as valid or at least inevitable and may subsequently act in ways that seem to confirm the teacher's opinion, thereby fulfilling the teacher's implied prophecy.

Such interpersonal interaction, with teacher and student influencing each other's behavior, sets off a cycle of reciprocal causes and effects that help establish the climate of the teaching-learning context.

As researchers plan studies to reveal person-environment interactions, they can profitably recognize the complexity of classroom interpersonal relations. Not only are the teacher's overtures to students affected by the teacher's beliefs about connections between students' observable characteristics and their personalities, but students' observations of the teacher's characteristics likewise help determine how students will act toward the teacher. Furthermore, students' perceptions of classmates can also significantly affect the learning environment. Therefore, research designs need to provide for the collection of information from the multiple vantage points of the persons who compose the social environment.

INSTRUMENT VALIDATION

Questionnaires are often intended to serve as short-cut techniques for learning about people's habits, preferences, and decision-making patterns. However, there is always a question about how accurately answers on questionnaires represent people's actual habits, preferences, and decision-making practices. In other words, do questionnaire responses truly mean what they say? To answer this query, investigators sometimes use direct observation as the basis for judging how closely people's behavior matches their questionnaire answers.

To illustrate, Ashley observed children's playtime behavior in order to judge the validity of the children's social status as charted on a sociogram constructed from the subjects' questionnaire answers. He first asked a group of 15 boys, ages eight through 11, to write down the names of the three classmates with whom they would most like to share a dormitory during a forthcoming field trip; the boys were also given the option of naming any classmates they would particularly wish to exclude from their dormitory. The results of their choices were plotted as a traditional sociogram as a diagram of who chose whom. The diagram enabled the researcher to categorize boys as *stars* (chosen many-times), as *average group members* (chosen by several classmates), and as isolates (chosen by no one).

To estimate the validity of the sociogram as a measure of the pupils' actual patterns of social interaction, Ashley observed each boy during a total of seven 15-minute sessions on the playground over a period of several months and coded each subject's social behavior on an observation schedule. The observation results were then compared with the original sociogram to show how well the data from the two sources matched. Ashley interpreted this comparison to mean that

As a source of information about behavior, sociometry, like any other form of asking people what they do, is unreliable. Popular children in sociometry do tend to have more interactions at playtime, but 'isolate' children are nevertheless engaged in fairly extensive interactions with groups and individuals the range or number of such groups differing little from that of the popular children. However, there are certain factors and patterns which can render sociometry useful. A child's own sociometric choices are a poor guide to the existence of friendships, but *mutual* choices are usually confirmed by observation and therefore considerably more reliable.

ALTERNATIVE CAUSE ESTIMATES

After describing the outcomes of their study, researchers often speculate about why such results occurred, with such speculation frequently including several alternative cause possibilities. In effect, interpretation takes the form of posing a variety of possible explanations of the results.

For instance, in an investigation of ways to teach children how to react to potential abductors, 62 preschool children were divided into three groups. The first group viewed five brief videotaped scenes, each involving an adult stranger seeking to lure a child to accompany the adult. After every scene, a teacher directed the group members in practicing ways of avoiding and retreating from strangers who sought to lead them away. The second group did not view the videotape but, rather, had a teacher read them an oral description of the five incidents and then practice how they should respond to strangers' overtures. The third group had no training in ways to react to such overtures.

The researchers adopted two methods of testing the effectiveness of the training procedures *self report* and *in situ*. For the self-report appraisal, each child was interviewed at home by a research assistant who described one of the five abduction scenarios, and the child reported how he or she would react in such a situation. For the *in situ* assessment, each child was in a public place, such as the child's front yard or a nearby store, and was there confronted by a stranger (a research assistant) who chatted briefly with the child, presented an abduction lure, and asked the child to go with him. In each situation, an observer rated the child for how appropriately he or she responded.

A comparison of children's verbal and *in situ* reactions revealed "low verbal/nonverbal correspondence, with over half of the children's verbal reports differing from their actual performances".

However, the results of both the self-report and *in situ* evaluations showed that the two training groups video and oral-description—reacted more suitably than did the no-training group. Furthermore, the oral description was more effective than the video, an outcome that prompted the researchers to propose two alternative perhaps mutually supportive causes for such a result.

First, children in the [oral-description] group listened to verbal scenarios about children in abduction situations and had to imagine the scenarios and the appropriate prevention responses. This imaginative responding was not required of children in the video group because the scenarios were visually presented to them. In part, children in the video group were engaged in passive learning. In contrast, the manual training method required a more active, possibly imaginative learning process. Second, it may be that training was more effective because more teacher-student interaction was involved. Presumably the teacher's attention was an established social reinforcer and therefore the children may have been more motivated to attend and respond correctly.

Such speculations about cause could then serve as hypotheses to be tested in future research projects.

BEHAVIOR AND ATTITUDE EXPLORATIONS

Some studies qualify as exploratory investigations because the researchers are guided only by very general questions rather than by specific hypotheses to test or precise questions to answer. As a consequence, interpretations of exploratory studies often include unanticipated conclusions. Such was the case in a study of the way a computer program, which functioned as students' personal tutor, altered teachers' and students' roles in high school geometry classes. The stimulus for conducting the study was the investigators' observation that there was a paucity of research exploring the impact of intelligent-computer-assisted instruction on classroom social processes.

The two methods of data gathering were intensive qualitative classroom observations and repeated interviews with students and teachers. This approach was selected because our knowledge of the likely effects of intelligent computer based tutors is so rudimentary that a flexible exploratory methodology seemed called for.

In analyzing data collected in eight geometry classes over a two-year period, the authors discovered a paradox—students claimed that a teacher provided better help than an artificially intelligent computer-based tutor, yet those same students preferred to use the tutor rather than study by traditional methods, and they appeared to learn more while doing so. The researchers concluded that three factors could account for the seeming paradox.

First, rather than replacing the teacher, the tutor provided an additional resource for students. Second, using the tutors allowed teachers to provide more individualized help. Third, students using the tutors had more control over the kind and amount of help they received from the teacher, with helping interactions becoming more private and potentially less embarrassing. None of these changes were envisioned by the tutor's developers, highlighting the importance of exploring unintended effects of technology on classroom functioning.

INTERPRETIVE TECHNIQUES FOR DATA ANALYSIS

The most common analysis of qualitative data is observer impression. That is, expert or bystander observers examine the data, interpret it via forming an impression and report their impression in a structured and sometimes quantitative form.

CODING

Coding is an interpretive technique that both organizes the data and provides a means to introduce the interpretations of it into certain quantitative methods. Most coding requires the analyst to read the data and demarcate segments within it. Each segment is labeled with a "code" usually a word or short phrase that suggests how the associated data segments inform the research objectives. When coding is complete, the analyst prepares reports via a mix of: summarizing the prevalence of codes, discussing similarities and differences in related codes across distinct original sources/contexts, or comparing the relationship between one or more codes.

Some qualitative data that is highly structured (*e.g.*, open-end responses from surveys or tightly defined interview questions) is typically coded without additional segmenting of the content. In these cases, codes are often applied as a layer on top of the data. Quantitative analysis of these codes is typically the capstone analytical step for this type of qualitative data.

Contemporary qualitative data analyses are sometimes supported by computer programs. These programs do not supplant the interpretive nature of coding but rather are aimed at enhancing the analyst's efficiency at data storage/retrieval and at applying the codes to the data. Many programs offer efficiencies in editing and revising coding, which allow for work sharing, peer review, and recursive examination of data.

A frequent criticism of coding method is that it seeks to transform qualitative data into quantitative data, thereby draining the data of its variety, richness, and individual character. Analysts respond to this criticism by thoroughly expositing their definitions of codes and linking those codes soundly to the underlying data, therein bringing back some of the richness that might be absent from a mere list of codes.

RECURSIVE ABSTRACTION

Some qualitative datasets are analyzed without coding. A common method here is recursive abstraction, where datasets are summarized, those summaries are then further summarized, and so on. The end result is a more compact summary that would have been difficult to accurately discern without the preceding steps of distillation.

A frequent criticism of recursive abstraction is that the final conclusions are several times removed from the underlying data. While it is true that poor initial summaries will certainly yield an inaccurate final report, qualitative analysts can respond to this criticism. They do so, like those using coding method, by documenting the reasoning behind each summary step, citing examples from the data where statements were included and where statements were excluded from the intermediate summary.

MECHANICAL TECHNIQUES

Some techniques rely on leveraging computers to scan and sort large sets of qualitative data. At their most basic level, mechanical techniques rely on counting words, phrases, or coincidences of tokens within the data. Often referred to as content analysis, the output from these techniques is amenable to many advanced statistical analyses.

Mechanical techniques are particularly well-suited for a few scenarios. One such scenario is for datasets that are simply too large for a human to effectively analyze, or where analysis of them would be cost prohibitive relative to the value of information they contain. Another scenario is when the chief value of a dataset is the extent to which it contains "red flags" (*e.g.*, searching for reports of certain adverse events within a lengthy journal dataset from patients in a clinical trial) or "green flags" (*e.g.*, searching for mentions of your brand in positive reviews of marketplace products).

□□□

11

Teacher Development and Educational Research

INTRODUCTION

We identify and critique a linguistic mode that is found in educational research pertaining to teacher education. We identify it as 'Aristotelian', and argue that its principles and methods captivate researchers. This linguistic mode has become very seductive, as it promotes the unification of teachers' consciousness with the objective world of their practical actions. The attraction to this mode is inspired by a drive to reduce the status of teachers' development to the level of a rational science. Important aspects of this academic project include the privileging of certain theories of language. Through a brief historical sketch, we show how figurative speech has been suppressed in favour of clear, rational explanation. This historical quest for rational, logical clarity is maintained in analyses of teacher education. We explain by outlining a theoretical argument on metaphor and dialectical reasoning before concluding with an alternative perspective rooted in Nietzsche. His perspective may offer the possibility of theorizing practice without relying upon theoretical mediation either of metaphor or of the confining path of dialectical reasoning.

THE FIGURATIVE LANGUAGE OF THE IVORY TOWER

In his pioneering work, Elliott observed how several metaphors for education (i.e. preparation, initiation, liberation, and guidance) originate in common cultural discourse. Education may be construed as: (1) preparation (for life, work, war, etc.); (2) initiation; (3) liberation; and/or (4) guidance. Each of these four metaphors for education involves proceeding towards some culturally sanctioned end. Preparation points towards outcomes that will benefit the learner, enabling her/him to meet expectations. Initiation assumes the existence of theoretical and practical knowledge, along with worthwhile public practices, and it moves towards getting the educated person to understand and love knowledge. Liberation moves towards freedom (e.g. participatory democracy or the dictatorship of the proletariat), and it involves 'empowering' the oppressed through enabling them to understand their alienated condition. Finally, guidance moves towards 'perfection' through imitation (usually of an individual who embodies a particular ideal). In all of these cases, metaphor fulfils a hortative and didactic function. For this reason, figurative language maintains significant status as a topic for educational research, especially as this research relates to teacher education.

The use of metaphor in curricula reaches back to ancient Greece. 'Metaphor' is rooted in the ancient Greek *metapherein*, which may be translated as 'transference'; and it shows up in the modern Greek *metaphora*, which may be translated as 'a vehicle of transport.' Thus metaphor may be seen as a vehicle that enables transference between experience and the language of thought. The transference between experience and thought has been the subject of many debates within the philosophical tradition rooted in Aristotle. Although Christian and positivist perspectives on language have complicated this debate, Aristotle's influence has been profound and exists to this day.

Johnson wrote that the late twentieth century interpretation of metaphor is directly connected to Aristotle's first extended treatment of the subject. Aristotle defined metaphor as a poetic art by which the poet provided knowledge through reflective intuition (from Latin, *intueri*, to look upon). In his *Poetics*, Aristotle wrote: 'Metaphor consists in giving the thing a name that belongs to something else'; the transference being either from generic to specific, or from specific to the more general, or from one specific category to another. This definition separated metaphor from a more literal truth, and this has complicated its value for the last 2,300 years. Since Aristotle, the drive for precise articulation has led to the dichotomy of accurate versus inaccurate knowledge.

Like Aristotle, Cicero saw metaphor as a misuse of words and as a flight from precise meaning. Latin rhetoricians valued metaphor chiefly as a linguistic ornamentation of argumentative proofs. Johnson added that medieval rhetoricians furthered this derisive interpretation of metaphor by referring to it as a stylistic device devoid of serious philosophical argument. They arrived at this opinion while attempting to establish the authority of biblical scriptures. Their attack was reinforced by a rising monastic tradition that emphasized the authentic outward expression of what were coming to be understood as intuitive truths of the mind. The scriptural basis for this orientation was to be found in biblical commandments against bearing false witness.

The belief that figurative expressions amounted to a deviation from orthodox meaning remained in the philosophical tradition of Europe and North America until the present century. It was reinforced during the seventeenth century when the foundations for ontological certainty began to shift from a belief in the unified sacred power of a monotheistic god to the belief in a unified secular power born of human consciousness. Rationalism and empiricism fueled the latter belief. Hence, while Descartes esteemed eloquence and loved poetry, he felt that both were underrated gifts of nature rather than fruits,of study. Those who reason most cogently, and who polish their thoughts to make them clear and intelligible, are always most persuasive, even if they speak only a provincial dialect and have never studied rhetoric.

Toulmin noted that, between 1600 and 1700, philosophy began to pursue universally valid answers by developing a distinct separation between rationality/logic and rhetoric/emotions. According to this distinction, a 'good reason' for correct practice had to be universally justified through the use of rationally logical syllogisms, which was dependent upon a linear form of reasoning. According to Toulmin, from the seventeenth century onwards, this type of reasoning ensured that philosophical validity was dependent upon the internal relations of logical arguments. The rhetoric of figurative language was disdained, as it was considered imprecise, misleading, and therefore not a source of dependable knowledge. This philosophical context fed an early Anglo-American enthusiasm for logical positivism, which only enhanced hostility towards figurative language. Logical positivism assigned 'meaning' to propositions that could be given a truth value that corresponded to 'reality'. In its quest for truth, positivism insisted that figures of speech were misleading and hindered clarity of meaning.

It was for Rousseau and the later German Romantics to revive an interpretation of metaphor that sought to address the relationship between emotionality and philosophical argument. According to Rousseau, truth may be a function of reason, but 'tropes' (i.e. the 'turning of phrases' from the ancient Greek *tropos*, 'a turning') are primordial because they are linked to the passions. It was Rousseau's recommendation, however, that such passions were to be sublimated into reason through proper education. While expressions inspired by passion were primordial, instruction was to lead learners to the world of self-conscious reason. Figurative language was the first language, but it had no truth value. Proper meaning could only be discovered with the assistance of reasoning. The relationship that Rousseau established between metaphorical language and reason was transmitted to nineteenth century German philosophy. In Hegel's view, a trope referred to a strategy for structuring explanations. It served, therefore, a structural function and required the presence of: (1) a judging subject, (2) a subject to be judged, and (3) a relationship between subject and its judged. The interaction between subjective and objective realms, mediated through metaphor, creates a new meaning - one that is distinguishable from the original idea as subjectively perceived. Hegel's methodology for a science of consciousness provides a foundation for popular contemporary theories of metaphor - theories that are part of a long heritage bent on uniting the intuitive subject with the 'objective' world. These theories are transcendentally spiritual, as they address processes of thought that can only be mediated through metaphor. For example, as a theoretical 'vehicle of transport', metaphor can re-signify experience figuratively in a way that makes an original name 'turn' into another idea categorically. The actual practices of teaching and learning, as Elliott mentioned, can be conceptualized ideally as any one of preparation, initiation, liberation, or guidance. A 'species' of educational practice, to use Aristotle's term, can be differentiatially categorized according to any one of such 'species' of mediated practices. All, however, fall under the general 'genus' of 'education'.

One of the most influential of contemporary perspectives on metaphor is that proposed by Lakoff and Johnson. They argue that metaphor is essential for interaction among conceptual systems. Lakoff and Johnson call these systems 'gestalts' but we understand these to be very similar to Aristotle's categorical distinctions of genus and species. In the case of educational research, traditional practices originating in the conceptual system of travel or biological growth would be understood to interact with the practical 'gestalt' of learning to teach in a school. Lakoff specializes in the study of conceptual systems the largely unconscious systems of thought that determine how we think. Metaphor, in this analysis, enables correspondence across conceptual domains, typically from concrete spatial domains to a more abstract domain. The study of metaphor, according to Lakoff, can yield a sort of dictionary of the unconscious. Lakoff assumes that there is an unconscious metaphorical language that functions separately from the body and its passions. Since there is no way to get conscious control over the unconscious, he suggests that we be aware of the components of our metaphorical systems and of what they entail. Adopting this advice, Sfard recommends examining the guiding metaphors of acquisition and participation (which are used to represent the abstract realm of learning), and she cautions against depending on one to the exclusion of the other.

Aristotle's drive for precise articulation was motivated by a need to provide adequate and consistent grounds for scientific inquiry. Universally valid answers demanded tools of reasoning which were sound and these required equally valid correspondence theories to unite object-as-perceived and idea-as-imagined. Metaphor, conceptualized as a hermeneutic vehicle of transport is intended to act as the intermediary between the conceptual domains that determine how we think. It would behove researchers, consequently, to examine the performance of these vehicles since they guide correspondence between the objectively experienced world and subjective, intuitive deduction.

FIGURATIVE LANGUAGE AND TEACHER DEVELOPMENT

One decade following Elliott's pioneering work, Bullough and Stokes identified several angles of research, most of which converge with regard to the preparation of teachers and all of which are concerned with how the latter identify themselves as pedagogues. These angles are 'images of self,' 'self- narratives,' and 'personal metaphors.' Bullough and Stokes begin by saying that metaphors can be used to represent and to reconstruct problems, and this assumes an implicit knowledge that needs to be made explicit. According to Bullough and Stokes, one of the most abstract of these implicit subconscious images is the preservice candidate's conception of him/herself as a teacher. The concrete experience of learning to teach requires a coherent self-image, and this develops through being socialized into the profession. Based on Lakoff and Johnson, Bullough and Stokes argue that metaphors are the vehicles that unify these diverse realms. They insist that a large part of self-understanding is the search for appropriate metaphors that make sense of our lives. In short, conscious practice is based on a correct understanding of subconscious images.

One aspect of research on metaphor and teacher development is particularly concerned with the role metaphor plays in teacher socialization. Self-narratives invoke the metaphorical vehicles that allow teachers to articulate images of themselves in a purposeful and coherent fashion. Metaphors shift the emphasis from internal 'vision' to external 'voice,' thus enabling teachers to see a reflection of themselves through language and to create 'a self ' in that image. Beyond enabling teachers to create personal identities, metaphors also enable them to construct images of their students and colleagues. Metaphor unifies their experience, therefore, and assigns a narrative coherence to teachers' lives, leading them to communal practices by enabling them to identify with colleagues. In short, metaphor is a rhetorical vehicle for the transcendental unification of teachers' experience and cognitive images of self.

Clearly, the theory of metaphor most useful to teacher education research is the one that treats metaphor as a vehicle for unifying conceptual realms (e.g. the conscious with the subconscious, the internal vision with the external voice, etc.). To be developed (prepared, initiated, liberated), therefore, is to be rationally guided by a methodology that navigates among these realms. Metaphor enables teachers to forge a link between external stimulus and internal synthesis. As Sfard recommends, the onus fall on researchers to locate, analyse, and sharpen this link by deciding which metaphors are most effective.

Aristotle's influence extends beyond a concern for accuracy of meaning as mediated through metaphor. We will argue, further, that researchers may be captivated by habits of practice that may marginalize alternative perspectives on learning to teach. These habits are maintained and defended in order to claim the status of 'genuine science' for teacher education pedagogy.

CATEGORICAL KNOWLEDGE ENDEMIC TO THE IVORY TOWER

Aristotle is concerned with knowledge as *episteme* (the etymological root of the term 'epistemology'). An episteme is a body of knowledge about a subject (for our purposes, about the documentation of knowledge as it pertains to teacher education), and it is organized into a system of proofs, or demonstrations. These proofs constitute a body of research, or 'science.' To 'know something' about a subject is to know why it is what it is, rather than something else. This conception of knowledge can rely upon the authority of a community of researchers, which, in turn, appeals to a common methodology for obtaining reliable knowledge. The science of learning to teach is, by implication, demonstrative, endlessly debating competing definitions of teaching and learning, all of which are based upon elaborate systems of classifying teachers' knowledge. Aristotle provides the rules for such a categorical debate in *Topics*.

Aristotle's 'categories' are, perhaps, his most heavily discussed notion, and their popularity is evident in research on teacher development. Most recently, Aristotle's perspective has been adapted by Orton; by Bell; by Schwab and, subsequently, by Connelly and Clandinin, and by Enns. Categories arise due to the human propensity to reflect on general questions concerning a given state. In our case, these questions concern the state of knowledge development as it relates to teachers. Aristotle's categories may be referred to as 'predicables' as each category provides one possible relationship between subject and predicate. This fits well with the meaning of 'category,' which is the ancient Greek word for predication (*kategoria*).

Think of primary categories of knowledge (i.e., of ontological predicates) in simple grammatical terms. Where a human being is a neutral 'subject', its verbal predicates may be any number of qualities that attribute to it an essential nature. The human subject can be categorically objectified in diverse forms. It can, for example, be (1) genus: the product of a divine creator, or differentiated into (2) species: a conscious agent of rational choice. The most dominant quality in contemporary literature on learning to teach assigns the teacher with the potential to be a conscious agent of rational choice. Assumed categories are usually hidden underneath everyday descriptions - descriptions upon which we rely in order to interact and write about teachers in practical ways. It is not necessary to refer to these fundamental biases in order to engage in everyday ethical and practical discourse, none the less, they remain as grounds for theories of knowledge and they locate teachers in a cosmological order of things. In other words, researchers assume that fundamental categories of knowledge support their theoretical decisions as much as their practical prescriptions.

Ontological categories determine conceptions of the nature and appropriateness of knowledge. For example, if we believe (1) that a divine masculine Creator determines human subjectivity, then we might ultimately consider how we should follow His commandments when seeking knowledge. If we believe (2) that subjectivity is a consciousness possessing rational agency, then we might consider 'reasonable' approaches to logically defined problems. If we believe (3) that we are children of a goddess, then we might perceive the earth as a natural living organism. As we have already indicated, option (2) is the dominant choice of much of the literature dealing with knowledge as it relates to teaching and learning.

Although one's fundamental ontology may remain implicit when one analyses knowledge and its development, one's interpretation of selfhood (what it is good to be), of ethics (what it is right to do), and of epistemology (what constitutes reliable knowledge) does not. It is from 'objective standpoints' that researchers make sense of teacher development and, we would argue, of their own. Without objective representations, discussions of what it would mean to 'develop' as a teacher would be senseless to both teachers and researchers alike. Archetypal predicates can, therefore, as cultural landmarks, come to represent the ethically sanctioned goals of an educational curriculum, and it is important to emphasize that privileged attributes define the tacit epistemological stance of any given culture. In other words, it is what is understood to be our essential nature and our practical, moral predicament that will provide the basis for an implicit doctrine of knowledge in an explicit research literature. For example, if we believe that we are the products of a divine masculine Creator, then we may tacitly deal with each other as archetypal saints or sinners - the idea being to educate and socialize as many saints and as few sinners as possible. If, on the other hand, we believe that we are self-conscious agents confronting a problem-presenting world, then we might try to get our educators to refine autonomous problem-solving skills. Researchers who focus on teachers, and who assume ontology of self-conscious agency, may construct teachers as reflexive or active. One of the most useful of these constructions was theorized and then elaborated upon in the 1980s by Donald Schon.

Clearly, researchers who write about teacher education as it relates to knowledge do so in the shadow of foundational goals and frameworks, the latter determining the correct procedures for attaining the former. Our foundational goals proclaim what it means to be a 'good' teacher, and these goals are framed by explicit epistemological prescriptions. All participants in the culture of the university will mutually accept the terms of reference, and they will provide codes of conduct within the 'ivory tower'. Conforming to these codes may be rewarded, while transgressing them may be met with penalty (often in the most subtle and insidious ways). Categories of knowledge function as guides for conducting research. According to these categories, researchers orient choices, decisions, and patterns of selection and analysis. (As in gendering, for example, a good illustration of how the neutral human being is burdened with all kinds of cultural baggage based solely on genitalia.)

The Aristotelian perspective on categorical knowledge and its development is driven by dialectical argument, and it is this type of argument that drives contemporary research questions concerning teachers' education. The term 'dialectical' comes from the ancient Greek verb *dialegesthai* (modern Greek: *dialektike*), which refers to a kind of exchange between opponents. In contemporary terms, such an exchange characterizes the university defence, wherein the doctoral candidate must 'defend' her/his dissertation against the questioning of his/her committee. Aristotle was Plato's student for 20 years, and the dialectic method refers to the way in which Plato's Socrates engaged in the search for knowledge: he drew responses to questions by engaging people in competitive dialogue. In the *Republic*, Plato refers to this method of practicing philosophy as 'dialectic,' and he proposes that the leaders of his ideal political state be trained in it. Aristotle's *Topics* presupposes a context of argumentation that involves rules and judges, with the respondent defending a thesis against those who attempt to refute it. The polemics of such an encounter were intended to be a method of learning within which participants were to be trained in the art of critical thinking. Smith observes that this form of practice serves the same purposes as do the exchanges that take place in scholarly journals and at academic conferences. Knowledge, as obtained through dialectical argumentation, serves as a means of socialization for, according to Aristotle, the premises of such argumentation must be accepted as orthodoxy. He defines orthodoxy as' accepted things [things that] seem so to everyone, or to most people, or to the wise either to all of those, or to most of them, or to the most famous and celebrated'. This definition characterizes the contemporary practice of scholarly 'peer review'.

The dialectical method enables one to deduce logical conclusions from premises conceded through argument. This works if (1) the desired conclusion follows from the given premises and (2) the respondent concedes those premises. Therefore, determining what various classes of researchers believe (especially what most believe and, most especially, what those considered 'most wise' believe) may enable us to predict which premises will be acceptable. It is necessary, therefore, to determine which class one's colleagues fall into and then to determine the scholarly argument most relevant to them. The dialectic, as standardized practice, consists in determining what is credible to various types of researchers. This being the case, it is necessary to find premises from which a desired conclusion will follow. In *Topics* II to VII, Aristotle provides a collection of argumentative rules, which he calls 'commonplaces' (*topoi*) a term that originates in ancient systems for memorizing lists of items by associating each item with a standard set of imaginary places. Smith elaborates:

> They rest on a classification of conclusions according to form: each gives premise-forms from which a given form of conclusion can be deduced... the dialectical method of the *Topics* requires the joint application of 'locations' and the inventories of opinions. To find an argument, I first look up a location appropriate to my desired conclusion and use it to discover premises that would be useful; then I consult the relevant inventory of opinions to see if those premises are found there. If they are, I have my argument; all that remains is to case it into the form of questions and present them to my opponent. Assuming that my inventories of opinions are properly constructed and that I have correctly estimated what type of person my opponent is, I can reasonably count on my premises being accepted.

Dialectical argumentation is, therefore, a competitive research activity involving strategy, tactics, and triumph. The fundamental characteristic of the dialectical game, however, is that arguments based on premises that lead to specific conclusions must be valid; that is, they must be acceptable to all players, so that the conclusions are a necessary consequence of the premises. With regard to dialectical inquiry, the existence of commonly held opinions is important. As Aristotle states 'a sufficient measure of correctness of an account is that it solve all the puzzles in the commonly held opinions about a subject and nevertheless retain as many of those opinions as possible'. To conclude this section, let us examine one significant account of how dialectical principles play themselves out in curriculum inquiry. Connelly and Clandinin attempt to recover the meaning of curriculum in Aristotelian terms and to embark on a discussion of the tools that are useful for such a recovery. As they write: 'when there appears to be a babble of voices about something that we all agree is significant, then what we need to help sort things out is a set of topics that help define the subject as experienced, while ruling no one's views out of order. We call these topics "commonplaces of curriculum". They identify these commonplaces as:

- Knowledge of subject matter (including methods)
- Knowledge of milieu
- Knowledge of learner
- Knowledge of teacher (or of self)

A quick scan of the literature reveals how teachers' education can be organized conveniently into these four categorical domains. For example, knowledge of subject matter and methods has been explored in depth by such authors as Shulman and Ayers. Over the years, the milieu of teaching has been the subject of writings by Ben-Peretz, Calgren and

Lindblad and Giroux, among others. Doyle, for example, as well as Martin and Kompf discuss knowledge of learners and their 'needs.' And, as I have shown throughout this chapter, Connelly and Clandinin, Carter, and Bullough and Stokes have researched knowledge of self (among others).

Connelly and Clandinin argue that, while there may be different foci within each category, and while arguments concerning curriculum may focus on a single category, categories are inescapable analytical tools when it comes to examining trends and conflicts pertaining to curriculum inquiry. Using categories for the sake of inquiry, they add, may involve mixing them so that theory may be demonstrated through practice. The recovery of meaning involves integrating theory and practice, which, in turn, reconstructs new, more productive relationships between thecretician and practitioner. Connelly and Clandinin explicitly propose a dialectic relationship for such a reconstruction. They argue that theoreticians and practitioners value 'good ideas' and 'good practice,' respectively, and that this forms a barrier between them. The barrier seems to concern two highly different educational contexts: the 'ivory tower' of the university and the 'trenches' of the school building and its individual classrooms.

We have doubts as to whether the foregoing two contexts are reconcilable; alternatively, we propose that theoreticians and practitioners do hold similar values when questions are raised regarding alleged differences between theory and practice. And we further propose that these similarities are rooted in common epistemological frameworks and biases. These similarities are visible in Connelly and Clandinin's suggestions. Both theoretician and practitioner honour the truth value of categorical knowledge as supported by transcendental cognition, and, it follows, they both utilize the latter in their attempt to attain the former. As we showed in the section on transcendental cognition, metaphor as a vehicle of thought is part of a philosophical lineage that unifies subjective and objective realm. Connelly and Clandinin attempt to show that theory and practice may be unified through the use of appropriate principles, strategies, and tactics. For example, they advise the practitioner to pose the following two questions:

- What does this stakeholder want me to do?
- What is the reason (the idea) that this stakeholder gives for asking me to do this?

They conclude by privileging personal knowledge as a useful approach to such integration, and they advocate the use of Aristotelian epistemology. The practical context, in their view, constitutes 'a kind of proof ', and the verification of this proof privileges praxis over theory. According to the principles of categorical knowledge as established by Aristotle, theoretical speculation should be modified according to the shifting exigencies of the practical world. 'The essential task of the dialectic', Connelly and Clandinin conclude, 'is to resolve oppositions'. The goal, then, is to involve researchers and practitioners as co-participants in the study of intentions, purposes, predispositions, and practices. The recovery of the meaning of curriculum, therefore, involves uniting both researcher and practitioner in a common plan dedicated to attaining a common goal.

We remain sceptical of the possibility of such a unification both in theoretical and in practical terms. Part of our scepticism comes from our concern over a theory of metaphor and a methodology for problem solving that is premised on the construction of linear paths of topical thinking. We especially have reservations as to the value of this categorical epistemology with regard to its evaluation of 'truth'. In short, what is the basis for the commitment to the truth-value of categorical knowledge and its accompanying methodologies of acquisition/mediation? In the final section of this chapter, we propose a more radical perspective on personal knowledge - one that Nietzsche elaborated upon and that cares little for strategies of mediation.

APHORISTIC KNOWLEDGE AND THE FRAGMENTARY LANGUAGE OF BABEL

Of all that is written I love only what a man has written with his blood. Write with blood, and you will experience that blood as spirit. Whosoever writes in blood and aphorisms does not want to be read but to be learned by heart. In the mountains the shortest way is from peak to peak: but for that one must have long legs. Aphorisms should be peaks - and those who are addressed, tall and lofty.

We remain curious as to why 'a babble of voices' poses a threat to the academic curriculum. Why must babble be harnessed within categorical terms before it is perceived as legitimate? It might be useful, given the academy's preference for transcendental cognition and categorically structured knowledge, to investigate a Nietzschean perspective on metaphor and knowledge a perspective that does not mandate strategies of reflective unification or categorical knowledge. This investigation may open paths whereby practice could be expressed without the necessity of some theoretical vehicle of mediation. Until Nietzsche, the theory of metaphor depended on interpreting human essence as a transcendental entity (a religious soul, a cognitive mind, or a reflective consciousness) that has the power to produce and to manipulate knowledge. Thinking, as articulated through interactive reflection, amounts to the metaphorical equivalent of feeling, intuitive seeing, and speaking or acting. First, the object of desire is perceived (i.e. it is visualized internally), then the abstract is vocalized and implemented in practice. It is taken for granted that the teacher is a conscious, thinking agent capable of accomplishing these tasks and that metaphor facilitates transference between the conscious and subconscious realms. Such a dialectical structure requires the constant refinement of strategies that seek to unify the subjective and the objective, the theoretical and the practical, as was evident in Hegel and, more recently, in Lakoff and Johnson.

According to Nietzsche, we imagine the existence of other things by analogy; that is, anthropomorphically. In this perspective, knowledge is comprised of socially determined conventions that are communicated through the use of customary metaphorical signs. Over a period of time certain linguistic habits become canonical and are always used when describing practices. Language, therefore, cannot be expected to correspond accurately to lived experience, and metaphor cannot be expected to be a dependable vehicle for the transference of authoritative knowledge. There is no transcendental intuition from which experience may be expounded.

Johnson's history of metaphor makes it clear that Nietzsche was attempting to counter the long heritage that has marginalized rhetoric and emotions, separating them from the process involved in generating truth claims. In Nietzsche's terms, metaphors are not involved in conducting transferences between meaning gestalts; rather, they spring from a primordial protosynthesis of physical/emotional sensations. From a research perspective, then, it is not the rational exercise of logical and categorical thinking that should concern us as educators, but the degree to which we can come to terms with our fundamental relationship to physical and emotional consciousness. Nietzsche's anthropomorphic mode of thought is affective and egocentric even when it is 'trained' to pattern itself according to social rituals (including academic research methodologies). From this hyper-organic perspective, metaphor still serves a purpose, but it is not to bridge the chasm between consciousness and the theoretically conceived objective world. Metaphor is not a vehicle that drives towards rational clarity; rather, it is the totality of all figurative rhetoric and springs from a basic connection between the body's needs and passions and the earth to which it is inextricably connected.

Learning, for Nietzsche, might be viewed vegetatively as if one is cultivating the soul. Language merely perpetuates conceptual schemata that abstract, simplify, and incorporates fallacious identities (Lakoff and Johnson's 'gestalts') for pragmatic use. Researchers seem to be much more concerned with organizing and legislating the epistemological boundaries of these schemata than they are with directly confronting the body's passions, not to mention those passions' relationship to the teaching and learning process. Such a confrontation de-emphasizes knowledge acquisition and emphasizes wisdom and its development, a capacity which we believe may be appropriate for considering the craft of teaching.

Learning to teach may be a pragmatic challenge, and the quest for authoritative, unified knowledge of the process that it entails may be elusive. We suggest that the researcher's desire to articulate teacher development and its relationship to knowledge through an analysis of metaphorical mediation and categorical knowledge cannot be fulfilled. Such a desire is as old as the notion of metaphor as a streamlined vehicle of consciousness. It descends from a desire to somehow grasp and control the flux of experience. A more authentic relationship to experience may produce novel perspectives on how one learns to teach. 'Novel perspectives' will necessarily be represented in different forms from those to which we are accustomed. Following Nietzsche, who attempted to articulate his perspective aphoristically, we offer an anti-structural perspective (the 'tower of Babel') on teacher development - one that originates in Nietzsche's highly personal style.

NIETZSCHE'S EDUCATIONAL CHALLENGE: SELF-OVERCOMING

In a letter to Georg Brandes, dated 19 April 1888, Nietzsche wrote that 'the person who does not find himself addressed personally by my work will probably have nothing to do with me'. Fourteen years earlier, Nietzsche had written that the only valid critique of a philosophy concerns whether or not one can live in accordance with it. Nietzsche was writing to himself and speculating on his own educational agenda; in essence, he was outlining and undergoing a program of personal research. It is not possible to imitate Nietzsche's personal agenda when one is in pursuit of one's own perspective. It is possible, however, to use Nietzsche's journey as an inspiration for reconsidering one's own path.

As in the usual academic tradition, such research begins by framing a context within which to locate one's study. But in this case, the context includes not only published secondary materials, but also one's own biography, which must be (re)evaluated along with any 'facts' that one may find. The methodology called for by such a programme of learning assumes a distinctive Nietzschean notion of self-concept - one that is balanced between essentialist and existentialist extremes.

Zarathustra's problem of 'self-overcoming' is related directly to his problem with temporality. In the prologue of *Zarathustra*, Nietzsche attacks the 'grave view' of the passage of time and its movement towards consummation. This attack is transferable to the 'grave view' of learning as a recurrent generation of dialectical thinking. Specifically, it is an attack on the concept of experience as a recurrent, forward moving rhythm that can be schematized as a progressive journey towards some specific end. It is for this reason that Nietzsche refers to aphoristic thinking as stepping from 'peak to peak' rather than as following a dialectical path. The fragmentary thinking of 'long legs,' which take the shortest route to knowledge, requires a different conception of thinking. It relates to problem posing rather than to problem solving. Generally, the rhythm of experience is interpreted in a dialectical fashion and the process of thinking is mediated through metaphor. This leads to severely limiting the possible paths of thinking as all methodologies can begin to resemble one another. This desire for correct and common understanding has religious undertones, but it originates in Socratic Platonism, specifically in the allegory of the devoted learner who, by following an ascending path, strives for a glimpse of the ultimate ideal of moral virtue.

Nietzsche calls for a new form of understanding - one that is more loyal to the body's obvious connection to earthly processes. The Nietzschean 'self ' is a middle ground between the two extremes of essentialism and existentialism. Nietzsche proposes 'the kernel' as a metaphor of being. And, of course, kernels must be germinated in order to grow. Unless held back by negative external circumstances, a germinated kernel will sprout. For Nietzsche, such negative external circumstances include transcendental cognition and the dialectic. Beginning with essentials, one must make a critical inventory, not of what one's peers value, but of what one values for one's self. Nietzsche refers to these values as 'idols'. Many may be reluctant to conduct such an inventory, for it demands honesty and may involve difficult admissions. Nietzsche concedes that 'writing in blood' is not for everyone, however, he promises rewards to those who can do it.

In order to satisfy the anti-essentialist extreme, one must collect, order, and destroy former values; in order to satisfy the existential extreme, one must cultivate one's true self. And if one wishes to be a philosopher in Nietzsche's sense, then one must become so through one's own striving. This involves renouncing the outer circumstances that impede development. The degree to which renunciation takes place measures the degree to which the way is made clear for the revaluation of those values committed to transcendental cognition and dialectical problem solving. To learn, we must overcome the 'self,' and for this we require the assistance of educators.

Two bodies of data are relevant to self-overcoming. The first is one's own biography, which often leads one to be contemptuous of one's cultural milieu and its values. We could say that this paper is intended to bring its readers to see transcendental cognition and dialectics as constraints on thinking and so to feel contempt for them. The second body of data is the philosophical tradition that has supplied the context for knowledge within the discipline of study. Begin by 'cleaning house,' by examining the texts that reared you as a researcher within the epistemologically 'common' place. Make an inventory of your values, including those that taught you the meaning of your life. Be relentless in your exhumation, and be honest about everything, especially when it hurts. Carry on until you begin to admit to thinking the bitterest truth of all: knowledge has no 'truth value.'

In Nietzsche's terms, then, one must paint a new existential picture of life, and this can be done in one's writing. Philosophical language is a significant medium within which to build the bridge to aphoristic, or fragmentary, thinking. However, our immersion in such philosophical language is, at this stage, contained within a specific linguistic mode one that seeks to grasp the outline of objects of perception through some form of mediation. Since Nietzsche believed that we think in terms of analogy (between ourselves and an anthropomorphic world), our investigation should begin with a critical examination of our own research texts.

CONCLUSION

Towards a Place for Fragmentation in University Curriculum Writing

Nietzsche, a trained philologist, taught classics and philosophy at the University of Basel, Switzerland, from 1869 to 1876. According to Nietzsche, if one document's one's own development, then one avoids the dialectical path of thinking and pursues an impetuous and aleatory notion of knowledge development. His penchant for this form of development explains his attempt to articulate his research in the form of thousands of fragmentary aphorisms, a style common to the Presocratic philosophers. Between 1878 and 1888, Nietzsche composed at least 5,000 aphorisms in published texts and unpublished notebooks. For Nietzsche, this had to do with engaging in a process of self-directed transfiguration. Much of his educational 'training' took place within the walls of esteemed research and teaching universities. Most of his writing, however, took place after he left the university setting (due to protracted illness and long-term disability). He was at liberty, some might say, to write what he chose regardless of his peers and colleagues.

We recommend a sympathetic reading of the Nietzschean perspective, for it could lead to novel interpretations of teaching and learning within the university setting. For this to be so, however, we must expect increased fragmentation in the expression of research practices, and these expressions may be initially shocking to some. One of Nietzsche's pedagogical projects was to fuel readers' doubts about the morality within which they had been raised. With regard to this, he is often misinterpreted. Nietzsche attacked the moral commitment to propositional and dialectic knowledge. He maintained that our allegiance to the truth value of knowledge was habitual, not unlike our allegiance to living a religious life style even after our belief in a deity has been long forsaken. What is required is a change in habits and practices. Our dedication to transcendental cognition through metaphor and dialectic thinking is simply an old habit.

Nietzsche's writings do not claim to provide universal or permanently useful knowledge. Unlike the analytic tool of the dialectic, there is nothing one can 'do' with an aphorism. But any utilitarian dismissal of Nietzsche misses the point of his works. Like Nietzsche, we argue that, to a large degree, our research is limited by a dominant linguistic mode and by a pervasive orientation towards transcendental, dialectical thinking. In many ways, our research is a repetitive faith in old cognitive habits. Nietzsche's style begins the project of undermining that faith and its morality, thus opening the way to experimentation in the fragmentary. It is time to explore where this way of thinking may lead us.

❑❑❑

12

Reconceptualising and Research on Comparative Education

INTRODUCTION

The most influential challenges that we have identified stem from dramatic changes in geopolitical relations; the intensifying pace of globalisation; the pervasive influence of market forces and neo-liberal economics; the changing roles and impact of international agencies; rapid advances in information and communications technology; demand for strengthened linkages between educational research, policy and practice; growing tensions between the economic and cultural dimensions of national development and social reform; and varied poststructuralist challenges to dominant theoretical and methodological frameworks. These challenges, it is argued, all call for urgent and critical reflection, and for a repositioning of the field of comparative and international education to better address contemporary priorities and meet the emergent needs of the twenty-first century.

In addition, it is argued that without a clear repositioning, the field remains open to critique and challenge from others with an active interest or involvement in the international dimension of educational policy and practice, and in the implications of globalisation for both educational research and development. To some extent this is a paradoxical dilemma because such interests – if well connected to the experience, literature and traditions of comparativists could in themselves be an important source of renewal and intellectual reinvigoration for the field itself. Such positive engagement, however, is more likely to develop if the distinctive comparative and international constituency can better demonstrate the continuing contemporary relevance of its work and if others engaging in related activities can then more clearly see the enduring significance of both the traditions and contemporary advances being made within the field. For such reasons a 'bridging of cultures and traditions' lies at the very heart of the reconceptualisation proposals articulated here. Moreover, it is emphasised that this is a bridging that implies a multi-dimensional process (between, for example, theoretical and applied arenas, policy and practice, micro and macro levels of analysis, historical and contemporary research, and studies of the North and the South), and genuine dialogue where all involved learn from the experience, practice and literatures of each other. From this perspective, those who see themselves working primarily within the field must actively look further outwards beyond conventional borders and, where appropriate, into other intellectual, professional and cultural territories and worldviews. It is in this critical but forward-looking and creative spirit that our case for the reconceptualisation of the field of comparative and international education is advanced here.

In doing this we are concerned to value diversity and not to overlook the very real strengths that have characterised the field from its origins in the nineteenth century plans and aspirations of Jullien and Sadler's 1900 benchmark lecture. As we have argued earlier, Sadler inspired many generations of comparativists on both sides of the Atlantic and beyond, including his student Isaac L. Kandel, with his then pioneering and interpretive social, historical and cultural studies of education. While academic territories can and do often limit creativity and intellectual advances, comparative education as a field can justifiably point to its long cherished, multidisciplinary foundations and traditions, as a notable strength on which to build in the future.

Previous efforts to synthesise challenges to the post-war empirical social sciences phase of comparative and international education were made by Altbach and Kelly in their compilation of relevant articles drawn from the *Comparative Education Review*. Reflecting upon what they then saw as the theoretical dominance of structural functionalism, combined with positivist methodological assumptions, Altbach and Kelly identified four main challenges that had emerged since previous 'state of the art' reviews of the field were published in 1977. These were seen as (i) challenges to the nation-state as the exclusive research framework; (ii) challenges to input-output models and reliance upon quantification; (iii) challenges to structural functionalism, and (iv) the emergence of new substantive concerns, most notably gender research, institutional studies and critiques, the content and processes of education and the legitimisation of educational knowledge. According to Kelly and Altbach, 'prior to 1977 these issues scarcely entered the discourse of the field and were not promoted through its major journals or texts'.

While this fourfold framework remains useful today, and can be used to categorise more contemporary work that has been carried out, clearly much has changed in the intervening years. The emergent nature of some of these changes is reflected in the contributions to a number of more recent edited collections. Our present discussion draws upon such work and our own related studies, but articulates an original, comprehensive and sustained analysis, within its historical and intellectual context, in advancing the case for a thorough reassessment and a fundamental reconceptualisation of the field overall. Since the nature and extent of the contemporary challenges have been discussed throughout the text, the present chapter focuses mainly upon their implications for the processes of reconceptualisation in practice, and upon possible ways forward for the field in the future.

RECONCEPTUALISING COMPARATIVE AND INTERNATIONAL EDUCATION

At the broadest level we have argued that it is the research dimension and research potential of comparative and international education that has underpinned the contemporary resurgence of interest in the field. Moreover, it is research activity, and related research training, that has played the most strategic part in the reinvigoration of the institutional base. From the work reviewed here, it can be seen, for example, that the relatively new Comparative Education Research Centre (CERC) established at the University of Hong Kong in 1994 has played a pivotal role during the 1990s and subsequently in stimulating and documenting comparative studies throughout Greater China and South-East Asia.

Building upon these research strengths in a more explicit way offers much for the future in a world where it is increasingly difficult to understand education in any context without reference to global issues and international trends and comparisons. But, in the light of the analysis presented here, there are clearly many questions to raise relating to both the focus of such research and the ways in which it might be carried out. The implications of such questions for the nature of the reconceptualisation process are considered below.

RESEARCH AND EVIDENCE-BASED POLICY

In addressing the contemporary critique levelled at social and educational research in general, comparative and international education can justifiably point to its traditional strengths as an applied, problem-oriented field. New and better ways, however, must be found to engage more directly, and critically, with the ongoing concerns and priorities faced by mainstream educational research and with the worldwide call for cumulative and professionally oriented, evidence-based research and policy-making. As Goodson argued, in speaking at the British Educational Research Association's annual conference, it is time for educational researchers to reposition themselves closer to practice. Since many mainstream educational researchers and policy-makers have also taken renewed interest in international trends, the potential for new partnerships and for a distinctively strategic, and possibly cautionary, contribution from comparative and international education has increased. Noah, for example, pointed out some time ago that while:

> *... comparative education is an applied field of study that finds particular justification in the service of evaluation, management, administration and policy-making. Like all fields, it is open to potential abuse by those who wish to use its results to support (or oppose) a specific program of change.*

Secondary analyses and politically inspired interpretations of the influential IEA Studies, as we have seen, illustrate such dangers well in a global context where relative positions on international league tables often tempt decisionmakers to consider the adoption of apparently successful pedagogic practice from foreign cultural contexts.

Comparativists can thus make a uniquely valuable contribution when reports of foreign educational policy are considered by reminding decision-makers that they can be:

> *... fully and fruitfully used in discussion only if they are seen as a part of a much broader enterprise, with HMIs [inspectors] contributing their particular insights along with others: scholars, researchers and students whose job it is to take more sweeping views, not necessarily tied to this month's policy problem the health of policy-making in an interdependent world must depend in part on the health of comparative education research in the broadest sense.*

The explicitly comparative IEA studies are particularly pertinent examples of the sort of large-scale, cumulative and evidence-based research that is advocated by contemporary stakeholders in education. This is partly because governments find it easier to seize upon eye-catching findings rather than to grapple with the complexity of many issues. Ironically, however, criticism (often relating to context insensitivity) of this highly influential, and still evolving model, has come more from within the field of comparative and international education than it has from without. Dialogue and discourse across professional and intellectual boundaries can thus be much improved. This critique is also valuable because it draws attention to the limitations of policy transfer and to further lessons that can be learned from the comparative perspective. It is in considering such issues that distinctive implications for theory, context and culture re-emerge with renewed force and relevance.

THEORETICAL IMPLICATIONS OF CONTEXT AND CULTURE

It should, perhaps, not be too surprising that the IEA comparisons of school achievement should have gained widespread recognition in the broader arena of policy-making. The sequence of assessment studies produced, since their origins in the early 1960s, have focused upon issues relating to the quality of teaching and learning that have increasingly come to dominate the priorities and agendas of decision-makers worldwide. Data have been systematically quantified on a large scale, core school subjects such as Science and Mathematics have received concerted attention and substantial resources have been invested in the research enterprise in countries drawn from a wide spectrum of developed and developing countries.

The critique noted above relates as much to the way in which findings have been used as it does to the methodological and theoretical limitations of the IEA studies themselves. Acknowledging this, Goldstein draws attention to the contextual relevance of IEA findings and the dilemmas encountered when attempts are made to focus upon comparisons of achievement across national systems of education. Such critiques draw more directly upon the core concepts of context and culture concepts that remain central to the work of those specialists in the field of comparative and international research that have long questioned the methodological rationale of the IEA model. It is possible, however, to argue, as does Cumming, that useful policy results can be more realistically derived from comparisons of differing groups within the same national education system data set and that such findings can be related to differences in social and cultural factors. In the light of such issues Kellaghan draws upon many insights and perspectives central to the comparative canon in outlining key parameters for those involved in the disciplined application of IEA findings in the policy arena. In doing this, Kellaghan helps to add renewed legitimacy to the distinctive characteristics of comparative and international research in education, in a policy context central to the management and performance concerns of governmental agencies worldwide. This discussion also draws attention back to the importance of contextual and cultural factors in cross-national research and to the dilemmas, long recognised by comparativists, associated with international transfer in all dimensions of educational research and development.

RAPPROACHEMENT BETWEEN COMPARATIVE AND INTERNATIONAL RESEARCH

A useful irony is embedded in the above analysis. Revealingly, the contextual critique emerges more strongly from the theoretically-oriented comparative tradition of the combined field of comparative and international education, than it does from the more explicitly applied and action-oriented expertise associated with international education. This, it is argued, is one of the most fundamental issues for consideration in the reconceptualisation of the combined field, for it simultaneously demonstrates the weaknesses of *both* established traditions, while identifying priorities for future attention in a way that is of considerable theoretical and methodological significance. As already indicated, in broad scope this relates to long-standing criticism of much international education for being too closely related to policy agendas of the day, and to the implementation of reform projects tied to development assistance agency assumptions and priorities. Counterpoising this perspective is the critique of the more explicitly comparative dimension of the field for being too preoccupied with abstract theoretical scholarship divorced from the real world of educational policy and practice. While the polarisation of this analysis may oversimplify the issues involved, it is revealing, and the latter critique is reminiscent of the broader challenge to educational research that calls for cumulative, applied and professionally relevant research that is clearly, and unambiguously, communicated to policy-makers and practitioners. There are, however, no simple answers here, even if a closer relationship between theoretical scholarship and applied research warrants careful exploration.

Experience within the international education arena also points, somewhat ironically, to the very real limitations of undue reliance upon applied, policyoriented studies. In many post-colonial countries greater degrees of austerity have long accentuated accountability, evaluation, project relevance and generalisability in research but, despite this, the success rate of many intended reforms has, as we have demonstrated, been disappointing, particularly with regard to their sustainability beyond periods of external funding. Moreover, it is argued here that it is the failure of many international development initiatives to give sufficient weight to the broad spectrum of theoretical insights, and to contextual and cultural issues that lies at the heart of this dilemma. It is only rarely that those working within the professional culture of international development co-operation have, to date, been able to apply the literature, experience and perspectives characteristic of the more detached comparative social science constituency in any challenging and sustained way. Unfortunately, the irony is greater still, for, while the comparative dimension of our combined field accords particular premium to such issues, it is this constituency that is most open to the ongoing challenge to mainstream educational research for not adequately addressing the policy issues and practical concerns of the day. In this context, and as noted earlier, the 1997 amalgamation of professional and academic constituencies that led to the formation of the British Association for International and Comparative Education (BAICE), represents important structural and organisational bridge building. This was a positive and practical movement towards reconceptualisation in itself, and one that helps further to consolidate efforts made to unite comparative and international education societies in the 1980s, while providing a foundation for more fundamental interpersonal, sub-cultural and intellectual advances in the future.

Perhaps more intractably the task of rapprochement will be more complex than this somewhat over simplified portrayal and analysis implies, for there are often sound reasons for the persistence of intellectual and organisational divisions between research cultures and communities. There are also well-established traditions and political and territorial imperatives to negotiate. As Furlong points out, educational research is 'constantly subject to fads and fashions, to competing, ill-defined and sometimes contradictory goals'. Moreover, to be realistic, we should recognise the limitations of research and not expect the impossible, or forget that:

> *The connection between research and practice is not one in which research influences practice, as many researchers might hope, nor one in which practice influences research as many might hope, but rather one in which both research and practice are influenced by and are perhaps even victims of the same shifting social and political context.*

Recognition of the impact of such changing socio-political trends, nevertheless, points to a more profound rationale for concerted efforts towards reconceptualisation and rapprochement in comparative and international education. This is especially so when old conceptual divisions between, for example, 'developed' and 'developing' countries are increasingly problematic, when global forces influence the educational arrangements of all nation-states, and when issues relating to culture, identity and context are challenging rationalism and modernist assumptions and development priorities worldwide. In such times the bridging of traditional divisions, the challenging of old certainties and the forging of new discourses is essential for the advancement of all fields of enquiry.

WIDENING THE DISCOURSE IN COMPARATIVE AND INTERNATIONAL EDUCATION

Central to the thesis developed here is the argument that the increasingly rapid pace of socio-economic change demands vastly improved forms of communication and interchange between human groups, organisations and cultures worldwide. This, as we have already noted, includes professional cultures, international agencies, policy makers, practitioners, paradigmatic frameworks, ethnic groups, the general public, periods of time, and researchers across all disciplines and fields. Such cross-cultural bridging is essential if we are to better conceptualise and understand the dramatic changes that contemporary globalisation processes have set in train. Indeed, in tune with Huntington it is argued that the changes now being faced across the globe are as profound as any previously encountered. Globalisation, spurred on by 'appeals to unfettered capitalism', is indeed progressing hand in hand with the poststructuralist challenges to the Enlightenment project, positivistic science and modernisation theory that we have discussed earlier. Tensions between ideas and developments that underpin globalisation on the one hand, and post structuralism on the other, thus generate, what we now reiterate, are some of the most fundamental of all intellectual challenges of the present day. Dealing with such challenges will demand the bridging of much more than intellectual traditions and cultures. It will require fundamental social change and new discourses that recognise the limitations of deeply embedded ways of thinking about the world, for as – we owe thanks to Phillip Jones, University of Sydney, for this evocative phrase.

Giddens points out, globalisation 'describes the increasing inter-penetration between individual life and global futures, something which is relatively new in history'. Giddens goes on to say that 'it is a wholly contradictory process' and that 'we are the first generation to enter a global age'. Discourses that can help improve our conceptualisation of globalisation processes, while engaging with the diverse challenges raised by poststructuralist critiques of meta-narratives have the potential to go beyond the well-known limitations of deconstruction and to contribute to advances that may be both affirmative and more effectively tuned to the cultural differences and multi-polar geo-politics of the twenty-first century.

Within the field of comparative and international education the reconceptualisation thesis articulated here thus suggests that there is much to be gained from a fundamental challenge to the barriers that limit wider debate and interchange, especially between what Altbach and Kelly labelled the 'new realists' and the post-modern proponents of critical scholarship. This is not to imply that comparative and international education should be too disparaging of itself for, within the broader field of education, it is particularly well placed to advance genuinely multidisciplinary research across cultural boundaries with an inherent concern for contextualisation and respect for differing social constructions of reality. Nevertheless, given the turbulence of the times in which we live there remains, as already expressed, much to be done and it is to the potential of a number of the more significant possibilities that we now turn in more specific detail.

LINKS BETWEEN RESEARCH AND SCHOLARSHIP

The broad epistemological issues raised above help to highlight the significance of strengthening linkages between the predominantly action-oriented, applied, international constituency of the field, and the more traditionally theoretical, comparative dimension. This also points to the importance of forging a more substantial dialectic between empirical research – from all paradigmatic foundations – and critical, in-depth, and theoretical scholarship. Unfortunately, intensified financial, managerial and micro-political imperatives have in recent years been notorious in increasing the pressures on researchers to compete rather than collaborate, and to seek new externally funded projects before sustained reflection upon the findings of 'completed' studies has been possible. Such missed opportunities and conflicts of interest can be costly in themselves, and undue haste, often generated by external pressures, does little to improve the range and quality of research dissemination repeatedly called for by concerned stakeholders. Efforts to bridge the research and scholarship divide also draws attention back to the limitations of prevailing research cultures that separate the study and conceptualisation of education in developing countries from other dimensions of comparative and international research – all the more so in a world where global forces have an increasingly influential impact in all socio-economic contexts. Despite encouraging organisational trends, barriers between the personnel, networks and literatures of researchers working on European and development studies, for example, remain pervasive and detrimental to the field as a whole. This is especially pertinent when faced with the questionable legitimacy of long-established socio-economic classifications, and the dramatic impact of major socio-economic transformations characteristics of the late twentieth century.

STRENGTHENED CROSS-DISCIPLINARY STUDIES

Discourses and studies that build upon the multidisciplinary traditions of the field are particularly apposite in times when cultural forces and political transformations are repeatedly demonstrating the limitations of linear, teleological assumptions about national and international development strategies. Holding significant potential for comparative and international education at this point in time are studies that combine the field's long engagement with language, literacy and culture with the advancement of the post-colonial critique. This has the potential to stimulate new developments that more firmly recognise the contemporary significance of intellectual frameworks that deal with issues of identity, culture, race, gender and class. Compatible with multi-level analyses, post-colonial studies can be advanced, for example, through critical ethnography and through further applications of the meta-level studies of critical theorists such as Bourdieu and Passeron, Bourdieu, Habermas, Giroux and Apple. As indicated in earlier chapters, post-colonial frameworks could also do much to challenge the Eurocentric profile of much post-modern theorising and the colonialist image of some ethnography, in a way that could better demonstrate their contemporary potential for applied, policy-oriented research. Indeed, as documented by Torres, for many years comparativists have sustained interest in the work of Freire and its implications for development processes. The cultural critiques of Mazrui, Thaman, Hickling-Hudson, Kumar and other non-Western analysts have also been acknowledged within the field – but the consistent application of such perspectives within the mainstream of international education discourse and development work remains limited or confined to the activities of non-governmental organisations (NGOs), detached theorists or polemical critics. On the other hand, there are some shifts in thinking and praxis inspired by the now worldwide influence of writers such as Freire, Chambers and others, that demonstrate ways in which more concerted post-colonial analyses may continue to advance theory while contributing in a productive way to the improvement of educational policy and practice in pluralist and multi-cultural communities. As with the post-modern critique and associated literature, however, the dangers of inaccessible theorising obscuring the applied potential of such cross-disciplinary and cross-cultural research deserve attention in their own right.

The mainstream challenge to what Becher has called 'academic tribes and territories', and reconsideration of the philosophical and historical traditions of Sadler's approach to comparative education also has much in common with the rationale and goals of contemporary socio-cultural studies of education. Closer working relationships between social scientists from different fields thus have much to offer, as reflected by the justification for the recent establishment in the United Kingdom of an Academy of Learned Societies for the Social Sciences.

The above discussion also demonstrates the potential of stronger linkages between social science researchers and those working within the arts and humanities. Much of the inspiration for post-colonial theorising, for example, is derived from the literature of cultural studies and Louisy an academic, and head of state, well illustrates this in her call for the rich cultural traditions of the Caribbean to play a more active role in shaping the future of comparative and international research. In urging Caribbean researchers to contribute more to the international debate she writes:

> *Cultural analysts and comparative sociologists should study in more detail the distinctive social, cultural or even economic circumstances that nurture, for example, the creative imagination of Jamaican Robert Nestor Marley and the musical and social phenomenon of Reggae, Rastafarianism and dreadlocks, that has permeated so many other countries both in the developed and developing world.*

In a different but similar vein, we have earlier noted how Kazamias applies concepts and insights from Greek mythology, develops a strong critique of positivistic approaches to social and educational research, and makes an impassioned case for 'reinventing the historical in comparative education'. For Kazamias, the displacement of history from the scope of much contemporary comparative education has contributed to its 'humanistic' impoverishment. This echoes a plea made by Watson in his 1997 Inaugural Presidential Address given to the British Association for International and Comparative Education (BAICE). Returning to these two examples usefully illustrates the case for the strengthening of linkages between the arts and the social sciences – and for stronger bridges to be built between current studies and disciplines, such as history, that may have played a more significant role for the field in the past. As Bourdieu's reflexive approach to sociology powerfully demonstrates, if we wish to understand each other better we also need to understand our own biographies, our own histories and, in doing so, where we are coming from. This, we argue, can apply as much to a field of study as it does to an individual agency. Contemporary researchers in comparative and international education can thus do much to remind policy makers of the importance of both philosophy and history.

Indeed, methodologically fruitful advances could also arise from more focused studies of the theory and practice of comparative methodology across faculties and disciplines. Oyen's work, for the International Sociological Association, is indicative of the methodological lessons that may be learned from other comparative fields, and this is appropriately related to Galtung's plea for pluralism in theory formation for social research.

At a more specific level, the potential for innovative cross-disciplinary comparative and international research is demonstrated by studies of cognition and culture that are beginning to open up new insights into the nature and implications of legitimate 'ways of knowing' in differing cultural contexts. Masemann echoed such principles on a broader platform in her Presidential Address for the United States-based Comparative and International Education Society, and Noah reminds us that:

> *A comparative approach enlarges the framework within which we can view the results obtained in a single country: by providing counter instances, it challenges us to refine our theories and test their validity against the reality of different societies; and, by providing parallel results, it can yield important confirmation of results obtained elsewhere.*

MULTIPLE FRAMES OF REFERENCE AND UNITS OF ANALYSIS

Early challenges to the nation-state as the primary unit of analysis have been sustained and reinforced in more recent years by the ethnographic movement at the micro-level and by the rapidly changing socio-political events of the 1990s.

Returning to the macro-level, the impact of intensified globalisation is, nevertheless, of particular significance as we have argued earlier. While the nation-state continues usefully to frame much research within the field, understanding the relationship between the state and globalisation as a process is currently of increasing importance and a global framework for analysis is especially pertinent for comparative studies. Dale thus suggests that 'it should be the central aim of comparative education to lay bare the nature of and the reasons for the different impacts globalisation has had in differing contexts worldwide'. To emphasise the significance and complexity of globalisation discourses he goes on to caution against simplistic alignments with the 'globalisation boom' and to argue for critical comparative analyses of globalisation's place in the 'knowledge economy' from the distance afforded by a 'very long spoon'.

Beyond this, much can also be gained from Bray and Thomas's plea for multi-level analysis, and from writers such as McLeish and Phillips who have focused upon frameworks relating to educational reconstruction in societies facing rapid socio-political transition. Others have seen potential in comparative studies of Pacific Rim contexts and of small states. Thus Cowen refers to 'transitology' and the need to give attention to forces beyond the nation-state, and to 'international and global structures associated with tendencies towards "post-modernity"' in his search for a 'new' comparative education. Paulston, as we have seen, also endorses the opening up of the comparative and international discourse to the debate of post-modern ideas, by accepting Rust's challenge with his advocacy of social cartography as a framework for comparative studies in education.

Miller also captures the importance of recognising the 'other' in similar terms when he applies place theory to the dilemmas faced by small states at the periphery of international decision-making, and argues that:

> *Marginal countries and marginal groups within these countries are in the most favourable position to take risk. They can convert disadvantage into opportunity and move to a more central place in the continued development of human civilisation.*

From this perspective it can be seen that much can be gained from alternative units of analysis and from intellectual frameworks that apply poststructuralist notions of, for example, place theory and social cartography. Watson's plea for clear applications remains important, however, if the advantages of innovative theoretical frameworks and units of analysis are to be realised and communicated in a way that is accessible to those seeking assistance in the qualitative improvement of educational policy and practice. This returns the debate to the initial critique of mainstream educational research, and to the call for more substantial, cumulative, applied and relevant evidence-based policy and research.

EDUCATIONAL RESEARCH, POLICY AND PRACTICE

In many ways the present analysis began with the call for a strengthening of the relationship between educational research, and policy and practice. Much has already been said on this core theme to demonstrate how comparative and international experience can make a distinctive contribution to the broader debate. In particular, it is argued that the tendency for much traditional comparative research to focus upon detached theory, or, at best, comparisons of policy and for much international work to eschew theory or implicitly adopt a modernist perspective, deserves concerted attention in the future. The poststructuralist debates articulated throughout this book, for example, help to demonstrate the potential and legitimacy of detailed qualitative research carried out within the field, of the opportunities presented by critical ethnography and of the centrality of cultural context in reputable studies designed to contribute to improved policy and practice. In this international arena the strengths of collaborative studies carried out by combinations of insiders and outsiders are enhanced. This is well demonstrated by the policy relevance of Broadfoot studies of perceptions of teaching in England and France, and Stuart efforts to improve classroom practice through action research in Lesotho. Strengthening partnerships between insiders and outsiders, researchers and practitioners and policy formulators and analysts could thus play an integral part in the reconceptualisation of the field as a whole.

In arguing this case it is acknowledged that comparative and international education has, once again, a credible track record. Wilson, a former President of the Comparative and International Education Society (CIES), for example, has long noted the emergence of the 'academic-practitioner' within the field:

> *... who has been equipped with a viable academic understanding of comparative education and who has used that orientation to further the* meliorative *function common to both international and comparative education in his or her subsequent international activities.*

Once again, such foundations provide an excellent platform for future development. However, while the case for the practitioner researcher is strong, Jarvis calls for broader scope within the field of education, and E.J. King warns comparativists that 'part of our conceptual reorientation lies in escaping from a purely pedagogical preoccupation: our "constituency" today includes not just other academics but a limitless array of participants'. Research strategies such as Participatory Rural Appraisal are thus finding increased favour in international development work focused upon non-formal education and other community empowerment activities. Such issues are explored at greater length by Crossley and Holmes with reference to contemporary trends in collaborative and participatory approaches to educational research, and to the potential of educational research partnerships, and international development co-operation.

In the international development arena, work of this nature highlights the importance of activities that contribute to the process goals of research capacity building, and the empowerment of local personnel. Achieving this in practice is, however, more complex than much of the partnership rhetoric would suggest – but it is here that a reconceptualised approach to comparative and international education has much to offer. At the forefront of such work is the influence of many non-governmental organisations (NGOs) such as the Swiss Commission for Research Partnerships with Developing Countries (KFPE). This organisation's *Guidelines for Research in Partnership with Developing Countries,* for example, identified 11 principles for successful research partnerships. Such guidelines point to innovative modes of operation for comparative and international researchers that require new levels of 'mutual respect, honesty and openness. The partners must be able to communicate effectively and must be able to commit themselves to a long-term involvement'.

Thus, in the development arena, research capacity building through partnerships between local and external personnel, could well prove to be one of the most effective ways of increasing context sensitivity and of bridging the gap between educational policy and practice. K. King certainly views such activities as the equivalent of a new model of development co-operation that can help reduce the knowledge gap between the North and the South and enable more symmetrical North-South partnerships. The attention of research must also encompass a much wider spectrum of teaching and learning sites and issues if it is to deal effectively with the uncertainties, technologies and imperatives of the future.

Moreover, as more educational researchers engage with comparative and international studies, many additional insights and benefits, both intellectual and professional may accrue. This is evident in the policy work by Ball in which he highlights the political motives for many cross-national studies where 'proposals and justifications for reform in one country provide resources for advocates and politicians interested in promoting change in others'. While Ball goes on to argue that, 'This is not so much a matter of policy exchange but the reinforcement of shared assumptive worlds', he also calls for 'more research and more theoretical development in the field of international policy'. Clearly, this identifies an important vein for future comparative studies but it also re-emphasises the dangers of uncritical international transfer, and of inadvertently reinforcing policy studies where a detailed knowledge of educational context and practice is often limited, and when the strengthening of evidenced-based policy is given a high premium by decision-makers and other key stakeholders.

Finally, it is argued that fundamental reconceptualisation must undoubtedly take greater cognisance of the advances in the field beyond the English language literature or dominant European discourses. As already argued, increased recognition of differing social constructions of reality, different cultural conceptions of development priorities and innovative work on teaching and learning in contrasting socio-cultural contexts can all help to improve our impact upon specific policy and practice, while strengthening genuinely global theoretical insights and understandings.

In this respect the reconceptualisation process can be most effectively advanced by greater support for the promotion of comparative and international research from a wider range of cultural perspectives, and by the more active dissemination of research carried out in this way. Illustrative of this is the attention given by Bray and Gui to the various comparative education traditions in Greater China. Also of significance is the example provided by the translation and publication of the collected works of Gu Mingyuan titled *Education in China and Abroad: Perspectives from a Lifetime in Comparative Education.*

Returning to our bridging theme, and in the light of the United Nations designated 'Year of Dialogue Among Civilisations', comparative and international education is especially well placed to pioneer new dialogue across cultures and between civilisations. Hayhoe and Pan's study is therefore most helpful for demonstrating how the field can help in giving 'voice' to three major Eastern civilisations - Chinese, Arabic and Indian in a way that generates a unique dialogue with the West on education, cultural differences and globalisation. Indeed, it can be argued that it is the changing nature of the dialogue between civilisations that has had the most profound implications of all for the reconceptualisation process advanced here.

As Hawkins points out:

> *To accomplish a truly democratic education, it is necessary to promote dialogues among and across different perspectives and academic communities around the world.*

VALIDATION

A central issue in qualitative research is validity (also known as credibility and/or dependability). There are many different ways of establishing validity, including: member check, interviewer corroboration, peer debriefing, prolonged engagement, negative case analysis, auditability, confirmability, bracketing, and balance.

ACADEMIC RESEARCH

By the end of the 1970s many leading journals began to publish qualitative research articles and several new journals emerged which published only qualitative research studies and articles about qualitative research methods.

In the 1980s and 1990s, the new qualitative research journals became more multidisciplinary in focus moving beyond qualitative research's traditional disciplinary roots of anthropology, sociology, and philosophy.

The new millennium saw a dramatic increase in the number of journals specializing in qualitative research with at least one new qualitative research journal being launched each year.

SUMMARY

In the light of our evolving critique of the nature and evolution of comparative and international education, the discussion in this chapter articulates ways in which the fundamental reconceptualisation of this multidisciplinary field can be advanced. At the outset of a new century it is argued that increasingly rapid socio-economic changes make such reconceptualisation essential. Tensions stimulated by the pace of globalisation and the simultaneous impact of poststructuralist critiques of social research, generate some of the most fundamental intellectual challenges of the present day. These tensions underpin the case for reconceptualisation in our field, although it is further enhanced by the contemporary emergence of a sustained challenge to the nature and worth of mainstream educational research and to its relevance and accessibility to those engaged in the improvement of policy and practice worldwide.

Looking to the future it is argued that the diverse and multidisciplinary traditions of comparative and international education make it especially well placed to deal with the increasingly complex, global and cross-cultural issues that will characterise the twenty-first century. It is, for example, a field that has long recognised the significance of global forces in educational research and development, and one that has consistently examined the dilemmas associated with the transfer of educational policy and practice from one cultural context to another. While some of the traditional strengths of the field provide a foundation for renewed growth, the case for fundamental critique and reconstruction, nevertheless, demands priority attention – if its potential to contribute to the improvement of policy and practice, or to advance theory in the educational and social sciences, is to be fully and effectively realised.

This process must necessarily involve a reconsideration of long accepted assumptions and sub-cultures within the field, and a reconceptualisation that engenders new priorities, discourses and modes of operation that are more closely in tune with the exigencies of the contemporary world. Of primary paradigms, theories and agendas also arise. This draws attention back to the field's distinctive strengths and expertise that relate to the importance of the two core concepts of context and culture. Indeed, for these reasons, it is argued that a reconceptualised field of comparative and international education will be especially well placed for the future study of issues relating to globalisation, culture and identity, and of the continued emergence and impact of international educational agendas. To some extent this further challenges the nation-state as the primary unit of analysis without, as demonstrated by Green, denying its continued relevance. A case is, therefore made for the reconceptualised field to be more explicitly associated with the socio-cultural study of education in context. This reaffirms the principle that context matters, but repositions the field to engage in the study of education in all its varied and new forms, with regard to contextual factors operating at all levels, ranging from the personal, through the organisational, to the global.

Returning to theoretical and methodological themes and to the debate relating to policy and practice, it is clear that there is much for all engaged in the educational arena to learn about the inter-relationship between theoretical scholarship and applied research from, and within, the field of comparative and international education. Firstly, the dangers of an either/or conceptualisation, tempting researchers to abandon culturally sensitive theoretical studies in the face of the contemporary applied critique, are well demonstrated by the cautionary experience of much policy-oriented research carried out in developing countries. However, tensions long existing between the comparative and international traditions also help to reinforce criticism of too much research becoming too divorced from the needs of policy and practice. The argument here is, therefore, for greater recognition of the interdependence between improved theory, policy and practice, and of the potential of related bridge building between the various research discourses and professional cultures involved.

As demonstrated above, the field of comparative and international education can add much to broad social science debates in this respect, and it can, and should, do this confidently in the light of its own distinctive experience and traditions. This will, in itself, contribute to the process of strengthening its own institutional base through the professional networks and research capacity building initiatives that it is equally well placed to support. This is not to imply that there is one definitive path to follow for, in sympathy with E.J. King, it is argued that any such proposals could 'divide comparative education's scholars from each other while distracting attention from urgent tasks, from new opportunities, and indeed from the need to continue our growth'. A strengthened institutional base may, therefore, be best seen as a core component of a thoroughly reconceptualised field, that welcomes the incorporation of multiple research discourses, recognises the potential of many different comparative educations, and simultaneously supports further advancement through disciplined comparative and international initiatives conducted in collaboration with a diversity of others, including mainstream educational researchers and their frameworks and organisations. Such a combined strategy for development and repositioning may well help the field to accommodate the systematic and rational impulse for renewed growth, with the inevitable strategic and political imperatives of all fields of study - in a way that is compatible with the respect for identity and difference that is so characteristic of the global era.

Contemporary qualitative research has been conducted from a large number of various paradigms that influence conceptual and meta theoretical concerns of legitimacy, control, data analysis, ontology, and epistemology, among others. Research conducted in the last 10 years has been characterized by a distinct turn toward more interpretive, postmodern, and critical practices. Guba and Lincoln identify five main paradigms of contemporary qualitative research: positivism, postpositivism, critical theories, constructivism, and participatory/cooperative paradigms. Each of the paradigms listed by Guba and Lincoln are characterized by axiomatic differences in axiology, intended action of research, control of research process/outcomes, relationship to foundations of truth and knowledge, validity, textual representation and voice of the researcher/participants, and commensurability with other paradigms. In particular, commensurability involves the extent to which paradigmatic concerns "can be retrofitted to each other in ways that make the simultaneous practice of both possible". Positivist and post positivist paradigms share commensurable assumptions but are largely incommensurable with critical, constructivist, and participatory paradigms. Likewise, critical, constructivist, and participatory paradigms are commensurable on certain issues (e.g., intended action and textual representation).

❐❐❐

13

Cross-cultural Development in Comparative Education

INTRODUCTION

The field of comparative and international education has, however, also undergone significant change during recent decades. It is, for example, not appropriately or accurately characterised, as it sometimes is, as an encyclopaedic and largely descriptive form of study concerned to improve the collection and dissemination of knowledge about different educational systems. Such studies may have played a part in its history, but, as our work demonstrates, they represent only one dimension of the much broader intellectual landscape that comprises the challenging and diverse field of today. Nor is the range of current activity as closely related to programmes of initial teacher education as it once was – or to positivistic notions of research as characterised in the Western literature during the resurgence of the empirical social sciences in the 1960s and 1970s. Indeed, most university teaching in the field is now closely aligned to a wide range of creative and ongoing research initiatives, and to related research training programmes.

On the other hand, comparative and international research in education is currently facing more fundamental challenges today than ever before. These challenges have been considered in detail throughout this volume. Some are externally generated while others relate more to internal debates and developments within the field itself. Significantly, they include the implications of changing geopolitical relations, the intensification of globalisation, advances in information and communications technologies, and paradigmatic developments across the social sciences and humanities. Moreover, the growth of interest in comparative and international research has both expanded the audience for such work, and broadened the constituency of the field of enquiry. Decision-makers, at all levels, are, as we have seen, increasingly looking to comparativists for practical applications of their work, and for guidance that may help to improve the efficiency or effectiveness of educational policy and practice. Indeed, this applies in many arenas, and it is therefore not uncommon to see new comparative initiatives and research centres emerging in a diversity of fields today. Indicative of this, for example, the International Social Science Council recently launched a comparative research programme focused on poverty and, in 2002, the University of the South Pacific established a new Regional Comparative Employment and Labour Studies Unit with support from the European Union. On a broader level, Giddens recognises the comparative and international ascendancy, and urges analysts of public policy to look outside their own systems in the search for critical insights relating to future policy and practice.

Attention to the applied and policy-oriented potential of comparative studies, however, brings with it further challenges, as noted by Cowen's previously cited observation that the field is now 'going through a dangerous moment', in a global climate displaying the re-emergence of simplistic assumptions about the transferability of policy and practice. Much of this, as we have shown, is driven by economic objectives, competitive motives and political advocacy. The dangers of intensified and ever faster uncritical international transfer thus loom large on the contemporary research agenda – further enhancing the need for critical, disciplined and independent comparative investigation. Moreover, to be done effectively, this needs time: time for indepth research, time for reflection. Policy makers, however, typically wish to make decisions quickly – and herein lies an ongoing tension. On the other hand, costly development mistakes will continue to be made if speed of action continues to inhibit high-quality, reflective work. In earlier chapters we have thus drawn attention to the dilemmas generated by the speed of technology transfer, to the implications of the increased power of international agencies over educational agendas worldwide, and to the need to recognise and document the differential impact of globalisation on education and society worldwide.

It is in this complex and rapidly changing global climate that, we argue, a more fundamental reassessment and reconceptualisation of the field of comparative and international education is essential. To return to Miller's pertinent reflections (as cited at the outset of the book) - and to reflect upon his insights more directly for this field:

> *The world is never static. Even in periods when everything appears to remain the same, streams of change, however small, exist. But in some periods myriad streams of change all flow into a giant river of transformation. Change becomes apparent when the different currents 'encounter' each other and the obstacles in their paths. All the streams of change that have been flowing quietly and even slowly during the century are now overflowing their banks.*

This somewhat poetic commentary reflects the central thesis of our book well. Recent and contemporary changes are indeed visible, but the challenges continue to rise, and the banks of the field of comparative and international education can now be seen to be overflowing. Deeper and more fundamental change is therefore necessary if comparative and international research in education is fully to realise its considerable potential to contribute to the advancement of both educational research and educational development in the future. Drawing from our own analysis, we here conclude by arguing that this requires fundamental, simultaneous and consistent reconceptualisation on four related fronts: the theoretical, methodological, substantive and organisational dimensions of the field.

We briefly reflect on these implications in turn, acknowledging that, because the issues and categories are so closely interrelated, it is often difficult, and inappropriate, to separate one from the other. This final analysis emerges from the more detailed considerations and proposals presented earlier. These intentionally brief concluding comments thus draw upon earlier discussions where appropriate, but focus more directly upon articulating and clarifying the broader scope of our overall contribution.

THEORETICAL AND METHODOLOGICAL IMPLICATIONS

'Globalisation, context and difference', we argue that tensions generated by the simultaneous intensification of globalisation and increased attention to the significance of cultural and contextual differences lie at the heart of many of the most fundamental problems of our age. If comparative and international research is actively to recognise this, it is to ways of respecting a greater diversity of cultural and contextual perspectives that we believe the field must look most carefully in the future. In this regard the dangers of dominant discourses emerge more strongly than ever and the importance of future work that priorities differing world views and cross-cultural dialogue is heightened.

There is already much evidence in the existing literature to suggest that, for example, improvements to the quality of education cannot be imposed, and that 'universally applicable' models of educational reform are highly problematic. Successful educational innovation, many now argue, is more closely related to mediated action, negotiation and collaboration between different stakeholders. See, for example, the socio-cultural and psychological perspectives articulated by writers such as Wertsch and Bruner on one level, and the case for greater cross-cultural dialogue in the wider arena of international development co-operation as advanced by Ward. The poststructuralist critiques that we have engaged with thus advance increasingly pertinent theoretical and methodological approaches to educational research and development that challenge learning theory, the contemporary hegemony of neo-liberal, marketisation policies and the increased power of international agencies.

The potential of collaborative research involving insiders and outsiders; the strengthening of research and evaluation capacity within the South; the prioritisation of context-sensitive research and evaluation methodologies; and the generation of independent and critically informed analyses of education and development.

Louisy's challenge to Caribbean researchers to engage more firmly in comparative studies from their own cultural perspective is particularly apposite in this context. Her respect for cultural sensitivity also reflects the influence of what has been called the 'literary turn' in the Social Sciences and the emergence of narrative research as a way of exploring the impact of cultural differences and identity on learning. For those wishing to pursue innovative studies of this nature, work by Jessop and Penny and O'Sullivan and recent doctoral research by Cross usefully illustrates the narrative potential within a comparative and international framework.

As with our review of problems and difficulties encountered in this field of study, in concluding here it is pertinent to emphasise the increased significance of theoretical and philosophical issues that has consistently emerged from our critical reflections. In doing this, however, we argue that greater attention to such issues also, somewhat paradoxically, holds much potential for the improvement of educational policy and practice. It is therefore again to improved dialogue and to a strengthening of the relationship between theory and practice that we look for advances in the future. As much of our analysis suggests, well-grounded theorising can make a most significant contribution to our collective understandings of problems, and to our assessment of appropriate ways forward in improving educational policy and practice.

To some extent this is well reflected in Apple's commitment to theoretical perspectives and the critique of neo-liberal projects - but, to cite his own words, in a way:

> *that examines their class,* and *race* and *gender effects at the level of who benefits from their specific institutionalisations and from their contradictory functions within real terrains of social power.*

Theoretical work on globalisation, as we have shown, also most clearly demonstrates the limitations of the traditional nation-state framework for analysis. Ilon's conceptualisation of three global (and hierarchical) tiers of education, for instance, has major implications for our understandings of new transnational class formations and for the implications of this for future work on inequalities relating to class, race and gender. This certainly demonstrates the potential of new comparative and international perspectives and the limitations of the more familiar and orthodox focus upon national level analyses.

Theoretical and methodological reconceptualisations also point down-wards as well as upwards in scale as Bray and Thomas's diagrammatic representation for multi-level analysis so well illustrates. In prioritising only selected themes here, however, our own concluding comments highlight the significance of studies that explore the relationship between the global, the national and, most importantly, the local levels. It is at the local level where, we suggest, differing perspectives, priorities and problems are more likely to surface given the greater likelihood of common values and world views being held by global and national elites.

With methodological implications more firmly in mind, the latter argument further reinforces our own commitment to participatory and qualitative forms of research that engage with a diversity of stakeholders and cultures at the grass-roots level. This can be interpreted in ways that focus upon the classroom and professional cultures of pupils and teachers or, in a broader way, to post-colonial analyses of the indigenous languages and cultures of marginalised groups in society. This has further potential to contribute to the democratisation of research processes, and highlights the increased centrality of reflexivity at all levels in our vision for the future of disciplined and context-sensitive comparative and international research in education.

Returning to our ongoing critique of the demarcation of historical phases for the field, increased reflexivity does much to reveal the benefits to be gained from a more cross-cultural reconceptualisation of the history of comparative and international education. This helps to demonstrate the diversity of comparative educations that our analysis recognises as, perhaps, one of the greatest strengths of the field. Such critiques also help to re-value the role of legitimate historical analysis in comparative and international education, as we ourselves, and writers such as Sweeting and Kazamias, advocate. Bray and Gui demonstrate, however, that there are many different histories of comparative and international education that are still to be written. This is, in itself, an exciting prospect for the future.

SUBSTANTIVE AND ORGANISATIONAL IMPLICATIONS

The articulation of our reconceptualisation thesis has equally diverse implications in substantive and organisational terms. It is not appropriate to revisit the detail of our earlier considerations here, but, in concluding, we can, again, usefully reflect upon their broader, collective significance. A diversity of substantive issues will clearly continue to command attention and emphasise the perspectives of different stakeholders in the future. Many of these issues will also continue to reflect current internationally recognised priorities, such as ongoing improvements to the quality of education, lifelong learning, advances in information and communications technologies, or the role of education in poverty alleviation worldwide. Consistent with our theoretical and methodological reflections, however, our earlier analysis suggests that many new research priorities will be derived from increased sensitivity to the impact of culture and context upon both educational research and educational development. A field that reconstructs itself along lines suggested here, will certainly prioritise new substantive issues for attention that are related to aspects of culture, difference and identity formation. Comparative studies of values education have, for example, recently pointed to the increasingly individualistic aspirations of elites worldwide even within cultures and systems that have traditionally emphasised collectivity. While we have shown that the latter decades of the twentieth century were dominated by economic priorities the impact of economic globalisation has, somewhat paradoxically, heightened awareness of cultural dilemmas that the field of comparative and international education is especially well placed to examine. Already, innovative cross-cultural research is beginning to show how intensified globalisation has different effects in different contexts adding further legitimacy for new themes in comparative and international research. Future research on the growing 'digital divide' within and between nations could illustrate this well, but case studies of globally inspired initiatives such as the African Virtual University are also pertinent.

The implications of reconceptualisation extend to the organisational arena in other related ways, reflecting the changes in geopolitical relations that we have noted throughout. Recognising worldwide advocacy for partnerships in all walks of life, the June 2002 G8 Meeting of world leaders, for example, emphasised its support for the New Partnership for African Development (NEPAD). Reflecting South African President Mbeki's rationale for the African Renaissance, the NEPAD initiative is itself based upon enhanced African self-determination and on active and critical engagement with the global economy. Similarly, in the arena of comparative and international education, it is argued that the revitalisation of the field will benefit greatly from the strengthening of partnerships between Northern and Southern agencies and personnel; from increased cross-cultural collaboration; from greater openness and permeability of disciplinary and professional boundaries; from new on-line and other international networks that may generate innovative forms of enquiry; and from greater collective efforts to advance the work of collegial and collaborative bodies such as NORRAG or the WCCES.

New journals that are being founded in both the North and the South are already contributing to the organisational revitalisation of the field. Taking advantage of computerised technologies, for example, a new on-line *European Educational Research Journal* was begun in 2002, aiming to foster clearer communication between researchers, policy-makers and teachers. Another such initiative is the on-line journal *Current Issues in Comparative Education* (CICE) run largely by graduate students from Teachers College, Columbia University, New York. This example also draws attention to the importance of the field finding new ways, such as this, to involve and induct future generations of researchers into the field. It is they who have many innovative ideas to contribute and on whom the future health of the field depends.

In a related vein, many of the changes that we have outlined have significant implications for university teaching related to the broad area of comparative and international education. As we have noted elsewhere, in many cases this teaching has also been directly influenced by the emergent research orientation. Today teaching in the field is therefore less closely associated with initial teacher education than it once was, and it is more likely to feature in programmes of continuing professional development or research training. This has implications for the organisation, focus and content of university programmes that deserve greater attention in their own right. Building upon Comparative and International Education Society (CIES) and WCCES deliberations about teaching within the field, a framework for analysis has thus been proposed in a related study to the present volume. In this, Tikly and Crossley examine 'whether or not it is appropriate to integrate comparative and international teaching more firmly into other courses and programs of study'. Recognising a diversity of possible responses, however, the overall aim of this work is to add to the ongoing debate about teaching, while exploring different ways of contributing to the future organisational strength of the field of comparative and international education. As with the present work, we hope this contribution will encourage others to engage with the issues, and advance the various debates, and related developments, further.

LOOKING TO THE FUTURE

It is argued that the current resurgence of interest in comparative and international education generates many exciting possibilities for the future. Our own intellectual journey in this volume suggests that the diversity of forms that are increasingly being encountered is perhaps best visualised as a creative, and multi-disciplinary, constellation of fields. While there is also much that lends coherence to the global field, there are, indeed, many comparative educations. This generates both strengths and weaknesses. Our core thesis further suggests that a thorough reconceptualisation of the field has distinctive theoretical, methodological, substantive and organisational implications. Central to this essential reconceptualisation process, we argue, is a need to bridge this diversity of cultures and traditions more effectively, in a way that capitalises more appropriately upon their combined potential. This recognises the creative strengths of differing perspectives, but acknowledges how improved dialogue across traditional boundaries – be they cultural, regional, disciplinary, paradigmatic, professional or other – has much to offer advances in comparative and international research in education for the future.

The analysis presented here inevitably reflects our own specific interests, backgrounds and experience, although, in the spirit of the book's original rationale, we have tried to capture and reflect upon the diversity and complexity of the field as a whole. In doing so the reconceptualisation that we envisage reveals both similarities and major differences between past and present work – and an imperative to look back, while anticipating new directions for the future. This is reflected in the re-valuing of philosophical, historical and cultural modes of enquiry that emerges consistently from our analysis. Thus, for example, while intensified globalisation has been largely financially and economically driven, we have argued that many of the contemporary human dilemmas that have been generated have, essentially, political and cultural foundations and implications.

To some extent this further underpins the resurgence, again in new and creative formations, of the humanitarian dimension of comparative and international research in education. As McCarthy points out in considering the place of culture in the future of education, 'the complexities of this world must not be masked, but addressed and confronted, in the multi-cultural world that rages into the twenty-first century'. Highlighting the relationship between education, cultural identity and the fragility of current international relations reveals much comparative and international evidence to suggest that, 'cultural pluralism within nations and cultural dialogue across nations is more urgent than ever before'.

Moreover, our review of changes in research approaches adopted within the field reveals how improved understanding of many contemporary educational problems is increasingly emerging from insights derived from innovative, constructivist, interpretive and critical research paradigms. Certainly, we can see how the field of comparative and international education has done much to demonstrate the dangers of overly positivistic assumptions, and the uncritical international transfer of educational policy and practice from one context to another. We do, however, suggest that this critique also applies more to the contemporary transfer of educational theory and research methodologies than is often recognised. The advancement of theoretical and 'scientific' knowledge is undoubtedly of great importance, but the comparative and international field is particularly well placed to highlight the complexities and dilemmas involved in knowledge transfer. In this regard, our own position acknowledges the insights that can be derived from the poststructuralist critique, and from the potential of the interpretivist – hermeneutic paradigm. We therefore agree with Stenhouse's helpful observation that comparative research 'deals in insight rather than law as a basis for understanding', and that such research is therefore best used to help 'tutor our judgement' on matters of policy and practice elsewhere.

There is, therefore, much to be gained from a re-reading of earlier work within this complex field – but in the critical light of more contemporary philosophical, epistemological and cross-cultural advances. The development of an innovative on-line library of classic, but out of print, comparative education texts by the Comparative Education Research Centre at the University of Hong Kong and Teachers College, Columbia University, New York, is thus one timely and pertinent bridge between past and present scholarship.

Our overall analysis, however, is distinctly forward looking and one that fundamentally challenges the linear phases representation of the field that is so prominent in much of the traditional Western literature. We therefore argue for a clearer future vision of the diverse field of comparative and international research in education, within which different paradigms and cultural perspectives can creatively co-exist. In proposing this, our reconceptualisation therefore calls for much improved dialogue between the various stakeholders and constituencies in the spirit of the bridging of cultures and traditions rationale articulated earlier. This we believe has considerable potential for both theoretical advancement and for the improvement of educational policy and practice worldwide.

This points, again, to the need for more holistic understandings of education in its diverse contexts, to the role of increased reflexivity and critical reflection in the research process, and to the related and still rarely addressed need for increased attention to the new ethical dimensions necessitated by the advancement of cross-cultural research. Bond, for example, draws attention to the difficulties faced in constructing contemporary pan-European statements of professional ethics, in a way that has considerable potential for comparative and international researchers in other fields including education.

The differences between past and future research that we envisage within the field of comparative and international education are therefore both deep and comprehensive. Our reconceptualisation thesis recognises the past achievements and the contemporary potential of the field, but it poses fundamental challenges that have substantial implications for the theoretical, methodological, substantive and organisational dimensions of comparative and international research in education. In examining these issues we have also suggested various ways forward, and have begun to explore how those engaged in such work may make further creative contributions in the future.

Finally, the arguments pursued here highlight the contemporary significance of context and culture throughout our analysis. Concern with context is perhaps the most enduring characteristic of disciplined comparative and international research in education. It is also central but in many different ways to the proposed reconceptualisation of the field. Increased sensitivity to context underpins the importance of new comparative work from a diversity of cultural perspectives. It is also central to post-colonial theorising; to the critique of globalisation; to the rationale for differing and multiple units of analysis; to the re-valuing of comparisons over time; to improved reflexivity; and to many proposed strategies to bridge the gap between research and educational policy and practice. In looking to the future, therefore, it is argued that context matters more than ever as we search – with justifiably renewed enthusiasm – for new directions in the field of comparative and international research in education.

❏❏❏

14

Pedagogical and Investigating Identity of the Teacher

INTRODUCTION

Values and norms form a complex field of personal existentialism, of principles that give people's life and community significance (values), and rules which regulate interaction between people (norms). In the past, public debate about the task of education in this matter has regularly cropped up in times of moral crises and disappeared again for a certain time.

The importance of the pedagogical task of the school appears to be increasing as a result of the processes of modernization. Many people have loosened themselves from social class, family, marriage, employment, politics, the church, and the neighbourhood. In addition, it is frequently pointed out that, as a result of various social developments (e.g., combined motherhood- employment, an increasing number of single-parent families), parents are spending less time on child rearing than before and children are spending increasingly more time outside the family.

In his book, *Building Community in Schools*, Sergiovanni suggests how teachers, parents, and school administrators can contribute to the development of a 'community of mind' with shared values and opinions on the school. The school community should, in the opinion of Sergiovanni, be rebuilt into a community in which moral obligations, trust, and communal behaviour replace the business, contractual, and formal organizational approach that currently predominates. Schools must take on more of the characteristics of a true community. Safe schools where children feel secure and at home are also advocated. 'Community formation' is said to be critical for the achievement, personal functioning (*i.e.*, greater well-being), and social participation (i.e., less absenteeism, greater social skills) of students. Moreover, the relation of the school and the social surroundings should be strengthened. A case is indeed increasingly being made for a 'community school' with anchors in the local community. Parents and school must work together to raise moral children.

In the discussion of the pedagogical task of the school, considerable importance is attached to the specific role of the teacher. In relation to the question of the significance for the teacher for the development of students' norms and values, it is important to determine teachers' perceptions of their pedagogical professionality and the goals of child rearing. It is important to consider how teachers think about the distribution of tasks between the school and family. Consideration of the pedagogical co-operation between the parents and the school is also important to consider.

The objectives of child rearing

The objectives of child rearing can be taken to be the general background criteria used by teachers to make choices and guide their behaviour. In the literature, a few hypotheses have been put forth with regard to the problematic relation between parents and teachers when it comes to joint child-rearing responsibility. From research by Cullingford, it appears that parents expect the school primarily to prepare their child for employment and concentrate on the acquisition of good manners. In contrast, teachers tend to attach more importance to the development of individual autonomy and social objectives. Teachers are of the opinion that the teaching of good manners is a task for parents. Goodlad had also concluded that, in contrast to teachers, parents place more emphasis on the professional as opposed to personal development of children. According to Kohn, a distinction can be made between two fundamental and mutually exclusive value orientations with regard to child rearing: self-determination versus conformity. This deeper distinction underlies apparently very different value orientations. In addition to the two value orientations of self-determination and conformity, attention will also be paid to opinions on social sensitivity.

In discussions pertaining to the pedagogical task of the school, considerable attention has been paid to the social aspects of child rearing. It is thus interesting in this connection to examine the extent to which an orientation towards self-determination is accompanied by an orientation towards more social goals. Independent students need not be socially sensitive students. To overcome a more egoistic form of self-determination in the present study, it was decided to include the category of social sensitivity. A fourth category of child-rearing objectives pertains to skills or the competence to think and communicate about values and norms. In various methods of value discourse, attention to such skills is assumed to be important. A final category of child-rearing objectives examined in the present research is the acquisition of such virtues as those propagated by proponents of 'character' education. This approach is concerned with developing virtue. The proponents of character education think that education should not engage students in complex moral dilemma's such as in Kohlberg's moral reasoning approach, but try to further the cause of virtue by positioning the teacher as moral authority.

Pedagogical attunement

Yet another basic concept utilized in the present research is pedagogical attunement (*i.e.*, the relation between the school and parents). The importance of this relation lies in the assumption that the attunement of ideas with regard to child rearing requires regular contact between parents and teachers on the issue. In research concerned with the relation between parents and school, attention is particularly paid to the activities that schools expect of parents and much less to the attempts on the part of the schools to improve the parent-school relation. The degree of participation by parents in school activities is frequently employed to categorize parents as involved or not involved. Research into the minimal participation of parents from lower social classes in school activities indicates a variety of reasons that underlie the phenomenon. Important causes of the observed discrepancy are the gap between the expectations of the school and the possibilities on the part of the parents to meet these expectations, the educational experiences of the parents themselves, status differences between the parents and the teachers, limited motivation for involvement, lack of time, and so forth. Research on the involvement of parents typically pertains to a wide variety of activities in which the parents can participate: hands-on assistance, administrative – technical help, directly educational activities, and educational steering activities. This sequence is also often adopted as the starting point to motivate parents via lower forms of participation (hands-on assistance) to higher forms of participation (educational steering activities). The problem is that all kinds of activities are expected of parents without mutual attunement. It is necessary, therefore, to examine the activities that schools develop to involve parents in the school and, in particular, meetings and thinking with regard to child rearing (*i.e.* educational steering activities). In this light, it is also important to examine the explanations offered by the teachers themselves for the lack of participation of parents in school activities and how the teachers interact with parents who are rarely or completely not involved in the school.

Framed against the above perspectives, the research reported in this chapter raises two central questions:

1. What are teachers' perceptions of the aims of child rearing and the distribution of tasks between the school and family?
2. What are teachers' expectations with regard to pedagogical attunement?

QUANTITATIVE AND QUALITATIVE RESEARCH METHODS

Respondents

A total of fifty-three teachers of children between 7 and 11 years of age participated in the present study. The research provides a broad picture of the various opinions of teachers with regard to the content (objectives) and attunement problems (family-school relations). With this aim in mind, it was deliberately decided to select a small number of schools (six) for study.

Design and variables

A combination of quantitative and qualitative research methods were utilized. First, the opinions of teachers with regard to the objectives of child rearing and pedagogical attunement were measured via the administration of a questionnaire in six schools. Second, the results of the questionnaire were explored in greater detail by undertaking group interviews with a select sample of teachers in all of the six schools.

The questionnaire

The questionnaire solicited the opinions of the teachers with regard to the objectives of child rearing and pedagogical attunement. The variables concerned with the aims of child rearing were operationalized as follows: *self-determination*: building self-confidence; taking responsibility; entertaining one's own opinion; perseverance; a desire to understand things, curiosity; independence; autonomy; *conformity*: obedience, listening to adults; sensitivity to order and discipline; adapting to rules and other views; respect for others; good manners; *social sensitivity*: helpfulness; respect for those who think differently; concern for the happiness and pain of others; consideration for others; non-discrimination of others; tolerance; solidarity with others; *skills*: be open to the opinions of others; think critically; promote one's opinions; deal with critique; *virtues*: honesty; justice; self-discipline; reliability; a sense of duty. The teachers were asked about the extent to which they considered these objectives important for child rearing at school or in the family. The items were measured with the aid of a five-point scale (not important, a little important, neither important/unimportant, quite important, very important). With regard to the operationalizing of the concept of pedagogical attunement, it was decided to formulate the items with respect to content aspects (objectives, measures), communicate aspects (providing information, listening) and pedagogical aspects (behaviour, values). A number of different statements were than presented to the respondents. The items were also measured with the aid of a five-point scale (disagree completely, disagree somewhat, do not agree/disagree, agree somewhat, agree completely). The response of the teachers was quite satisfactory. More than 75 per cent of the teachers (*i.e.*, fifty-three teachers) participated in the questionnaire research. Of the participating teachers, 69.5 per cent were female and 30.2 per cent were male.

The group interviews

Group interviews were undertaken with teachers in all of the schools to gain greater insight into the results of the questionnaire. Considerable attention was paid to clarifying the manner in which the teachers interpreted the notions employed within the questionnaire. In all of the schools, interviews were undertaken with a group of six teachers in the autumn of 1997. A prerequisite for participation in the group interview was completion of the questionnaire.

Analysis

The questionnaire data were examined using factor and descriptive analysis. For the analysis of the group interviews, the audio recordings were fully transcribed. The answers to all of the questions posed as part of the protocol were then categorized into the relevant rubric. For purposes of reliability, all of the transcribed texts were analyzed by two researchers and agreement sought where discrepancies occurred.

QUANTITATIVE RESEARCH RESULTS

The objectives of child rearing

In the questionnaire, the opinions of the teachers regarding the objectives of child rearing were measured by way of three rubrics: (1) the importance generally attached by teachers to a specific child-rearing objective; (2) the attention to be paid to a specific child-rearing objective at home; and (3) the attention to be paid to a specific child-rearing objective at school. Factor analyses revealed two factors for each rubric. The factors explained 40.2, 43.5, and 43.9 per cent of the variance from the general, home and school rubrics, respectively. The interpretation of the factor solutions appeared to be the same for the different rubrics. The first factor consistently reflects a pattern of opinion concerned with self-determination and social sensitivity. The second factor consistently refers to aspects of obedience and conformity.

Table 14.1. Varimax-rotated factor matrix, communality (h2), and percentage variance explained for the General Child-Rearing rubric.

Child-rearing objective	**f1**	**f2**	**h2**
General			
Justice	0.52	0.16	0.30
Respect for those who think differently	0.67	0.15	0.47
Taking others into consideration	0.57	0.26	0.40
Non-discrimination	0.61	0.16	0.40
Tolerance	0.62	0.27	0.46
Solidarity with others	0.54	0.31	0.39
Openness to the opinions of others	0.61	0.11	0.38
Critical thinking	0.61	?0.07	0.38
Capacity to justify one's own opinion	0.64	?0.03	0.41
Able to handle critique	0.57	0.24	0.39
Carrying responsibility	0.52	0.17	0.30
Have one's own opinion	0.53	0.15	0.30
Desire to know why certain things occur, inquisitiveness	0.50	0.16	0.28
Independent thinking and behaviour	0.54	0.07	0.30
Obedient, listens to adults	0.04	0.72	0.52
Feeling for discipline and order	0.16	0.65	0.45
Adapt to applicable rules and opinions	0.14	0.73	0.56
Respect for your elders	0.15	0.74	0.57
Having good manners	0.21	0.59	0.39
% Explained variance	30.3	9.8	40.2

Pedagogical attunement

Factor analyses produced two factors, which together explained 49.3 per cent of the variance. Given that the factors highly correlated (0.65) after oblimin rotation, the factor matrix following such rotation was utilized in further analyses. The factors can be described as follows. The first factor pertains to the accessibility of the school and the teachers for parents and the general information provided by the school and teachers. This factor is therefore referred to as service institution. The second factor specifically concerns the contact that the school has and maintains with the parents with regard to values, norms, and other child-rearing matters. This factor is, therefore, referred to as communication on child rearing.

To determine the internal consistency of the questionnaire scales, reliability analyses were undertaken. For each scale, a scale score was calculated in the form of an average item score. The reliability estimates for the scales related to the rubrics of general, home, school and pedagogical attunement are reported. All of the scales appear to be reliable.

Table 14.2. Factor matrix following oblimin rotation (pattern matrix); communality (h2) and percentages explained variance for the rubric pedagogical attunement.

Pedagogical attunement	f1	f2	h2
Parents are adequately informed with regard to practical matters	0.43	0.13	0.27
The teacher is prepared to listen to parents	0 .92	?0.17	0.68
If problems occur at school, consultation is possible	0.52	0.21	0.46
Parents are not taken seriously by the school	?0.47	0.10	0.29
The school provides parents with little information on the work attitude of their child	?0.34	0.15	0.20
The school administration is accessible	0.68	0.07	0.52
The school administration is prepared to listen to parents	0.69	0.13	0.62
I'm very accessible	0 .91	?0.14	0.69
Parents can participate in discussions of value and norm questions	0.04	0.72	0.57
I always contact parents in cases of a problem in time	0.22	0.56	0.52
Parents can influence the child-rearing ideas of the school	?0.01	0.65	0.41
Parents are adequately informed with regard to content matters (objectives, manner of working)	0.13	0.64	0.54
Parents are adequately informed about the values and norms that the school considers important	?0.08	0.84	0.64
% Explained variance	41.9	7.4	49.3

Descriptive statistics

In Table 14.4, the descriptive statistics for each of the scales are presented. Most striking is that the teachers consider all of the child-rearing objectives to be important. At home and school, attention should be paid to the development of independence, social sensitivity and more conformity-directed objectives. The respondents appear to be satisfied with the school as a service institution (score: 4.59). With regard to communication on child rearing, however, teachers are less satisfied (score: 3.92).

QUALITATIVE RESEARCH RESULTS

Group interviews

As already mentioned, a protocol for the group interviews with the teachers was developed on the basis of the questionnaire results. The following questions were posed: Why do you think attention to self-determination and social sensitivity are important?

What do the notions of self-determination and social sensitivity mean? Do you think it is logical for self-determination and social sensitivity to go together? What is the importance and meaning of the notion of conformity? What is the distribution of tasks between parents and school in the domain of child rearing? Are you satisfied with this distribution of tasks? Why are you less satisfied with communication on child rearing? Are parents sufficiently informed about the child-rearing ideas of the school? How could communication on child rearing be improved?

Objectives of child-rearing and distribution of tasks

Teachers consider attention to the development of independence and social sensitivity both at home and at school to be very important. Educational and professional demands make the realization of these objectives a necessity in the eyes of teachers. A society that is continually getting harder and thereby demands that you stand up for yourself is also continually mentioned: 'You have to take a stand certainly in this society. Things are getting so hard if you look around you. A kid has to stand up for himself 'cause if he doesn't he ends up in the middle of nowhere.' In addition, the realization of the aforementioned child-rearing objectives is considered important for the functioning of children at school, allowing all kinds of group activities to run effectively and for the personal development of the child.

Table 14.3. Reliability estimates (Cronbach's Alpha) for scales representing the opinions of teachers with regard to the objectives of child-rearing and pedagogical attunement (N=328)

Category	Number of items	Cronbach's Alpha
Child-rearing objectives		
Self-determination/social sensitivity	14	0.8864
Conformity	5	0.8293
Child-rearing objectives Home		
Self-determination/social sensitivity	16	0.9185
Conformity	5	0.8289
Child-rearing objectives School		
Self-determination/social sensitivity	14	0.9066
Conformity	5	0.8246
Pedagogical attunement		
Service institution	8	0.8603
Communication with regard to child rearing	5	0.8484

When asked about the meaning of the notion self-determination, teachers think of making one's own decisions, solving problems, performing tasks independently, expressing one's opinion, and thinking critically. When asked about the meaning of the notion of social sensitivity, consideration for others and helping one another are mentioned in particular. Another qualification involves the embedding of the notion of self-determination within a particular social context. According to many teachers, self-determination is primarily aimed at the development of the personality of the child in current times with some room for social sensitivity while the notion had a much more individualistic reading in the sixties.

Table 14.4. Descriptive statistics for opinions on the objectives of child rearing and pedagogical attunement for teachers.

Source	Teacher n=47	
	mean	**sd**
Objectives		
Self-determination/social-sensitivity (G)	4.63	0.32
Conformity (G)	4.18	0.73
Self-determination/social-sensitivity (H)	4.57	0.37
Conformity (H)	4.28	0.72
Self-determination/social-sensitivity (S)	4.52	0.39
Conformity (S)	4.03	0.74
Pedagogical attunement		
Service institution	4.59	0.34
Child-rearing communication	3.92	0.45

Teachers are also of the opinion that such notions as self-determination and social sensitivity cannot be considered independent of each other. They agree that the development of independence without some social sensitivity can lead to an egoistic form of individualism: 'Independence alone threatens to become something egoistic. You can be independent but you have to have a certain social feeling because you simply have to do things together at times.' Conversely, it is argued that the development of social sensitivity without attention to independence can lead to submissive behaviour and the neglect of one's own interests. 'When only social sensitivity is aspired to, you get people who completely ignore their own self-worth.' The meaning of the notion of social sensitivity should not, in the opinion of teachers, be construed as being blindly oriented towards the group.

In addition to these objectives, teachers emphasized the importance of attention at both home and school to more conformist objectives. The motives behind this lie in the battle against the indifference and survival mentality that prevail in the current chaotic and complex society. Most teachers consider conformity a 'condition' for functioning in society in general and in the school and family in particular. Rules, agreements, and good manners are needed to live together. Conformity is similarly seen as a prerequisite for the personal development and social behavior of students: 'You cannot have respect for another or express such respect without good manners. You are also more quickly pushed aside in a group, I think, when you behave rudely or without manners. In other words, it is good to have good manners.' The notion of conformity is interpreted as the provision of structure and creation of a peaceful and secure environment in which the formulation of rules, making of concrete agreements with children and consistent behaviour on the part of teachers are taken to be of great importance.

Of particular importance for pedagogical attunement are the opinions of the teachers with regard to the distribution of tasks in the area of child rearing, values, and norms. According to many teachers, a strict division does not exist between the two. The child-rearing role of the school is generally viewed as an extension of the child-rearing role of the parents or caregivers. The child-rearing tasks overlap and should, according to teachers, be attuned as much as possible to each other. The school and the parents should also supplement each other whenever and wherever necessary. Teachers are, nevertheless, of the opinion that the primary responsibility for child rearing lies with the parents.

The interviews with the teachers showed them to be quite critical of the manner in which parents raise their children. Teachers are of the opinion that parents provide their children with too little structure and impose insufficient demands on their children: 'A general experience for me is that children from families where real rules dominate and life is very secure, very structured and very pleasant but five o'-clock is five o'-clock tend to get along better and easier with other children than children who are left to decide for themselves. The latter miss the security needed as a base for functioning.' Teachers thus plead for greater peace in the family (*i.e.* children are saddled with too many social obligations according to teachers) and more consistent behaviour on the part of the parents when rules are broken or agreements are not met. A consequence of such child-rearing behaviour is, according to teachers, a shift of responsibility from the family to the school. According to teachers, parents brush their child-rearing responsibilities aside too easily and currently invest insufficient time in the rearing of their own children. The school is thus forced to invest extra time in child-rearing tasks to compensate for various shortcomings. 'I think we are more and more busy with child-rearing objectives that are obviously part of our task but not to the degree that we are now sometimes saddled with. I consider learning to listen and being motivated while you work to be child-rearing objectives as well. We have to fight much harder now to get children to a certain point. They don't get this from home. Some of them do, of course, but many of them don't.'

Pedagogical attunement

Parents are informed of school activities and expectations through information booklets, newsletters and information evenings as well as through parent evenings, some of which are organized around specific topics. The results of the group interviews show teachers to be generally happy with this aspect of the pedagogical attunement. A complaint shared by teachers concerns a particular group of parents.

The questionnaire showed teachers to be less satisfied with the relationship between parents and school when it comes to communication on child-rearing tasks. According to many teachers, child rearing is only an issue when a concrete problem presents itself (e.g., disagreements, bullying); parents are generally not aware of the child-rearing ideas of the school itself. 'I think that parents don't know how we work. I sometimes notice this in conversations. They are suddenly much more enthusiastic when they know how we are working with the children, although this depends on the individual parents.' Most schools also lack a useful child-rearing policy. Two reasons for the lack of communication were presented in the group interviews. First, the emotionally charged nature of the topic, which gives a discussion on the topic a threatening character. 'Child rearing has certainly become a subject of discussion over the last years but as a failure in the eyes of some if one was to be honest: yeah, I have a problem with my child and wonder what I should do.' In addition to this, an (unconscious) presupposition exists on the part of teachers that the communication of information sufficiently meets the needs of parents. This appears to be a misconception in most cases. There is generally too little consultation. Teachers know virtually nothing about what the parents think of the child rearing at school. Teachers also make very little effort to understand the real reasons why parents are not more involved in the activities and policies of the school.

SUMMARY

Teachers consider all of the child-rearing objectives to be important. At home and school, attention should be paid to the development of independence, critical thinking, social sensitivity and more conformity-directed objectives. The interviews strongly suggest that the objectives of self-determination and social sensitivity are not independent of each other. Self-determination without social sensitivity can lead to an egoistic form of individualism. In the child-rearing expectation of teachers, the citizenship ideal of autonomy appears to be attached by definition to the carrying of social responsibility. The interviews indicate that teachers consider attention to conformist objectives particularly important to combat currently prevailing indifference in our complex society. The notion of conformity is not associated with (authoritarian) behaviour aimed at the creation of submissive behaviour. Rather, it appears that teachers consider the child-rearing objective of conformity to be a prerequisite for functioning in society, the family, and the school. Attention to conformity is also considered a prerequisite for the personal development and social functioning of the child.

Teachers believe that parents neglect attention to conformist ideas while this is partly a consequence of inadequate communication between parents and schools when it comes to child-rearing issues. Parents generally know too little about the child-rearing ideas of the school; teachers know virtually nothing about the child-rearing ideas of the parents. Child rearing is only an issue when a concrete problem presents itself. As a consequence, teachers form images of parents that are far removed from actual child-rearing practice. It is obvious that such images do not contribute to adequate pedagogical attunement between school and family.

How should the results now be evaluated? It is clear that no single procedure exists to realize adequate pedagogical attunement between school and family. Teaching and child rearing are much too complicated for this. Various studies have shown that involvement on the part of parents positively influences the general well-being and school achievement of students.

However, in a climate where there are increasing and often conflicting demands on teachers, to the point of overload, time for better and more frequent communication between home and school is not propitious. This situation is exacerbated by present-day discussions with regard to school effectiveness that, in turn, influences parents in their choice of school. In research concerned with the effective school, the cognitive achievements of students stand central. The educational-learning process is thereby reduced to the pursuit of objectively measurable and comparable knowledge goals. Such a vision of education is particularly welcome, moreover, in these times with an emphasis on productivity, efficiency, and return. In the discussion of school selection motives, consideration of parents as consumers on the educational market is also increasingly the case. Parents are continually confronted with the question of which criteria should be used to select a school for their children. To lend parents a helping hand, the different research directions are often now connected to each other in social science and public discussions. The achievement performances of schools are presented in guidebooks to enable parents to make a responsible choice on the basis of objectively determined information. Once again, the information pertains to cognitive achievements only of students in different schools. The evaluation of schools on the basis of these criteria only constitutes a very limited approach to the problem. In such an approach, the social, moral, aesthetic, and affective aims of education are continually marginalized. One possible consequence is that schools direct themselves at the cognitive aspects of the educational process because they are evaluated in these terms. In other words; if attention to the non-cognitive aims of education is not appreciated, then teachers will not invest much time or energy in the establishment of a child-rearing dialogue with parents.

Another dimension of this issue concerns the specific knowledge, skills, and attitudes that teachers require to conduct a well-structured dialogue with parents on the issue of child rearing. Research has shown traditional forms of participation (information evenings, report consultations, parent nights) to be generally characterized by a one-sided transfer of information from the school in the direction of the parents. For the establishment and maintenance of a dialogue between the school and parents on the topic of child rearing, it is more important to place the accent on the mutual exchange of information and experiences. To realize this, traditional forms of participation should be critically examined and alternative possibilities carefully considered. Of central importance, of course, is the creation of a climate in which both parents and teachers feel free to talk about their visions on child rearing. Research shows communication on child rearing to be experienced by many teachers as emotionally charged and therefore silent. Familiar relations must be created for a dialogue on the topic of child-rearing to be successful. Many teachers may experience feelings of impotence because they are insufficiently qualified for the realization of such initiatives. In addition to this, many teachers may experience a discussion with regard to pedagogical attunement as a clear threat to their pedagogical autonomy. Nevertheless, successful pedagogical attunement between school and family means that teachers must account for their pedagogical practices much more than before. Schools are not very interested in critiques of their policies. Communication on such a sensitive topic as child rearing is possible only when all of the parties concerned consider that their perspectives and concerns are being taken seriously.

To get values' education at school and the pedagogical attunement between schools and families sufficiently off the ground, research will have to concentrated on school activities intended to stimulate the pursuit of the social, emotional, affective, and esthetic objectives of education. It will also be interesting to consider the extent to which attention to the non-cognitive aims of education affect the well-being and non-cognitive development of students. The possible connections between the non-cognitive and cognitive achievements of students should also be examined in future research. Such research should also address the different organizational and professional facets of school practice that may hinder communication within the school with regard to child-rearing issues. Finally, there is need to investigate how teachers can increase their competence and confidence to establish and maintain a dialogue with the external school environment.

15

Sources of Teachers' Learning

INTRODUCTION

Teachers need technical skills to work effectively with their students in the information age. Teachers need to be up-to-date in their subject area. Teachers at all levels and across disciplines need to be able to teach reading. In policy circles, 'knowing more' often is treated synonymously with 'teaching better'.

Certainly, knowledge of new practices is essential for teachers to improve instruction for today's classrooms and prepare students for a productive role in the twenty-first century workforce. Yet more or better content knowledge by itself cannot necessarily accomplish much. For one, simply having more and better knowledge resources available does not mean that teachers will or can use them effectively in their classrooms. But equally as important, teachers require more than content knowledge to construct the sorts of educational environments reformers hope for and contemporary students need. For example, teachers need to know how to engage students in content knowledge, how to allocate time and attention, how to articulate standards appropriate for practice. Teachers need to know where to place instructional priority, how students are responding to their classroom choices, how to make adjustments when student achievement disappoints.

Conceptions of teachers' learning that inform policy and practice are similarly underdeveloped. Research on teachers' learning generally is decontextualized and silent on the question of environments that stimulate or frustrate it. Relatively little research looks at how sites and sources of teachers' learning affect teachers' ability and motivation to learn and use new knowledge. Likewise, research on teachers' learning typically is more concerned about the content of teachers' learning than with the processes that stimulate, support and sustain it.

The position that reform initiatives aimed at improving teaching and learning involve distinctly different forms of knowledge, and that these forms of knowledge are generated at different sites and play strategically different roles in teachers' learning and change. I then turn to the character of school communities of practice as both medium and context for teachers' knowledge use, generation, learning and change. This descriptive analysis highlights ways in which policy can affect teachers' learning and support the knowledge they find useful as they seek to make change at their school and in their classrooms.

WHAT KINDS OF KNOWLEDGE DO TEACHERS NEED TO IMPROVE THEIR PRACTICE?

Marilyn Cochran-Smith and Susan Lytle distinguish among three substantively and strategically different conceptions of the knowledge associated with teachers' learning and change: knowledge for practice, knowledge of practice, and knowledge in practice. Cochran-Smith and Lytle define knowledge for practice as the formal knowledge and theory generated by researchers and university-based scholars. Some of this external knowledge comprises new programs or strategies – for example, Success for All, or Reading Recovery programmes are examples of such university-produced knowledge for practice. Other externally developed knowledge for practice involves new theories of learning or instruction, such as reciprocal teaching, cooperative learning, or peer instruction. Knowledge for practice also includes assessments, strategies for research and evaluation, or other inquiry tools such as running records to score students' reading progress.

Knowledge of practice conveys yet another form of knowledge and image of teachers' learning. This second form of knowledge comprises neither formal nor practical knowledge. Knowledge of practice is generated when teachers treat their own classrooms and schools as sites of inquiry and examine them in terms of such broader social and political issues as equity, patterns of student achievement, or school supports for students' futures. Knowledge of practice may be produced by teachers themselves, or may involve data and analysis provided by outside evaluators or researchers – working with or without teachers' involvement.

Knowledge in practice – a third kind of knowledge – is what teachers come to understand as they reflect on their practice, and is situated in their own classrooms. It is practical knowledge. Action research and other forms of classroom-based inquiry support teachers' learning of this sort. Knowledge in practice is individual knowledge, stimulated by teachers' own questions about their own classrooms.

Calls for reform in teaching and learning implicate all three forms of knowledge. Without knowledge for practice, teachers lack the new ideas, skills and perspectives they need to evaluate, enrich or change their practices. Yet, without knowledge of practice, teachers are constrained in their ability to exploit external knowledge, situate it in their particular school workplace, or even understand the need for new ways of doing things. Teachers often do not know what they need to know to address questions of whole school change and to move a faculty forward in a consistent manner. Knowledge of practice enables a faculty to see problem areas in their practice, and to identify opportunities for inquiry and innovation. Knowledge of practice points a faculty to needed external resources and areas for internal improvement.

However absent teachers' knowledge in practice, new ideas may have only uneven or marginal effects on individual classrooms, since they may not reflect the needs and issues specific to any one classroom setting, or since any individual teacher may or may not be interested in how his classroom is located in school-level data. Knowledge in practice informs individual teacher action and reflection, and guides teachers in tailoring resources to best support their everyday work.

ENGAGING MULTIPLE FORMS OF KNOWLEDGE

Most strategies or policies concerned with enhancing teachers' knowledge and learning are single-focus and disjoint. Research and Development efforts aim to provide teachers with the latest in best practices but pay little attention to teachers' motivation or capacity to use that knowledge or sustain changes associated with it. Action researchers focus on teacher-produced knowledge about their classrooms. Yet these individual efforts are seldom seen in terms of the broader school context, or as parts of a whole picture of practice at a site. Reform strategies such as site-based management or school improvement programmes centre attention on school-level knowledge for action, but focus little if at all on the content of those changes and the knowledge resources necessary to support them.

What would a strategy look like that attended simultaneously to all three knowledge domains as sites and sources of teachers' learning? The Bay Area School Reform Collaborative (BASRC) provides the opportunity to see how different forms of knowledge can or do work together to support teachers' learning and change. BASRC, a 5-year reform effort involving schools throughout the 118 district Bay Area region, seeks to 'reculture' schools in ways that support whole school reform.

BASRC strategies aim to change the way schools do business. Merrill Vargo, BASRC's executive director, likes to ask people to complete the sentence: 'The problem with schools today is ' BASRC's design for reform finishes the sentence 'their culture' and posits a missing element in schools' cultures as evidence-based decision making centred on a focused reform effort. BASRC's overall strategy uses a cycle of inquiry to inform school reform efforts, and marshals diverse forms of knowledge to support teachers' learning and change.

The initiative exposes teachers to diverse forms of knowledge for practice. Much of it is content knowledge – resources and technical assistance in such domains as literacy, mathematics, technology and writing. These knowledge resources generally are carried to schools and teachers through so-called Support Providers, organizations contracted by Leadership Schools using their BASRC funds.

The initiative also attends to the learning skills that teachers will need in order to make effective use of that content knowledge. In an effort to foster teachers' capacity and comfort in generating knowledge of, teachers receive training in asking probing questions, in developing an accountability framework to guide their school's cycle of inquiry, and in constructing standards against which to measure their school's progress in their focused reform effort. They practice these skills in many BASRC events. For example, regional meetings of hundreds of Bay Area teachers, administrators, parents, support providers and funders were convened to score schools' portfolio applications for BASRC Leadership School status. Subsequently, regional preparation and reviews Leadership Schools' Reports of Progress immersed teachers in the use of rubrics to evaluate the process on five dimensions of whole school change.

A number of teachers told us that evaluating the portfolios with teachers from around the Bay Area 'was the best professional development I have ever had'. One said, for instance, 'Just reading about other schools and using that rubric forced us to use it well. It taught me about standards and accountability, skill I could take back to my school.' Critical friends visits - a BASRC strategy that brings two or three schools together to consider each others' practice - involve teachers in both giving and receiving critique of practice and school culture. As one teacher put it, '(our Critical Friends) enabled us to look at evidence from a different perspective; we learned about gaps and about what we didn't know'. Affinity groups engaged teachers from across the region in research on topics of their choosing. Through summer institutes for faculty teams from Leadership Schools, BASRC gave teachers tools in other areas important to their success in generating knowledge of practice in their schools - how to run a meeting, how to facilitate a discussion, how to deal with the 'politics of data'.

Teachers' skill in and experience with generating knowledge of and in practice was stimulated initially by their schools' preparation of the Portfolio Application for Leadership School status. BASRC required schools to provide evidence of their status along five dimensions of whole school change and in support of the 'focused effort' they selected to frame their reform efforts. Subsequently, BASRC required that each Leadership School develop and carry out a 'Cycle of Inquiry' to inform their school's reform efforts and to provide data for what BASRC calls an 'accountability event', where the school reports its progress annually to its community - faculty and parents.

BASRC's strategy places as much emphasis on developing teachers' learning and inquiry skills as it did on connecting them with relevant content knowledge. These tools and learning skills, BASRC hoped, would equip teachers to begin to ask questions about their own practices, gather evidence to address those questions, and situate reform efforts in their analyses. In other words, BASRC provided teachers with exposure to and practice with the skills and experience they would need to generate knowledge of and in practice at their own school site.

HOW DID TEACHERS USE NEW KNOWLEDGE TO SUPPORT LEARNING AND CHANGE?

What happened as a result of BASRC's efforts to reculture schools around habits of inquiry and whole school change? Across BASRC Leadership Schools we observe different patterns and processes of teachers' knowledge use, and so of their learning, change efforts and outcomes associated with them.

Not all schools or teachers were able to receive or use knowledge resources in the same way; schools and teachers also differed in the ways in which they approached engaging or generating forms of knowledge in their reform efforts. Some teachers or schools were relatively sophisticated in their thinking about inquiry-based reforms; some teachers wondered out loud 'What's data?' Few schools had experience with the school-based cycle of inquiry and accountability BASRC required – they were experienced in accounting for compliance's sake, but not for their own community of practice.

Over the course of the initiative's 4 years, we have begun to see in Leadership Schools different overall patterns of teachers' knowledge use as well as varied patterns of relations among forms of knowledge. Associated with these different patterns of knowledge generation and use, we find different consequences in terms of changed practices at school and classroom levels. Four general patterns emerged across BASRC Leadership Schools: First Steps, Beginning Inquiry, Getting Comfortable with Inquiry, A Cycle of Inquiry. I sketch them below and highlight the processes of knowledge use and learning we observed in Leadership Schools.

First steps in using knowledge to support learning and change

One pattern could be called 'First Steps'. For some Leadership Schools, BASRC involvement comprised the faculty's first efforts to think about whole school change - either in substantive or strategic terms. First steps were apparent especially in secondary schools where schools rarely thought in whole school terms, but rather in terms of departments, student academic placements or grade levels. Common to secondary schools are so-called Christmas Tree reform efforts, which collect multiple but usually unrelated reform efforts.

The evidence and inquiry BASRC requires of its Leadership Schools was both foreign and threatening to many teachers. 'Why are we doing this data collection stuff?' one teacher asked as she began her involvement with BASRC and was introduced to expectations for assessment and analysis. 'We're not methodologists', said another. This teacher, like many if not most of her colleagues, knew nothing about how to develop standards for assessment, how to go about systematic inquiry into the consequences of practice, or even how to construct the indicators that would be most meaningful to practice and action.

In schools taking their first steps towards whole school change based on a cycle of inquiry, teachers engaged support providers to provide assistance with their focused effort and made tentative, usually difficult and painful, efforts to think about what evidence and inquiry at the school level would mean or require. Teachers in these schools attended BASRC workshops on accountability and standards, but often found them inadequate in the light of their inexperience and anxiety about inquiry at the school level. These faculties often turned to their support providers for help with figuring out what measures would be meaningful in their schools, and strategies for collecting evidence about their work.

A major element frustrating the inquiry process in 'first step' schools was a contrary normative climate of the school which made teachers' work and student outcomes largely a private matter, and cast accountability as something done to, not for, the school. The learning most evident as schools began their journey as Leadership Schools was about new forms of practice. For many teachers, it was the first time in many years they had taken a hard look at what they were doing and thought about alternatives. For example a veteran teacher, working in a tough elementary school setting told us that BASRC opened my mind to certain strategies and I have been teaching for more than a quarter century but I didn't realize there were other outlets – that I could use much better strategies. So I became a strategy-seeker. I was open to the fact that it's not my way or the highway any more. I am opening up new approaches to my students.

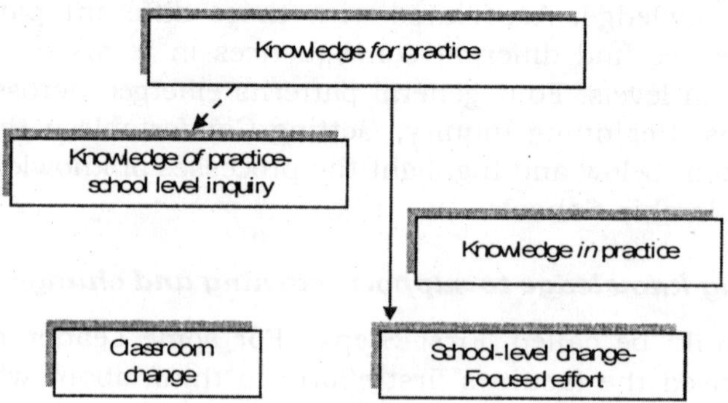

Figure 15.1. First steps

Another teacher commented on the expanded view of her work and career promoted by BASRC's various assemblies, institutes and other learning opportunities: 'Being a part of BASRC has forced me to see some areas of professional growth that I wasn't aware of before.' Another said: 'BASRC has provided the intellectual challenge that I need in my work. A couple of years ago, I was really thinking [of leaving teaching] and BASRC was a good vehicle for me to get recommitted ... so now it's become challenging and intense.'

As these comments suggest, in schools just getting started with the challenges of using and generating knowledge, much of the 'learning' we heard about was at individual rather than at school levels. Notice, too, that sources of knowledge for teachers in 'first steps' schools were external, located in BASRC workshops or institutes, or brought into the school by the Support Providers hired with BASRC funds.

Beginning school-level inquiry and change

For many if not most of the BASRC Leadership Schools, their BASRC involvement was their first venture into looking at their school-level practice. A second pattern we observed in Leadership Schools could be called 'Beginning school-level inquiry and change.'

These schools had started with their cycle of inquiry, and were struggling with questions about appropriate indicators for their focused effort, sources of data, and strategies for data collection. We see norms about evidence and uses of data changing from the culture of privativism seen in First Steps schools, to openness on the faculty's part to consider new ways of looking at their practice at the school level. Teachers in schools just beginning remark on what they have learned about the power of data to illuminate their own practice and student accomplishments school wide.

We are starting to ask what are our data and inquiry strategies really telling us about our children? What do we want to know about our children? We have finally been able to ask ourselves: What do we really want them to know about and be able to do when they go out the door at the end of the year?

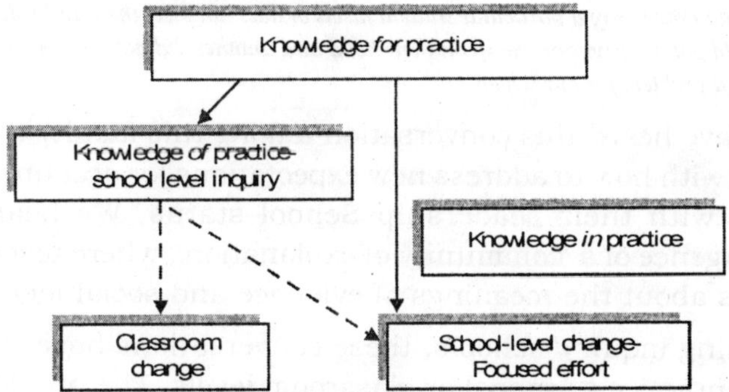

Figure 15.2. Beginning school-level inquiry and change

Teachers in schools just beginning substantive engagement with a cycle of inquiry were having some of their first conversations about data, using new language, and working to generate evidence of practice as a faculty.

In many of the Leadership Schools at this point, teachers tell us that this was the first time that 'every single teacher' had some form of assessment data for his or her class, and that for the first time, baseline data were collected across the school. Teachers also point to the changed lens they have now:

I never could see what a good school this is because I was so into my own classroom. I never had the broad picture. And until I saw that, when I could really sit down and see the whole school, that's when the light went on. You know, we have some holes, we have some gaps, but boy, we're okay!

In schools described by 'Beginning school-level inquiry' we saw how BASRC affiliation helped faculty deal with the politics of data.

The data part of this has been hard for our school a real challenge we have some teachers who will pass any child who breathes. We have to be very creative in how we look at data. BASRC is a real help [as a shield]. BASRC says 'data, data, data'.

BASRC's requirements about evidence and accountability allowed teachers eager to generate knowledge of practice make objective fact of what before had been seen as personal and subjective evaluation, where it was seen at all – most especially problematic evidence about particular classrooms or student groups. Teachers commented on how BASRC's status as 'outsider' and BASRC requirements for Leadership Schools enabled their schools to wade into the difficult waters of equity, outcomes and ties to practice.

Where schools began to see the value in site-level data, most remarkable to us was the shift in teachers' discourse. The language of inquiry and data thread through faculty conversations. Teachers use evidence-based standards comfortably, and we hear new standards brought to evaluation and planning sessions. For example, this snippet of conversation among members of the leadership team at a BASRC school reflects serious effort to take a hard look at data and learn from it:

> *Do all students meet or exceed the standards? What plan should we make to figure out who isn't or is and why? We need to understand how to say a particular student meets or does not meet the standard. We should be able to explain why one child got a particular stamp on their head and another did not. If standards aren't understood by teachers, then it's a problem for our school.*

We would not have heard this conversation among this faculty the year before, when they were grappling with how to address new expectations for accountability and decision-making associated with their Leadership School status. We hear this discourse as evidence of the emergence of a 'community of explanation', where teachers share language and understandings about the meanings of evidence and social facts.

In some 'beginning inquiry' schools, these conversations have started to make their way into change in practice at school or classroom levels. The problem most pressing in terms of knowledge generation and use in 'beginning inquiry' schools is the character of the community of practice in the school. Many reform-minded faculties in these schools wrestled with rifts in their community; not all teachers bought into the 'whole school' character of the reform. Moreover, in some schools most especially high schools– reform leaders acknowledge that not all of their colleagues really believed that 'all students could perform at challenging standards', a central tenet of BASRC's whole school reform vision.

In these schools, the community of explanation was emergent only, since teachers viewed the same disappointing data about student performance in different ways some see it as a warrant to re-examine practice and others view it as evidence about students' abilities and motivation. Yet, in schools such as these, the sites and sources of teachers' knowledge and learning are moving, if only in tentative ways, inside the school. Outside knowledge resources remain important to teachers' thoughts about how to change, but energy in these communities focused more at this stage on establishing priorities for data collection and reform.

Getting comfortable and capable with data

A third pattern of relations among knowledge, learning and change could be called 'Getting comfortable and capable with data'. Some Leadership Schools entered the Initiative already comfortable with inquiry and experienced with school-level reform.

But for most of the Leadership Schools where we found faculty comfortable with using evidence from their own inquiry to rethink their practices, we saw significant learning on the part of individual teachers and the faculty as a whole. We also found faculty struggling with their inquiry processes, but around different issues than were schools less experienced with inquiry. In some schools, the most important learning was about inquiry itself. For example, at the end of their first year of inquiry a high school faculty realized that they had chosen the wrong measures to assess their focused effort. In their second year, they returned to questions of indicators and evidence, but with concrete experience about internal validity to guide their decisions.

In this and other schools, we saw that the cycle of inquiry often was not sequential as a 'cycle' image might imply. Faculty had to revisit first questions before proceeding to data collection and analysis. Faculty gained confidence and competence as data collectors and analysts. One teacher said, for instance:

> *'It's hard to know what is good evidence. But the more you do it, the more you are able to identify what's good evidence.'*

An elementary school teacher's remark speaks volumes about the new knowledge and skill teachers have acquired through BASRC, in this instance the reading assessment tool of running records.

It will be interesting to compare running records across teachers to see whether the evaluations are reliable – we all need to be speaking the same language and looking at kids work in the same way ... next year we want to get people to the table understanding data ... it will be a 'so what' year. We have been working on collecting data to take action.

In many schools, we see that the results of their inquiry process have led to new knowledge and understandings about practice in their school and classrooms. For example, an elementary school faculty looking at student work samples based on BASRC rubrics saw both examples of 'high levels' of instruction in some classrooms, but also identified issues of co-ordination within and across grade levels. Based on this knowledge the faculty took steps to 'evaluate where our kids are and what we are going to do to move them forward'.

Teachers' new knowledge of their practice motivated more inquiry and commitment in some instances. Faculty in a number of Leadership Schools told us that 'there is a lot of buy-in [to reform] from doing these assessments'. Teachers formerly resistant to collecting baseline data, or engaging in the assessment effort at all, are energized by seeing growth in their students as well as by identification of concrete problem areas for the school to grapple with. What had been generic 'problems' became more concrete – they took on names and faces. They also became more amenable to action as teachers began to agree on the nature of the issues facing the school and a range of possible responses. Teachers in schools comfortable with new learning skills and norms of discourse readily admit that such conversations did not and could not have taken place prior to their involvement with BASRC nor could have expressions of collective responsibility for all students in the school.

This teacher's comment makes apparent, for instance, how teachers' problem-solving skills developed though the BASRC rubrics can affect faculty discourse and attention:

We gave a writing sample to all students last fall. All staff learned how to score it. From that experience, all teachers, even art teachers, realized how important writing is. It was interesting to hear history teachers debate with the art teacher about whether [student work] was a 3 or a 4 [on a rubric of 1 to 4, with 4 being high].

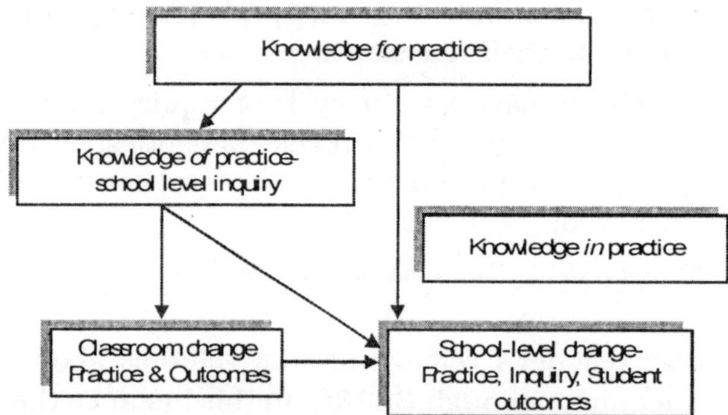

Figure 15.3. Getting comfortable and capable with data and reform processes

An elementary school made substantial progress in their students' achievement once they disaggregated scores by ethnicity and re-evaluated the literacy programs they were using. In 2 years, the school's Limited English Proficient students moved from 44 per cent scoring at grade levels on a reading comprehension test to 73 per cent achieving at or above grade level. In this and in other Leadership Schools, we find positive signs that changes in practices at school and classroom levels are reflected in student achievement. Eleven of the first cohort of fourteen Leadership Schools report student achievement gains in their annual Review of Progress.

Sites and sources of teachers' learning found in these schools 'Getting Comfortable' are both internal and external. Faculties have begun to internalize norms of inquiry and habits of evidence. Teachers ask for data to support decisions and inform discussions about practice. By their language and action, faculty in schools described by these relationships between knowledge, learning and change appear to have become communities of explanation.

Cycle of inquiry, learning and change

In a few of the Leadership Schools we see a fourth pattern of relations between knowledge generation, use and change. In these schools, the Cycle of Inquiry has begun to mature into an accepted, iterative process of data collection, analysis, reflection, and change. These schools function as 'learning organizations', and themselves constitute teachers' essential site and source of learning.

As the double-headed arrows in Figure 15.4 suggest, learning is ongoing and recurrent and the three forms of knowledge are strategically interrelated. These schools appear to be 'recultured' in the way BASRC's theory of change envisioned. The whole school is both the site of inquiry and the focus for change; the community of explanation incorporates most of the faculty, not just a smaller group of reformers. Discourse about students' standard-based achievement and expectations about evidence are everyday rather than exceptional. The sites and sources of learning are internal and external - and mutually informin.

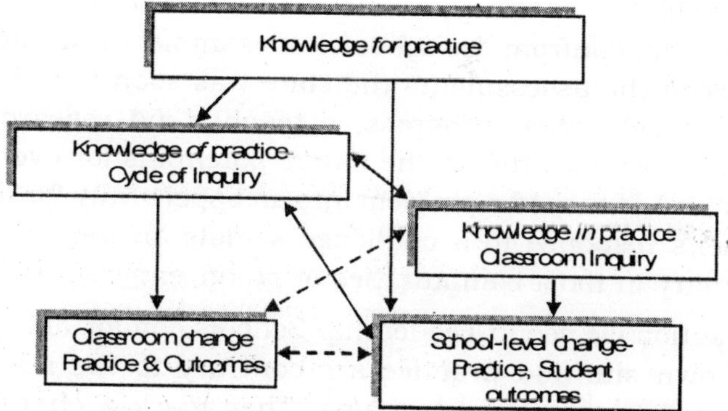

Figure 15.4. Cycle of inquiry, learning and change

Knowledge for practice is both sought and filtered through knowledge of practice. Teachers' new knowledge of their practice enables them to see ways in which they need to improve, and the kinds of resources [or knowledge for practice] they need to begin making those improvements. One teacher commented, for example, that the links between their focused effort on literacy, and their students' work has allowed them to 'see connections' they had not seen before, and make much more specific demands for assistance from their support provider.

Teachers in such schools have become particular and demanding in terms of what their school needs by way of knowledge resources from the outside, and in what form they should be provided. Knowledge of their practice has made them more powerful as consumers, as the double-headed arrow implies.

We observe a number of other things in schools whose patterns of relations among knowledge, learning and change resembles those depicted in Figure 15.4. We see that teachers' generation and use of knowledge of practice often comes before systematic production of knowledge in practice. A hunch based in this observation is that the collective experience of inquiry at the school level may stimulate more inquiry at the classroom level. Teachers' involvement with and acceptance of inquiry at the school level both lends cachet to the norms and mental attitude teachers need to do the work in their own classrooms, and provides the experience, skills, and comfort necessary to ask tough questions of one's own practice - and to share the results.

In a few schools, school level inquiry is making its way into classroom-based inquiry and change. For example, a high school science teacher who had long assumed the disappointing achievement of many students in his culturally diverse classes was a consequence of indifference or laziness, was provoked by literacy data collected at the school level to take a look at his own class through that lens. What he found forced him to fundamentally re-evaluate his practice. He discovered that a significant number of students in his science classes read at a level insufficient to grasp the material. Yet, as the dashed arrow suggests, teachers' systematic collection and analysis of their classroom data to inform both their practice and school-level decision-making is not yet routine in any BASRC Leadership School.

In schools comfortable with inquiry, we also find instances of teachers using inquiry tools to address issues that confront the school. For example, in the face of concern about the relationship between the assessments the state was soon to require, and those the school was using to assess their progress, a teacher did research on the overlap, congruence and conflict between them. She found 'potentials for overlap and a different way of looking at this' and so turned a problem into an opportunity for the school to deepen its work. This teacher's response to a challenge signals an inquiry stance new to the school and extraordinary in most communities of practice.

The inquiry and action we see in Leadership Schools comfortable and confident with learning from their own site and practice are contrary to the norms of privacy and individualism characteristic of school teaching. They mark a changed school culture, and generate a number of questions based on institutional traditions. Why would such things as portfolio readings or critical friends' visits translate into new forms of inquiry at the school level? Why would site level data about problematic patterns of achievement among students encourage teachers to face up to their own effectiveness and look at the gap in their classrooms between intention and accomplishment? Why would teachers expose their own uneven student results to their colleagues?

COMMUNITIES OF PRACTICE

We find some answers to these questions in the character of the school's community of practice and relations among teachers. These communities of practice have become communities of explanation by virtue of their collective inquiry; they also are learning communities where reflection about current practice and habits of inquiry prompt change at schools and classroom levels. They are communities of teacher learners where learning and change are a social process of active participation in inquiry.

BASRC Leadership Schools suggest how patterns of knowledge use and learning define the culture of the community of practice at the school-level. We see seven interrelated elements of the school's community of practice that influence whether or how teachers could use knowledge for practice, whether or how they developed knowledge of or in practice.

In schools where we find teachers using data about their students and their practice to inform their decisions about directions for their school and about the sorts of external resources that would be most useful, we find that a majority of the faculty hold clear and shared goals for their students and their performance as a faculty. Faculty conversations about priorities for their school's reform effort, evidence to support their strategy, portfolio application and designing a cycle of inquiry to assess their progress fostered clarity and buy-in on school goals. They also stimulated active communication within the faculty, across grade levels and departments. Faculty communication continued to address these classroom-specific concerns, of course, but in addition regularly engaged whole school issues, most especially patterns of student performance and faculty responses to disparities by students' ethnicity.

Communities of teacher learners explicitly adopted what Cochran-Smith and Lytle call an inquiry stance towards their own practice as well as towards their broader workplace environment. In these communities we found instances where 'problems' were transformed from 'immutable facts' to subjects for inquiry and problem solving. This transformation was most apparent in high school faculties where explanation for poor student performance moved from those based on beliefs about students' attitudes, backgrounds or capacities to the 'fit' between what their students needed to learn and achieve and what was provided them.

Communities of teacher learners possessed and used a number of resources. They developed the learning skills necessary to pursue inquiry and analyse evidence; they had a growing body of knowledge about aspects of their practice and continued to add to that understanding. These skills and knowledge were broadly distributed across the faculty community, not merely the assets of an isolated sub-group of teachers.

Communities of teacher learners also had a store of knowledge about 'best practices' and were able to distinguish on technical grounds among alternative practices available to them. They knew not only what kinds of resources best suited their school, they also knew where to build or rebuild their own core technical capacity. This technical knowledge, combined with knowledge of their school site and classrooms, combined to make teachers adept at evaluating the kind and quality of knowledge for practice available to the school, and was central to what Donald Schon called the 'reflective transfer' of knowledge from outside the school.

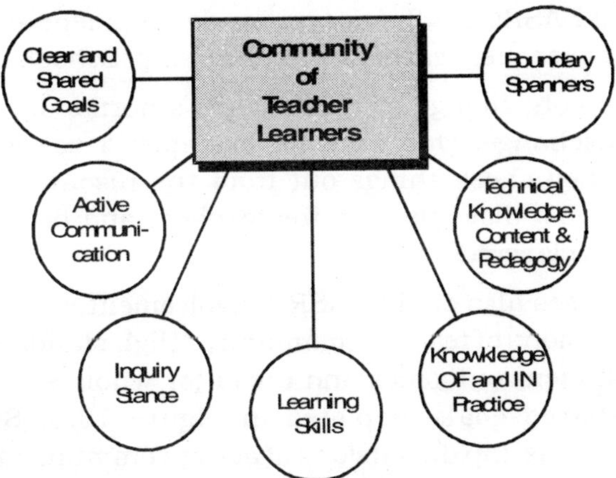

Figure 15.5. A community of teacher learners at the school-level

Finally, communities of teacher learners were communities open to the environment. In one or another form, they had boundary spanners, individuals active in the context outside the school who brought new ideas as well as challenges into the community.

These elements of the communities of teacher learners we encountered among BASRC Leadership Schools were mutually reinforcing and deeply interdependent. Technical skills alone did not enable a community of practice to be learners, or teacher learners to make productive change in their practice. Teachers required common values about inquiry, goals for their school, and shared conceptions of 'good' work and a 'good' colleague.

The high levels of social participation are signal to communities of teacher learners. We saw how communication and co-ordination among teachers extended the shared understanding (or community of explanation in Donald Freeman's terms) that generated both action and inquiry. Communities of teacher learners used active participation to forge common ground about the meaning of the evidence they generated, and agreements about a course of action at both individual and organizational levels. Further, the teachers' quest for shared goals and common perceptions of the facts of the matter, involved both individual accommodation and learning. Individual teachers' learning, in this sense, is part and parcel of their involvement in reflecting on and inquiring into the practices of their school community.

BASRC'S STRATEGY STIMULATES COMMUNITIES OF TEACHER LEARNERS

Many of these elements of a community of practice where teachers are learners often are thought to be outside the purview of policy, and to operate in the domain of school leadership - most particularly, school-level clear goals, communication, stance towards learning and inquiry. Certainly, we find, with the rest of the research community, that leadership matters. Strong principals were a feature of almost all of the Leadership Schools successful in forging new relationships, making progress with a Cycle of Inquiry and whole school change. However, we also find clear evidence in our interviews, observations and surveys of BASRC's influence on the development and functioning of all elements of communities of teacher learners in Leadership Schools.

A number of principals note change in their faculty's norms of communication and attitudes of sharing and exchange. One said, for example: 'I see my staff asking one another more questions. They check things out from the resource lab. A teacher will walk in to get materials, have a dialogue with the teachers and before you know it, one will be stopping by another's classroom.'

Principals' survey responses also credit BASRC involvement with substantial change on a number of critical dimensions of teacher community. 'High standards for all students', 'Teachers' consensus' on student outcomes and areas for whole school change tap the presence of 'Clear and shared goals' depicted in Figure 15.5. Similarly, 'Teacher leadership' and 'Staff discussions' tap dimensions of active communication among faculty. 'Working with outside change agents' provides an indicator of 'Boundary spanning', and 'use of data as a basis for decision-making' captures principals' views about change in their faculty's inquiry stance, learning skills, and knowledge both about their practice and appropriate resources to enhance their work.

Principals also report that they have some distance to go in order for their schools to be characterized by a community of teacher learners.

In a nutshell, Leadership School principals say that their school's involvement with BASRC has resulted in important changes in their schools' cultures – but that especially in the area of 'consistent standards for all students', and inquiry stance, much change has yet to take place.

Table 15.1. Leadership school principals' report of changes associated with BASRC involvement (N=63).

	Strongly Disagree		**Strongly Agree**		
High standards for all students	0%	0%	10%	62%	28%
Teachers' consensus on desired student learning outcomes	0%	0%	10%	53%	37%
Teachers' consensus on needed areas for whole school change	0%	0%	3%	52%	45%
Teacher leadership	0%	0%	10%	47%	44%
Staff discussions of teaching and learning	0%	0%	5%	49%	46%
Working with outside change agents to support reform goals	0%	0%	12%	53%	35%
Use of data as a basis for decision making	0%	0%	8%	50%	42%
Note: These data are from a Winter 1999 survey of all Leadership School principals.					

Support providers also see new, stronger communities of practice taking form in Leadership Schools. One said, for example:

> *What difference do I see in BASRC schools? The main difference I see is that those schools and the district, to a lesser extent, are slowly turning towards gathering and using evidence in a formal accountability system. I think teachers, individuals, have been turning that way. And it's been neat to get a whole school community to pay attention and give that level of priority.*

Teachers' comments and our observations of faculty meetings and planning sessions point to the emergence of a significantly different community of practice in many Leadership Schools. These new communities of practice have formed around the knowledge resources associated with BASRC new skills and capacities, new knowledge of the school as an educational setting and the community itself serves as a resource to generate new practices and invent ideas for reform. A number of teachers commented, for example, on how the diverse perspectives within their community enable them to see gaps in understanding that would otherwise be invisible. One said, for example:

> *I know that I'm not perfect, but my standards are higher because of my colleagues. Also, I found out that there are many different ways to do something amazingly well [through our teacher community] I found out that a person who writes a whole lot differently from me can be amazingly successful and although I found out that I need to improve a lot I also found a couple of ways that work.*

Teachers also comment on the power of distributed expertise within the teacher community. One middle school teacher said, for example:

> *By sticking together, someone comes up with something and we try it. When you start in this [teaching] business you are isolated and think in the box. [Because of the teacher community in my school,] I have learned to think outside the box. We have hit a lot of curves, but we feel like we are a group that can work through them. When you talk together it is a powerful problem-solving group. There are things to be gained from this [community of practice] that cannot be gained from working alone.*

Many teachers attribute the stronger teacher learning communities at their schools to the tools and processes they learned at BASRC's Summer Institutes, most especially skills in facilitation, reflective dialogue and conflict resolution pragmatic skills important both to generating new knowledge and understanding about practice and in making effective use of the knowledge resources available to members of the Bay Area School Reform Collaborative.

Table 15.2. Principals' report of existing conditions in leadership schools (N=63)

	Strongly Disagree		Strongly Agree		
This school has high standards for all students	0%	3%	21%	49%	27%
This school has consistent standards for all students	5%	14%	44%	29%	8%
Teachers are engaged in systematic analysis of student data	2%	8%	27%	38%	27%
Teachers in this school regularly examine school performance	2%	16%	22%	41%	20%
Teachers take steps to solve problems, they don't just talk about them	3%	8%	23%	30%	36%

LESSONS FOR POLICY ABOUT SITES AND SOURCES OF TEACHERS' LEARNING

It draws upon our evaluation of BASRC to provide elements of a descriptive theory of how different forms of knowledge relate to one another, how teachers interact with these forms of knowledge and with each other to foster learning and change. The patterns of knowledge use and elements of teachers' learning communities associated with BASRC's experience contain important lessons for reformers.

Patterns of knowledge use

Looking across the different patterns of knowledge use and generation in BASRC Leadership Schools, it is evident that forms of knowledge are path dependent. We notice that the knowledge teachers bring into the school and the knowledge and learning generated at the school site builds on what they know and can do. Wesley Cohen and Daniel Levinthal use the term 'absorptive capacity' to signal the critical role prior knowledge plays in an organization's ability to use external knowledge to remain vigorous and stay ahead of the competition. Their conception of how organizations identify and use knowledge corresponds with our observation that what teachers already know mediates between external knowledge and teachers' capacity to use it effectively or even to recognize – relevant external knowledge resources.

This view of knowledge, teachers' learning and educational change makes it evident why 'solutions' cannot be 'imported' into schools or classrooms with any significant effect if internal capacity in the form of prior knowledge is not already there. Without foundational, situated knowledge of and in practice, teachers lack effective hooks to pull new ideas into their workplace. In other words, what teachers know about their own practices, and about their school as an educational environment, shapes fundamentally what and how much they can learn from knowledge for practice.

These diverse but interrelated images of knowledge complicate policy investments in teachers' knowledge since they implicate different sites and supports for teachers' learning. A successful school reform effort, in this view, would need to supply or foster knowledge of all three sorts – for, of and in practice in order for teachers to learn what they need to know to initiate, deepen and sustain change.

Communities of practice

A description of relations in a community of practice illuminates age-old problems of knowledge use. Change agents and reformers have long been frustrated that teachers too often make little or only superficial use of the knowledge resources available to them. Knowledge resources evidently are not self-enacting nor do they necessarily engender learning. And learning does not necessarily lead to productive change in practice. What happens to knowledge brought into or produced by a community of practice depends fundamentally on the character of that community and relations among its members.

BASRC's experience highlights the many ways in which a community of practice is both the medium and source of learning, reflection and new knowledge about practice. It also illustrates the situated character of the community of explanation created at a school. In each of the Leadership Schools where we found a community of teacher learners we found a community of explanation we heard language and understandings particular to and shared by that community.

One important implication of the central role we see for communities of practice is their centrality to reformers' visions of how to stimulate and sustain change. Policies need to consider how strategies can provide occasions, tools and resources for building a community of teacher learners. BASRC's design is remarkable in that it provides teachers with the tools they need to learn how to learn, to forge new conversations and accommodation among faculty, and with a 'focused effort', the work essential to constructing shared goals and understandings. Few reform policies keep communities of practice in their vision or acknowledge the pivotal role of a community of explanation to knowledge use, learning and change.

Another important implication of the situated character of these communities is that they cannot simply be regrouped or combined with other communities without attention to the rebuilding of shared understanding and language. Policies aiming to bring different communities of explanation together – be they different school communities or more obviously diverse communities such as researchers and practitioners, policy makers and practitioners, or knowledge providers and knowledge users must attend at the outset to building common understandings. BASRC accomplished some of this in its first years through the Portfolio Review process, where parents, educators, researchers, business people and others first spent time together calibrating their responses to schools' portfolios and talking about why they saw the same evidence in divergent ways. Only after some level of mutual understanding was achieved did the group move on to their common work. Teachers' assessments of these Portfolio Reviews as 'the best professional development I've ever had' lay in the process of participation and joint sense making it entailed. These strategies for developing shared understandings and standards for good work not only created new communities of explanation among individuals based in other ones, they also play a critical role in generating a regional understanding of the goals and elements of school reform in the Bay Area. BASRC experience illuminates the trap of *de facto* assumptions about common language and explanations across communities of practice. Simply convening stakeholders from different organizational or institutional communities may be efficient, but will probably accomplish little by way of learning and progress without opportunity for them first to have conversations about their different perspectives and understandings.

A related lesson: BASRC's experience also suggests how teachers' participation in multiple communities of practice/explanation can promote more durable structures for knowing and learning. Teachers from Leadership Schools who have participated in conversations throughout the region have been able to hear multiple perspectives on practice and reform and integrate them into their own. Participation in multiple stakeholder groups enables teachers to take them into account as they go about work in their own school communities. Access to multiple communities makes teachers' own understandings more durable because they are more cosmopolitan and so less vulnerable to external 'shocks' to their beliefs such as new or contradictory ideas about practice.

BASRC's experience and the practical theory of learning it suggests stand in direct contrast to professional development or school reform policies that frame teachers' learning as solely an individual matter. We see in BASRC Leadership Schools that learning is a social process, where the process in critical ways is the product, and where the knowledge generated by the community is more than a sum of individuals' learning. Communities of practice generate knowledge and understanding that is different in kind from that produced by individuals alone. Likewise, individuals' learning is a matter of their participation in a community of practice engaged in reflection and inquiry. In summary, observations of relations among teachers and forms of knowledge in BASRC schools suggest a different perspective for policy, one rooted in communities of practice as sites and sources of teachers' learning.

❑❑❑

16

Understanding and Expressing Teacher Knowledge

INTRODUCTION

These assertions 'ring true' with teachers who have adapted and interpreted them in a variety of ways to shape and inform their teaching practice. They have also served to encourage further research by PEEL teachers. From the early days of PEEL, the use of language was important and teachers found the term metacognition to be both acceptable and usable. Metacognition had meaning for the participants as they saw their teaching as a way of pursuing the enhancement of students' metacogntive skills.

The nature of PEEL necessitated a language for the sharing of ideas and practice as discussion associated with ways of recognizing and responding to the dilemmas of practice became windows of opportunity for better understanding the nature of teaching and learning. Through the ongoing collaboration between the academics and teacher-researchers, many of these windows of opportunity have been grasped and this led to the formation of the PAVOT project. PAVOT (The Perspective and Voice of the Teacher) has become an important bridge to accessing teachers' professional knowledge and has created opportunities to articulate and disseminate this knowledge to others.

Table 16.1. Assertions about learning

1	Learning outcome is determined by decisions made by the learner.
2	Inadequate learning is due to inadequate decision-making.
3	Learners often are unaware of their learning problems. This lack of awareness generates poor attitudes.
4	It takes energy to learn with understanding, or to unlearn a misconception.
5	Increasing awareness of the nature and process of learning leads to improved attitudes and procedures.

PAVOT has been an interesting project as it has built on the solid foundations of the PEEL project and specifically aimed to develop ways of introducing the voice of the teacher into the research literature by communicating the findings of their work through their writing about their research.

The form of research and documentation in PAVOT has been influenced by case methodology which allows teachers to 'unpack' the complexity of teaching and learning, and, through case discussions, to develop insights into their own practice. Case writing and the use of cases have been helpful for PEEL and PAVOT teachers and has been another impetus for the development of a language of learning through the need to articulate and communicate the knowledge underpinning the practice.

This chapter then is one attempt to illustrate how the professional knowledge of teachers has developed through involvement in PEEL and PAVOT. This development has been as a result of the recognition and response to the need to share and learn with one another as they have begun to understand better and value their practice, and therefore, the knowledge that is at the heart of these understandings.

PEEL GROUPS

The participants in this study were drawn from three different groupings of PEEL teachers. The three groupings each comprised three teachers who volunteered to be interviewed (at times convenient to them) about their understanding of their teaching practice and the principles which underpinned their actions. Each of the three groupings is an attempt to establish general categories of involvement including beginning PEEL teachers, experienced PEEL teachers and PAVOT teachers (PAVOT teachers being experienced PEEL teachers who choose to pursue teacher-research in a systematic and organized manner).

The first group (beginning PEEL teachers) included David and John (all participants have pseudonyms) who were English and humanities teachers and were recent graduates with 2-3 years teaching experience, and Sophie who taught mathematics and humanities and had been teaching for 8 years.

The second group comprised experienced PEEL teachers with more than 5 years involvement in the PEEL project. All had at least 15 years teaching experience. The teachers interviewed in this grouping (Olivia, Andrea and Jack) taught a range of subjects including mathematics, science, social studies, and technology studies.

The final group was made up of experienced PEEL teachers who had also been involved in conducting their own PAVOT projects. Two of these teachers (Jen and Joan) were elementary teachers, the third (Callum) was a high school mathematics and science teacher. All three of these teachers had been involved in developing and delivering professional development programmes for schools and had also been involved in presenting nationally and internationally at conferences for both teachers and educational researchers.

These groupings offered one way of viewing the development of teachers' professional knowledge through the PEEL project across the continuum of experience from early PEEL to PAVOT. All interviews were conducted at a time and place convenient to the teachers. Interviews were audio-taped then later transcribed for analysis.

FINDINGS

The three groupings of teachers are presented separately in attempt to illustrate the changes in their knowledge in concert with their experience in PEEL.

Beginning PEEL teachers

These teachers, like many beginning teachers, were enthusiastic about their work and their hopes for their students. They were also a little critical of some of their more experienced colleagues whom they characterized as teaching in 'routine' or 'non-thinking ways'. Each of these teachers illustrated a desire to teach in ways that they saw as extending themselves beyond the 'norm'. Obviously this is not necessarily a trait peculiar to beginning PEEL teachers, but in their particular case a defining characteristic of their views was that they had an underlying purpose that directed their approach to teaching.

This sense of purpose that directed their practice was based on a genuine commitment to student learning derived largely from an understanding, or at least a recognition, of the poor learning tendencies which were the basis of Baird's initial work.

In the case of these teachers, involvement in PEEL created a situation with which they could readily identify. They came to see the relationship between teaching and learning as something important for their practice and therefore actively pursued ways in which to better understand the links. Consequently, they began to focus as much on learning as on teaching and this is a considerable shift in the manner of conceptualizing one's own practice. I would argue that it is much more common for teachers to explore teaching in terms of new or interesting activities to use in the classroom rather than specifically apprehending the implications for learning. This focus on learning was important in both conceptualizing teaching and discussing their developing practice and subsequent knowledge.

Learning: a basis for pedagogical reasoning

Amongst all three participants was a sense that the development of learning as an organizing principle of practice was something they had come to understand through reflection on their early teaching experiences. David was perhaps the most forthright in his views on this development:

> Now I choose activities to meet the learning outcomes I'm hoping for, whereas earlier I think I saw PEEL as offering a *smorgasbord* [of procedures] and I'd just try them all out, you know, to break up the routine a bit. But the class makes a big difference to what you do.

John (who worked for a time between his initial degree and his teacher education program) believed that his use of teaching procedures as activities, rather than as purposeful choices to enhance learning, had been much more limited due to his experiences in the workplace before becoming a teacher. In any case, all three recognized that they had experienced a progression in their practice from managing the dailyness of teaching, through to the use of teaching procedures in order to break up the normal routine, to their present approach of explicitly linking their teaching practice to the intended learning approaches and outcomes they were hoping for.

One way that this development had been enhanced was through the support structure of PEEL. The fact that they met on a regular basis to discuss their teaching and their students' learning was an impetus for reconceptualizing their classroom practice. These meetings helped them to access a range of teaching procedures, but more importantly, through discussion, encouraged an understanding of the use of these procedures as much more than simply being a smorgasbord of classroom activities.

PEEL is a way of staying in tune with the profession. It keeps your enthusiasm. *(John)*

It's a support base. The teacher talk and support matters. *(Sophie)*

It's other teachers going through the same things as you. You find out what's important to your colleagues and it makes you ready to reflect. *(David)*

The individual recognition of this shift in thinking and associated practice was perhaps most apparent to David as he had vivid memories of trying to do something different each lesson (in his first year of teaching) simply to maintain students' interest. His current understanding of his teaching had shifted such that he believed – just because a particular teaching procedure was used in a class did not mean that a student's approach to learning necessarily changed. He felt there was a need to both understand the procedure and to use it appropriately so that it encouraged learning, not just to maintain (or create) student interest. John concurred with this view.

Kids get sick of concept maps just as much as chalk and talk. At some PEEL meetings a good idea might come up and if we all rush in and do it the kids say, 'we've done that in the last three lessons!' So, we need to use a procedure for a particular purpose and not all do it because we are keen to try it out. You have to think about what you're doing and why. *(John)*

A language of learning

This shift from the use of teaching procedures as activities to reasoned selection of teaching approaches particular to the anticipated learning has also become a basis for a language of learning - not unlike that described by Macdonald. As these teachers have come to align their teaching with their intentions for their students' learning, they have developed a language to communicate these ideas with their students. Hence, the names of teaching procedures (for example, concept maps, venn diagrams, semantic maps) and terms such as metacognition, chunking and processessing have become a part of their teaching vocabulary. This was necessary so that students could be conscious of, and responsible for, their learning behaviours and so that the learning intentions could be better understood, communicated and realized in practice.

Negotiation with students is important. We discuss what we are going to do and why, and then how to do it best. *(David)*

You have to let the students know what you think a particular teaching approach is designed to do, they have to know what you mean. *(Sophie)*

To enhance students' metacognitive skills it is important to be able to highlight examples of them as they occur in the classroom. Therefore, there is a need to label them so that a sense of recognition and meaning can be conveyed. For these early career PEEL teachers, this language of learning was clearly being developed and used in their teaching and was a feature of their growth and professional development through PEEL.

You come to know what you know about teaching through experience and then there is a need to be able to express this. Normal teachers operate by instruction and organization as a focus for their teaching, we focus on learning and discuss this with our students. Perhaps we create and see things as a learning environment, it's not a threatening sort of thing – but I can see how some teachers would see it that way talking with students about learning [is important] so that they know how to learn and when they are doing things that help that, that's the point of talking about metacognition. *(David)*

We encourage student learning [so] metacognition is important because you need to recognize the type of learner you are and PEEL groups help us develop the language to articulate what's happening. It's trying to move them into more use of higher order thinking skills and that. *(Sophie)*

Students suffer more from not knowing about their learning and so we need to help them to learn and to see and use a learning language too. *(John)*

At this stage in their development, these teachers recognized the value of a learning language as a way of communicating ideas with other PEEL teachers at their school. They had not yet begun seriously to consider how this use of language might vary across PEEL groups in different locations, but through our discussions, there was little doubt (for me) that they believed that a language of learning was important and was helpful for professional dialogue and the development of understanding about teaching and learning.

Sophie in particular explicitly related her views of teaching for enhanced metacognition to her pre-service teacher preparation programme in which metacognition and higher-order thinking skills had been an explicit organizing principle. Therefore, metacognition, as an important signpost of PEEL, was a label that created recognition as it echoed the intentions for teaching which she had identified within her teacher preparation programme.

Both David and John had come from a teacher preparation programme in which PEEL was an explicit approach for teaching about teaching. However, they did not link their current views on teaching to their teacher preparation programme in quite the same 'matter of fact' way that Sophie did, but they did note that PEEL was something they were aware of as a result of their teacher preparation programme. Perhaps then it is reasonable to suggest that for these teachers, the PEEL seeds had been planted and that when they found themselves in a sufficiently conducive environment, germination had been initiated.

Experienced PEEL teachers

The three experienced PEEL teachers (Olivia, Jack and Andrea), described their approach to teaching as 'flexible' in that they believed their main motivation for the way they organized their lessons was influenced by their students' learning needs and, as such, came before the specifics of the curriculum. This was not meant to imply that the curriculum was not important but that - as a result of their experience – they were skilled at carefully scrutinizing that which was 'on offer' (content wise) and appropriately adjusting it to the learning needs of their students. This issue was particularly highlighted through their descriptions of their purpose for the way they thought about, organized, and structured their lessons.

I'm not into busy work [time-consuming work with little engagement in learning]. We have made science relevant and exciting by developing our own curriculum so that it is meaningful. My repertoire is [built around] quality practice which generally is designed to get the kids thinking at a higher level – so they put an effort into their learning. I have taken on the PEEL strategies and I suppose I find [at times] that I can take for granted the way things like POEs and concept mapping work, they've just become part of my practice. (*Olivia)*

The need for school work to be relevant and meaningful seemed to be an expectation of their practice so that, as a result, their students could link their learning experiences to their existing knowledge in ways that would make it, 'useful and relate to their lives'. This approach to teaching was considered to be important if their students were to, 'think and be independent learners' and they constantly encouraged this by drawing on their students' own experiences.

By being able to explain these issues in the way that they did, they clearly illustrated a use of language that carried an understanding of both their views of professional practice and of student learning.

Explicitly linking teaching and learning

Like the beginning PEEL teachers, these teachers used a number of terms (*e.g.* seeing the big picture, linking, analysing learning, complexity of processing, synthesizing, students' need for a sense of progress and delayed judgement) that were accepted descriptors and a natural part of their vocabulary they did it in an almost 'matter of fact' way. They were also aware that they did have a vocabulary that encompassed ideas about teaching and learning that were not so common amongst all of their colleagues.

These experienced PEEL teachers' range of language seemed more diverse and carried specific meaning and was more explicit and more extensive than the beginning PEEL teachers.

In considering a particular concept, you are aware of the context of the situation, the Poor Learning Tendencies they [students] display, the Good Learning Behaviours you try to encourage to tackle these and the teaching procedures you use to address the situation having an opportunity to discuss and share ideas helps to challenge the isolation of teaching. *(Jack)*

This response by Jack was indicative of the language and thinking about teaching and learning that was apparent amongst these three interviewees. In effect, what their language illustrated was how they had refined their understanding of their approach through PEEL and how they then conveyed their understanding to others. The essence of their message seemed different to 'normal' teacher talk because they spoke in specific rather than global terms about their knowledge.

Kids have to be active, interested and involved in their learning, they can't just be expected to soak the learning up they have to learn to challenge teachers' chalk and talk approaches. *(Andrea)*

I've come to know that people learn in different ways I now know what is happening when someone is a good 'swatter' for exams while others need connections between ideas, or relevance to their life so increasing experiences for students really matters and you need a wide range and use of questioning techniques there's a difference between knowing and understanding. *(Olivia)*

You come to see that teaching and assessment can be at odds and causes a conflict that you need to respond to if you want your students to learn, and to value the learning. *(Jack)*

It was noted that in some instances their use of language caused problems when talking to non-PEEL teachers because, as Olivia stated, there was a big difference between talking about good ideas and classroom activities and talking about enhancing specific aspects of learning through carefully chosen and well-understood teaching procedures. This led to a selective use of language in some situations:

I'm almost bi-lingual, so I'm a bit selective about what [language] to use to talk about teaching and learning and where to use it. There's a big difference between saying here's a good idea or activity as opposed to talking about concept mapping, linking, etc. – some people would just see it as a wank. *(Olivia)*

Olivia offered an example that illustrated the value and importance of language when she explained her 'backsides' communication strategy. On the back side of the school's daily memo she had initiated discussions to help develop and share the knowledge of practice. She had found that asking teachers to write up their thoughts for this task had not been easy as there was an inevitable struggle for many to find a language to explain their ideas in conveying their message. She had therefore developed some key questions to help teachers do this such as, 'What was the concern that caused you to reconsider your practice? What did you observe before and after the change? How would you describe the practice? How have you analysed the procedure? How have you come to see your practice now?' Clearly, these questions require a language and an understanding of teaching and learning that prompt a reflective and meaningful response rather than the simple transmission of a 'good teaching activity'. Hence, she highlights the important difference between teaching as a series of interesting activities and the use of particular teaching procedures for specific reasons.

[Through the use of backsides'] you can see that you come to know teaching procedures and the way they underpin your teaching also talking at conferences is a big boost to your confidence and ability to share knowledge and because it is from your own practice and you examined and researched it, you begin to better understand what's happening. *(Olivia)*

An issue which emerged was how the PEEL group served different functions. The first function was as a general forum for issues of teaching and learning:

> *PEEL offers a social dynamic to teaching and supports a development of learning about teaching, you get an energy from PEEL groups, especially here with the large number of PEEL teachers and groups that all support each other.* (Jack)

The second function was in response to a need for teaching and learning issues to be particularly well understood in terms of specific content – perhaps alluding to something similar to Shulman's notion of pedagogical content knowledge.

I sometimes want to take PEEL and have my own science group [of teachers], to take another step, to want to link back again into science so that we can feed on the specific things that are different for teaching procedures just in some special science content things. *(Olivia)*

This issue highlighted an aspect of the value of PEEL which all three saw as important, an understanding of teaching and learning in a way which supported the development of specific professional knowledge for individual teachers in their own way in their own content fields. As most PEEL groups are cross faculty, the range of creative responses to different situations offers teachers opportunities to consider their content base in new and challenging ways. However, within individual subjects, there is a need to recognize and understand the way particular teaching procedures impact on specific content learning issues.

This development of teaching procedures with a particular focus on (and relationship to) specific content was well illustrated by Andrea who related how she had come to develop a case in which her understanding of the content knowledge was enhanced. She recognized through this process that:

> *Cases cause you to stop and think and present knowledge in ways that also help others to get the idea and that sort of feedback helps you to see – and challenge – misconceptions and assumptions. Some other teachers read my case and said it helped them understand the topic in a way they hadn't understood it before.* (Andrea)

What Andrea had created in her case was a way of drawing on her wisdom of practice within her content field and writing it up in a way that demonstrated an intimate understanding of both the specific content knowledge and issues of learning which when combined, clarified what was for many learners a difficult concept that (Andrea believed) was often taught but not understood.

The development of experienced PEEL teachers (like these three interviewees) to a point where their professional knowledge is able to be well articulated and communicated (in various forms) to others is, in some instances, a platform from which a decision to explicitly research practice emerges.

Teachers can see the value to themselves and their students. I now know the difference between learning and understanding you can teach kids to do a task but how they arrive at understanding is a different matter. (*Olivia)*

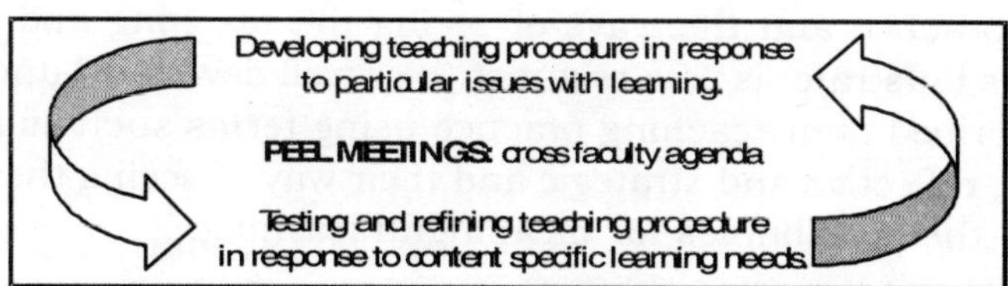

Figure 16.1. The dual agenda of shifting teaching needs addressed through PEEL meetings

The knowledge that these teachers have of their practice is drawn from a recognition of, and response to, teaching and learning situations in which the need to understand practice better and the outcomes of learning demand (through interaction with colleagues in PEEL meetings) a language through which to share the knowledge being developed.

PAVOT: PEEL TEACHER RESEARCHERS

The final grouping of PEEL teachers were members of PAVOT. These were experienced PEEL teachers who chose to further their professional growth and knowledge by purposefully researching their teaching and their students' learning. These teacher-researchers had been involved in a large range of professional development and leadership roles within PEEL, and the profession generally, and were also actively researching a range of issues within their classrooms.

For these experienced PEEL teachers, 'purpose' was a most important and unifying theme in their practice. This was most evident in the view that 'busy work' was not a common feature of their classes. Their emphasis on learning as the purpose for their work meant that a commitment to helping students learn necessarily ruled out teaching approaches which 'wasted students' learning opportunities'. Their image of busy work was that it was counter-productive as it did not encourage students to view school learning as engaging and meaningful.

Considering the fact that Jen and Joan were both experienced at teaching a range of elementary grades and that Callum had taught all high school grades, their expectations for student learning (and their expectations of teaching) obviously confront and challenge some of the 'taken for granted myths of teaching' *e.g.* that students can not concentrate for extended periods of time, that working independently only happens in the (at best) latter years of schooling, and that students are dependent on teachers for decision-making and for directing (and/or controlling) the learning.

... we've got so much to do and get through we can't waste time doing busy work. And that doesn't mean all that we do has to be intellectually challenging [all the time], but it has to have a purpose. It's not [like in some classes

where it's] let's take the kids so that they can do busy work, I mean that's what play times are for [besides] the kids will tell us when they need to rest because they'll say my brain hurts, or we've had enough thinking or whatever. (Jen)

This sense of purpose has helped all three to reconceptualize their teaching in ways that have made their practice illuminative for others. However, what they see in their teaching is somewhat different to that which others might initially see. In many ways, the insights into practice and the ways of seeing the teaching and learning situations that these teachers illustrate, is as a result of their well developed understanding of their role. All three described their teaching practice using terms such as focused, motivated, idealistic, creative, reflective and strategic and their way of seeing their practice certainly appears to extend the possibilities for meaningful learning.

We quickly saw that what they took away was ideas of activities that they could do and we were really entirely frustrated because they were not seeing what we saw was happening in the classroom in terms of the kids being more reflective. we're so intent on [students] making links and knowing what linking means and how to use their prior knowledge and how to use it to help their new learning. and because we were keen to make kids understand the value of questioning as a tool for learning and that they had a role in making decisions in the learning process, they became our important understandings about how kids learn. But the other teachers didn't see that, they, at that time, would see the activities by which the kids were displaying those behaviours to us, but they didn't see the [actual] behaviours, they just saw the activities and because the kids were performing on those quite well they thought it was the activities that led to the changed behaviour. They [the teachers] really often commented on how the kids didn't seem to interrupt and nag us over what we call irrelevant interactions and they just thought we'd trained the kids well. Whereas we believe that they're [students] deciding that they don't need to ask those questions because they can solve their own problems. So it's also about people looking at the same thing in a different way. We had a forum for discussing things that came up, having a critical friend and a collaborative working relationship. And the outside discussions we had with other people through PEEL, I think you need the support, ongoing support and opportunities like mine. I know that to make teaching better we need to have quality interactions with other people. (*Jen*)

Learning: a basis for practice

The teaching style illustrated by these teachers is based on knowing about teaching and learning in ways that draw the two together in a relationship such that their classroom 'manner' is based on an understanding of learning that leads to teaching practice styled on expectations of learning. For example, terms often associated with learning such as linking, prior knowledge, reflection, purpose and independence (all used extensively by the interviewees), are translated into their teaching so that there is a direct correlation between these attributes of learning and the teaching used to foster their development.

My teaching practice has changed. I am constantly aware of what I'm doing, I've spent a lot of time out of the classroom thinking through what the kids have done, why it's happened that way, reflecting on what happened in the classroom. I also describe myself as a learner in my own classroom that's really important and it never ever bothers me if we're working on something and I am not the dispenser of knowledge. I want to see what happens in a classroom with this sharing between me and the kids and I write, I intentionally write assignments and things in terms of 'we' and not 'you' it's [also] very reflective, I spend a lot of time thinking about what's happened when I trained as a teacher they taught us how to plan lessons, so the notion that we were given was that the teacher directs it, it's like conducting an orchestra, you go in and you make it happen your way and you come out and the kids have learnt something. But there is nothing in that about looking at what the kids are doing, listen to what they're saying, sharing that learning with them. It was all teacher directed so I have no doubt I started off that way and I know there's been a shift, but that shift didn't just come out of PEEL, that shift [also] came out of not being entirely happy with a classroom that didn't seem to meet the [learning] needs of all kids [so] what PEEL gave me is this structure for thinking about what happens in my classes. (*Callum*)

This description by Callum is indicative of the development of understanding of classroom teaching and learning by all three of these interviewees. Their understanding of learning shapes their teaching and, for Jen and Joan in particular, also shapes the physical nature of their classrooms.

It is not uncommon in elementary classrooms for the walls to be decorated in a variety of ways to make an attractive and stimulating room. However, in many instances, although these decorations may comprise some student work, the students do not necessarily share ownership of the room, rather the teacher displays the products of particular activities. For Jen and Joan, they see the classroom as containing resources that will benefit students' learning so their intention is always to assist students' recollection of that learning, 'through linking'. Therefore, they see students' work as an opportunity for providing resources for the class. These resources are readily available because through their class work students are continually constructing them. The resources come in the form of posters and materials that when displayed in the room provide a stimulus for remembering particular learning episodes and approaches. Further to this, these resources are only kept on display if they are being used by the students. If they are not being used then Jen and Joan believe they should no longer be taking up valuable wall (resource) space. In contrast to the image of a 'normal' elementary classroom, this is a clear change in understanding of what the physical environment of a school classroom has to offer.

This change in approach to the physical environment came about from looking more specifically at the way students linked (or did not link) their prior knowledge in order to enhance their learning. For Jen and Joan, they started examining their own practice and noticed that most of their 'best teaching', or the processes of 'building up a chart' or a 'sheet of information or teaching procedures', was erased from the chalkboard at the end of a lesson/day. Now they see the value in turning these learning experiences into resources that are useful in the classroom. Hence, the walls in their rooms have learning posters and student work which illustrate linking, venn diagrams, semantic maps, fact charts (and much more) and this has emerged in their practice from looking closely at how their students learn. The physical set-up of their rooms now explicitly fosters linking to both decrease the reliance on the teacher as the knower and to enhance student decision-making and independence.

A visit to these classrooms shows students (as young as 6 years of age; grade 1) working in ways that illustrate an independent approach to learning. Students can be seen discussing how they might embark on a task, they might then do a 'print walk' to review learning procedures illustrated on posters (that they have constructed) in order to decide how they might approach their work, they will also choose the individuals they decide to work with to complete their task – such decisions being made for a number of important reasons; who can they learn best with, what skills are needed to do the task, and so on.

Articulating the language of learning

To convey this understanding of teaching to others is not a simple task. Callum describes how he has developed in this regard:

> *you just come to question your teaching from another direction. I can see that through working with a PEEL group and the discussion that you have with them you start to take on a new language of learning and you're able to articulate what you're doing much better. So I think being able to articulate what happens in my classroom comes out of a couple of things, one is when you're in a PEEL group and you've got to put into words as clearly as you can what's happening in your classrooms, you find the language to describe it. And you [also] take on the language of the academics through the PAVOT groups, but I'm sure a lot of it also came out of just the need to articulate to the PEEL group what was happening. And I know I can remember looking for words and terms to express what was happening ... now I have a way of doing it ... you're trying to convey a very important message to people, and you've got to say it as clearly as you can. And you can't, you couldn't go and take any classroom teacher out of the classroom and have this conversation, I mean I'm not saying that what we're doing is exceptional but they couldn't have this conversation and articulate as easily what's happening in their classroom because, well 2 things, number one they haven't had the time, this is a teacher who perhaps hasn't been through the experience of you know discussion of everything else [that we have through PEEL and PAVOT] because they haven't had the time to frame the answers in their mind. They would be saying Oh I've never thought of it like that, or that's an interesting question I'll have to think about it. But when you've been through that discussion, you know the issues, you know how you feel about it, and then the second thing is you find the terminology to express it so there's a knowledge base of teaching and there's evolving [for me] now this new language of teaching.*

And that language is of great importance when you do things, things like turn up for your annual review like when I was interviewed for the job I have now, I'm sitting there talking teaching and learning and people's heads around the room are nodding because when you can articulate your professional knowledge well, people like to hear about it.

The way that these three teachers came to recognize, understand, and articulate their professional knowledge is important. It would seem that for each this development happened best when they had time to talk; with individuals and in discussion groups. In this way they were communicating their knowledge and that which they understood through their insights in their classrooms. Callum, for example, recognized his own development through the need to help a young teacher who wanted assistance. He noticed how he needed to use his knowledge to give some insight into what might be happening in the other teacher's classroom. He was easily able to recollect the way he spoke with the younger teacher and noted how different this was from the experience of many other teachers.

And it gets back to what I said before, I don't think most teachers have had the experience of having to think through the issues to such a level that PEEL teachers have and therefore they are not in a position to say, oh well I think this might be what's happening. *(Callum)*

In essence, all three, through their involvement in PEEL and PAVOT, have been placed in situations where the need to be able to articulate and communicate their knowledge has been important. Their involvement gave them a need, and an opportunity, that almost demanded that they be able to articulate their practice, 'it cannot be shared if there are no words to do that'. So there was a clear need to develop a language to share as what they had to say was significant.

Further to this, these teachers also needed to see that what made their practice different was a way of knowing what to look for in order to move to the depth of understanding (illustrated in Jen's open day experiences). Primarily, their growth had to do with helping their students come to understand their role in the learning process which led to a corresponding development in Jen and Joan's understanding of their role in the teaching and learning process.

So yes, now I'm very confident in being able to say that I've got something to say about what's different about my practice. There were times of personal growth, our points of consolidation, and they really are where we had to sit down and work out what it is that we wanted to say and where we'd come from and where we are at now. And it was because we had to share our practice with other people and it didn't really matter whether it was colleagues at school, or in a board of education, or community, or at the university, we had to have an explanation or reasons for why we were doing what we did. So each time we had to do something like that, we came a little bit further we had to dig through what we thought was essentially different [in our teaching] from what we wanted to share with other people. The first time we had to write, and that's another form of communication, and that was really hard and, as you know, the writing skill is not easy for us, but I suppose we're a bit better at it now than what we were.

The other thing about communicating our practice and the reasons for having to articulate it was so that we could reproduce it for ourselves we don't have to [continually] re-invent the wheel. And we now realise the benefits of organising our thoughts so really to reproduce it so that next year in my teaching when something comes up I can base it [on my knowledge] so I'm maximising the thinking that I've done before. That's been really critical for ourselves as well as for others. *(Joan)*

SUMMARY

There has been a growing recognition of the value of teacher research and of school-university collaboration as well as the need to include the voice of the teacher in the academic literature. PEEL and PAVOT are examples of such work starting from a desire by teachers to improve their students' learning. This chapter has illustrated some of the professional growth and development of knowledge of teachers through their involvement in such projects. In this case there are some clear similarities and difference in the three groups of PEEL teachers interviewed for this study. It seems reasonable to assert that they all conceptualize their teaching in terms of learning and it would appear that both the development of their practice and the manner in which they have learnt to articulate and communicate it to others are indicative of different points along a continuum.

For the beginning PEEL teachers there is a clear shift from seeing teaching procedures as activities to focusing on learning as an impetus for the appropriate use, and choice of, teaching procedures. Through this development they have also begun to develop a language to share their understanding, a language which is based on learning but is explicitly linked to teaching in order to lead to meaningful teaching and learning interactions. The experienced PEEL teachers illustrate an understanding of teaching and learning that is based on an extensive knowledge of learning and requires a well-developed language to enhance this understanding through practice. Their refined ability to articulate their approaches to teaching and learning go hand in hand with their confidence in, and growth of, their professional knowledge both in terms of learning generally and particular aspects of learning in relation to specific content. The PAVOT teacher-researchers illustrate how instructive the recognition and valuing of professional knowledge can be for practice and how choosing to extend and validate their knowledge is enhanced through researching their teaching and their students' learning.

❑❑❑

17

Professional Autonomy and Bureaucratic Accountability

INTRODUCTION

The self-managing school is emphasized as an important means for school improvement and school effectiveness. This focuses on potential effects of changed decision-making structures on the relationships between principals and teachers, and how this may be connected to school improvement. Two upper secondary schools were selected as cases to investigate the questions. They are within the same county, yet possess different course structures; one school offers general subject courses and the other offers both general and technical vocational courses. Both schools are noted, by the county director, for their good organization and leadership. Interviews have been used as the main method of investigation. All those holding formal administrative position in addition to some teachers have been interviewed. In addition, policy documents have been examined.

THE SELF-MANAGING SCHOOL

In developing the concept as well as offering a normative model of a self-managing school, Caldwell's work and research have played an important role. In *Leading the Self-Managing School* he and Spinks presented a model of school planning as a means of achieving school effectiveness that was used in an extensive programme of training for parents, principals and teachers in Victoria (Australia). Caldwell emphasizes that the concept of the self-managing school also implies a powerful role for central agencies in respect to formulating goals, setting priorities and building frameworks for accountability. He defines the self-managing school as the systematic decentralization to the school level of authority to make decisions on the allocation of resources, defined broadly, within a centrally determined framework of goals, policies, priorities, standards and accountabilities. The centre may remain concerned about the ends for education, but those at the school site are responsible for the means of education and for demonstrating their success at achieving goals set both locally and centrally. Based on his research, he concludes that the trend towards self-management has resulted in greater awareness of what resources schools receive and why. He argues that the findings reveal effects on capacity for self-management, on improved learning outcomes for students, and that these effects have important implications for the role of school leaders. The move towards decentralization of governance has also implied unfulfilled expectations and lots of problems for principals, for instance, frustration at 'bureaucratic interference', inadequate resources, and intensification of work. Nevertheless, his research reports that the overwhelming majority of principals would not wish their schools to return to previous arrangements.

Based on his research on decentralization and school-based management in Canada, Brown found that principals and teachers generally agreed on the strengths and weaknesses of decentralization. The strength was the flexibility, while the weakness was the time requirement. Often external constraints imposed on schools under decentralization limited their flexibility. Brown's research also showed that the participation of teachers and support staff in the budgetary process varied a lot. When the principles of decentralization are applied to schools, they match Mintzberg's divisional form quite well, but decentralization has tended to die at the principal's desk.

Current discourses of self-managing schools incorporate notions of democracy, participation, choice, community and society. Critics have emphasized that the self-managing school is not fundamentally about choice and grassroots democracy, but the reverse where the process is about tightening central controls through national curricula and frameworks, national and state-wide testing, teacher appraisal and curriculum audit. In reality there is no shift in central power. Particularly the frameworks of accountability have constrained decision making at school level instead of empowering schools. The notion of democracy seems to have been reduced to a simplistic concept of parental choice, and the move towards the self-managing school can be characterized as part of a discursive trick where schools control their own decline. What has occurred is that there has been a rhetoric of devolution in a context of centralism and managerialism.

Smyth refers to studies in Canada, USA and UK which support this argument. In Canada, for instance, school-based management seems to result in a reduction in the overall quality of educational provision, because there is no longer any provision for ensuring an equitable balance of services and facilities within the system. Resources are allocated to schools before educational needs are assessed. According to Smyth, power, control and resources are kept at the centre; while responsibility, blame and guilt are decentralized to the schools. In the USA where there is support for school-based management, the support tends to come from school administrators, not from teachers and the wider school communities. In the UK budget cutbacks have accompanied devolution, and heads say that self-managing has increased their administration, and schools are forced to supplement their funding from private sources. Herein lies the equity issue: schools have vastly different capacities to do this owing to their socio-economic make-up.

Smyth argues that the discourse of self management has a different Bill of Sale depending upon who it has to be sold to. To the principals and teachers it is put as a form of empowerment, made possible by removing bureaucracy. In addition, it is a way for principals of reclaiming control over the day-to-day running of the school. To the parents it is said to be a way of making schools more accountable and giving them a greater say over what is happening to their children. At the same time, the devolution to self-management has been accompanied by centralizing tendencies, and the struggle between political and professional power over education has been sharpened. A crucial question is, therefore, who at the local level obtains more autonomy; the principal, the teachers, the parents or the students?

Lundgren has pointed out that a decentralization of the educational system, irrespective of motives, puts in focus the balance between political and professional power over education. It shows four main models for governing education: central, local, professional, political. In Lundgren's grid, the horizontal axis refers to the tension between political versus professional power over education, while the vertical axis refers to central versus local governing of schools. The first quadrant shows a system of central governing where the politicians are in command. The second quadrant shows a centralized system where the educational bureaucrats in the governing boards have the power. The third quadrant shows a model for local governing where the professionals set the agenda, and in the fourth quadrant the local politicians have obtained the power.

The movement towards decentralization has focused questions around the professional ability of teachers, and the diffuse borderline between political and professional responsibility seems to represent a major problem. Conservatives see opportunities for potential abuse in school-level control, particularly if teachers are able to capture the process of school governance. If school-based management is to be introduced, they suggest that lay control must be assured. From the left it is argued that deregulation, choice, local control will ultimately favour those with greater personal and family resources. Greater inequality will result, with the best getting better; the education gap between rich and poor will widen. At the same time, blame will be decentralized. Central agencies will no longer carry the political burden of confronting those who accuse them of ineffectiveness and inefficiency.

The model of decentralization chosen in Norway is one where the political authorities state the goals to be achieved, whereas local authorities or professionals have the freedom to pursue the practice that they find most suitable to achieve the objectives. Decentralized governing is praised, but schools work to fairly detailed curriculum guidelines in terms of timetable and syllabuses, and with central approval of textbooks. During the early 1970s these specifications were replaced by looser guidelines from the centre. However, in the 1990s curriculum guidelines have become more detailed again. A tight-loose management approach is used to set standards, while encouraging local initiative in fulfilling the objectives. So far it is uncertain who at the local level, obtains more autonomy the principal, the teachers, the local school authorities, the parents, or the students. Different municipalities have chosen different approaches to school-based management from a small to a large amount of district resources. What is clear, is that evaluation has become an important method both of reconstructing the role of the centre and the role of local politicians.

CONCEPTIONS OF ACCOUNTABILITY

The concept of accountability means having to 'answer for one's actions, particularly the results of those actions'. During the 1980s both politicians and top administrators have raised doubts about the extent to which teachers are making claims on behalf of their clients, or perhaps rather on behalf of their own interests as a group. The politicians use the notion of 'provider capture' in this connection. It implies that those who provide the service, capture the benefit. This is probably the reason why external evaluation of education at various levels has come into focus in recent years. Education policy could no longer be based on widespread trust in the professional competence of educators, their performance should be controlled and judged according to criteria established outside the profession.

Thus, policies of decentralizing the governance of educational systems, seem to carry the seeds of their own contradictions. Weiler has analysed three arguments or models which one normally encounters where decentralization in educational governance is discussed. These arguments are: (1) the redistribution model, which has to do with the sharing of power; (2) the efficiency model, which is geared to enhancing the cost-effectiveness calculus of the educational system through a more efficient deployment and management of available resources; and (3) the cultures of learning model, which emphasizes the decentralization of educational content. He concludes that there is a need to go beyond these kinds of arguments in understanding the political dynamics of centralization and decentralization in educational policy. He says that decentralizing 'the implementation of educational policy affects in very important ways the nature and the interests of the state, particularly its ability to cope with the dual problems of policy conflict and the erosion of its own legitimacy' (p. 61). Against this background he examines the relationship between decentralization and external evaluation, and argues that evaluation tends to be used for its legitimating rather than its informative capacity. The linkage between external evaluation and control is obvious, and therefore evaluation enters into a competitive relationship with the basic premises of decentralization.

Accountability can be understood as an obligation for professionals in teaching. Sockett distinguishes between bureaucratic accountability and professional accountability. Bureaucratic accountability can be compared to a salesman model which has very limited applicability within schools. In this view, accountability refers to 'an agent's responsibility to a provider, the provider being the beneficiary as measured by the results produced through the agent's skill in handling resources'. The salesman is only accountable to the owner of the shop. Teaching as a profession requires an alternative model of accountability because the exercise of teaching demands greater autonomy than the salesman model would allow, and there are many different constituencies of accountability for the teacher. Sockett has articulated an approach to the question of professional accountability that is consonant with teaching as a moral endeavour. He argues for four main positions: (1) accountability is akin to moral obligation; (2) trust is a primary condition for the development of professional accountability; (3) a professional code of practical guidance could provide a vehicle for accountability; and (4) a moral stance toward professional accountability is central. This accountability includes not only classroom conduct, but also relations with colleagues, parents, and the community. A professional teacher will try to find ways of explaining achievements and failings in recognition of the need to build trust in the practice and in the judgments made.

In Norway accountability issues related to the school sector were put on the public agenda after the OECD evaluation of our educational policies in 1988. The government still praised decentralization of education, but proposed that evaluation should become a key element in the improvement of Norwegian education. This led to a long debate about the potential and the dangers of a strong evaluative system. In December 1997, a committee on behalf of the Ministry of Education, Research and Church Affairs launched a proposal to a new national evaluation system. The White Paper based on the hearing of this proposal was postponed several times, but, eventually, in June 1999, it was presented to and discussed by Parliament.

The proposal was in line with a new management practice in Norwegian schools, which has been combined with greater concern for documenting results. It stated that all levels should show their efficiency by what results they have obtained, and the idea of a Norwegian inspectorate body with the Scottish system as a model, was carefully mentioned. The committee also underlined the importance of school-based evaluation, but clearly the tendency was towards greater emphasis on external accountability. The White Paper, on the other hand, focuses on the importance of giving the control of curriculum development and teaching back to teachers. It criticizes conceptions of accountability that appear to be couched in terms of a bureaucratic audit. The White Paper emphasizes school-based evaluation as the key element in improving schools. At least rhetorically this White Paper represents a shift in educational policy. It argues for professional accountability, and states that external evaluation should not be used as an instrument for direction and control. There is a risk in being so preoccupied with measurements and tests, that we forget to evaluate quality issues that cannot be measured so easily but are more often the object of sound judgment.

However, it remains to be seen what local politicians will decide to do in this connection. It will take time to implement a new practice. For more than 10 years there has been a focus on school self-evaluation in the educational debate and in in-service-training for teachers and principals in Norway. In an evaluation of the upper secondary school reform in Norway, Monsen found that schools which have succeeded in developing their own model for school-based evaluation, are still exceptions within the Norwegian school system. According to his research only 20 per cent of the schools are doing some kind of systematic school-based evaluation. So far Norwegian teachers, to a very little degree, have entered the public debate with their internally defined criteria of teacher professionalism. They are angry and tend to concentrate on pragmatic matters relating to their use of time.

PERSPECTIVES ON PROFESSIONAL IDENTITY

Teachers and administrators, at various levels within schools, have different functions and knowledge, but they have a joint responsibility for providing pupils with a quality education. The professional identity one develops, becomes apparent through interaction with others working at the same school, with other schools and other areas of the education system.

In his analysis of quality within the education system, Dale has focused on the relationship between the identity one develops at work, the reference frames one uses in defining each others' duties, and the joint effort made to develop quality in schools. He views this identity in relation to four dimensions which form the basis for a social system: collaboration, stability, homogeneity and communication. In contrast to these, Dale places individuality, mobility, heterogeneity and isolation; hence, creating a series of contentions. If a system consists solely of contentions, an imbalance arises, preventing a common professional identity. However, a certain amount of contention between collaboration and individuality, between stability and mobility, between homogeneity and heterogeneity is required for school development.

When examining different layers of school bureaucracy, it becomes apparent that teachers, principals, local, regional and central leadership constitute different sub-cultures with different jargons, problem definitions and loyalties. Professional identity is to a large degree defined locally by tradition, and separated groups define separate identities. Dale's main argument is that there must exist a common knowledge of technical language and concepts used for discussing quality within education. He claims that today there is a lack of common reference frames among those working at different layers within school bureaucracy, and he argues that communication between sub-cultures must be rooted in teaching-related criteria. This can only be acquired through an extensive formal socialization in the theory of education. Otherwise, there will continue to be low permeability between the different groups.

THE SCHOOLS IN THE STUDY

Soltun Upper Secondary School was built as a combined, upper secondary school in Oslo. The modern buildings encompass comprehensive study facilities. The student population is 700, age 16-19, and 150 trainees are attached to the school. There are ninety teachers. The school offers foundation courses for general and business studies, building trades, health and social studies, mechanical trades and technical building trades. Advanced course 1 includes general studies, car mechanics, hair-dressing, carpentry, skin-care and general care. Advanced course 2 includes general studies and skin-care. In addition to this there is the trainee school for building trades and scaffold construction. There are also unemployment courses.

Soltun recruits students primarily from its local catchment area, although the vocational training course students do tend to come from further afield. Thirty per cent do not have Norwegian as their mother tongue. According to the staff, this creates tensions because different cultural groups have conflicting behavioural norms. The school is situated on the city's outskirts, which appears to influence the recruitment of general course students. At present, the city centre schools appear to be most attractive to students. There is competition for students among schools, and Soltun is struggling against a negative reputation established by the media. As a result, teachers are working extra hard to encourage students to be proud of their school.

Good inter-faculty relations have always been encouraged to avoid divisions and cliques occurring. However, an awkward conflict arose a couple of years ago when a quarrel within the administration team led to a rift among the staff. Discrimination and whispering behind closed doors resulted in the head's resignation and the appointment of a new head. The new principal, who was recruited internally, had worked at the school since its opening. Following this upheaval, it became vital for the school to regain administrative stability and order.

Borgen Upper Secondary School is an old, respected school which was built as an upper secondary school more than 80 years ago. It is located in Oslo's centre. The school's exterior is impressive, but refurbishment is required internally. Borgen offers mainly general subject courses and courses for music, drama and dance. It is very popular, and competition for entry is tough. The student population is 450, age 16-19. On average, the students have extremely good, lower secondary school grades, and they come from all over Oslo. The school has almost no foreign-language speaking students. Fifty teachers are working at Borgen.

Many of the school's past principals have been described as pioneers of school politics. The instruction of more traditional subjects is deeply rooted, and many believe much of the traditional Latin school remains. The school is built upon strong subject identities with a high academic emphasis. The present principal was appointed 2 years ago, after having been principal at a combined, upper secondary school, within the same county.

REORGANIZING THE LOCAL ADMINISTRATION AT SCHOOL LEVEL

Running an upper secondary school is a complex task. Therefore, it is usual to consider the management as a team effort, with numerous members of staff fulfilling different administrative roles. The larger the organization, the more important it is to distribute administrative duties. A position of faculty head was established in the 1970s to help the teachers co-ordinate teaching activities within each faculty. Responsibilities included co-ordinating department meetings, promoting subject/pedagogical collaboration among teachers, supervising the preparation of internal examinations, initiating work placement contacts and co-ordinating budget plans and faculty purchases. The main purpose was to improve quality in teaching. In practice, the tasks have primarily been administrative. An award of 29 March 1996 led to a decentralization of internal organization. Schools were given greater freedom to appoint faculty heads. At some schools, this resulted in a reduction of faculty heads, whereas at other schools, it resulted in an increase in number. There has been a general tendency to introduce a system of middle managers instead of faculty heads. The principal appoints these middle managers, while the faculty heads were elected by their peers. There is a wish to abolish the 'tacit deal' where teachers and administrators generally respect each other's 'zones of influence'. To a larger degree both teachers and leaders should collaborate in improving the quality of teaching.

Soltun school has reorganized its local administration, and the principal has appointed eight middle managers and has abolished the old system with faculty heads. Every second year contracts may be renegotiated. Positions are now regarded as part of the school's administration team. They are no longer solely the teachers' representative, as they have often been regarded before. The faculty head is in charge of pedagogical affairs and has the task of coordinating teaching and ensuring directives are followed. In addition, they prepare local curricula, internal examination papers and oversee budgets and teaching materials but, as yet, personnel responsibility is not part of the position.

The old administration team at Soltun consisted of the principal and four deputy heads. They have all been actively and strategically involved in setting up this project. They are convinced it will cause both pedagogical and administrative duties to be carried out effectively. The principal points out:

The school has become autonomous. We have financial management and complete responsibility for personnel and property. Indeed, everything concerning the management of the school is part of our responsibility. Therefore, we have many more duties. The running of a large, combined upper secondary school, such as this, requires management similar to corporation management. The top management is removed from individual affairs, whether they concern teachers or students, due to the incorporation of intermediate level. This is what we are working on. It is impossible for the head of a large school to supervise, for example, 800 students and 120 members of staff.

Another administration team member argues:

The reorganization of the administration is exciting. It will award greater responsibility to faculty heads. Previously, the faculty head functioned as an administrator dealing with course inquiries and taking necessary action, discussing the written exam and other mundane tasks with little definite responsibility.

The newly appointed middle managers at Soltun feel they should have educational leadership responsibilities connected to specific subjects, but so far, they have been acting in a purely administrative capacity. The principal wishes to see them as part of the formal administration team, whereas many teachers still want to go on with the old system where the faculty heads were their representatives.

One of the middle managers explains:

For many teachers, the faculty head or the middle manager is the sorter and the fixer: 'Set things up for me, make sure I have books, find things for me, always know what is written in the circulars', and so forth. I prefer to be an educational leader. Today, there is often a lot of improvisation. People come and seek advice when they are unsure how to grade work, or about subject related matters. I like these kind of inquiries. It becomes an extension of my role as a teacher. At the moment, we are debating whether the middle manager should have personnel responsibilities. The concept of personnel responsibilities is complex, and there are some things I am glad we do not have responsibility for, for example, granting leave. It is quite all right that it is decided centrally; particularly when the middle managers' responsibilities comprise different subject areas; sometimes one teacher can actually be accountable to three different middle managers. In time, individual staff hours could be handed over to the middle managers. I think that would be wise, but not yet. None of us are ready for that yet. There is strong resistance among some of the teachers.

Thus, the support for these structural changes seems to come from those in formal leadership positions. The teachers are more divided in their feeling towards the reorganization. Some fear it will be difficult to adhere to the administrative links, the distance between them and the principal will be increased and contact reduced. Nevertheless, two teachers have positive expectations and other teachers regard the faculty head's possible personnel responsibility as both positive and negative. The following quote captures this sentiment:

Now they are talking of the faculty head being given greater control over personnel. This has both positive and negative aspects. We will have a closer relationship with the faculty head in a teaching situation, but the distance to the rest of the administration will be increased. Sometimes, you want a little more distance between you and the person who has personnel responsibility above you. Yet, on other occasions, it can be advantageous to have them more closely involved in your teaching. They get to know the pupils so they can provide pupil-related advice, especially if it concerns a specific pupil. On the other hand, a middle manager does not have the same weight of authority as the others in the administration team.

The following quote summarizes the scepticism among the teachers:

The faculty heads are now to function as intermediaries; … I am rather sceptical towards this because of the many steps between you and the person you really want to deal with. I find myself asking: Is it really necessary to have more administrative levels at our school? How many more are going to control us?

At Borgen school, so far, no steps have been taken formally to introduce a new local administration, and the traditional system of elected faculty heads remains. However, their framework has been enlarged, as have their responsibilities. Each faculty head has been given several pedagogical duties by the principal. She has meetings with the faculty heads approximately twice a month and they have been assigned the responsibility of setting up planning days, following up local curricula work and initiating collaboration. The administration team considers it necessary to make demands upon the faculty heads to realize the reform.

But the faculty heads do not think their allocated tasks are in keeping with the administrative resources available to them:

The instructions we receive are so vague you can do almost anything and nothing. During the few years I have been faculty head, my tasks have grown in number. For example, budgeting was never my responsibility, but now I am forever called upon to draft budgets, sign requisitions and oversee orders. The faculty head is called upon in connection with numerous matters. We have heard that now there is to be an intermediate level. I feel we are about to become intermediaries without being given the time and economic resource required. As a result, I go around with a constant guilty conscience. I feel it is affecting my teaching. Neither am I able to do all the things I am supposed to as faculty head. I either don't get the work done on time, or I don't get it done at all. I go around with a bad conscience thinking of all the things I should have done or followed up. It is very frustrating.

The teachers consider the faculty head as their representative. This opinion is shared by the faculty heads, as exemplified by the following quote: 'I am a teacher, not a manager, so I will always be loyal to my teachers. That is where I belong. I am a kind of spokesperson for them, against the administration if need be.' The debate surrounding faculty heads is not an issue among the teachers at Borgen. But they will probably soon have to face it. The county administration is following carefully the experiences of other schools such as Soltun.

The above describes how the principals at both schools have opted for different strategies. The principal at Soltun has appointed middle managers, and they are regarded as part of the administration team. Borgen still has the old system where faculty heads are elected and look upon themselves as spokespersons for teachers. This may be due to a combined school being a complex organization and better suited to a divisional structure. Many of the vocational subject teachers have experienced an intermediate arrangement in the private sector before they applied for a job as a teacher. The altered administrative system will be nothing new to them. The crisis within Soltun's administration team, which occurred several years ago, may have quickened the process to establish a new administrative system. The principal at Borgen school was recruited externally and, therefore, must learn to handle an established culture before proposals for change may be promoted. In addition, the need for an intermediate structure may not seem so pressing when the school has mainly general subject studies. Both schools experience the pressure towards more administration, and the principal has to respond to external pressure. Both principals, interviewed in the study, are critical of what they call 'bureaucratic interference of local politicians', and both have experienced difficult relationships with these local politicians. Even though the main purpose of the structural changes was to improve quality in teaching, the effect, so far, is that more time is dedicated to administrative duties, and less time is left for pedagogical purposes.

Teachers' experience is that the quality of personal relations with the principal owing to his or her presence around school is reduced. To a larger degree, the principals feel they have to choose to define their role in relation to outside constituencies and audiences. The result is that they are seen as absentee heads.

WHO AT THE LOCAL LEVEL OBTAINS MORE AUTONOMY?

The self-managing school within the Norwegian context has meant that principals have become targets as well as agents of change in a drive for improved standards in schools. They are responding to external imperatives while trying to create conditions for staff to participate in organic school development. It is quite obvious that the principal's role as employer, personnel manager and educational leader cannot be fulfilled effectively with the present organization structure in school. The administration team at Soltun views the intermediate administrative level as the key to solving problems surrounding regulation of staff collaboration and evaluation of individual teachers. However, established zones of influence are challenged, and the extra administrative level disrupts the school's flat organizational structure and traditional distribution of power and duties. Hierarchical structures and administrative duties seem to be intensified. When this is coupled with external regulatory demands from society, the teacher's traditional autonomy is threatened.

So far, principals seem to have strengthened their formal power, and the administrators in this study seem to support the move towards a self-managing school. However, all over the country increasing demands and intensification of work has led to a recruitment crisis. There are very few applicants for each vacancy, on average less than three, and often the applicants do not have the required competency. In 1998, because of high work loads, low salaries and high stress levels, one in four principals quit the job to go back to classroom teaching, because there was too much stress connected to the job as principal. Chief Education Officers, Teacher Unions and politicians see this as a great problem. Right now principals' salaries are the focus of debate. The Ministry has announced that a White Paper about recruitment to teaching and leadership jobs will be launched in September 1999.

At the same time a continuing struggle between political and professional power over education goes on. As Tiller has pointed out, trust should be a central term in a decentralized school system, but some uncertainty has been spreading lately. During the seventies it was correct to talk about bottom-up strategies in school development. Today it is seen to come from above, but the talk is about decentralization. Politicians and educational bureaucrats at municipal level seem to have a strong belief in top-down strategies in order to improve schools. They argue for more regulation of classroom activities, and reports are seen as a means to guarantee educational quality in schools. Tensions are heightened, and this explains the resentment felt by some teachers towards the revision of local administration at school site. It has come to symbolize the authorities' lack of confidence in teachers. Decentralization is perceived and experienced as rhetoric.

Lack of confidence coupled with putting the market alternative in education on the political agenda. Right-wing parties, which now hold power in Oslo, would like to see more private schools receiving state support at all levels, to give state-maintained schools more competition. They wish to give students freedom of choice among schools. Throughout the country it is, so far, more talk than action. But in the future Norwegian education will probably see more differentiation and more privatization. There may be a deterioration of some public schools, and an emerging market for private schools.

The politicians want to reduce the professionals' power over education. For instance, in Oslo they established local governing in January 1994, giving the principal a lot more power and autonomy, but in January 1999, the politicians introduced a board between the local school and the Chief Education Officer, restricting the principal's autonomy and with the intention of empowering parents. This board consists at primary and lower secondary level of three parent representatives, two teachers (or other employees) and one external representative. At upper secondary level there are three external representatives, three students, and two teachers (or other employees). Using Lundgren's models for governing of education, this can be understood as a move from central and professional governing to local and professional governing and now to local and political governing. It might result in less power for principals, but not necessarily. The competency of board members will probably be crucial. The school principal is the board's secretary and has to prepare all meetings, and the power may still be in the hands of the professional. So far, it seems that the board has turned out to be an important support group for the school against the local politicians. When external representatives experience how small a budget the local school receives, they are ready to fight together with teachers for their school. However, participating in this board is time consuming, and it results in more administrative work for principals and less time for educational matters.

QUALITY IN TEACHING – WHO IS SETTING THE STANDARDS?

The struggle between political and professional power over education includes a power struggle in society for who should define qualitative teaching. From a political perspective, there are other social groups wishing to define educational quality, but, as yet, they have had little bearing upon practice in schools. Intensified administration, in the form of external regulation, might solve some problems, but new problems will undoubtedly appear. In the long term, there is the risk that teachers' enthusiasm and commitment will be lost a far greater problem for schools. It has still to be proved that intensified administration produces better schools. Education cannot be developed mechanically with administrative decrees and regulations.

However, teachers continuing fight for their individual right to set their own standards for teaching does not correspond with the conditions of professionalism. It is not the individual who is awarded autonomy, but the profession. And as a profession teachers should enter the public debate with their critique and internally defined criteria of teacher professionalism. In addition to their efforts of voicing protests against more managerialism in schools, teachers should lead the drive to resolve the tension between public and professional control by promoting forms of accountability that are publicly acceptable.

A GAP BETWEEN ADMINISTRATION AND TEACHING

Dale claims that a lack of reference frames for discussing quality in schools makes collaboration difficult. Is this the case if we analyse the educational background of those who work in schools? To hold an administrative position in Norwegian schools, one must have three years teaching experience and formal teacher training. Therefore, one would imagine that both administrators and teachers have the background Dale describes. However, an upper secondary school teacher's education is primarily in their specialized teaching subject(s) and not in pedagogy. The majority of upper secondary school teachers have only 6 months practical pedagogical education, in addition to 5 to 7 years of their specialized subject studies. It is true that most teachers identify closely with their subjects, and they have developed pedagogical identities that are congruent with their subject being communicated in strongly academic ways. At the same time, administration teams, to a larger degree, identify with new constructs of educational leaders as managing directors.

Communication is unproblematic within a group possessing homogeneous reference frames and interests, but difficulties arise when the administration team and the teachers develop different reference frames. There is a risk of discussions becoming centred around administration matters when management does not have an identity connected to educational theory. According to **Dale**, *the gap between administration and teaching increases when the administration team identifies itself with the co-ordination of school activities through administration and regulation, and the teachers identify themselves with teaching their specific subject areas.*

This tendency has been emphasized lately. At county level, for instance, further education courses for school administrators are often based upon general management and administration strategies used in the private sector. And school administrators at county and municipal level do not have to have an educational background as a teacher anymore. People with education in economy and law are in particular demand. As Rovik points out, in his report about modernization within the public sector, the same solutions are applied in both public and private sectors, and in large and small companies. If an organization is to prove its worth, it must be seen to incorporate the latest administrative strategies. Organizations create meaning and belief through symbols, including myths. Such myths are thought to be objective, but, in reality, they result from specific social and political definitions and dominance. They are circulated to promote legitimacy in areas of inconsistency. For example, outwardly, a new administrative system is seen to indicate renovation and increased efficiency within schools. But modernization often runs the risk of discarding the old before fully understanding the new. The key management concepts for the 1990s were total quality management and quality assurance, and these stem from economic rather than educational theory. This would support Dale's claim that the education system lacks a common identity.

However, the Ministry of Education, Research and Church Affairs has outlined competence objectives for educational leadership within schools, as part of the administrative programme. These include educational politics, curricula theory, evaluation and advisory topics, and may counteract the general tendency towards managerialism when it comes to governing of education. This type of knowledge is equally important for all teachers as it is for administrators, but it will take more than a few, brief courses before it is firmly established. So far, that seems more like a vision for the future.

SUMMARY

The trend toward the self-managing school is probably irreversible within the Norwegian context. However, it is less evident as to who is likely to obtain more autonomy at the local level. The introduction of a board between the local school and the Chief Education Officer in Oslo could be a step towards more managerialism and less power to professionals, but not necessarily. The competency of board members will be crucial. So far schools have experienced the board members as a support group against politicians.

The new arrangement with middle managers allows the principal to take a greater educational leadership position, but that may strengthen the hierarchical management structure in schools. It may lead to a sharper division between the administration team and teachers. Furthermore, school administrators will be more closely linked to the county administration that probably will expect school administrators to enforce their directives.

The question is whether or not the education policy lays down a managerial rather than an educational agenda. Will it be an emphasis on 'school image' rather than 'educational vision'? School democracy and teacher professionalism are emphasized in national curriculum guidelines. However, other things like requirements of assessment reports from local schools, detailed descriptions of how to do things, new agreements on regulation of teachers' work time, which are happening simultaneously, may reduce the educational emphasis. Right now the political wind is shifting, at least rhetorically, from control to trust.

Attacks on teachers in the media and the political will to regulate classroom activities appear to have drained teachers of their enthusiasm. Unfortunately, energies are being concentrated upon the protection of established practice as opposed to educational improvements. Both parents and students wish to make their voices heard in the schools. Teachers voice their protest against managerialism, but without initiating school-based evaluation and promoting alternative forms of accountability. When this occurs, they loose the opportunity of coopting parents as their alliances. There is a tension between the teachers' demand for autonomy, for an independent right to draw up and discuss the ethics of professional practice, and the control of this practice by the democratic state. This should mobilize teachers in collaboration with principals to enter the public debate with their critique and internally defined criteria of teacher professionalism. A professional role entails professional responsibility, and this implies that teachers make their experience more visible. Within the Norwegian context there are still spaces and opportunities for teachers to promote alternative forms of accountability that are publicly acceptable.

❑❑❑

18

Curriculum Planning and Sharing by Teachers

INTRODUCTION

There are two main approaches to studying the curriculum. It can be examined in the traditional sense as a course of study or as teachers prefer to do as an educative experience. In their work, teachers revise and apply continuously the written curriculum to create unique educative experiences for their pupils. Ultimately, application of the curriculum is always a question of the quality of learning and teaching, and of what or how the pupils learn, how they advance, and how their learning can be supported most effectively.

The curriculum, therefore, can be studied as a text or as a process where pupils and teacher(s) interact in order to implement the objectives of education. In Finland, the curriculum has often been defined as 'a dynamic *process* that is constantly reacting to the results of evaluation and changes in the environment. The aims that have been set show the direction in which to go, but they are not to place restrictions on the tuition'. Defining the curriculum as a process accentuates its significance as an instrument for developing school. This emphasis is also an important starting point in this chapter, where teachers are examined both on an individual and group level, as developers of the curriculum of their school and thus, also, as developers of their own work and the entire school community.

In Finland the curriculum is an important instrument for directing education policy and promoting educational equality: 'The curriculum is an expression of the local decision-makers' political will as part of the national education policy'.

Finnish schools draft their own curricula independently on the basis of national guidelines. The foundations of the national core curriculum determine the social and cultural changes central for the development of the education system, and the value basis of schoolwork. When the society as a whole is in a continuous state of change, curricula also need to be flexible. The significance of local decision-making and expertise and the needs of local actors have become strongly accentuated. The teachers have a high level of professionality and are experts on the possibilities and restrictions for successful schoolwork in their own working community and municipality. In this sense, they are the best possible experts for planning the curriculum for their own school.

CONTINUOUS CURRICULUM REFORM

The interval between reforms of the national guidelines for curriculum has become shorter and shorter in Finland. This accelerating change is represented in Figure 18.1.

Since the mid-80s the responsibility for drawing up a curriculum increasingly has been transferred to the teachers. Since 1994, the national development work of curriculum has been informed by ongoing evaluation of the reform process.

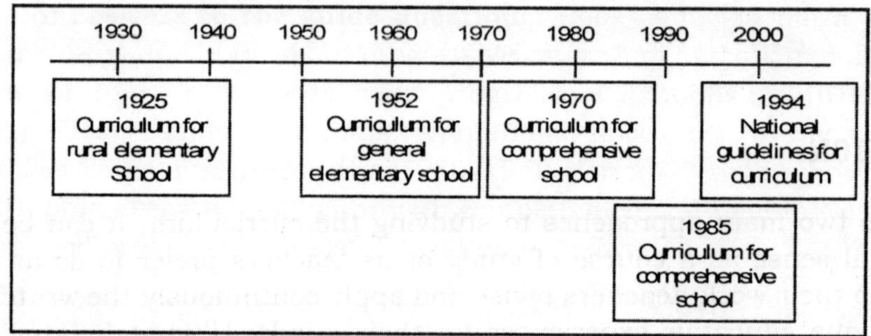

Figure 18.1. Curriculum reforms in the Finnish school system

The next national curriculum development projects are related to pre-school education. During the years 2000-01, every Finnish child under 6 years old gains the right to pre-school education. The curriculum work began in autumn 1999, and the new national guidelines for curriculum had a planned date for introduction of 1 August, 2000 when legislation on pre-school education was to be enacted. After the publication of the guidelines for curriculum, the providers of education have 1 year to prepare the local curricula.

TEACHERS AND THE TEACHER COMMUNITY IN THE SCHOOL-BASED CURRICULUM PROCESS

The idea of the teacher as the maker of his or her own curriculum has been a consideration when drafting curriculum guidelines. It has been presumed that this might transform the teacher's work from practices dictated by habits and traditions into a more reflective direction. The process itself has been seen as a strategy for supporting the professional growth of teachers. The work and role of a teacher are not necessarily collegial and reflective. Teacher isolation, indviduality, presentism and conservatism have been identified as characteristic of teacher's work. It is essential in developing school, as in developing the school's curriculum, to provide teachers with instruments for analysing their working community and individual work. An important dimension of this work is to expose embedded beliefs and routines to enable teachers to reflect critically on their practice. More traditional approaches to teacher learning and curriculum development are contrasted with this reflective turn in Table 18.1. What characteristics are evident among Finnish teachers as they engage in the curriculum process? In this chapter, on the basis of two extensive empirical studies, the status and significance of individual teachers, teacher community in the curriculum process and in developing the school are critically analysed. Data are selected from the following studies:

- A study that combines quantitative and qualitative approaches while focusing on individual class teachers as planners of their teaching and users and developers of the written curriculum.
- An ethnographic case study that includes interviews, observations and document analysis of a primary school teacher and the teacher's school community as planners and developers of the curriculum.

Evidence from both of these studies is presented separately.

FROM INDIVIDUAL TO COLLABORATION: TEACHERS AS CURRICULUM PLANNERS

The essential factors in developing curriculum and schools are individual teachers, groups of teachers, and the teacher community. The aim of Kosunen's study was to understand primary school teachers' interpretations of the intended curriculum and to ascertain how the intended curriculum and curriculum development are related to their instructional planning and teaching practices. Curriculum knowledge was examined as an integral part of teachers' practical knowledge.

The theoretical background of this study can be found in studies of teachers' thinking, studies of primary school teachers' work and studies of teachers' professional development. In addition, theoretical aspects applicable to the study are found in curriculum studies and studies of teachers' instructional planning. Accordingly, the most important theoretical aspects and main concepts in this study are found in three models: Calderhead's model of Knowledge Use in Teaching, Jaggar's model of Teachers' Sources of Knowledge and Ways of Learning and Cornett model of Analysis of the Impact of Teacher Personal Practical Theories on their curricular and instructional decision making.

The methods used to determine the views of primary school teachers were both quantitative and qualitative: a questionnaire with attitude scales and open questions (n=85), in-depth theme interviews, journal writing, and thinking aloud techniques in authentic instructional planning situations.

The results indicate that teachers' sex, the amount of working experience they have as well as their participation in curriculum development projects were connected with attitudes the teachers have towards the use and development of the curriculum. In addition, the three background factors mentioned above were related to the willingness of the teachers to put the curriculum into practice.

Experienced teachers possess a broad and many-sided body of knowledge related to learning and instruction. They use this practical knowledge in constructing their teaching practice. Professional experience and broad knowledge of instructional and management routines seem to enable experienced teachers to understand essential ideas and principles written in the curriculum and to put them into practice. Accordingly, experienced teachers are able to process 'the spirit' and the goals of the curriculum in planning their instruction. Experienced teachers are more able than their less experienced colleagues to connect curricular goals with pupil learning and learning situations.

Of special interest was how the experienced teachers, as members of planning teams developing the curriculum, interpreted the written curriculum. These curriculum-makers had internalized the core idea of the curriculum innovation. They used student-oriented teaching methods more often than other teachers and were more often development-oriented. They tended also to individualize and differentiate their instruction more often than their less experienced colleagues. The curriculum-makers stressed the importance of using the written curriculum as a basis for their instructional planning. They also showed consideration for collegiality in their work and in developing the curriculum for school. In this study teachers were considered as potential breakers of the isolation of teachers' work. In addition they were seen as developers of the curriculum, their own professional practice and school.

Table 18.1. Teacher community vs. teacher isolation

Teacher community in the school's curriculum process	Teacher isolation in the school's curriculum process
The community has the ability to analyze itself and to conduct open, reflective discussions	Openness and reflectivity do not reach the entire community; there is little professional dialogue
The community is willing to develop its culture of practice in order to improve its basic task	Teachers create their own curriculum without input from others
The community is able to work interactively- all members actively participate in the planning process with a critical perspective	Interaction is limited

The findings on the vital importance of collegiality and teacher groups inspired Huusko's study, which concentrated on studying the teacher community's activity during the planning process of school-specific curriculum.

COMMUNITY OF TEACHERS IN THE CURRICULUM PROCESS

Huusko's study investigated the organizational characteristics of the teacher community and analyzed dominant characteristics of school culture. The teacher community was examined as a loosely coupled expert organization in which a shared and pervasive school culture is prevalent. In such a case, the improvement of the school – the enhancement of learning and educating the pupils – is understood primarily as the improvement of the school culture, a process in which the teacher community plays a central role in defining the characteristics of a desirable culture. Educational dialogues clarify the direction of development. In addition to specifying the tasks of the school, they define the views of 'up-to-date' teaching and learning, teachership, and the direction of the curriculum process.

Huusko's inquiry is a qualitative case study consisting of interviews of the teacher community, observations and analyses on documents mainly related to the preparations of a school-based curriculum. From the standpoint of the curriculum, the most interesting area of study was observing the teacher community planning the school-based curriculum. In addition to the teachers' own views of themselves (interviews), also their activity (observations) and products (document analyses) were examined.

The study indicates that the activity of teachers is guided by good practice norms a culture shared within the teaching staff, directing its observations, interpretations and behaviour. This was summarized in a model of the interaction of the teaching staff. The model consists of three levels: (1) job satisfaction - liberalism: the positive experience of the community based on the markedly autonomous status of the individual teacher; (2) auto-censorship as a tool for maintaining and preserving the community spirit; (3) small groups, forming 'cliques,' which function as a realization method and a discharge channel for the need for development.

The basic assumption in this model is that the teachership maintains the feeling of satisfaction and community spirit by means of preventing and avoiding conflicts. The teacher avoids expressions of his or her own opinion, thus practising auto-censorship. In this situation, development work and dialogue are essential for transfer from the community level to small groups. In these groups, the teachers' efforts for development are supported by like-minded teachers. Pedagogic like-mindedness and common objects of interest are crucial criteria for the teachers' grouping, forming 'cliques'.

The character of the interactive culture in the teacher community leads to the question of whether school practices could become more reflective through curriculum reform. To evaluate this, the teacher community and its activity can be examined by means of a three-level model related to interaction between teachers.

First level: job satisfaction - liberalism

Teachers share an idea of the curriculum and its significance as the disposition of the teacher's work. At this point, the written curriculum is seen as the framework of activity, liberal and responsive to diversity. Within the framework of the curriculum, an individual teacher can work according to his or her own internal, idiosyncratic visions and values. It is regarded merely as a series of recommendations, from which an individual teacher can get ideas that influence his or her own work.

Second level: auto-censorship

At this level the teaching staff does not want to, or is unable to, comment on the activity of their individual members in the curriculum process. The eagerness of individual teachers to participate is considered a private matter, and the other teachers do not regard it as appropriate to comment. This indicates a lack of community-level discussion on the content of curriculum. Practical, everyday matters are discussed while teaching, learning and whole-school issues are avoided. Examination of the teacher community as a whole, therefore, does not reveal the activities of teachers or groups of teachers. It is, therefore, necessary to shift the focus from the level of the entire school to small groups - the 'cliques'.

Third level: commitment to the activity of small groups - forming 'cliques'

The school curriculum is drafted on several separate levels, even in individual schools. The 'official' curriculum groups are divided by subject and/or by class. In practice, the working intensity of curriculum groups fluctuates considerably. In Huusko's study, only some groups of teachers implemented the process to create 'a somewhat acceptable result'. Some groups of teachers tackled the task in a more active manner with the intention of bringing about real changes even in the pupil's work and methods.

In their own opinion, the target-oriented teachers gained more personal benefit and satisfaction from the curriculum process. These teachers compared the drafting of curriculum to professional guidance, or regarded the process as 'a valuable forum for professional discussion'. They found the effects of the curriculum work positive and productive as well giving direction to the overall development of the school. More passive teachers did not grasp this connection between the development of the school and the curriculum work. They did, though, mention that the school-specific curriculum work was 'one of those rare situations, where you can honestly talk about your job with your colleagues'.

For the development of school it is essential that all the members of the working community learn from the productive co-operation of the active teachers. At the community level, this means acknowledging members' heterogenic activity in the teacher community. The teacher community of Huusko's study took its first steps towards a more active and open development of school. The curriculum process enabled collegial, professional discussion between the teachers. On the basis of the study material, however, it seems as though the need for professional dialogue disappears as quickly as it comes into existence.

COMMUNITY DIMENSIONS OF CURRICULUM DEVELOPMENT

Problems have been detected regarding teacher's participation in the drafting of the curriculum. Firstly, the teachers are poorly acquainted with the theory of curriculum. There are courses on curriculum, or at least on matters directly linked to it, in teacher education programmes. Unless in-service training on the drafting and use of curriculum can be provided for the teachers, the 'know how' in this area may remain deficient. Secondly, the lack of process thinking has proven problematic in the drafting of curriculum. The teachers do not appear to understand the drafting of curriculum as a continuous, dynamic process evolving through evaluation. Rather, the curriculum is too easily regarded as a one-off product, using the principle of 'over and done with'.

What, then, has been achieved through school-based curriculum work during the past five years? What are the effects of the curriculum reform on teachers' professional practice? Has the process of making school-based curricula been successful from the point of view of teachers and school organization? And, finally, has the process of making school-based curricula empowered the teachers to reflect on their practice and profession both individually and collectively and thus provided 'added value' to their professional growth?

In Huusko's study, the level of commitment to the curriculum process of individual teachers was very inconsistent and fragmented. The collegial groups that were used for multilateral co-operation in their work concentrated on the process. The teachers in these groups felt that they acquired tools for their own pedagogic development and reflectivity. A majority of the teachers in the study did not, however, show an adequate communicative/reflective competence to advance into real development discussion during the process. For these latter groups the process did not meet anticipated outcomes. Curriculum work did not increase these teachers' capacity for curriculum and school development.

The teachers were quite unanimous in their opinions, stating that the process was an event where they were obliged to discuss work, the development of school and its future. This was perceived as a positive and useful experience that was expected to continue.

However, observation of these group meetings indicate that the hopes for continuing the curriculum process were not fulfilled. In this community, the school-based curriculum was seen as 'finished for good', and the process was not continued after the complementation of the written curriculum. This process automatically excludes new teachers in the community from the school-based curriculum process, thus leaving them without any possibilities to influence the commitments referred to in the school-based curriculum.

One of the objectives of the curriculum reform was to increase the collegial cooperation between the members of the teacher community. However, self-censorship within the school was a barrier to altering its culture.

We have identified a number of strategies that may be useful to teachers to continue their curriculum work.

Acknowledging dominant interaction patterns

Open communication is prevented by unconscious sets of actions. In order to alter these models it would be necessary to acknowledge the structures and their effects, after which they could be detected and worked on. The starting point for development must be the present state of the community with its specific features.

Methodological approach

The objectives and activities of schools can be documented. A school-based curriculum process provides an excellent framework for community-level professional discussion. A possibility to participate in the decisions made concerning making the activity more efficient, principles for activation and development areas must be worked on for all members of the community. The community should also cultivate shared ownership of the development process. Commitment to the development work of individual teachers must be commonly accepted. The input of active teachers and teacher groups as the gatherers of development experience becomes significant towards these ends.

Utilizing 'cliques'

The school development work becomes easily concentrated in the cliques created by active teachers. The existence of different teacher groups should, then, be acknowledged and accepted, thus increasing the openness and manageability of the teacher community. Even teachers outside the cliques should be communicated with on the work and observations of the various cliques.

Leadership

The principal of the school is a central person in the school's development. The central elements in the activity of the leader of the school are the creation of development opportunities, support for development work by the leader's own example, and the acquisition and allocation of the resources needed for development work.

The function of a school-based curriculum process as contributing to teachers' reflective approach to work is quite problematic. Current patterns of present a formidable challenge. To create a universal development model is particularly problematic in a situation where the capabilities of both individual teachers and teacher communities are different, and when the learning environments of schools differ significantly from each other. The East Anglia Center for Applied Research in Education evaluated the success of the Finnish curriculum reform. The evaluators stated that when they first visited schools in early 1995, the curriculum process was only beginning. At that time, many of the schools lacked a strategy for curriculum work. There were no common strategies for negotiating curriculum targets, and no agreement on the measures for implementing the objective of change. Many of the teachers had not read the curriculum guidelines and did not understand their implications for their teaching. Norris noted significant differences between schools and teachers in their ways of utilizing the possibilities inherent in the curriculum reform. They concluded that: 'Only in a minority of schools was there an explicit recognition that developing the curriculum might involve a continuing cyclical process of innovation, evaluation, and development'. Particularly interesting in the Norris study was the division of schools into five different classes in relation to the development of the curriculum. These are summarized as follows.

1. **Non-starters** – schools that have little or no conception of the framework for the comprehensive school, have not started implementing the reform nor do they have the organizational capacity or staff to do so.
2. **False starters** – schools that have adopted some of the features of the reform (e.g. options or consulting parents) but are not in tune with its spirit and do not have the organizational capacity for school-based curriculum development.

3. **Slow starters** – schools that understand the main themes of the curriculum reform and have started to implement some of its features but appear to lack the organizational capacity or vision to take things much further.
4. **Up-and-running** – schools that have the organizational capacity for school-based curriculum change, have made progress in developing the main lines of the reform but have yet to engage the issue of classroom change.
5. **There or thereabouts** – schools that are engaged in school-based curriculum development, in changing classroom practice and appear to have organizational capacity to sustain such work.

SUMMARY

It seems that basing one's hopes on school-based curricula as a conduit for improving teachers' reflective capacity development expertise is not entirely without foundation. However, there is need for further research on how teachers interpret curriculum frameworks and to support the development of strategies to promote ongoing professional development. However, improving the curriculum and the school in a way that provides effective education requires patience and time. As Olson suggests new ideas are shifts in orientation, new sets of unclear meanings, whose implications take time to emerge. What these meanings are we must learn from teachers who can tell us what they understand the new ideas to be and what significance they attach to them. We need to see how the intentions of teachers are connected to problems they are trying to solve.

In view of the continuous development of the curricula, information collected by means of continuous evaluation is essential. More external evaluation is needed both for national development and international comparison. Evaluation is vital also for internal feedback as a formative professional influence.

There are several opportunities inherent in the processing of school-based curricula. The 'slow starters', 'up-and-running' and 'there or thereabouts' schools, identified by Norris, are not a problem. However, the 'non-starters' and 'false starters' schools present a more obdurate challenge to a reform process that is premised on a school-based approach. However, the expertise of active teachers and groups of teachers should be better utilized and school principals need to be more aware of their pivotal role in the process.

Curriculum planning is a vital element of effective teaching. When planning a curriculum, teachers create a detailed outline of what they are going to do with the students throughout the school year. Preservice teachers need to be instructed in curriculum planning so that they can effectively compose curricula once they enter the teaching profession. By clearly explaining the steps in curriculum planning and allowing pre-service teachers to practice the act of planning a curriculum, instructors can ensure that pre-service teachers will be able to effectively write a curriculum.

INSTRUCTIONS

1. ***Explore the standards :*** Each state has set curriculum standards that dictate what students should be taught in each subject and grade. Explain to pre-service teachers that they need to consult their standards prior to planning the curriculum.

2. ***Compose a yearly plan :*** Prior to starting a school year, all teachers should compose a yearly plan. This plan should consist of a list of all of the weeks of the school year. Next to each week, the curriculum planner should list what activities the students need to complete as well as which standards they will teach during that time period. Ask pre-service teachers to practice this skill by composing a yearly plan for a hypothetical school year following this format.

3. ***Write a weekly plan :*** As teachers move through the year, they compose weekly plans. These plans are more specific than the yearly plan. To compose a weekly plan, teachers list the days of the week, and for each day they list the activities that they will ask the students to complete in numbered order. Below the numbered list of activities, teachers list the standard or standards that they will cover that day. Ask pre-service teachers to create a weekly plan by selecting one of the weeks from their yearly plan and writing it out in this more specific format.

4. ***Prepare a daily plan :*** Teachers write a daily plan for each day in the weekly plan. The daily plan is even more specific than the weekly plan. This plan includes an objective, or statement, that explains what will be accomplished on that day, a list of required materials, a scripted outline of what the teacher intends to say and do during the class and a listing of the standard or standards covered. Instruct pre-service teachers to give daily lesson planning a try by taking one of the days from their weekly plan and composing a daily lesson plan containing all of the required elements.

5. ***Encourage reflection :*** After trying a lesson plan, teachers should reflect upon the effectiveness of the lesson. Ask pre service teachers to participate in reflection once they begin teaching by taking a few minutes after presenting a lesson to students and writing notes about the lesson. In these notes, they should include what parts worked well as well as how they would change the lesson in the future to make it more effective.

19

Improving Accuracy in Education

INTRODUCTION

The discussion identifies eleven trends in the evolution of research technologies trends toward greater digitalization, speed, accuracy, capacity, sensitivity, miniaturization, versatility, popularity, and ease of control. An additional trend involves the dollar expense of devices a mixture of both increased and decreased costs.

DIGITALIZATION

The word *digital*, when applied to electronic devices, refers to the manner in which information is processed in a device (computer, camera, audio recorder) and communicated to other devices. The implications of digital systems is perhaps best exemplified in electronic computers.

Computers are of three classes analog, digital, and hybrid. Analog computers operate on the basis of continuous variables, just as a thermostat functions along an unbroken array of temperatures, ranging from very cold to very hot. In along an unbroken array of temperatures, ranging from very cold to very hot. In contrast, digital computers operate on the basis of discrete variables, just as the typical electric-light switch can assume only two positions completely on and completely off. Hybrid computers combine certain features of both analog and digital devices. But because analog computers are rarely used in the field of education or in the social sciences, our concern in educational research is limited to digital varieties (even though digital machines may include some analog elements).

In computer parlance, each binary on/off switch in a digital circuit is called a *bit.* Because a bit has only two possible positions (the digit *1* for on, the digit *0* for off), it cannot hold or convey much information. However, when eight bits are clustered to form a unit called a *byte*, the large quantity of on/off permutations that this 8-bit cluster assumes can represent a great variety of symbols. For example, a single meaningful character such as a letter of the alphabet, a number, or a punctuation mark can be assigned a set code of eight on/off (1/0) combinations. The byte pattern representing letter A is 01000001, the pattern for letter B is 01000010, and so on. Furthermore, in order to provide more flexibility in defining symbols manipulated by computers, byte size has been extended from 8 to 16 bits in recently designed systems.

Because great quantities of bytes are needed for the complex operations of the computer, bytes are usually not referred to as single units but, rather, as *kilobytes*, a term often abbreviated as K or KB. The prefix *kilo* normally means 1000. However, a digital computer's counting system is binary, based on the number 2 rather than on the number 10 in the decimal system, so one kilobyte contains 1024 individual bytes (since 2 multiplied by itself nine times equals 1024). The operating capacity of computers is often referred to in terms of kilobytes or in such larger units as *megabyte* (one million bytes), *gigabyte*, (one billion bytes), and *terabyte* (one trillion bytes).

In summary, one trend in digitalization has been that of increasing the number of bits that comprise a byte and of increasing the number of bytes that a given computer has available for manipulating and storing data. A researcher who in the early 1980s operated a desktop computer that had a maximum of 128 kilobytes of working memory was, at the end of the 1990s, operating a notebook-size computer that provided a few dozen megabytes of working memory (random-access memory) and several gigabytes of long-term storage on a hard disk.

A further trend has been the digitalization of an increasing variety of research devices that formerly operated on principals other than the digital computer's 0/1 binary principle. The recording of visual images, which traditionally has depended on film, is increasingly recorded in digital form in both still cameras and motion-picture cameras (television *camcorders*). A digital camera that is operated as easily as an instamatic camera enables a person to photograph scenes that are captured into the camera's random-access memory or on a special diskette and then transferred into a personal computer. The computer displays the picture on its screen, where the researcher is able to edit the scene adding, altering, or eliminating elements and then print out the result as a full-color photograph.

The recording of sound (speech, music, sounds in nature) that traditionally took the form of vibrations in grooves on a plastic disk (phonograph records) or magnetic impulses on a wire or tape (tape recorder) increasingly depends on digital devices. For example, the grooves on a compact disc contain pits that a laser beam reads as either of two depths, one signifying *1* and the other signifying *0*. The quality of these digital visual and sound representations is superior to that of their non digital predecessors.

SPEED

One of the more dramatic impacts of modern technologies on research activities is that of increasing the speed of operations.

Transistors began replacing vacuum tubes in computers in the early 1960s, making it then possible for computers to execute up to 100,000 instructions per second. Since then, the speed of computation has increased many fold. Desktop computers within seconds perform calculations that would require months of time with a hand calculator. In no more than a second, mainframe computers carry out billions of calculations, with the speed of such devices continuing to increase by the year. As a result, determining the degree of correlation among several thousand students' test scores in a variety of subject-matter areas is a task requiring no more than a moment.

The velocity of transporting information from one site to another also continues to accelerate. Whereas postal service can require days or weeks to carry messages, facsimile copies of documents are sent instantaneously via telephone lines and satellites to nearly any city in the world. Electronic mail provides researchers a similar quick way to exchange ideas.

Although traditional methods of producing photographs and motion pictures have required a delay of hours or days for the film to be processed, researchers now can immediately see the results of their photographic efforts. A snapshot of a school building (taken with a Polaroid or digital camera) or a motion picture of a student dance performance (taken with a television camera a camcorder) can be viewed the moment after it's recorded.

ACCURACY

Although bank tellers, supermarket clerks, and insurance adjusters are apt to blame mistakes of computation or billing on "computer error," it is rarely the case that something wrong with the computer's hardware is at fault. Computers are generally highly accurate and reliable. In the great majority of instances, when errors do occur, the fault lies either with the person who wrote the software program which carries out the computations or else with the people who are operating the computer. There is always the danger that a computer programmer out of ineptitude or malice will insert malevolent instructions into a program which subsequently act as a virus, harmfully infecting the operation of other computers with which that machine communicates. Virus protection programs have thus been developed to cope with this danger of viruses. But again, the blame for viruses must be borne by people, not the computers themselves.

In sum, computers are far more accurate than are people in performing computations, storing quantities of information, and verifying the storage operations; and new methods for ensuring accuracy continue to appear.

CAPACITY

In 1974, the Intel Corporation's 8080 computer chip that represents the heart of the system contained 4,800 transistors. In 1993, Intel introduced its Pentium chip that provided 3,200,000 transistors, with future chips promising to expand such capacity at an accelerating rate. On the average, each newly developed computer chip doubles computer operating capacity every 18 months. Consequently, educational researchers are able to manipulate and store ever-growing quantities of complicated variables. For example, carrying out computations involving multiple scores for thousands of students who inhabit complex and diverse environments has become increasingly feasible.

SENSITIVITY

Recorders for capturing sounds and sights provide a good example of the increasing sensitivity of electronic devices. The passing years witness advances in the ability of audiotape devices and video cameras to record events from greater distances and in difficult environments.

In the past, the task of editing a research report for publication required that an editor first peruse a handwritten or typewritten document in order to mark corrections and make format changes, then have the material set in type for printing. However, today a document can be digitized into a computer by means of an image scanner equipped with an optical character recognition function (OCR software). Each page of the author's document is thereby transformed into an image on the computer screen so that an editor can read and alter the material as if it had originally been typed into the computer. The more sophisticated present-day OCR programs are highly sensitive, able to distinguish the shapes, sizes, and pitch of symbols including handwriting and to learn from experience. The edited, newly-formatted version of the material can be printed as typeset copy, ready to be photographed for printing in a final published form.

Although a universal OCR machine is not yet available to read all versions of even a single alphabet, the likelihood that such software will be perfected seems bright.

The ability of computers to achieve reasonable translations of documents from one language into another can be expected as well, a great boon to researchers whose own foreign language skills are limited.

MINIATURIZATION

To house a computer in the 1950s, a large room was needed to accommodate the forest of vacuum tubes that performed the machine's data manipulation and storage. By the 1990s the size of computers had so dramatically decreased that an electronic gadget smaller than a deck of playing cards could carry out far more operations and far more quickly than had its 1950 ancestors. Two inventions made such miniaturization possible. First was the creation of transistors to replace vacuum tubes. Second was the development of integrated-circuit chips into which multiple transistors could be encased. By the 1990s, millions of transistors could be imbedded in a single silicon chip no larger than an infant's finger nail.

Audio and video recording equipment has likewise become more compact each year. The widespread adoption of wire and tape-recorders in the mid-20th century eliminated the need for a bulky collection of machinery to record and playback speech and music. Since that time, audio recorders have become increasingly small and sensitive. By the end of the century, tape recorders no larger than a small child's hand and weighing no more than a few ounces were commonly used by researchers to record interviews and group discussions. Such devices were voice activated, starting to record only when someone spoke, then stopping until another voice was heard, thereby permitting a researcher to record intermittent conversations without being immediately present to personally start and stop the instrument.

Miniature video cameras, placed in inconspicuous locations and operated by remote-control devices from a distance, enabled investigators to record sights and sounds of a classroom, office, or discussion group without intimidating the participants with the presence of onlookers or highly visible equipment.

VERSATILITY

Tasks that were performed by individual instruments in the past are increasingly being performed by a single device. Prior to the advent of "talking pictures" in the late 1920s, motion-picture cameras recorded sights but not sounds, whereas phonograph recording devices captured sounds but not sights. Since those early years, the ability of a single, combining instrument to carry out multiple functions has markedly improved. Therefore, by the end of the 20th century, a relatively inexpensive video camera (camcorder) could simultaneously record the sights and sounds of an event, either up close or at a distance (via telephoto lenses and remote microphones), with the results immediately available for display on a computer screen and ready to be edited portions eliminated, sequences altered, details enlarged, and the pace of events slowed or quickened.

POPULARITY

The pace at which attractive technological innovations are disseminated can be illustrated with the worldwide distribution of computers over the decade 1985–1995. In 1985, an estimated 38.1 million computers were in use throughout the world. The total grew by 260% to 129.4 million in 1991 and by 575% to 257.2 million in 1995. The expected total by year 2000 was projected at 535.6 million, 14 times greater than the number sold 15 years earlier. However, the distribution by nations has been very uneven, with the United States in 1995 having 345 computers per 1,000 people, a number expected to reach 580 by year 2000. Following the United States, the nations with the highest per capita incidence of computers by year 2000 are expected to be Australia (526 per 1,000 population), Norway (515), Canada (512), Denmark (510), Finland (505), Sweden (109), New Zealand (500), and Great Britain (441). Less favored am such countries as Mexico (66 per 1,000), Russia (62), Brazil (48), and China (11). The worldwide rate has been predicted at 90 per 1,000 people by the opening of the 21st century.

EASE OF CONTROL

The electronics industry made rapid progress over the last half of the 20th century in rendering their projects more "user friendly," with further progress due in the years ahead.

During the 1940s, producing a monaural phonograph recording required a special studio, complicated equipment, and the services of a skilled technician. By the close of the century, a child with minimal training could produce a stereo sound tape-recording of far greater fidelity than the skilled technician's phonograph disk of the forties.

During the early 1960s, producing a black-and-white television sequence required a complicated, weighty camera and a trained operator. If the sequence was to be saved for transmission at a later time, it had to be recorded on motion picture film as a *kinescope*. But by the 1990s, nearly anyone with a few minutes' instruction could successfully produce a full-color television sequence by means of a lightweight camcorder that conveniently fit into the palm of the hand and simultaneously converted the pictured scenes into digitized codes on magnetic tape that could be saved for later viewing.

In the 1970s, an investigator who wished to use a computer to calculate the frequency of a large quantity of respondents' answers to questionnaire items and to compute correlations among types of items was obliged to enter the data and calculation instructions into a mainframe computer by means of a rather complicated programming language, such as Fortran. By the 1990s, that same task could be accomplished on a laptop personal computer equipped with an easily understood statistical program that provided the user with far more kinds of information than would a mainframe computer 25 years earlier. Furthermore, the personal computer allowed the investigator to insert the outcome of the computations into the research report which the author was currently writing on the machine and include full-color graphic displays of the summarized data.

COST

With the passing of time, the purchase price of a technological innovation typically assumes a familiar pattern—very high cost at the outset, with the cost then progressively diminishing as the device is mass produced, improvements are effected in its design, and competition heats up among manufacturers.

A mainframe computer that filled a large room and cost $1 million in the 1960s could be replaced in the 1990s by a desktop personal computer that was 1,000 times cheaper but had comparable computational power. In the mid-1990s a $2,000 laptop computer was more powerful than a $10 million IBM mainframe computer 20 years earlier. In the mid-1970s a handheld electronic calculator that could only add, subtract, multiply, and divide cost $250 at an office supply store. In the 1990s, an even smaller calculator that performed far more operations than the 1970 model cost $2 at the corner supermarket.

In summary, the 21st century should witness the improvement of such technology at an accelerating pace, equipping researchers with an expanding range of devices that improve the speed and accuracy of collecting and storing data, classifying information, and publishing the results.

RENDERING COMPLEXITY UNDERSTANDABLE

Most thoughtful people likely recognize that (a) every educational event is the result of a host of causal factors, (b) each event can contribute to a diversity of after-effects, and

(c) any event can be viewed from a variety of vantage points, each of which yields a different understanding. In short, educational activities are extremely complicated phenomena.

Not only does every event involve multiple variables and many facets, but no event is static—frozen in time. Each is in continual transition, shifting from one status to another as its constituent variables interact. Consequently, a student's achievement-test scores are valid only for that one testing occasion and can be expected to change as the student gains experience and views matters in a different light. Likewise, the pattern of decision making in a nation's ministry of education is bound to alter, at least in subtle ways, as the days pass. And the amount of effort a group of pupils devote to their learning tasks can differ with the advancing moments.

When educational studies are cast against such a backdrop of reality the reality of a highly complicated and ephemeral world it becomes apparent that all research projects represent only bits and pieces of a constantly shifting picture puzzle. Hence, scholars are confronted with two daunting tasks how to encompass all of this complexity and how to render such complexity understandable to their audience. The ability to perform such tasks is constrained by the limitations of the human mind and the fallibility of human communication. People's capacity to simultaneously interrelate a host of variables is restricted, because their minds are engineered to consider one thing at a time. Although ideas may follow in rapid succession, they still generally march in single file. Furthermore, human memories as the raw materials of most thought—are elusive and often imprecise. Consequently, a researcher trying to accomplish the goal of completely elucidating educational events in all their tangled complications is rather like the man, in Stephen Crane's verse, who chased the horizon. Yet, however impossible the goal may be, the need for people to understand and manage educational affairs requires that the goal be pursued, even though, for the sake of practicality, it must be reduced to a more modest and achievable aim. Such a modest aim can be that of designing studies which accommodate as many influential variables and viewpoints as feasible and of admitting the limitations of the conclusions.

Thus, the position adopted here is that investigators cannot legitimately dismiss complexity simply with such clichés as "Other things being equal" or "Setting other factors aside." The trouble is that "other things" are never equal "other things" affect outcomes in either large or small ways. Nor can "other factors" be set aside without risking inaccurate interpretations of results. Consequently, researchers can at least attempt to place their projects within a broader domain of related events and to estimate not only what their work means within that domain but also to propose which features of the domain are not addressed by their work.

This modest aim of expanding the purview of a research project beyond the data collected in the project itself involves placing the project in a broader context by such methods as (a) literature surveys, (b) meta-analysis, (c) classification systems (typologies and taxonomies), and (d) explanatory theories. As methods, all four of these have been used in the past; so, as general Few, however, give any indication of the means by which they selected studies for review.

The term meta-analysis can be applied to any quantitative integration of empirical research results. The two most popular approaches to defining the domain of pertinent studies and calculating the commonalties and differences among studies are those described by Glass, McGaw, and Smith and by Hunter, Schmidt, and Jackson.

Proponents of meta-analysis note that the technique has equipped researchers to reveal consistencies in several bodies of studies in which narrative reviewers were only able to discern marked variation, suggesting that wider use of the technique may "help reestablish public faith in the efficacy of empirical research in education by making clearer what has already been achieved" by schools.

Larger quantities of increasingly precise meta-analyses can be expected as computer networks provide investigators access to so many more studies and as more refined statistical programs are produced. The ability of computers to calculate complex relationships among a host of variables within the space of a few seconds will equip researchers with the capacity to conduct meta-analyses that would have been impossible a few years ago.

CLASSIFICATION SYSTEMS—TAXONOMIES AND TYPOLOGIES

The intention of such schemes is to provide a complete mapping of a realm, with the realm usually identified by such a label as "types of affective educational objectives", "forms of differential education of the gifted", or "taxonomies of misdeeds, sanctions, and aims of sanctions".

Although computer networks expand the variety of studies available to researchers, that expansion does not render the realm of a researcher's topic more readily understood. Indeed, an expansion of collected studies can easily do the opposite increase the difficulty of comprehending the additional variables that an augmented search typically produces. This means that, in the future, investigators need to devise new classification schemes that lucidly portray the extended variety of variables comprising a domain of interest.

There are two principal approaches to creating a classification scheme by logical deduction and by a method of statistical comparison known as numerical *taxonomy.* Logical deduction consists of a person inspecting a collection of data (in the present case it's a collection of studies in some domain of education) and proposing enough categories to accommodate all of the data (all of the studies). The categories generally form a hierarchy, with more specific classes subsumed under more general ones. In contrast, the numerical-taxonomy approach consists of a person (a) identifying a series of defining characteristics of the collected data, then (b) statistically comparing the individual items (studies) to determine how much one is like another in terms of those characteristics. The greater the correlation among items (studies), the more they belong together within the same category or within closely related categories. In way of illustration, the characteristics to be compared among studies that comprise the domain *school finance* might include (a) size of a school system's enrolment, (b) size of the school budget, (c) budget categories, (d) sources of income, (e) accounting procedures, and such. Producing a numerical taxonomy of school finance would consist of calculating the degree of similarities among research studies in terms of the array of characteristics.

The logical deduction approach has been by far the more popular method. However, with the capacity of computers to calculate complicated relationships, numerical approaches to constructing taxonomies may be more widely adopted in the years ahead.

One important way researchers use a classification system is to show where within a domain of knowledge their particular study is located. In other words, taxonomies help investigators portray how their research project fits into the pattern of other studies conducted in a particular area of education.

EXPLANATORY THEORIES

Whereas taxonomies and typologies are designed to show relationships among phenomena without accounting for the causes of such connections, *theories*—as the term is used here—serve as formal explanations of why educational events occur as they do. More precisely, the relationships depicted in theories are assumed to be cause-and-effect linkages among phenomena. For instance, a theorist may assert that the nation's lack of progress in furnishing adequate educational facilities for all learners has been caused by a combination of economic recession, skirmishes between political parties, and a reactionary educational bureaucracy. Another theorist may account for an adolescent's sudden spurt of progress in school by changes in the boy's environment-encouragement from an admired teacher, the youth's election as a class officer, and his parents' promise to buy him a car upon graduation if he earns a place on the academic honor role.

To create an explanatory model, a theorist abstracts from a type of educational phenomenon the assumed key components of that phenomenon and then proposes how such components interact to produce the phenomenon's outcomes. Thus, a theory of educational administration proposes the sorts of units (people, departments, agencies) that make up the administrative structure and the manner in which those units influence each other. Statements of influence take the form of speculation about who is responsible for what actions, who has authority over whom, how information flows among the units, what sanctions one unit can impose on others, and more. In like manner, a theory of student discipline identifies the units that participate in any instance of student misbehavior and postulates the kinds of interactions among those units that produce the results of the event. What, then, does the theorist's expanding ability to compile studies and theories portend for the future? That ability can:

a. Increase the sophistication of theories (increasing the components that theories include and the interactions envisioned among components) by obliging theorists to consider a greater diversity of variables found in a wider range of studies conducted with different people in different contexts.

b. Enhance the ability of theorists to compare their models with others' versions, thereby assisting them in recognizing shortcomings of their own proposals that invite correction, revision, and explanation.

c. Challenge researchers to explain increasingly complex relationships in ways that other people can readily understand, particularly by utilizing the capacity of computers to display animated graphic versions of complicated models.

One way to compare theories is in terms of the range of phenomena they intend to explain. From such a perspective, theories can be arrayed along a scale extending from the most encompassing macro theories at one end to the most restricted mini theories at the other end. To illustrate, in the field of biology, Darwin theory of how all living species evolved over eons of time embraces more phenomena than does Wenner's theory of how honey bees communicate to their hive-mates the location of a bed of nectar-rich blossoms. Darwin's proposal, in effect, belongs toward the macroend of the scale while Wenner's belongs toward the mini-end. In the realm of education, Carroll's model of school learning is a macrotheory that focuses on teaching toward any sort of objective, whereas Downing model of teaching beginning reading is a mini theory focusing on structural (phonics) and semantic features of written language.

The chief advantage of macro theories is that they are designed to explain a wide range of events on the basis of a relatively few components and principles. However, in proposing to explain so much in such a simple way, they can fail to account for exactly how a specific event in a particular context has occurred. For this reason, some critics in the fields of human development and education contend that minitheories are apt to have greater explanatory and predictive power because they are obligated to explain a narrower range of variables than are the all-embracing macrotheories. Thus, one challenge theorists face in the future is to bridge the gap between mini- and macrotheories by depicting how more precise sub-components and sub-principles fit within more general components and principles. Theorists' improved ability to survey the professional literature, combined with the capacity of computers to manipulate variables, should contribute to greater integration of the macro and the mini.

DISTANT SOURCES

In the mid-20th century, the postal service, telephone, and airplane were the most influential media for extending researchers' capacity to collect data from a distance. At the close of the century, fax machines and such computer networks as the Internet and World Wide Web eclipsed those earlier devices' ability to reduce the distance barrier in researchers' data-gathering activities.

Furthermore, improvements achieved in the more traditional media permitted researchers to conduct a greater range of distant business from their own office or home. For example, the invention of telephones that furnished a television image of the speaker at the other end of the line enabled interviewers not only to conduct inquiries from any distance, but also to see the individuals with whom they were speaking. In addition, the devices already in widespread use to record phone conversations on tape could soon be replaced with ones that recorded both the telephone-transmitted sounds and sights in a computer for storage and display.

SIMULATED SOURCES

A simulated source is a substitute for an actual data source that cannot be studied directly. The researcher's aim in creating a simulation is to make the significant characteristics of the substitute source resemble as closely as possible the significant features of the original source. Prominent among forms of simulations bearing on education are studies of artificial intelligence.

Artificial intelligence (AI) has been described as "the science of making machines do things that would require intelligence if done by men". The machines in this instance are electronic computers. Developers of artificial-intelligence schemes assume that if they can devise computer programs that arrive at the same answers to problems that humans would provide, the steps of logic in those computer programs are likely similar to if not identical to the steps of human thought. In the field of artificial intelligence, the term *expert systems* refers to the patterns of information and decision-making rules applied by human experts to arrive at their solutions. A system necessary for solving one sort of problem can be different from the system for solving another. For instance, the information and rules employed by a chess master are not identical to those employed by an adroit reader of French literature, an adept auto mechanic, or a skilled teacher of children who suffer from dyslexia.

Noteworthy success in creating computer programs that solve complex problems has been achieved in the playing of such table games as checkers, tictac-toe, and chess. For example, consider the development of chess-player simulations. After three decades of efforts, computer scientists by the early 1990s had created a chess program named Deep Thought that could defeat 99.9% of human players. Designers then began working on a new version that would deploy integrated-circuit chips one thousand times faster than those available in the mid-1990s, chips that would inspect about one billion chess positions per second. But the scientists' joy in creating a machine that could defeat all but the most adept grand masters was dampened by their realizing that the machine's success derived from its exceptional speed of computation and not from its use of human-like logic. Hence, while success with computer chess failed to meet the researchers' "hopc of learning about the human mind it nevertheless led them to discover thinking processes different from our own [a discovery illustrating] the serendipity of science".

Undaunted, computer scientists and psychologists continue to pursue the challenges of artificial intelligence, including challenges relating to human learning issues important to educators. However, up to now Every prediction about major advances in artificial intelligence has proved to be overly optimistic. Today even simple learning tasks still go well beyond the world's most capable computer. When computers appear to be intelligent it is because they have been specially programmed to handle some task in a straightforward fashion like trying out billions of chess moves in order to play master-level chess. The computer has the potential to be a tool to leverage human intelligence for the foreseeable future.

One advantage of computers in this pursuit is their demand for clear thinking. Formulating a hypothesis so precisely that it will run on a computer forces crystal clarity on it. Computers tolerate neither hand waving nor fuzzy thinking and keep you honest. Unrealized, implicit, or unspoken assumptions are mercilessly weeded out. Weaknesses of construction appear as if under a magnifying glass.

A second advantage is the computer's ability to isolate aspects of mind in the form of simulated mental functions, enabling researchers to evaluate theories about how people learn and how they store and recall memories. In doing so, computers can organize and compare far larger masses of data scores, measurements, symptoms, behaviors in a far shorter time and more accurately than can humans, thereby providing investigators better tests of their theories than would otherwise be possible.

Educational applications of artificial intelligence have already appeared in the field of instructional design, particular in the analysis of the structure of subject matter areas and of students' thought patterns as they solve problems.

SUMMARY

As the contents of this chapter suggest, educational research faces a bright future as a result of technological advances that enhance the scope, speed, accuracy, and complexity of collecting and manipulating information and that foster greater worldwide communication among researchers.

20

Statistical Analyses and Future Sampling of Education

INTRODUCTION

The following discussion first identifies a variety of descriptive statistics that are useful in research, then turns to matters of inference. The aim of the chapter is to suggest which types of statistics are most suitable for answering different kinds of questions. However, the aim does not include explaining the mathematical foundations underlying those statistical procedures nor to tracing in detail their methods of computation.

USING DESCRIPTIVE STATISTICS

The descriptive statistics included in this section are percentages, percentiles, measures of central tendency, measures of variability, measures of skewness, and correlation techniques. The presentation of each type opens with questions that the statistic is designed to answer. The discussion then continues with an explanation of the statistic's nature, its advantages and limitations, and examples of its application in comparative studies.

PERCENTAGES

The research question: What proportion of a variable (such as students, schools, equipment, events, or the like) display a particular characteristic?

Among the 300 female students surveyed, 35% would condemn the war criminal to death. Among the 114 males surveyed, 49% would put him to death.

The annual urban population growth rate in Argentina is 1.65%, in Afghanistan 4.84%, and in Tanzania 9.59%.

Nicole's test scores were: 86% in language usage, 68% in mathematics, 72% in science, and 93% in social studies.

The annual school budget allocated 67% of the funds for personnel salaries, 13% for equipment and supplies, 8% for transporting students, 7% for administrative expenses, and 5% for miscellaneous costs.

A valued feature of percentages is their ability to translate disparate measures into a common coin that permits easy comparisons among the measures. For instance, in the case of students' opinions about a war criminal, 105 females and 56 males would put the man to death. But the question of whether females were more prone than males to recommend execution cannot be answered until we know the number of each gender in the survey (300 females, 114 males). Even then we are unable make an accurate comparison until the figures are translated into a common denominator. Translating the quantities into percentages provides the solution—35% of the females and 49% of the males advocated executing the man.

Another advantage of percentages is that they are a familiar part of the general public's everyday living, so research results expressed in percentages can be readily understood by a very broad audience.

As Figure 20.1 shows, pie-shaped charts are often useful for graphically conveying the meaning of percentages.

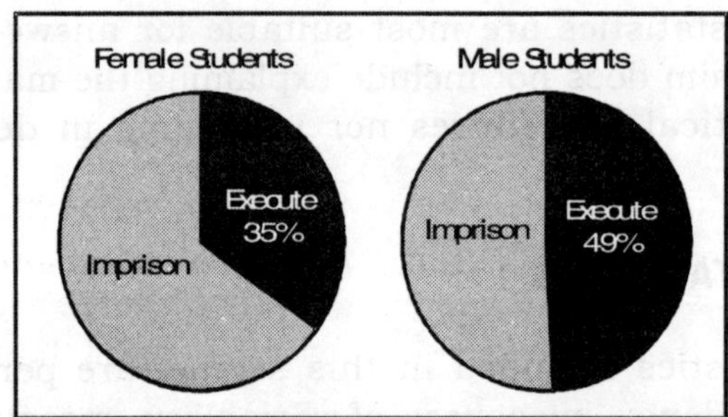

Figure 20.1. Pie Charts for Displaying Percentages

PERCENTILES

The research questions: What proportion of a variable falls below a designated point on a 100-unit scale? Within a collection of items (people, institutions, objects, events, or the like) where does one item rank in comparison with the others?

The meanings of *percentage* and of *percentile* are closely linked but not identical, which is a distinction sometimes missed by people not well acquainted with the two terms.

Whereas a *percentage* tells the proportion (on a 100-unit scale) of a variable that displays a given characteristic, a *percentile* is the point on the scale below which a given percentage of people, objects, or events are located. Thus, a percentile tells where a particular person, object, or event stands in relation to the total number of other persons, objects, or events in terms of some specified feature. Let us say that Nicole was in a class of 33 students. Of the 50 items on the language-usage test, Nicole answered 43 (86%) correctly. However, 16 of Nicole's classmates did better than she by answering 44 or more items correctly. This meant that in the class of 33 students, 16 of them (48.5%) scored higher than Nicole and 16 (48.5%) scored lower. Hence, Nicole was in the middle, at the 50th percentile the point below which nearly half of the students' scores fell. In like manner, we could determine Nicole's percentiles in the other three subject areas by computing where she ranked in relation to her classmates on the math, science, and social-studies tests. Furthermore, by learning the annual urban-population growth rates of an additional 17 countries, we could determine the percentile ranks of Argentina, Afghanistan, and Tanzania in comparison to the others. We could then conclude that:

Nicole's percentile ranks in the four tested subjects were: 50th percentile in language usage, 15th percentile in math, 67th percentile in science, and 88th percentile in social studies.

In urban-population growth rate for 20 developing nations, Argentina is at the 10th percentile, Afghanistan at the 65th percentile, and Tanzania at the 95th percentile.

Percentiles thus provide a convenient way to show one unit's (person's, school's, nation's, or such) position on some measure in relation to the other units in the group under consideration. Like percentages, percentiles allow a researcher to compare disparate rankings in terms of a single, readily comprehended scale.

GRAPHIC COMPARISONS

As Figure 20.2 demonstrates, bar charts sometimes called *histograms* are convenient devices for graphically comparing groups and for comparing individuals within groups. Even a brief glance at the distributions of reading-test scores in the three rural schools shows that students in School B generally performed better than students in Schools A and C. Furthermore, those in School C were distributed somewhat more evenly across the range of scores than were students in either School A or School B. The bar charts also aid us in comparing students. When we learn that Anne earned a score of 68 in School A, we recognize that she was one of the better readers among her classmates. But if she were in School B, she would be slightly below average. And judging from the test results, one of the two best readers was in School B and the other was in School C, since each of them earned a score of 75.

Although we can derive a good deal of information from the bar graph, we are left without detailed answers to several questions: Precisely, which school was the better overall, A or C? In which school were the scores most bunched together, A or B? In which school were the scores balanced better around the average, A or C?

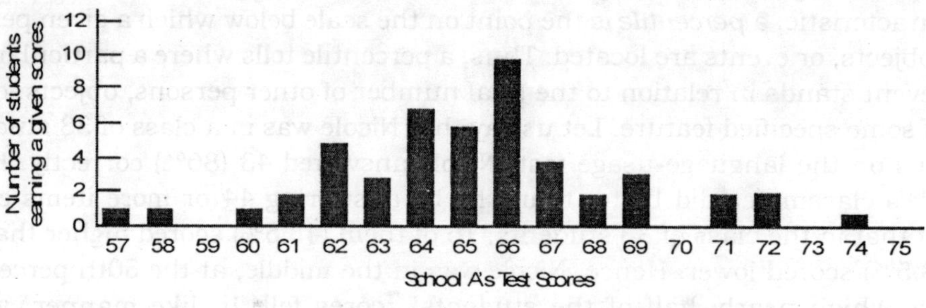

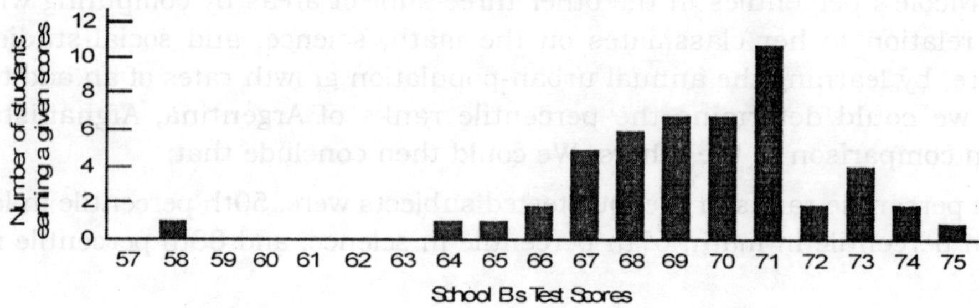

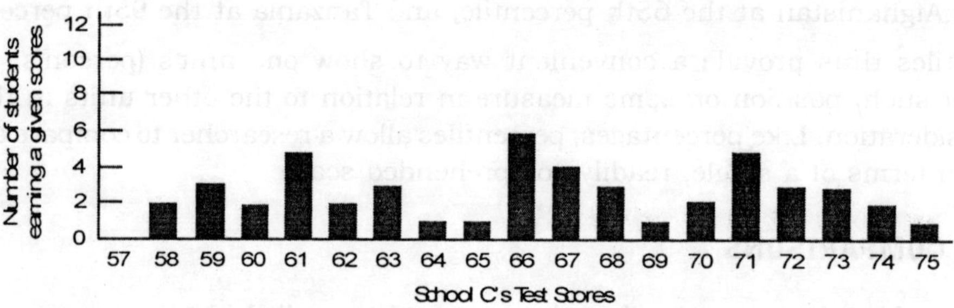

Figure 20.2. Distributions of Reading-Test Scores in Three Rural Schools

To answer these queries, we can turn to statistics describing central tendencies, variability, and the balance of score distributions that is referred to as skewness.

MEASURES OF CENTRAL TENDENCY

The research question: What single number can show the level reached by a group in terms of some measure? The measure in question can be any one of many kinds—achievement-test scores, per-pupil costs for school supplies, numbers of day teachers were on sick leave, incidence of students' illicit drug use, football team scores, and much more.

The three most commonly used central-tendency statistics are the *arithmetic mean*, the *median*, and the *mode*. Each is designed to answer a particular central tendency question.

THE MEAN

The research question: What was the average among the measures of some characteristic?

Ratings on sportsmanship among pupils in the discussion groups were 17.3 points higher on average than ratings of pupils in the lecture groups.

Textbook costs throughout the school system this year rose $13.56 over last year.

The average class size in Monarch City is 25.7 students, in Desert Wells is 30.8, and in Langston 33.7.

The arithmetic mean is computed by adding together all of the measures attained by the members of a group, then dividing the sum by the number of members. Groups can then be conveniently compared in regard to how well they performed in general or in the main or on the average. For the three rural schools in Figure 20.2, the mean reading scores were 65.30 in School A, 69.5 in School B, and 66.26 in School C. Earlier, by inspecting the bar graphs we were unable to judge whether students in School A earned higher scores than the ones in School C. However, after computing the means we now recognize that School C students scored higher on the average than those in School A, and we know precisely how much higher.

THE MEDIAN

The research questions: What score separated the upper half of the group from the lower half? Which score fell in the exact middle of the group's distribution of scores?

Whereas the mean for a group of students that took a test is computed by totalling their scores and dividing by the number of students, the median is determined by listing the students' test scores from the highest to the lowest, then counting up this list to find the halfway point. The median is that halfway score (if there is an uneven number of students) or it is the space between the two scores that lie just above and below the middle (if there is an even number of students). The median obviously is the same as the 50th percentile.

The median income of Preston High School graduates is $41,000, and of Marline High School graduates is $57,000.

The median times spent on homework assignments by sophomores over the past month were: mathematics 25 hours, science 16 hours, foreign language 22 hours, and history 19 hours.

In Figure 20.2, the medians for the rural students' reading performance fall at score 65 in School A, 70 in School B, and 66 in School C. Thus, the comparative success of the students in the three schools as pictured by the medians is quite the same as that furnished by the means. Hence, either the mean or median in this case would answer our research question equally well. The median is the easier to compute from inspecting the distribution of scores in a bar chart we simply begin counting individuals from the bottom of the distribution (or from the top) until we reach the halfway point. Thus, for sake of convenience, the median might well be the statistic we would choose to calculate. However, sometimes the mean and median give rather different impressions of what occurred, as will become clear when we discuss skewness.

THE MODE

The research questions: Which is the most popular score in a distribution of scores? Which is the maximum number of items required to fill some educational need?

The term *mode* identifies the score or amount that appears most frequently in a distribution. Thus, in an array of test results, the mode is the score the greatest number of students earned. In the rural-school example, the modal score for each of the schools is shown by the tallest bar. For School A the mode is 66 (9 students earned that score), for School B it is 71 (11 students), and for School C it is 66 (6 students).

Consider, also, how the mode serves to identify the maximum number of items required for some educational function. If the school librarian learns that the modal class size in the school is 37 (the class with the largest number of students), then she knows that 37 chairs are needed in the library to accommodate an entire class at one time. Obviously, if there are enough chairs to seat all members of the school's most populous class, there will be quite enough to seat all students from any class. Likewise, if the athletic instructor learns the size of the largest physical education class, he can order enough jerseys to outfit all members of any class that arrives.

As a measure of central tendency, the mode is less helpful than either the mean or the median, because the mode might occur at any place in the distribution other than near the middle.

MEASURES OF VARIABILITY

For many research interests, it is not sufficient to learn only the average of an array of measurements. It is also important to learn how much the measurements are bunched together or spread out. For this purpose, we need statistics that summarize the extent of variability or dispersion in a distribution. Several kinds of variability measures are available. Those described in the following pages include the total range, distance between percentiles, inter quartile range, standard deviation, and variance.

RANGE

The research question: What is the distance between the highest score and the lowest one?

The range or total range is calculated by subtracting the lowest quantity in a distribution from the highest quantity.

At first glance, it might appear that the range is a desirable measure of dispersion, since it is easy to compute and understand. However, the range is determined entirely by the two scores at the opposite ends of a distribution. Consequently, it fails to show whether the bulk of the scores between those extremes are bunched together or spread out. For example, in Figure 20.2, the arrays for the three rural schools all have the same range (17 points), yet the picture of variability of scores from one school to another is very different. Most of the scores in School B are clustered within a 7-point spread, whereas most scores in School C are distributed across 11 points. The fact that one student in School B scored far below his classmates on the reading test accounted for the range in that school matching the ranges of the other two schools.

When people ask for a report about the variability within a group's performance, they typically want to know about the group in general, not simply about the two extreme individuals at the opposite ends of the array. Thus, in educational research, the range is rarely useful. Unlike the range, the following statistics depict the variability of the bulk of the items in a distribution, not just the two items at the extreme ends.

DISTANCE BETWEEN PERCENTILES

The research question: How many units of measurement or of scores lie between a selected percentile in the upper half of a distribution and another selected percentile in the lower half?

As explained earlier, along a 100-point scale, a percentile is the point below which a specified fraction of the measurements or scores are located. A girl who is taller than 78% of her agemates is at the 78th percentile in height. A boy who runs faster than 43% of other 9-year-olds is at the 43rd percentile in speed.

The distance between selected percentiles can be used to describe the extent of variability among measurements in a distribution. To choose which percentiles to use, we need to estimate what portion of extreme scores at the opposite ends of the scale we wish to disregard in order to report how much the majority of the scores were spread out or clustered together. If we decide that eliminating 10% at each end would be sufficient to prevent extreme scores from affecting the impression of group variability, then our measure of dispersion will consist of reporting the distance between the 10th percentile and the 90th percentile, thereby encompassing the middle 80% of the scores in our report. Or if we think it best to disregard 15% at each end, we will report the distance between the 15th percentile and the 85th percentile, thus focusing on the middle 70% of the measurements. In choosing which pair of percentiles to adopt, we wish to (a) prevent extreme measurements outliers or deviants from distorting the picture of variability for the group in general, but at the same time (b) avoid cutting off so many measurements that we end up telling more about central tendency than about dispersion. For instance, reporting the distance between the 45th and 55th percentiles would focus on only the central 10% of measurements and would ignore how the remaining 90% clustered together or spread out, thus failing to reflect the extent of variation within the group as a whole. The effects of such choices are illustrated in Figure 20.3, which displays the array of science test scores for students at Bay City High School and Linvale Preparatory Academy. (So there will not be an excessive number of intervals across the baseline of either bar graph, each interval along the baselines represents two adjacent scores, thereby forming a sequence extending from the lowest score that any student achieved [48] to the highest [84]. Consequently, the interval labelled "48" includes students who earned scores of 48 and 49, interval "50" includes students who had scores of 50 ad 51, and so on across the scale.)

In the Bay City distribution, the middle 80% of students fell between scores 56 (10th percentile) and 76 (90th percentile), a distance of 20 points. In the Linvale distribution, the middle 80% fell between scores 60 (10th percentile) and 72 (90th percentile), a range of 12 points, thereby reflecting a considerably tighter bunching of scores at Linvale than at Bay City. The distances between the 15th and 85th percentiles likewise depict less variability among the Linvale students 18 points at Bay City and barely 12 at Linvale.

One popular version of distance-between-percentiles is the interquartile range, which reports the distance between the 25th percentile (first quartile) and the 75th percentile (third quartile). The interquartile range, therefore, reflects the extent of dispersion among the middle 50% of a distribution's measurements. Sometimes the interquartile range is divided by 2, producing the *semi-interquartile range.*

The interquartile range for the Bay City High students is 14 points (75th percentile minus 25th percentile), so the semi-interquartile range is 7 points.

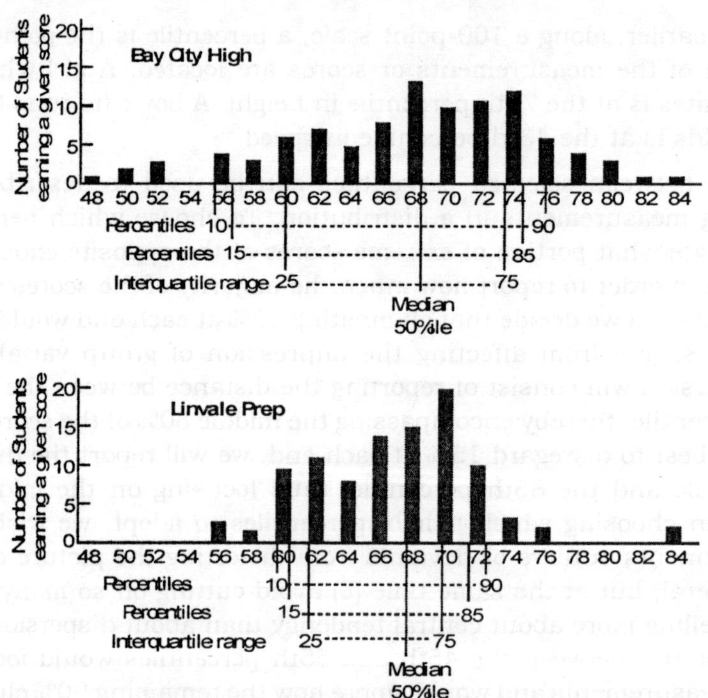

Figure 20.3. Distance-Between-Percentiles as a Measure of Variability

It is useful to note that the principal types of central-tendency and variability measures form two families of statistics. First, in the percentiles family the measure of central tendency is the median (50th percentile), while variability is determined by some version of distance between percentiles (including the interquartile and semi-interquartile ranges). Therefore, if the median is used to report the general success of a group of students, the accompanying measure of variability can reasonably be a version of distance between percentiles.

STANDARD DEVIATION AND VARIANCE

The research question: How much do measurements or scores in a distribution stretch above and below the mean?

As noted above, calculating the median and allied percentiles consists of counting the number of scores extending from the lowest and highest. In contrast, computing the mean involves totalling all the measurements or scores, then dividing the sum by the number of measurements or scores. Three measures of dispersion related to the mean are ones determined by calculating how far a distribution's scores deviate from the mean. These measures are named the *average deviation, variance*, and *standard deviation.*

Although the average deviation is rarely used in statistical analyses, inspecting its computation can be helpful in explaining the meanings of variance and standard deviation. The average deviation tells how far, on the average, all the scores or measurements in a distribution are located above and below the mean. To calculate the average deviation for the dart-game data in Figure 20.4, we first need to recognize that each of the scores in the left column represents an interval. The score number is the center of that interval. Therefore, the number 4 identifies the center of an interval extending from 3.5 to 4.5. The number 3 interval extends from 2.5 to 3.5, and so on with the rest of the scores. When we add all of the dart-game scores together and divide that sum (132) by the number of students (36), we find that the mean of the distribution is 3.67. Thus, the mean falls in the lower portion of the 4 interval exactly .12 above the lower limit (3.5) of that interval. To calculate the average deviation for the dart-game distribution, we need to determine how far each student's score deviates from 3.67. So, if a student earned a score of 4, we find how much that differs from the mean by subtracting 3.67 from 4 (4 – 3.67 = .33). In the same way we find that a student's score of 5 deviates from the mean by 1.33 points (5 - 3.67 = 1.33). And a score of 2 deviates from the mean by 1.67 points (3.67 – 2 = 1.67). By carrying out these calculations for all 36 scores, and summing the results, we obtain a total of 46.66, which is then divided by the number of students (36) to yield the average deviation (1.30) of scores from the distribution's mean. This 1.30 might then be used to compare the 36 students with students from other classes in order to determine which group demonstrated greater variability in throwing darts. Assume, for instance, that the average deviation for a second class was 1.78 and for a third class was 0.92. It is thus apparent that the scores in the second class spread out far more than did the scores in either the Figure 20.4 group or the third class. The tightest bunching together of scores appeared in the third class with its 0.92 average deviation.

In contrast to the average deviation, which is seldom employed in research, the variance and standard deviation are very popular, since both provide important advantages.

The method of computing the variance is similar to that used for the average deviation—except with the variance, each score's deviation from the mean is squared before the deviations are added together. The squaring process increases the weighting of deviations as their distance from the mean increases. Thus, the variance is the average of the scores' squared distances from the mean.

Once the variance has been calculated, the standard deviation is easy to determine. You simply find the square root of the variance. Note in Figure 20.4 that the standard deviation of 1.77 is the square root of the variance of 3.14. The conventional symbol for the standard deviation is the small Greek letter sigma (σ), and for the variance it is sigma-squared (σ2).

Scores	Number of Students Earning Each Score	
9		N= 36 students
8	/ /	Mean = 3.67
7	/	Average deviation = 1.30
6	/	Variance = 3.14 = σ2
5	/ / / /	Standard deviation = 1.77 = σ
4	/ / / / / / / / / / / /	
3	/ / / / / / / / / / /	Range = 8
2	/ / /	Median = 4
1	/ / /	Mode = 4
0	/	

Figure 20.4. Students' Scores in a Dart Game

THE NORMAL DISTRIBUTION CURVE

Over the years, large numbers of people have been measured to determine their status on such physical characteristics as height and weight or their relative standing on a test of some mental ability general intelligence, academic aptitude, or the like. The results of such measurements have shown that the distributions of scores have tended to assume nearly the same configuration. The bulk of the group cluster around the middle, with the remaining people's scores gradually diminishing as they deviate farther above and farther below the majority. Because so many human characteristics seem to result in such a configuration, this common arrangement of measurements has been called the normal distribution curve.

The relationship of the standard deviation to the normal curve provides researchers with useful information. The area of the curve lying one standard deviation above the mean contains slightly more than one third (34.1%) of the scores or measurements reported in a given research project. The same proportion of scores is found in the area within one standard deviation below the mean. Hence, slightly over two-thirds (68.2%) of the scores lie in the area between +10 and –10 from the mean; 95.4% of the measurements will be found in the area +20 and –20 from the mean; and nearly all (99.7%) will be within +30 and –30 from the mean. The closer a distribution approximates the form of a normal curve, the more these proportions can be trusted.

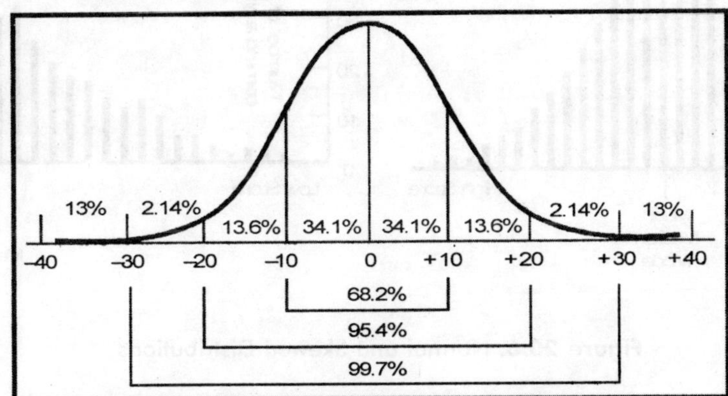

Figure 20.5. Standard Deviations and the Normal Curve

The standard deviation and the variance are not only convenient statistics to report for portraying the comparative variability of several distributions of scores or measurements, but they offer particular advantages for the inferential use of statistics, as we will see later in this chapter.

SKEWNESS

Research questions: How symmetrical is the array of measures? In other words, how closely does the shape of the lower half of the distribution match the shape of the upper half?

The statistical concept reflected in these questions is *skewness.* Figure 20.6 shows two distributions of scores. In the one labelled *normal distribution,* the form of the lower half of the array of scores is a mirror image of the form of the upper half. In the example labeled *skewed distribution,* the lower half of the array is rather like a tail, whereas the upper half is humped. When the tail-like form is in the lower half of the scale, the distribution is said to be *negatively skewed.* When the tail is in the upper half of the scale, the array is called *positively skewed.*

Measures of skewness report how much a distribution deviates from perfect symmetry. The degree of skewness of the normal distribution in Figure 20.6 is 0.0, because the scores are not skewed at all. However, such is not the case with the reading scores for the three rural schools in Figure 20.2. There, the distribution of scores is least symmetrical in School B, where the students tended to bunch toward the top of the scale (–1.16) The closest to symmetry is School C (–0.01). School A is between the other two, with scores slightly skewed toward the high end of the scale (+0.18).

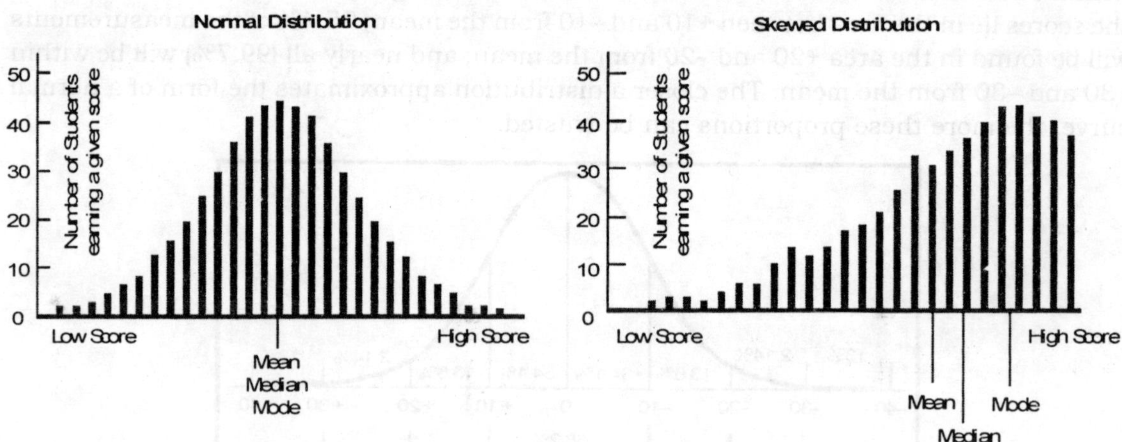

Figure 20.6. Normal and Skewed Distributions

In Figure 20.6, the skewed distribution depicts Samoan high-school students' performance on a Samoan-language reading test. The degree of skewness is –0.78. The abundance of students bunched together at the high end of the distribution suggests that the reading test did not sufficiently challenge the best readers' skills. It seems likely that the students who earned perfect or near-perfect scores were actually not all alike in ability. Probably some of them were better than others, but the test lacked a sufficient number of difficult items to separate the very good readers from the superior ones. In the future, the test constructors would be advised to put more *top* on the test by including some items that demand more subtle reading interpretations than do the questions on the existing test. Figure 20.6 illustrates the way skewness influences the relationships among the mean, median, and mode. In a symmetrical array, the mean, median, and mode are all at the same location. However, in a typical skewed distribution, the median will lie between the mode and the mean. The mean is tugged toward the tail end of the scale by the extreme scores that lie in that direction. The greater the skewness, the larger the separation among the three measures. In a markedly skewed array, the median is likely the best of the three statistics to represent the central tendency of the distribution. In the skewed display in Figure 20.6, students' scores range from a low of 2 to a high of 27, with 27 representing a perfect score. The median is 21 and the mean 19.87. The standard deviation is 5.31, and the interquartile range is 7.

CORRELATION TECHNIQUES

The research question: The general question that correlation statistics are designed to answer is: When a change occurs in one variable, how much change if any occurs in another variable? The general question, when recast in terms of particular variables, results in such queries as the following:

- *Ethnic status and academic achievement*: Are students from certain ethnic groups more successful at academic studies than students from other ethnic groups?
- *Television viewing and violent behavior.* What is the relationship between the amount and kinds of television programs children watch and the amount and types of violent acts in which children engage?
- *Mothers' intelligence and daughters' intelligence.* How closely do mothers' IQs (intelligence quotients) correspond to their daughters' IQs?
- *Identical twins' academic achievement.* In pairs of identical twin girls, how does the level of academic achievement of a typical girl compare with the academic achievement of her twin sister?
- *Administrative style and teacher satisfaction*: Are school principals' administrative styles related to the degree of satisfaction expressed by teachers who serve under those principals' supervision?

A variety of statistical procedures are available for answering such questions. Which procedure will be appropriate in a given case depends on the kind of data found in the variables that are being compared. Variables appear in three principal forms: (a) as a series of scores or measurements ranging from low to high, (b) as a series of rankings extending from first to last, or (b) as a dichotomy, pitting two or more separate categories against each other. Table 20.1 indicates which correlation process is suited to which pattern of data. Each of the correlation procedures listed in the right-hand column of Table 20.1 is described briefly in the following pages.

Table 20.1. Kinds of Data and Correlation Procedures

Variable A	Variable B	Correlation Technique
Measurement series	Measurement series	Pearson product-moment (*r*)
Ranks	Ranks	Spearman rank-order (*rho* or *p*)
Measurement series	Dichotomy	Biserial (r_b)
Dichotomy	Dichotomy	Phi coefficient (φ)

PEARSON PRODUCT-MOMENT CORRELATION

The research question: What is the degree of relationship between two variables if each variable consists of measurements along a scale that consists of a series of equal intervals?

In judging whether the Pearson product-moment method (symbolized by the letter *r*) is appropriate for a given study, the researcher needs to decide whether both of the variables being compared represent equal-interval scales. Strictly speaking, an equal-interval scale is one in which the distance from one step to the next step is precisely the same throughout the entire length of the scale. Measures of height fulfill this equal-interval requirement, since the distance from 25 centimeters to 30 centimeters is exactly the same as from 60-cm to 65-cm or from 105-cm to 110-cm, and so on. Measures of temperature, of weight, of time, of speed, of dollars, and of distance on a running track also involve equal unit scales. In contrast, some scales used in the field of education and in the social sciences may appear at first glance to be composed of equal intervals, but upon closer inspection it becomes clear that they are not. The scoring of intelligence-test results in terms of IQ levels is a familiar example. The difference in intellectual ability between an IQ of 100 and one of 105 is not the same as the difference between 120 and 125, because the questions that make up the test are not all of equal difficulty. Test items that differentiate between IQs 120 and 125 are probably more demanding than those that distinguish between IQs 100 and 105. Likewise, a distribution of scores on a test of English usage or of science facts does not produce an *equal-interval* scale in the strict meaning of the term, because the items that differentiate between scores 80 and 90 are likely more difficult than those that differentiate between scores of 30 and 40. In effect, a 10-point difference in one segment of the scale is not equal to a 10-point difference in another segment.

This distinction between truly equal-interval scales and scales that contain intervals that are only approximately equal has caused some critics to condemn the use of the Pearson method in a great many of the studies that have employed the procedure. (More than 90% of all correlation coefficients reported in the research literature within the behavioral sciences are Pearson *r*'s.) However, Heermann and Braskamp analysis of a host of investigations suggests that using *Pearson*'s technique with variables involving intervals that are no more than approximately or partially equal is still warranted. Glass and Hopkins have observed that the critics' "disenchantment with the classical methods was premature." Thus, it is generally acceptable to apply Pearson's *r* in studies whose variables consist of test scores or involve ratings of performance or of attitude.

Our purpose in this section is not to detail the technique involved in calculating *r*. Such information is found in the statistics books listed at the end of the chapter. Here we confine our attention to a brief description of what different magnitudes of *r* can mean.

The size of *r* can range from 0 to 1.00. An *r* of 0 means that change in one variable is associated with no change in the other. For instance, it seems likely that the *r* between college students' political attitudes and their shoe sizes is 0.0, meaning that there is no link between the two variables. Hence, knowing a student's shoe size offers no clue at all about the student's political views, nor will information about a student's political attitudes aid us in estimating that individual's shoe size. However, *r*'s that approach 1.00 can aid us a great deal in estimating a given individual's position on one variable from knowing his or her position on the other. But before demonstrating that point with some illustrative *r*'s, we should note that two variables can be related in either a positive or a negative manner.

A positive *r* means that high scores on one scale are accompanied by high scores on the other. Likewise, low scores on one variable are associated with low scores on the other. In contrast, a negative *r* means that low values on one dimension are related to high values on the other.

For example, a study of the IQs of identical twins raised in the same home has yielded an *r* of +.91, so that if we know the IQ of one member of the pair, we can safely judge that the other member's IQ will be nearly the same. However, for identical twins raised in separate homes, the *r* found between their IQs was only +.67. This means that, whereas there is still a tendency for the twin of a person with a high IQ to have an above-average intelligence-test score as well, our estimate of what that score will be is less accurate than if the *r* were +.91 or even +.80 or +.75. Still less confidencc can be placed in predicting a child's IQ if we know the IQs of the child's brothers or sisters, because evidence about the *r* between siblings raised together suggests a relationship of only +.50. And if the siblings havc been raised apart, the *r* descends to +.40. There is even less connection between the IQs of unrelated children who are reared in the same home (*r* +.23), and no connection at all between unrelated children who are reared in separate homes (*r* 0.00). Hence, in the case of two unrelated children who have been raised apart, estimating one child's IQ from knowledge of the other's IQ is no more than a wild guess.

Negative correlations can also range from 0 to –1.00. But in this case, low scores along one scale are associated with high scores along the other. Among people from ages 50 to 90, there is a negative relationship between age and muscle strength, because with advancing age, people's strength diminishes. As in the case of positive *r*'s, the closer a negative *r* approaches –1.00, the more accurately a score on one variable can be predicted from knowing a given score on the other variable.

Consider these two examples of *perfect* correlations, one positive and the other negative.

Pearson *r*	**Variable 1**	**Variable 2**
+1.00	Centigrade temperatures	Fahrenheit temperatures
-1.00	Students' correct answers on a science test	Students' incorrect answers on a science test

SPEARMAN RANK CORRELATION

The research question: What is the degree of relationship between two variables if each variable consists of ranks along a scale rather than measured intervals?

Frequently research data are not in the form needed to compute a Pearson *r*, because one or both of the variables consist of ranks instead of measured amounts. Sometimes the data are originally collected as rankings, as when teachers are ranked in terms of popularity with students, basketball players ranked by overall ability, and nations ranked by the prestige of their higher education systems. Other times the data are collected as quantities which are then converted into ranks for convenience of computation. Thus, provinces can be ranked by per-pupil expenditures, colleges by their graduation rates, and students by their grade point averages.

The most popular method of computing correlations between pairs of ranked data is the Spearman procedure, symbolized by the Greek letter *p* (rho). Spearman coefficients, like Pearson *r*'s, can range from 0 to 1.00 in either a positive or negative direction. Interpreting magnitudes of *p* is much like interpreting similar magnitudes of *r*.

BISERIAL CORRELATION

The research question: What is the degree of relationship between two variables if one is measured in a graduated fashion so as to produce a sequence of quantities and the other variable is in the form of a dichotomy?

Two computational techniques for determining the association between such variables are the *biserial* and *point-biserial* methods. Each method yields correlation coefficients that are estimates of what the Pearson *r* would be if both variables were normally distributed arrays rather than one of them being in the form of a dichotomy.

Deciding whether the biserial technique is appropriate in a given research situation depends on the researcher's assumption about the nature of the dichotomous variable. The biserial method is not appropriate in cases of *true* dichotomies, such as sex (male/ female) or students' class attendance on a particular day (present/absent). However, it is applicable when the dichotomy appears to be an artifact of crude measurement. For instance, in a survey of parents' opinions about teaching birth control methods in high school, data may be collected in the form of a dichotomy (*agree/ disagree*). But it is likely that parents' opinions are actually far more varied than the resulting data suggest-some parents will have strong objections to birth control instruction, some will disagree moderately, others will object mildly, some will agree but with serious reservations, and so on. If a more precise scaling approach had been used in gathering opinions, the results would have assumed the form of a distribution of graduated steps. In effect, the dichotomous variable in this instance was not truly discrete. Therefore, it is this latter type of spurious, crude-measurement dichotomy for which the biserial correlation technique is designed. Because coefficients resulting from biserial computations are estimates of Pearson *r*'s, the interpretation of biserial coefficients is similar to the interpretation of *r*'s.

On the other hand, if the dichotomous feature is truly discrete (male/female, citizen/ alien, fourth-grade pupil/non-fourth-grade pupil), an estimate of *r* can still be obtained by applying the *point-biserial* method.

PHI COEFFICIENT AND CONTINGENCY COEFFICIENT

The research question: What is the degree of relationship between two variables if both of them are dichotomous?

The phi ($r\varphi$) coefficient is the product-moment correlation between two variables when each variable is scored as discrete points rather than as a series of measured steps. For example, imagine that we wish to determine among students in a junior high school the direction and degree of relationship on a given school day between two variables: (a) family type and (b) homework diligence. We identify two types of families (single-parent and two-parent) and two levels of homework diligence (homework completed and homework not completed). For convenience of computation, we arbitrarily assign the score 0 to students in one-parent families and the score I to those in two-parent homes. Likewise, we assign the score 0 to students who failed to hand in their completed homework on the particular day and a score of I to those who completed their assignment. Then we can locate in a 2-by-2 contingency table the number of students who fit each of four conditions: (a) 1-parent family and missing homework [0-0], (b) 1-parent family and completed homework [0–1], (c) 2-parent family and missing homework [1–0], and (d) 2-parent family and completed homework [1–1]. Assume that we collect family-type and homework-completion information from 200 students and enter the data into a contingency table (Figure 9.7). We see by the totals at the bottom of table that there were 90 students from 1-parent homes and 110 from two-parent families. By applying a standard formula for computing the phi coefficient, we learn that in this case of our fictitious junior high school the $r\varphi$ = +.06. The positive value of $r\varphi$ indicates that students with 1's on home-type were a bit more likely to have 1's also on completing homework. In effect, there was a slightly greater tendency for students in 2-parent families to complete their homework than for those in 1-parent families. But the magnitude of the phi is so small that its usefulness for drawing generalizations about the relationship of family type and homework diligence would be of no practical value.

For sake of comparison, let us now assume that we next collect information about a different set of 200 students on a different day's homework assignment, then enter those data into Figure 20.8. The resulting phi coefficient is $r\varphi$ =+.17, showing a somewhat higher tendency than in Figure 9.7 for students from 2-parent homes to hand in homework in comparison to students from 1-parent families.

The data used in contingency tables need not be restricted to two discrete positions on each of the variables. For instance, a table comparing high school students' grade levels (10th/11th/12th) and those students' use of alcohol during a given week (did drink vs. did not drink) would produce a 3-by-2 table. In like manner, other variables represented in discrete types or steps could produce larger size contingency tables—4-by-4, 3-by-6, and such.

OTHER CORRELATION OPTIONS

The correlation methods described in the above paragraphs are only four of the more commonly used techniques. Numerous other approaches found in statistics textbooks and journal articles are designed to suit additional conditions of the data that a researcher has at hand. For instance, in some situations the relationship between two series of measures may not assume the shape of a straight diagonal line. As scores on one variable increase, the scores on the other do not increase regularly in a similar manner. Such a relationship results if people's ages over the life span are compared with their eye-hand coordination scores. Whereas age increases in regular steps, eye-hand skills do not; instead, such skills increase in early life, remain at a high level for much of adulthood, then decline in old age, thereby rendering their progression *curvilinear.* In such cases, an eta (η) coefficient should be computed to reflect the association between the variables.

As a second example, under certain conditions a tetrahoric coefficient (r_t) rather than a phi coefficient can usefully be calculated to determine the magnitude of the relationship between two variables, each of which is a dichotomy.

Homework Completed?	Type of Home: 1-parent [0]	2-parent [1]	Total
No [0]	42	42	75
Yes [1]	48	77	125
Totals	90	110	200

Figure 20.7. Family Type and Homework Diligence—Example 1

Homework Completed?	Type of Home: 1-parent [0]	2-parent [1]	Total
No [0]	42	33	75
Yes [1]	48	77	125
Totals	90	110	200

Figure 20.8. Family Type and Homework Diligence—Example 2

The term *factor analysis* identifies several alternative procedures for estimating which features are common to a series of correlations that have been computed from a variety of measures of a group of individuals. For example, a large number of students can be administered tests intended to assess their mental abilities. Correlations can then be computed to determine which test items are highly related to each other and which ones appear to be mainly independent of each other. The assumption is that when certain items are closely associated (so that students who do well on one item in the cluster also do well on the others, and vice versa), a particular mental ability or mental *factor* underlies that group of items. Typically, a label is assigned to that cluster of closely related items, with the label intended to reflect the cognitive skill or *factor* that binds the cluster together. For example, the labels applied to factors found in such test batteries as the Primary Mental Abilities and Differential Aptitude Tests are: number comprehension, verbal reasoning, verbal comprehension, abstract reasoning, clerical speed and accuracy, mechanical reasoning, space relations, language usage, and word fluency.

In applications in education, factor analytic studies have been undertaken in such diverse areas as prose style, administrative behavior, occupational classification, attitudes and belief systems, and the economics of education. The technique is still in extensive use in the exploration of abilities, in the refining of tests and scales, and in the development of composite variables for use in research studies. Its most promising applications in recent years, however, have been concerned with the testing of explicit hypotheses about the structure of sets of variables, as in the study of growth models. It has also facilitated the comparison of the factorial structure of different subpopulations, allowing investigators to determine whether the factorial structure of a given set of variables varies, for example, with sex, age, ethnicity, socio-economic status, or political affiliation.

For steps to follow in calculating the correlation coefficients mentioned in the foregoing pages, and for explanations of the conditions under which each method is appropriate, readers can consult such books as those listed at the end of this chapter.

DRAWING INFERENCES FROM SAMPLES

As mentioned earlier, descriptive statistics summarize in a concise form the results of measurements of a group of individuals or events. Sometimes researchers are interested only in what such statistics tell about that group. However, other times they want to apply the group's results to a larger population. In other words, the measured group is considered to be a sample of a larger population that has not been measured. Hence, from testing the reading ability of 200 nine-year-olds, an investigator may intend to draw inferences about the reading skills of all of a city's or state's nine-year-olds. From a statistical summary of 350 college students' expressed attitudes about the use of marijuana, a researcher may hope to estimate the attitudes toward illicit drugs of all students in that particular college—or perhaps of all students in all of the nation's higher education institutions. However, extending the conclusions about a tested group to a larger population always entails a risk of error, since the sample group may not truly represent the larger population. In effect, the sample may be biased. Therefore, it is important for researchers to have ways of judging how likely the statistics gathered about a sample will accurately portray the features of an intended population. Or, stated as a question, what is the probability of making an error when using descriptive statistics as the basis for drawing inferences about a population? The procedures for answering such a question are called *inferential statistics*.

It is useful at this point to consider the sources of errors that may distort the conclusions drawn from assessing people or events. In the case of descriptive statistics, inaccurate conclusions derive from measurement errors. For instance, the purpose of having students take a history test is to discover precisely their knowledge of historical facts, concepts, trends, theories, and the like. However, various kinds of errors can render the assessment inaccurate. The directions for taking the test may be unclear, some test items may be badly phrased, noises in the classroom may disrupt students' attempt to concentrate, the time to complete the test may be too short, the tester's method of correcting the students' answers may be faulty, and more. Such measurement errors can be reduced by careful attention to the preparation of the test, to the manner of administering it, and to the method of correcting it. However, if the results of testing a sample of students are used as the foundation for drawing inferences about the broader population of students from which the sample was drawn, another source of inaccuracy can distort the inferred picture of the population's knowledge of history. That source is *sampling error*, meaning the degree to which inferences about a population likely deviate from the true characteristics of that population.

ESTIMATING SAMPLING ERROR

A researcher can never know for sure how accurately one sample drawn from a population reflects the characteristics of that population. The only way to know positively how closely the mean of 100 pupils' test scores represents the mean that would be achieved by all 50,000 pupils in a county's school population would be to test all 50,000. But since testing the entire population would likely be considered impractical, the best an investigator can do is to estimate the probability that the sample mean is close to the population's true mean. Inferential statistics are designed to furnish that estimate. We will briefly inspect two of the ways to arrive at such estimates—the *t*-test and the analysis of variance.

THE T-TEST

Researchers often compare two groups in terms of their means. If the means are found to differ, the question arises: Does each group represent a different population in relation to the characteristic that was measured, so the difference in these sample means reflects an actual difference in the means of the underlying populations? Or are the two groups simply two slightly biased samples from the same population, whose true mean we really don't know? To illustrate, imagine that 50 women and 50 men are enrolled in a college class entitled "Methods of Logic." On the final test at the end of the semester, the mean for the women is 83.6 and for the men 78.9. We may now ask whether these scores reflect a difference only between female and male members of that particular class, or is the population of the kind of college women who enrolled in the class generally more adept at learning the methods of logic taught in the class than is the population of the kind of college men who enrolled? The *t*-test provides an estimated answer to this query.

To perform a *t*-test, we first compute the standard deviation for the women's and men's distributions of final-test scores and find that the women's $\sigma = 6.7$ and men's $\sigma = 6.3$. Next, by applying the appropriate computation procedure (found in nearly any statistics textbook, a procedure requiring the two groups' means and standard deviations), we learn that there apparently is less than I chance in 1000 that the two groups represent the same population and that the obtained means are different simply because of bias in drawing the samples. In other words, our results support the conclusion that the population of women (of the kind enrolled in the logic class) is on the average somewhat more skilled at learning the methods of logic taught in the class than is the population of men (of the kind that enrolled). There is a 999 chance in 1,000 that this conclusion is warranted.

However, if the means for women in our hypothetical logic class had been 81.0 and the men 83.6 (with the standard deviations still $\sigma = 6.7$ and $\sigma = 6.3$), we would learn that there are likely 5 chances out of 100 that there is no real difference in the means of the populations from which these women and men were drawn. In effect, there are 5 chances in a 100 that the difference between 81.0 and 83.6 is simply the result of sampling error—the men's sample just happened to include more adept logic learners and that both the men and women represent the same population in terms of ability to master the logic techniques taught in the class. But there are 95 chances in 100 that the obtained differences actually do reflect a difference that would be found in the mean scores of the two populations of the kinds of women and men who took the test.

Thus, the *t*-test is designed to help researchers estimate the probability that measures of a sample of people or events accurately portray the broader populations of people or events from which the sample was apparently drawn. In addition to testing the representative ness of obtained means, there are *t*-tests for pairs of percentages, standard deviations, correlations, and measures of skewness.

In the above brief sketch of the *t*-test procedure, I have not taken the space to point out several important assumptions about the way samples are drawn from populations, assumptions that significantly affect the appropriateness of *t*-tests in particular studies.

ANALYSIS OF VARIANCE

As explained earlier, *variance* (σ^2) is a description of how much measurements spread away from the center of a distribution. Specifically, the variance is the average of the squared measurement-deviations from the mean.

We have seen that the *t*-test is used to estimate whether the means from two samples represent the same population or two different populations. The analysis of variance (ANOVA) is a statistical procedure for simultaneously testing how likely three or more means represent samples drawn from the same population or, in contrast, are means representing different populations. One example of comparing three or more means is found in a study of attitudes toward a 10-o'clock curfew law as expressed by parents, teachers, police officers, and teenagers. Another example is found in a study of mathematics test scores of high school students representing six ethnic groups Anglos, Latinos, Afro Americans, Asians, Native Americans, and Pacific Islanders.

Not only does ANOVA permit the simultaneous comparison of multiple means, but the results are more accurate than if *t*-tests were applied to each pairing of the multiple means being studied. Glass and Hopkins point out that "ANOVA is the most common of all inferential statistical techniques in education and the behavioral sciences."

ANOVA results are interpreted in much the same way as those of the *t*-test, that is, in terms of the probability that a difference between sample means are the result of sampling error rather than the result of a difference in the true means of the populations from which the compared samples were drawn. Thus, a difference among sample means that could occur by chance (by sampling error) at a probability level of only 1 time in 100 gives the researcher more confidence in believing that the means of the represented populations are truly different than does a difference among sample means that could occur by chance 5 times in 100 or 10 times in 100.

ANOVA can also be extended to test the likelihood of interactions among factors. For instance, one researcher used ANOVA to discover whether teachers' ethnic status affected their perceptions of how adaptable Anglo and Latino students were. The results showed that there was indeed interaction between teacher and student ethnic types. Latino teachers more often judged Latino students as more adaptive, whereas Anglo teachers more frequently considered Anglo students more adaptive.

WAYS OF DRAWING SAMPLES

The types of research in which concerns about sampling are most important are experiments and surveys. Among numerous methods of drawing a sample to represent a population, five are described in the following paragraphs. They bear the titles *simple random, multistage, cluster, systematic,* and *convenience.*

SIMPLE RANDOM SAMPLING

In the field of education, the populations that investigators choose to study can usually be defined in terms of their (a) content, (b) units, (c) extent, and (d) time. For instance, in a study of the reading habits of Canadian college freshmen, the population can be specified as: (a) all first-year college and university students, (b) in all higher-education institutions, (c) in Canada, (d) in 1998. Or, in an investigation of the student-discipline policies in Philippine private secondary schools, the population can be described as consisting of : (a) all discipline regulations, (b) in all private secondary schools, (c) in all of the Philippine Islands, (d) in 1998.

Consider, then, how we might proceed to compile information about Canadian college students' reading habits. We quickly recognize that the task of gathering data from all Canadian freshmen is well beyond the resources we command. Thus, we decide to study only a sample of Canadian freshmen. To help ensure that our sample truly represents the pattern of reading habits of the student population, we decide to use a random sample. The basic rule in drawing a random sample is that every individual in the population must have an equal chance of being selected. One way to fulfil this requirement would be to obtain the names of all 1997 first-year college students and assign each an identification number, starting with I and continuing until we reach the total number of students. We then decide what size sample will (a) provide a sufficiently large group to offer a trustworthy estimate of the population characteristics and (b) at the same time will fit our budget, staff, and time constraints. On the basis of these considerations, we choose to gather data from 300 respondents. Our next step is to obtain a list of random numbers, either from a table in a statistics book or from a computer program that generates random numbers. The first 300 numbers in that list identify which students (in terms of their assigned identification numbers) from throughout Canada would be included in our survey.

The advantage of drawing a simple random sample of the population is that we can now make a good estimate of sampling error (by such techniques as the *t*-test or ANOVA) and thus know how well the results of our sample likely reflect the reading habits of the nation's entire population of first-year college students. The disadvantage is that carrying out such a sampling plan would entail far more expense and difficulty than the results of the study would warrant. I doubt that all of the nation's post-secondary institutions would be willing to send us the names of their freshmen. In addition, drawing students randomly from across the nation would necessitate our collecting reading-habit information (by mailed questionnaires, phone calls, or face-to-face interviews) in many different sections of the country. Therefore, unless a population is quite limited in size and distribution, direct random sampling is usually not practical.

MULTISTAGE AND CLUSTER SAMPLING

One way to simplify our problem of drawing a random sample of students would be to carry out the selection process in stages. That is, a population often can be described in terms of a hierarchy of sampling units of different sizes and types. In the case of our reading-habits study, the hierarchy could consist of two stages or levels: (1) colleges and universities and (2) first-year students within those institutions. First, we list the names of all colleges and universities. Then by a random-selection process, we choose five institutions. Next, we obtain the names of all first-year students in those five institutions, and from that list we randomly select 300 students to be surveyed. This procedure meets the basic requirement for random sampling (each student has had an equal chance to be chosen) and has much simplified our task of conducting the survey. A number of variations of multistage sampling are available to accommodate the conditions of different studies and different types of populations.

Cluster sampling is similar to multistage sampling. In both methods, the first step is the same the population to be investigated is divided into groupings referred to as clusters. For the Canadian example, each college or university would be a cluster. In both multistage and cluster sampling, the number of clusters to be included in the sample would first be chosen by random selection. But the two methods differ at the second step of the process. Whereas in the multistage procedure, the second step consists of randomly selecting units (students) within each of the clusters, in cluster sampling all of the units in a selected cluster become members of the sample. In effect, every first-year student in a selected college would be interviewed.

SYSTEMATIC SAMPLING

Within relatively small populations, a systematic sample usually will represent a population's characteristics as accurately as will a random sample. Consider, for example, a secondary school with an enrollment of 1,400 students. The dean of students wishes to collect students' opinions of the new dress code that the school is proposing to adopt a code requiring students to choose their garb from among two styles for boys and three styles for girls. Rather than soliciting the opinions of the entire population of 1,400, the dean plans to interview only 35 students or 2.5% of the total. To select the 35 who will participate in the study, he assigns each student in the school a number, ranging from 1 to 1,400. Then he writes numbers 1 to 20 on a sheet of paper and, with his eyes closed, touches a pencil point to the sheet. The pencil points to number 7. That number identifies the first student to be included in the sample. And because 2.5% of 1,400 is 20, the 20th student from 7 (student 27) is the second one to enter the sample. The 20th student beyond 27 (student 47) becomes the third. And in like manner, each subsequent 20th student is chosen until the desired 35 have been identified.

Because only chance errors, rather than other sources of bias, are apt to affect how closely the interview results approximate the population's opinions about the dress code, the statistical techniques described earlier for estimating sampling error (*t*-test and ANOVA) can be appropriately used with systematic sampling.

CONVENIENCE SAMPLING

A great many studies in the field of education involve what have been called *available, convenience*, or *accidental samples*. Such is the case when teachers in an elementary school test sixth-graders' mastery of computer keyboarding, when a graduate student assesses a group of kindergarten children's methods of settling disputes, or when an anthropologist analyzes the instructional roles played by members of three families. In these instances, the particular elementary school, kindergarten, and families were chosen because they were convenient to study, not because they were randomly selected representatives of a defined population. Therefore, the value of such studies resides in what they tell about the people who participated directly in those investigations rather than in generalizations that might be proposed about a population of sixth-graders, kindergarten children, or families. In effect, there is no available statistical procedure for estimating how well convenience samples reflect the pertinent characteristics of whatever population a researcher may wish to speak about.

The best a researcher can do in such situations is to (a) identify the features of the sample that seem to be causal factors (factors that influence keyboarding, ways of settling disputes, and family members' roles), then speculate about whether those same factors might obtain in other groups (representing a population) that could be studied. For instance, the teachers who evaluated the Keyboarding skills of their school's sixth graders might suggest that results similar to the ones obtained in their research would perhaps be found in other schools that displayed similar and apparently influential conditions, such as, (a) the same computer facilities, (b) the same computer-literacy instruction, (c) teachers with similar training, and (d) pupils from similar socio-economic backgrounds. However, such generalizing from an available or convenience sample to an assumed population is a very risky venture, since there is no clear way of identifying and measuring the factors that may have biased the sample's results.

SUMMARY

To estimate how accurately a sample of people or events represents a population about which the researcher wishes to speak, and to draw samples from populations. The chapter's presentation of these matters has admittedly been cursory at best.

Bibliography

Adams, D. (2000). From the international year to a decade for a culture of peace and non-violence. *International Journal of Curriculum and Instruction Special Issue, 2*(1), 1-10.

Altbach, P.G. & Kelly, G.P. (1986). Introduction: Perspectives on comparative education. In P.G. Altbach & G.P. Kelly (Eds). *New approaches to comparative education* (pp.1-10). Chicago & London: The University of Chicago Press.

Altbach, P.G. (1991). Trends in comparative education. *Comparative Education Review, 35*(3), 491-507.

Archer, Eileen A. ed. *Commonwealth Universities Yearbook 1992*. London: The Association of Commonwealth Universities, John Foster House, 1992.

Arnove, R.F. (2001). Comparative and International Education Society (CIES) facing the twenty-first century: Challenges and contributions. *Comparative Education Review, 45*(4), 477-503.

Assefa, A. Mariam. France: *A Study of the Educational System of France and a Guide to the Academic Placement of Students in Educational Institutions of the United States.* Washington, D.C.: AACRAO, 1988.

Ball, S.J. (1998). Big policies/small world: An introduction to international perspectives in education policy. *Comparative Education, 34*(2), 119-130.

Bjerstedt, Å. (Ed.). (1993). *Peace education: Global perspectives.* Stockholm, Almqvist & Wiksell.

Brock-Utne, B. (1988). Formal education as a force in shaping cultural norms relating to war and the environment. In A. Westing (Ed.). *Cultural norms, war, and the environment* (pp. 83-100). Oxford University Press.

Burns, R.J. & Aspeslagh, R. (Eds). (1996a) *Three decades of peace education around the world. An anthology.* New York/London: Garland Publishing.

Carnoy, M. & Rhoten. D. (Eds). (2002a). The meanings of globalization for education change. *Comparative Education Review Special Issue, 46*(1): PAGE NUMBERS?.

Chinese Education Association for International Exchange. *Chinese Universities and Colleges, Second Edition.* Beijing, China: Higher Education Press, 1994.

Choy, Eppie. "Grading and degree classification Hong Kong University of Science andTechnology." Personal email. (8 August 2001).

Cook, B.J., Hite, S.J. & Epstein, E.H. (2004). Discerning trends, contours, and boundaries in comparative education: A survey of comparativists and their literature. *Comparative Education Review, 48*(2), 123-150.

Cowen, R. (Ed.). (1996). Last past the post: Comparative education, modernity, and perhaps post-modernity. *Comparative Education Special Number (18), 32*(2), 151-170.

Crossley M. & Watson, K. (2003). *Comparative and international research in education: Globalization, context and difference.* London/New York: Routledge Falmer.

Crossley, M. & Broadfoot, P. (1992). Comparative and international research in education: Scope, problems and potential. *British Educational Research Journal, 18*(2), 99-112.

Crossley, M. & Jarvis, P. (Eds). (2000). Comparative education for the twenty-first century: An international response. *Comparative Education Special Number (23), 36*(3).

Dale, R. & Robertson, S.L. (Eds). (2005) Globalisation and education in knowledge economies and knowledge societies. *Comparative Education Special Issue (30),* 41(2).

Davies, L. (2005). Schools and war: Urgent agendas for comparative and international education. *Compare, 35*(4), 357-371.

Dean, Michael. Vietnam. *A Study of the Educational System of Vietnam and Guide to the Academic Placement of Students in Educational Institutions in the United States.* PIER. Washington, D.C.: AACRAO and NAFSA, 2000.

Devlin, Edward. *Australia: Education and Training.* An AACRAO country guide. Washington, D.C.: AACRAO, 2004.

Educational Research, Methodology and Measurement: An International Handbook. 2nd ed. Edited by J.P. Keeves. New York: Pergamon, 1997.

Elvin, L. (1979). International understanding. *International Review of Education, 25,* 461-476.

Feagles, Shelley M. *A Guide to Educational Systems Around the World.* Washington, D.C.: NAFSA, 1999.

Fingar, Thomas. *Higher Education and Research in the People's Republic of China: Institutional Profiles.* Washington, D.C.: Committee on Scholarly Communication with the People's Republic of China and NAFSA, 1981.

Gannon, Philip J. Korea: *A Study of the Educational System of the Republic of Korea and a Guide to the Academic Placement of Students in Educational Institutions of the United States.* Washington, D.C.: AACRAO, 1985.

Gray, Collen. Peru: *A Study of the Educational System of Peru and a Guide to the Academic Placement of Students in Educational Institutions of the United States.* Washington, D.C.: AACRAO, 1983.

Halperin, D.S. (Ed.). (1997). *To live together: Shaping new attitudes to peace through education.* Paris. France: UNESCO: International Bureau of Education.

Harber, C. (1997). International developments and the rise of education for democracy. *Compare, 27*(2), 179-191.

Heater, D. B. (1984). *Peace through education: The contribution of the Council for Education in World Citizenship.* London/Philadelphia, Falmer Press.

Higbee, Homer and Winters, Marjorie K., eds. *The Admission and Placement of Students from: Hong Kong, Malaysia, Philippines, Singapore.* Report of a Workshop, February, 1979, Baguio, Philippines. Washington, D.C.: The Joint Committee on Workshops, NAFSA and AACRAO, 1980.

Holmes, B. (1985). Trends in comparative education. *Prospects, 15*(3), 325-346.

Hopkins, John D. "The Educational System of Finland: Background, Structure, Equivalencies, and New Directions." *World Education News & Reviews.* Winter 1990.

International Companion to Education, Edited by Moon, B. Ben-Peretz, M & Brown S. London & NY: Routledge, 2000.

International Encyclopedia of Adult Education and Training. 2nd ed. Edited by Albert C. Tuijnman. Oxford, UK; Tarrytown, NY: Pergamon, 1996.

International Encyclopedia of National Systems of Education. 2nd ed. Edited by T. Neville Postlethwaite. Tarrytown, NY: Pergamon, 1995.

International Handbook of Educational Change. Edited by Andy Hargreaves, et al. Boston,: Kluwer Academic Publishers, 1998.

International Handbook of Educational Leadership and Administration. Edited by Kenneth Leithwood, et al. Boston: Kluwer Academic, 1996.

International Handbook of Research in Arts Education. Edited by Liora Bresler. New York: Springer, 2006.

International Handbook of Teachers and Teaching. Edited by Bruce J. Biddle, Thomas L. Good, Ivor F. Goodson. Boston,: Kluwer Academic Publishers, 1998.

International Handbook of Women's Education. Edited by Gail P. Kelly. New York: Greenwood Press, 1989.

Iram, Y. (Ed.). (2003). *Education of minorities and peace education in pluralistic societies.* Westport, CT/London, UK: Praeger.

Jones, P.W. (1998). Globalisation and internationalism: Democratic prospects for world education. *Comparative Education, 34*(2), 143-156.

Kandel, I.L. (1933). *Studies in comparative education.* London/Bombay/Sydney: George Harrap and Co.

Kelly, G.P. & Altbach, P.G. (1986). Comparative education: Challenge and response. *Comparative Education Review, 30*(1), 89-107.

Koenig, Ann M. *An Overview of the Educational System of Albania.* Milwaukee, Wl: Educational Credential Evaluators, Inc., 1993.

Lukas, Karen H. Austria: *A Study of the Educational System of Austria and a Guide to the Academic Placement of Students in Educational Institutions of the United States.* Washington, D.C.: AACRAO, 1987.

Marginson, S, & Mollis, M. (2001). "The door opens and the tiger leaps": Theories and reflexivities of comparative education for a global millennium. *Comparative Education Review, 45*(4), 581-615.

Mashiko, Ellen E. Japan: *A Study of the Educational System of Japan and a Guide to the Academic Placement of Students in Educational Institutions of the United States.* Washington, D.C.: AACRAO, 1989.

MBoungou-Mayengué, D., ed. *Directory of African Universities.* 5th edition. Accra: Association of African Universities, 1988.

Mehta, S. & Ninnes, P. (2003). Postmodernism debates and comparative education: a critical discourse analysis. *Comparative Education Review, 47*(2), 238-257.

Open File (1989). Comparative education: A provisional stocktaking. *Prospects, 19*(3), 351-406.

Page, J. (2004). Peace education: Exploring some philosophical foundations. *International Review of Education, 50*(1), 3-15.

Peisert, Hansgert and Framhein, Gerhild. *Higher Education in the Federal Republic of Germany.* Bonn: Federal Ministry of Education and Science, 1990.

Popovych, Erika I. *A Directory of Higher Education in Armenia, Azerbaijan, Belarus, Estonia, Georgia, Kazakhstan Kyrgyzstan, Latvia, Lithuania, Moldova, Russian Federation, Tajikstan, Turkmenistan, Ukraine, Uzbekistan.* Washington, D.C.: PIER, 1995.

Raby, R.L. (2005). Reflections on the field: A review of the 2004 *Comparative Education Review* bibliography. *Comparative Education Review, 49*(3), 410-418.

Ray, D. (Ed.). (1988). *Peace education: Canadian and international perspectives.* London, Ontario: Third Eye Publications.

Reardon, B.A. (1987). From international understanding to peace education and world order studies. *Reprints and Miniprints No. 579,* Department of Education and Psychological Research, Malmö School of Education, University of Lund.

Reed, Linda A. *Education in the People's Republic of China and U.S.-China Educational Exchanges.* Washington, D.C.: NAFSA, 1988.

Regional Education Profile: Central America. Institute of International Education. New York, NY: 1986.

Ross, H. (2002). The space between us: The relevance of relational theories to comparative and international education. *Comparative Education Review, 46*(4), 407-433.

Rust, V. (2001). Editorial. *Comparative Education Review, 45*(3), iii-iv.

Rust, V., Soumaré, A., Pescador, O. & Shibuya, M. (1999). Research strategies in comparative education. *Comparative Education Review, 43*(1), 86-109.

Schriewer, J. (Ed.). (2006). Comparative methodologies in the social sciences – cross-disciplinary inspirations. *Comparative Education Special Issue (32), 42*(3), FAGE NUMBERS?.

Sellew, Kathleen T. *Dominican Republic: A Study of the Educational System of the Dominican Republic and a Guide to the Academic Placement of Students in Educational Institutions of the United States*. Washington, D.C.: AACRAO, 1987.

Sepmeyer, Inez Hopkins, ed. *The Country Index: Interpretations for Use in the Evaluation of Foreign Educational Credentials.* Alhambra, California: Frank Severy Publishing, 1986.

Simkin, K. (1998). Education for intercultural understanding: Some implications for comparative education. In R.A. Peddie (Ed.). *Looking at the past, looking to the future: Educational change in comparative perspective. Proceedings of the 26th Annual Conference of the Australia and New Zealand Comparative and International Education Society.* Auckland, New Zealand: University of Auckland, 6-9 December, 157-173.

Stedman, Joann B. Malaysia: *A Study of the Educational System of Malaysia and a Guide to the Academic Placement of Students in Educational Institutions of the United States.* Washington, D.C.: AACRAO, 1986.

Sweeney, Leo J. and Kallur, Ravi: *India: A Special Report on the Higher Education System and Guide to the Academic Placement of Students in Educational Institutions in the United States.* Washington, D.C.: PIER, 1997.

Tamminen, Arvi, ed. *Higher Education in Finland: Guide for Foreign Students.* Helsinki, Finland: Ministry of Education, 1982.

Taylor, Ann C.M., ed. *International Handbook of Universities and Other Institutions of Higher Education.* 12th ed. New York: Stockton Press, 1991.

Tikly, L. & Crossley, M. (2001). Teaching comparative and international education: A framework for analysis. *Comparative Education Review, 45*(4), 561-580.

Tikly, L. (2001). Globalisation and education in the post colonial world: Towards a conceptual framework. *Comparative Education, 37*(2), 151-172.

Torres, C.A. (2001). Globalization and comparative education in the world system. *Comparative Education Review, 45*(4), iii-x.

Tsang, Monica. "Degree classification scheme Lingnan University." Personal email (1 August 2001).

Turner, Solveig and Frederick, Antoinette. *Education in Ireland: Admission and Placement of Irish Graduates.* Boston, MA: CED Publications, 1994.

Villa, Kitty M. Mexico: *A Study of the Educational System of Mexico and a Guide to the Academic Placement of Students in Educational Institutions of the United States.* Washington, D.C.: AACRAO, 1982.

Vriens, L. (1990). Peace education in the nineties: Revalution [*sic*] of values and options. *Paper presented to the International Peace Research Association Conference, Groningen, The Netherlands,* 3-7 July.

Welch, A. & Masemann, V. (1997). Editorial introduction. *International Review of Education, 43*(5-6), 393-399.

Welch, A.R. & Burns, R.J. (Eds). (1992). *Contemporary perspectives in comparative education.* New York/London: Garland Publishing.

Welch, A.R. (1985). The functionalist tradition in comparative education. *Comparative Education, 21*(1), 5-19.

Wellington, Stanley. Colombia: *A Study of the Educational System of Colombia and a Guide to the Academic Placement of Students from Colombia in Educational Institutions of the United States.* Washington. D.C.: AACRAO, 1984.

Wilcox, Lee. *Arab Republic of Egypt: A Study of the Educational System of the Arab Republic of Egypt and a Guide to the Academic Placement of Students in Educational Institutions of the United States.* Washington, D.C.: AACRAO, 1988.

Williams, C. (2000). Education and human survival: The relevance of the global security framework to international education. *International Review of Education, 46*(3-4), 183-203.

Wilson, D.N. (1994). Comparative and international education: Fraternal or Siamese twins? A preliminary genealogy of our twin fields. *Comparative Education Review, 38*(4), 449-486.

Woolston, Valerie A. and Dickey, Karlene N. Denmark: *A Study of the Educational System of Denmark and Guide to the Academic Placement of Students in Educational Institutions in the United States.* PIER. Washington, D.C.: AACRAO and NAFSA, 1995.

Zachariah, M. (1979). Comparative educators and international development policy. *Comparative Education Review, 23*(3), 341-354.

Zajda, J., Majhanovich, S. & Rust, V. (Eds). (2006). *Education and social justice.* Dordrecht, Springer.

Index

D

E

F

G

U

V

W